Applying Decision Research to Improve Clinical Outcomes, Psychological Assessment, and Clinical Prediction

Applying Decision Research to Improve Clinical Outcomes, Psychological Assessment, and Clinical Prediction

DAVID FAUST
UNIVERSITY OF RHODE ISLAND; WARREN ALBERT MEDICAL SCHOOL OF BROWN UNIVERSITY

HAL R. ARKES
OHIO STATE UNIVERSITY, HARDING CENTER FOR RISK LITERACY

CHARLES E. GAUDET
VETERANS AFFAIRS BOSTON HEALTHCARE SYSTEM

(WITH ANA BRIDGES, DEPARTMENT OF PSYCHOLOGICAL SCIENCES, FULBRIGHT COLLEGE OF ARTS AND SCIENCES, UNIVERSITY OF ARKANSAS, SERVING AS FIRST AUTHOR FOR CHAPTER 9 AND GABRIELE FARIELLO, DEPARTMENT OF MANAGEMENT IN DIGITAL AND NETWORKED SOCIETIES (MINDS), KOZMINSKI UNIVERSITY, SERVING AS FIRST AUTHOR FOR CHAPTER 10)

OXFORD
UNIVERSITY PRESS

OXFORD
UNIVERSITY PRESS

Oxford University Press is a department of the University of Oxford. It furthers the University's objective of excellence in research, scholarship, and education by publishing worldwide. Oxford is a registered trade mark of Oxford University Press in the UK and certain other countries.

Published in the United States of America by Oxford University Press
198 Madison Avenue, New York, NY 10016, United States of America.

Library of Congress Cataloging-in-Publication Data
Names: Faust, David, 1952– editor. | Arkes, Hal R., 1945– editor. | Gaudet, Charles E., editor.
Title: Applying decision research to improve clinical outcomes, psychological assessment, and clinical prediction / [edited by] David Faust, Hal R. Arkes, Charles E. Gaudet.
Description: New York, NY : Oxford University Press, [2024] |
Includes bibliographical references and index.
Identifiers: LCCN 2023017314 (print) | LCCN 2023017315 (ebook) |
ISBN 9780197694237 (paperback) | ISBN 9780197694244 (epub) |
ISBN 9780197694268
Subjects: LCSH: Psychology, Industrial. | Organizational sociology. |
Psychology, Applied. | Decision making—Psychological aspects.
Classification: LCC HF5548.8 .A727 2024 (print) | LCC HF5548.8 (ebook) |
DDC 158.7—dc23/eng/20230711
LC record available at https://lccn.loc.gov/2023017314
LC ebook record available at https://lccn.loc.gov/2023017315

DOI: 10.1093/med-psych/9780197694237.001.0001

Printed by Marquis Book Printing, Canada

FSC www.fsc.org MIX Paper from responsible sources FSC® C103567

To Paul E. Meehl and Leslie J. Yonce:

For the many gifts you both have given to me, both intellectually and personally, which have enhanced my life remarkably and made such a difference. I will always be grateful.—David Faust

To all my teachers, from Ms. Gibbons in the first grade to Professor Walker in graduate school.—Hal R. Arkes

To Jody and Chuck, thank you for your unwavering love and support.—Charles E. Gaudet

CONTENTS

PART I

Introduction and Foundations

1

The Benefits of Decision Research for Clinical Practice: Framing the Issues

GETTING BETTER: SOME ILLUSTRATIONS OF WHAT DECISION RESEARCH CAN OFFER

A client facing very difficult circumstances develops suicidal ideation and comes to you, their therapist, for help. Your immediate tasks are to ascertain the risk of suicide and to intervene as needed. Suppose the client is facing a challenging and troubling situation at work that could go very wrong. The client has a history of sexual abuse and intermittent loss of anger control, although her self-control has improved considerably as treatment has progressed. The client works at a small, family-owned company. Her boss, although usually supportive, has made a number of insensitive comments. These comments have triggered powerful emotional reactions and thoughts of self-destructive actions. The client, who desperately needs her job but finds the situation intolerable, has made a firm decision to talk with her boss. The concern is that the boss will respond badly, the client in turn will respond with uncontrolled anger, and things will go downhill rapidly from there, potentially eventuating in a suicide attemp.

We realize that this brief scenario falls well short of capturing the details, nuances, or fine texture and context of a clinical encounter, but scenarios like these can elucidate important decision making principles that can be very helpful when considering intervention choices and their implications. Thus, simplification can serve as a useful starting point. With that noted, suppose we are considering three factors that may impact the likelihood of a suicide attempt: the boss will respond badly, in response the client will lose emotional control, and the client will have access to lethal means. Again, for the sake of the example, assume the chances of these three things happening are:

1. The boss responds badly 50%
2. The client loses emotional control 10%
3. Access to lethal means 90%

If all these things must occur for a suicide attempt to take place, and treating these variables as independent events (again, for the sake of the example), then the probability of an attempt is: .50 × .10 × .90 = .045, or 4.5%. This likelihood is relatively low, but almost surely much higher than we would like given the potential or ultimate harm that could result. We have posed the following question to many students and professionals: Assume, given the practicalities of the situation, you can only focus on one of the three risk factors or variables, and that whichever one you place your focus on, you will have the same absolute level of impact. Which factor would you select?

A very typical response is to focus on the factor with the highest risk, and a much more unusual response is to focus on the factor with the lowest risk. The highest risk factor is often the most salient variable, and one's first thought may well be that this variable merits our focus. However, consider the following. If you can lower any of these factors by, say, 5%, then there is limited return if one focuses on the most likely factor. If access to means decreases from 90% to 85%, the result is as follows: .50 × .10 × .85 = .0425, or 4.25%, or compared to the original 4.5%, a decrease of ¼ of 1%. Calculated another way, the change from 4.5% to 4.25% is a proportionate drop in risk of about 6% (.25/4.50). In contrast, if one selects the least likely variable, one achieves far greater risk reduction. A 5% reduction changes the risk of the least likely variable from 10% to 5%, with an overall result as follows: .50 × .05 × .90 = .0225, or 2.25%. Here, the decrease is 2.25%, or nine times greater that the reduction realized by selecting the most likely variable. When expressed as a proportion, the change converts to a 50% reduction, which is obviously far more robust than the 6% proportional drop achieved by selecting the most likely variable. The principle being illustrated here is: if a series of two or more things that are independent of one another all must happen for a bad outcome to occur, than all else being equal, lowering the risk of the least probable variable creates a disproportionally greater reduction in overall risk than lowering the risk of more likely variables.

This disproportional impact can become even more dramatic if, for example, one can achieve greater change than illustrated above, such as a 9% reduction in any one of the variables. Here the results achieved by selecting the least likely variable would be: 10% – 9% = 1%, hence: .50 × .01 × .90 = .0045, or 0.45%, or about 1 in 220. That decrease is nine times greater than the change achieved by selecting the most likely variable (90% – 9% = 81%, hence .50 × .10 × .81 = 0.0405, or 4.05%).

The inverse of this principle is that if a series of two or more things that are independent of one another all must happen for a good outcome to occur, than all else being equal, increasing the probability of the least likely variable creates a disproportionally greater increase in the overall chances that the desired outcome will occur. For example if, as things stand, a prospective student must overcome three obstacles to be admitted to a graduate school program, all else being equal, one should increase the likelihood of the least likely of these elements (such as the probability of obtaining adequate funding).

We realize that life is usually more complicated than these simplified scenarios. For example, one might be able to double the absolute level of change in one of the variables as opposed to another one, although in some cases focusing primarily on the least likely variable may still have a greater payoff (e.g., if the most likely variable is 80%, the least likely 5%, and the absolute change 10% versus 5%, respectively, as one can confirm by performing the calculations). Alternatively, the components may not be independent of one another, instead having varying degrees of codependence. However, these important potential complexities aside, and acknowledging that ambiguity often characterizes real-life situations, knowing such principles can provide extremely helpful guides for decision making. Put another way, despite its counterintuitive nature, knowing that the greatest benefit may be obtained by focusing on the least likely (and possibly least salient) variable may lead to considerably greater overall success than what is often the more intuitively appealing alternative, which is to focus on the most likely (and possibly most salient) variable.

Furthermore, real-life ambiguities often do not change the relative merits of emphasizing the least versus most likely variable, and if anything, may increase the advantage of the former course of action. If all the complexities and ambiguities that exist when focusing on the least likely factor are similarly present if one instead focuses on the most likely factor, then focusing on the most likely factor remains the far more flawed approach. Often the greatest value of decision research is not when it confirms things we already know, but when it overturns false beliefs and provides us with better alternatives.

As a second example, suppose a study suggests that a test achieves an overall accuracy rate of 85% (and a corresponding error rate of 15%) in distinguishing between individuals with and without delusional disorder. (Alternatively, we could use a structured interview technique or a particular diagnostic sign instead of a test for this example, but that would not change the principles under consideration.) The study involves evenly divided groups of individuals who do and do not have the disorder. Assume further that among the general population, the prevalence of delusional disorder is about .2%, or 1/500 (according to the *Diagnostic and Statistical Manual of Mental Disorders,* American Psychiatric Association, 2013). A term that can be substituted for prevalence rate is *base rate,* which simply is the frequency of occurrence (whether the matter at hand involves a disorder or other kinds of entities or events, such as the percentage of sunny days in San Diego). If we incorporate base rates into the analysis, a very different picture of accuracy emerges than the 15% error rate obtained in this study of equal-sized groups.

Assume we are screening members of the general population for delusional disorder using the test from the study. Given the very low base rate of the disorder, if 500 individuals are tested, the 15% error rate results in a mean of 75 individuals being misclassified. In contrast, if we simply assume that no individual among the 500 has the disorder, we would only make one error on average, or instances in which we failed to identify an individual with the disorder. Hence, using the test would result in 75 times more error than simply going with the base rate and assuming that no one has the disorder. We realize that such an approach would miss the positive case, and that other steps might be warranted to try to avoid this error, especially with serious conditions. Putting these legitimate concerns aside for the moment, the example illustrates that determinations of diagnostic and predictive accuracy need to take into account the base rates of occurrences. When the base rates in studies for those with and without disorders, or for differing outcomes, vary from the base rates in settings of use, study results can create a very misleading impression about the success achieved in actual practice. When base rates change, accuracy rates change.

Suppose one rejects this example and considers missing the positive case as unacceptable, despite the consequences of making far more erroneous identifications (the latter of which could cause as much, or perhaps far greater, harm). Here we would note that the same principles apply to differential diagnosis. For example, some psychological disorders are far more frequent than others. Suppose the differential is between two disorders, one of which is 10 times more frequent than the other, and further that missing either disorder is about equally bad. If diagnostic signs and indicators point equally toward the two disorders, then always selecting the more frequent disorder will yield an accuracy rate that will almost certainly be considerably higher than selecting one or the other disorder on a case-by-case basis, and 10 times higher than always identifying the less frequent condition.

Hence, level of diagnostic and predictive accuracy is not solely a product of validity coefficients or the robustness of methods. Accuracy also depends, sometimes to a substantial degree, on prevalence or base rates. As the research described in Chapter 6 indicates, clinicians across an array of fields often underweight or disregard base rates. In Chapter 6, we discuss the power of base rates, how they can be used to enhance diagnostic and predictive accuracy, sometimes multifold, and specific methods for incorporating base rates into decision making.

A final example is the common belief that one should integrate and consider as much information as possible, and that adding further information to the information already at hand can only improve judgmental accuracy. For example, suppose a test developer designs a measure that is 70% accurate in distinguishing between the presence versus absence of clinically significant depression. This 70% hit rate easily exceeds the 50% rate one would achieve without the measure, or by chance, when evaluating an overall group evenly split between individuals who do and do not have significant depression. Here, the measure reduces the error rate from 50% to 30%, or diminishes error substantially.

But does the measure's 70% accuracy rate always provide an advantage? Assume for the purposes of this example that about half of the errors misidentified significantly depressed individuals as not being significantly depressed (or resulted in false-negative errors), and about half of the errors misidentified individuals without clinically significant depression as being significantly depressed (or resulted in false-positive errors). Now suppose that 85% of the clients in a treatment setting had clinically significant depression, and one simply assumed that every client was depressed. Consequently, one would achieve an 85% accuracy rate, or a higher rate of accuracy than the test. Alternatively, if there was a second test that yielded a 90% accuracy rate among this group, and we used that test alone, we would do better than we would using the other test or assuming all clients were depressed.

Perhaps instead we might combine the two tests to try to do better than either test alone. If the two tests generated the same result for a client (e.g., significant depression present), there is no inconsistency to resolve. However, if the accuracy of the better test is 90% and the weaker test 70%, they have to generate conflicting results in at least 20% of the cases, because otherwise the better test could not be 20% more accurate than the weaker test. In fact, it is possible that in every case in which the two tests disagree, the stronger test could be correct and the weaker test wrong (with the two agreeing on the correct identification 70% of the time and agreeing on the wrong identification 10% of the time). More generally, if we always deferred to the weaker test, we would increase the error rate threefold. Given the presence of measurement error and other contributing factors, it seems incontrovertible that different sources of information can be flat-out inconsistent or contradictory. For example, one of the outcomes may simply be wrong (e.g., the client actually may not have a history of repeated violent behavior); therefore, how could one "integrate" a correct and incorrect piece of information (the client does and does not have a history or repeated violent behavior), or how likely is it that additional, but mistaken, information will enhance judgmental accuracy?

So why not just defer to the weaker test when the stronger test is wrong or seemingly wrong? In most situations, we simply do not know when that is the case. In order to know when the better test was wrong, we would probably need a stronger method than the better test, which we likely lack, otherwise we would be using the stronger method in the first place. Thus, we are reduced to guessing when the stronger test is wrong. Given the weaker test's error rate of 30% and the stronger test's error rate of 10%, the chances of beating the 3:1 odds against us across multiple cases are very poor, which is almost surely why it is so difficult to find supportive examples in the literature. Thus, although the weaker test is valid, we are generally going to be better off, and perhaps far better off, by not using it and instead using only the stronger test.

Furthermore, the oft-accepted "given" of throwing all information into the decision pot can be, and often is, counterproductive, as will be discussed in greater detail in various sections of the text. Rather, a better question to ask is something like this: If I add this new source of information to the best available information, will my accuracy improve (potentially making it worth it to do so), stay the same (which creates an inefficiency that may drain our resources and capacity to help individuals), or decrease (in which case its use may well be counterproductive)? Thus, the common emphasis on collecting and integrating large amounts of information, although sometimes productive and worth pursuing, and despite its near omnipresence endorsement in the field and seeming self-evident truth, can also lead us in the wrong direction, increase error, and encounter major limitations and reservations.

There are times that we struggle, perhaps more than we might realize, with integrating complex information optimally given the range of difficult obstacles often faced in the mental health field, such as the complexities of the human mind and human behavior, the level of inference that may be required in appraisal, and limitations in our still-emerging science (see Chapter 7, "The Integration of Information: Strengths and Limitations"). Many professionals struggle with the types of examples we provided, not due to any limits in intelligence or capabilities, but simply because they may be counterintuitive and infrequently covered in training or presented in a contrary fashion. It is for exactly this type of subject matter that decision researchers, quite a few of whom are also practicing clinicians, have directed their talents toward developing knowledge and tools that enhance clinical decision making and prediction. This book is dedicated to this spirit of doing better and improving care, with the following section on the importance of prediction serving as the jumping-off point.

GREAT QUESTIONS IN PSYCHOLOGY

If one opens up almost any introductory psychology text, one almost inevitably finds a paragraph, and perhaps the first one in the book, setting forth the great questions in the field. Those questions commonly include the understanding, prediction, and control of behavior. Perhaps the great irony is that a reader probably will not find any mention in these texts that one of the three questions, the one addressing the prediction of human behavior, has already been answered, at least at present. If the matter is addressed at all, it is probably to advise readers that the answer is wrong, although it was provided by the preeminent psychologist Paul Meehl—the recipient of the American Psychological Association's award for Outstanding Lifetime Contribution to Psychology, arguably its most prestigious approbation; the youngest president in the history of the organization; and the stated hero of a Nobel laureate, psychologist Daniel Kahneman. Most texts disregard or reject Meehl's answer despite the massive evidence favoring it. This is unfortunate because awareness of that answer can be of great benefit to mental health professionals and others who have dedicated their lifework to improving the human condition. A fundamental intent of this book is to discuss that answer, to share what is (and is not) known about predictive methods and strategies, and to do so in the most balanced manner we can achieve. We discuss the background research and the fascinating, often counterintuitive, outcomes that the research has generated, and we lay out practical applications of that knowledge for improving human welfare and enhancing intervention outcomes.

Some decision researchers have used this research and knowledge in an attack mode, to convey the strong message that we are doing things wrong or proceeding irrationally or foolishly. That seems to be an odd and ineffectual way to present good news, like telling someone they're becoming emaciated for lack of nutrition without emphasizing that "By the way, we brought something good for you to eat." How the situation ever got so twisted, so that a body of knowledge that can help us perform our jobs more effectively is sometimes presented as the plague, we do not know, but it is something we hope to avoid repeating. Perhaps in support of our more optimistic as hopes about receptiveness to this work, one group of clinical students in a Ph.D. program with an applied emphasis, when surveyed a number of years after they graduated, rated the course they took in clinical judgment and decision making the single most useful class they completed during their graduate training.

WE'RE IN THE PREDICTION BUSINESS

Much of applied psychology rests, at least partly, and sometimes vitally, on prediction. An obvious example is the prediction of suicidal potential, which helps a clinician take needed steps to avoid tragedy. Many clinical and everyday situations engage individuals in predictive tasks, from the relatively mundane to the more consequential. If one fails to predict rain, one may need to change clothing, or if when trying on a pair of shoes one mistakenly predicts that the shoes will gradually stretch and fit comfortably, the cost of that error can be a few blisters and a return to the store. In contrast, picking the right investments, choosing safety equipment for a car, or opting for a risky surgical procedure can obviously have life-altering consequences.

Many judgments and decisions hinge on prediction, although we may sometimes fail to recognize the omnipresence of predictive activities if they are not explicit, but implicit. For example, if I'm trying to pick the winning horse or politician, it is pretty obvious I'm engaging in prediction. In contrast, if I'm selecting from among alternative interventions for a client, or deciding whether or not to seek consultation with a colleague, it may not be so clear or apparent that prediction is typically involved. For example, if I select treatment A over B, all else being equal, I should pick the one with the greatest prospects for success. Making that selection thus involves predicting the outcome of the respective actions. Surely, in many cases, it would be odd to tell a client, "Treatment A and B are similarly costly and risky, but my advice does not hinge to any degree on how often one versus the other achieves a good outcome." At a more fine-grained level, even an interpretive statement in a therapy session, or the decision to make or not make such a statement, often comes with an underlying belief that the course of action selected is likely better than the alternative rejected. Whether based on explicit contemplation, or almost instantaneously based on tacit knowledge or belief, the decision that is made still often rests at some level on the intent to achieve a positive outcome, and hence involves a core predictive element.

Even tasks that may seem largely descriptive, such as determining whether a person has a certain psychological disorder or characteristics, may have limited value unless knowing the answer provides some degree of predictive utility. For example, what value is an "established" psychiatric diagnosis if it does not allow us to predict anything important, such as the likely course of the disorder, the degree (if any) of functional impairment, or better versus worse treatment choices? Our intent is not to argue that meaning or value hinges solely on pragmatic utility, because that most decidedly is not our view. Furthermore, we realize there is much more to applied or clinical psychology than prediction, such as providing empathic links with individuals, and that varying skills and competencies may intersect minimally with predictive judgments.

Recognizing there is more to psychology and life than prediction, however, does not counteract the potential importance and pervasiveness of predictive undertakings. Being able to predict often helps us prevent negative outcomes or alleviate conditions. Even when prevention or negation is not possible, prediction may at least allow us to reduce harm or implement compensatory approaches, as might be the case if one knows one will never recover full strength in an injured limb, and thus one needs to make certain changes in lifestyle or occupational activities. Knowing a hurricane is coming will not prevent it. However, advance warning can still make a considerable difference. An erroneous prediction of the minimal potential for flooding in the summer hurricane of 1900 led citizens of Galveston to stay in the city and consequently pay the ultimate price. Prediction can matter, sometimes a great deal.

DOES THE ACCURACY OF PREDICTION REALLY MATTER IN PSYCHOLOGY AND ALLIED FIELDS?

Limits of Extreme Empiricism and Relativism

The view that accurate prediction can be beneficial may bump up against extreme versions or stereotypes of alternative epistemological assumptions in psychology or against beliefs about methods of knowing. On one side is hardcore empiricism, which is easy to bash when represented, or misrepresented, as individuals holding the narrow-minded view of science as the method for learning the Truth. Such adherents supposedly believe that Truth is revealed when science is performed capably by those upholding core scientific values, and who thereby act in an objective and unbiased manner, unswayed by personal predilections, life experiences, or cultural background. Such a portrayal is little more than blatant stereotyping, although in less extreme forms it can capture common scientific blind spots. For example, it would not be unusual to find scientists who underestimate the potential influence of culture on scientific conceptualizations and leanings.

An opposing counterpart to extreme empiricism is extreme relativism, the view, or supposed view, that all knowledge claims are equally valid or warranted, and that beliefs are merely a product of such factors as one's background, culture, and personal experiences. (One of the authors had a graduate student in a class argue that *brain tumor* did not refer to anything material but was primarily a social construct.) It is hard to give credence to either extreme relativism or extreme empiricism, or, to put it differently, to expect either of these polarized views to take much of the research on decision making very seriously (for reasons that might not seem apparent in the case of the extreme empiricist, as discussed momentarily).

Those who take extreme relativistic views would seem unlikely to place much value in decision research. Nonetheless, although acknowledging the limits of our evidentiary base, we have encountered multiple instances in which individuals who voice such views have been quickly convinced to reconsider their position. For example, one of the authors had a student who, upon first arriving at graduate school, argued that gravity was a completely artificial concept. However, when asked if she would therefore find it perfectly acceptable to flip a coin to determine whether to leave a 10-story office through the window or stairs, she quickly realized she did not really embrace the extreme version of relativism she was articulating. That same student later reported that a professor had recorded her exam grade incorrectly and that she was absolutely sure she had gotten a 97, hardly the assertion of an extreme relativist.

Likewise, none of the authors embraces an extreme form of empiricism. For example, it seems patently absurd to believe that scientists approach complete objectivity, are free of biases, and regularly discover immutable and final truths—that is, that the scientific method and scientists are infallible. The present authors have written books and articles on the limits of scientific judgment, and on potential problems with such scientific activities as journal review, grant review, and the appraisal of scientific theories. Human beings, scientists surely included, suffer to varying degrees from the flaws and limits of human cognition, the very problems decision making research is often directed to address and attenuate.

Rather, we endorse the view that a (or the) main aim of science is verisimilitude (i.e., truthlikeness), that is, to reach as close an approximation to the truth as possible. (Note that *truth* here is spelled with a lower-case *t*, although it is conceivable that there are rare instances, which are problematic to recognize, in which the upper-case *T* just might apply). Hence, one might say we are semi-demi-quasi-hemi-scientific realists, which means that we believe that an external world exists beyond ourselves or our perceptions, and that a central goal of science is to come as close as possible to capturing the external world accurately, just as the concept of verisimilitude conveys. These views do not align with extreme relativism or empiricism, and they do not rule out, and instead recognize, that a myriad of background factors and biases can derail human thinking. In addition, in our view, such flaws and limitations apply not only to people on the street, but also to individuals in all walks of life and across the full range of professions, with scientists and mental health professionals certainly not being exempt. To acknowledge, however, that no one is free from the limits and fallibilities of human judgment is not to argue that all ideas, thinkers, and decision making processes are equivalent. It is one thing to assert that different things may also have something in common, and another to argue that these different things are equivalent in all ways. It is exactly the differential effectiveness of varying approaches to decision making that provides the fundamental underpinnings and justification for this book and that serves as the main guide in the selection of materials that follow.

Finally, we take what seemingly should be the noncontroversial position that evidence counts, although what evidence counts, and how much it counts for, can raise deep questions and ambiguities. With that said, some basic distinctions seem worth making here. First, in our opinion, statements like "because I say so and believe so" by themselves, should count for little. As research on confidence and accuracy shows compellingly, self-confidence is often a shaky guide to accuracy, and the most confident individuals are sometimes among the least accurate decision makers or prognosticators. Second, it can be helpful to distinguish between the context of discovery and the context of justification or verification. A rough equivalent is generating hypotheses versus testing hypotheses. (Of note, the work of Reichenbach [1938], the philosopher of science often cited as elucidating the distinction between the context of discovery and verification, does not necessarily match its frequent portrayal.)

In many cases, relaxing evidentiary standards when generating new lines of thought helps avoid rejecting them too hastily, especially ideas that may have great value. Of course, turning idea generation into a complete free for all, especially beyond its early stages, has potential costs. Evaluating each erroneous idea may take time and effort away from developing ideas with greater promise. Nevertheless, novel ideas are often the driving force in scientific breakthroughs, yet they may be very difficult to evaluate initially. Consequently, in a range of situations, especially those in which progress seems to have been thwarted, one might be willing to accept a high risk of error for a potentially high payoff.

Failure to distinguish between the context of discovery and the context of justification leads to unproductive arguments and unwarranted criticisms, as are all too common in psychology. For example, if one is trying to generate ideas to solve a novel problem, it often makes sense to initially relax evidentiary standards to a degree and not worry too much about just how promising they seem, especially to those other than the person or persons who generated the possibility. However, there often are substantive differences between approaches that are effective for generating ideas as opposed to testing them. Methods and processes for generating ideas often provide limited or faulty means for testing them, just as applying more formal and rigorous methods for testing ideas can impede the initial steps of discovery or the generation of novel problem solutions. Hence, problems often arise when standards for evidence or evaluation are not adjusted in accord with the context under consideration.

Someone who applies relaxed standards to both contexts and forgoes more rigorous methods to test new ideas is almost doomed to make too many errors. Conversely, one who applies overly strict standards of evidence in the context of discovery may often fail to get very far on especially challenging problems because potentially fruitful ideas are rejected prematurely. Thus, if a case conference or single case study is used to generate ideas, and less so to test them, a critic who impugns the process due to its lack of rigor is probably missing the mark, just as someone who does not tighten up approaches for testing the proposed ideas has probably made the obverse mistake. Put simply, methods for generating ideas can be weak approaches for testing ideas, and thus applying the same standards across the two contexts is likely to be counterproductive and may promulgate unfair and overly general criticisms of individuals who adjust rigor depending on the context under which they are operating. Certainly, some of the greatest discoveries in a field like neurology originated from case studies or work with a single individual, such as various insights into functional neuroanatomy. However, many ideas or hypotheses arising from such methodology turn out to contain significant error, or to be just plain wrong, when subjected to more rigorous testing. Many patients have benefited from the elimination of compelling but mistaken beliefs that have been replaced by more accurate ones. Throughout this book, we describe many conditions that create high risk for error, as well as ways of identifying them and reducing the likelihood of mistakes.

Two fundamental questions about the status of knowledge claims are almost always worth asking: "What is the evidence?" and "How strong is the evidence?" As already discussed, just how strong evidence needs to be in order to support alternative courses of action will often vary depending on whether the primary interest is generating versus testing potentially useful or novel ideas. Beyond that, at least for now, we do not wish to enter into the far more complex question of judging knowledge credentials, except to suggest that the following might serve as a useful rule of thumb: If a reasonably large and consistent body of well-conducted research contradicts personal impressions about a hypothesis or clinical conjecture, in most cases the research will be right, and the personal belief will be wrong. Note that we use the qualifier *in most cases*, and not such words or phrases as *always* or *almost always,* and we have not extended this guide to situations in which the scientific evidence is tenuous. However, if one will not even accept this modest rule of thumb as a sound generalization that holds more often than not, then it seems that one has largely rejected the scientific method. One is not truly incorporating scientific knowledge if one accepts scientific findings only when they align with one's personal impressions and rejects them when they do not. Given such practices, except perhaps for the sake of appearance, there would seem to be little point in reviewing scientific evidence on almost any issue, despite working in a field that that frequently claims to use science as a major foundation for applied work.

Greater Accuracy Often Results in Better Outcomes

Returning now to the question of whether accuracy matters in psychology and allied fields, it seems almost self-evident that the answer is sometimes not very much, but in many other instances more than a little, and sometimes a great deal. For example, if a neuropsychologist mistakenly lists a prior childhood illness as roseola and not rubella, it may not make a whit of difference in the current assessment of a potential neurodegenerative disorder. That benign error is very different from concluding that a police officer has re-established psychological stability and therefore should have authorization to carry a weapon reinstated, when that officer has minimized ongoing struggles with homicidal ideation, emotional flooding, racial hatred, and shaky self-control.

Mental health professionals, to their credit, often take on vitally important work, roles, and challenges. In many such undertakings, predictive accuracy can improve the prospects for positive outcomes and reduce the chances of harm or tragic outcomes. Even a short list of psychologists' and other mental health professionals' common activities and undertakings provides compelling examples:

- Prediction of suicide and implementation of steps to prevent self-harm
- Consultation with parole boards
- Evaluation of airline pilots
- Child custody evaluations
- Evaluation of potential child abuse
- Identification of cognitive dysfunction and potential causative factors (e.g., assisting in differentiating reversible versus nonreversible causes of cognitive decline)
- Design of treatment for severe depression
- Design of treatment for severe, incapacitating anxiety disorders
- Design of interventions for modification of life-threatening health behaviors (e.g., compliance with diabetic treatment protocols)
- Design of treatment for substance abuse or addiction
- Evaluation of the need for involuntary hospitalization
- Evaluation of potential danger to others
- Evaluation of fitness for military duty
- Evaluation of testamentary capacity
- Determination of whether juveniles should be tried as adults
- Differentiation between legitimate mental disorder and feigned "insanity"

Such a list could be expanded considerably, and for each item it would be easy to show that the chances of positive outcomes would likely be enhanced by increasing the accuracy of prediction or evaluative judgments. Evaluative accuracy itself often fits lock and key into a predictive context, because often a major purpose for conducting evaluation in the first place is to help with some implicit or explicit prediction (e.g., if an officer is returned to duty, will weapons be handled appropriately?). Given the predictive component of these various professional activities and the gravity of the situations involved, the help that decision science can provide is a fortunate addition to the resources at our disposal.

STRIVING FOR CONTINUING IMPROVEMENT

There is an extensive literature on the accuracy of clinical judgment that we will cover throughout the book, but for the moment, suppose that in a particular area studies generally yield a 75% accuracy rate in differentiating between three possible outcomes or conditions. For example, suppose the differential is between slowly resolving cognitive dysfunction secondary to protracted alcohol abuse, the early stages of an irreversible dementia, or metabolic dysfunction that would likely remit if proper treatment was provided within a limited time window. For the sake of this example, assume that the three possibilities occur with equal frequency, and hence if one lacked any useful knowledge and was merely guessing, accuracy would be about 33%. In such circumstances, achieving 75% accuracy is a major improvement, reducing the error rate from about 67% to 25%, or something approaching a threefold reduction. If, in turn, improved accuracy helped considerably in intervention choice or selection of the most efficacious treatment, it might benefit many individuals, and could even be life-changing.

Suppose the accuracy rate had remained at about 75% for a number of years, with a breakthrough then occurring that improved accuracy to 85%. Suppose further that the new method is inexpensive and essentially risk-free. Now assume you are consulting with a healthcare professional on behalf of a loved one, with this three-way differential diagnosis at issue. If the healthcare professional states that the 75% accuracy rate is pretty good already, so why bother implementing the new method, would you find that a satisfactory position? As the example illustrates, asking how we are doing with commonly used methods is incomplete. We should almost always be asking in addition whether we can do better if we combine or supplement the frequently used method with other available methods. All things being equal, if adding the new method increases accuracy and enhances outcomes, it typically should be embraced.

The importance of comparative questions may be overlooked. For example, knowing whether a psychological assessment method has validity may be much less helpful in decision making than knowing how it compares to other methods. Suppose a method achieves 70% accuracy. If an alternative method achieves 60% accuracy, and if combining the two methods does nothing to bolster the accuracy achieved by the better method, than all else being equal, the better method should be used rather than the relatively weaker method. However, if an alternative method is available that achieves 85% accuracy, then the situation is very different. Here, and again assuming all other things being equal, the method achieving 85% accuracy should be selected over the method that achieves 70% accuracy, or the two should be used together if joint use elevates accuracy to over 85% (which may or may not occur, as discussed in various sections of the book, such as chapters 6 and 13).

Even small increments in accuracy, such as a change from 75% to 85%, may not seem very impressive, but can be well worth the effort. How many decisions does a practicing professional make over a career? Surely thousands. A change from 75% to 85% accuracy, or a reduction in error rate from 25% to 15%, especially when accuracy impacts outcomes, can realize much human good. There is a story told in many variations that goes something like this: As the tide goes out, a young child sees that hundreds of starfish are stranded on the rocks and will suffer or die from sun exposure. The child starts gathering starfish and placing them back into the water. A grandparent turns to the child and comments that the undertaking is far too great to get very far, at which point the child holds up a starfish she is about to save and says, “It makes a difference to this one.”

For various reasons, relatively subtle changes in rates of positive outcomes can be very difficult to discern accurately in the context of day-to-day clinical activities. Often the greatest obstacle to recognizing the impact of positive changes in decision practices is that one does not know what would have happened if one had done otherwise, or had changed one's usual procedures. If we apply the methods we believe are best, there is no problem if we've made the right choices, but how can we know whether our choices are optimal if we rarely or never implement methods we think are not as good? In such circumstances, how can one learn best from experience alone if our choices preclude examining alternatives that could be as good as, or better than, the choices we make?

One of the greatest benefits of many well-designed studies is the inclusion of a comparison group, which helps us circumvent a major factor that frequently compromises, and sometimes enfeebles, our capacity to learn from experience or when operating in naturalistic circumstances. (We recognize that moving from naturalistic environments to study settings also comes with disadvantages that merit serious attention.) In a study, for example, a properly formed control group, or an alternative intervention group, helps us learn what might happen if one does not intervene, or when an alternative intervention is used. If the study is well done and other studies replicate the findings, we then may have a strong basis for comparison, and we may find that the original intervention is far better than no intervention at all, not different at all, or actually causes more harm than good. One might think that the latter outcome would be easy to recognize without formal study, but that is not always the case. For example, if almost everyone is treated with a widely accepted intervention that has an 80% positive outcome rate (thereby seemingly verifying utility), it might not be easy to know that the positive outcome rate without intervention is 85%. Along these lines, despite the wide array of helpful medical interventions that have been developed, there are still numerous examples in the history of medicine in which interventions presumed to be helpful on the basis of clinical experience either did not change the outcome or were harmful.

Although beliefs about the efficacy of clinical decision making can vary widely, almost surely most would agree that seeking further improvement is a worthy objective. As we describe, certain strategies for enhancing accuracy often backfire. For example, we may abandon established methods for methods that have a compelling appearance of effectiveness but that actually degrade accuracy. That such counterproductive outcomes sometimes occur in no way negates the worthiness of the underlying commitment to improvement, but rather calls for careful review of the best available evidence when selecting strategies. As it turns out, there are often readily available methods that are underutilized and can help us do better, such as the integration of base rates into decision making, although they may come in relatively plain wrappers. Thus, rather than focusing on how well we are doing by placing primary reliance on clinical judgment, if we start by finding common ground in the pursuit of improvement, we need not get waylaid before even getting started with evaluating the evidence and options.

Finally, before overviewing the organization of subsequent book materials in the last part of this chapter, one area remains to be covered first. We wish to provide two exemplars of the types of challenging and messy problems common to applied settings, and for which decision research can be especially useful. A common source of divisiveness between those conducting clinical research and those being asked to implement that research is that studies may strip away many of the complexities that create the very difficulties for which practitioners are seeking help and that may well be the original rationale for the research. For example, suppose a study on neuropsychological impairment after concussion excludes potential participants who show any one of multiple potential confounding factors, such as a prior history of learning disability or major psychiatric disorder. However, many clinic patients evaluated for concussion may have three, four, or five exclusionary conditions. As a consequence, when looking to the research for help, it may be extremely difficult to know if a patient's closer match with the concussed group versus the normal group was due to the condition of interest, the deleterious impact of the multiple other confounding factors, such as sleep apnea or past substance abuse, or some combination of both. None of the concussed individuals in the study were known to have these other conditions, and thus how does the clinician isolate potential causative factors? Such a determination, for example, might be central to qualification for benefits or to treatment choice. More so, the accuracy of clinical decisions, and the need for enhanced methods, may vary markedly depending on the difficulty of cases. The two circumstances we describe can have a major impact on case difficulty and are among common situations that make clinical decision making more difficult than it might appear to nonpractitioners.

CASE DIFFICULTY: TWO INFLUENTIAL FACTORS

Conflicting Indicators

Cases in which everything points in the same direction are about as unusual as they are easy. For example, how often is every test result abnormal, and how hard would it be to differentiate normality and abnormality under such conditions? If every sign points to depression, or posttraumatic stress disorder, or a markedly heightened propensity for violent acting out, accurate classification or characterization should rarely be a problem. The same is true if Treatment A is superior to Treatment B along every evaluative criterion or in every respect, if Test A is better than Test B across the board, if Theory A is better than Theory B in all regards, and if Study A is better than Study B across all comparative features and the two have generated conflicting outcomes. The problematic situation, and where expertise is often needed, occurs when things are not so clean, such as when (a) Treatment A is better than Treatment B on some evaluative criteria but worse than Treatment B on other criteria, (b) standing on other criteria is ambiguous or unknown, (c) there is limited information on which criteria might trump other criteria, and (d) there are significant gaps in knowledge about a range of factors that might determine outcome. These are the types of complex and messy problems that all too often confront us in the clinic, where the correct choice may enhance the chance of a good outcome substantially, and where we need to use the best tools at our disposal; it is also where decision research can often provide a critical edge. In entering into such decision domains, we start with the example of conflicting normative data.

Although one might think there are uniform or standard normative data sets for many tests, that is frequently not the case. Rather, different studies may have yielded different, and at times widely contrasting, results, as illustrated in Figure 1.1. Here, two different sets of norms for the same test generate very disparate outcomes. The test at issue (the Category Test) is designed to appraise nonverbal conceptual ability, the capacity to shift mental sets, and the productive use of feedback. The test has 208 items and is scored primarily based on the number of errors. Consequently, the higher the score (i.e., number of errors), the worse the level of performance. For purposes of this example, suppose that a score that falls more than a standard deviation (SD) below the mean is set as the cut-off for relative weakness or abnormality.

According to the study cited at the top of Figure 1.1 and represented in the top half of the figure, 35 errors places a person right at the cutoff point, or at the 16th percentile. The 16th percentile falls below about 5 of 6, or 6 of 7, individuals. Anything more than 35 errors exceeds the cutoff. In contrast, according to the study cited at the bottom of Figure 1.1 and represented in the bottom half of the figure, a score of 35 places one at the 88th percentile, which surpasses about 8 in 9 individuals. According to this same study, one would have to exceed 94 errors to fall outside normal limits, but according to the study at the top of the figure, such a result falls almost 6 SD below the mean, which theoretically occurs in far less than 1 in 1,000,000 individuals.

The example is genuine but certainly extreme, although there are many cases in which different studies generate contrasting normative data. In some cases, the choices are relatively easy because one set of norms may provide a far better match with the examinee on various sociodemographic dimensions associated with test

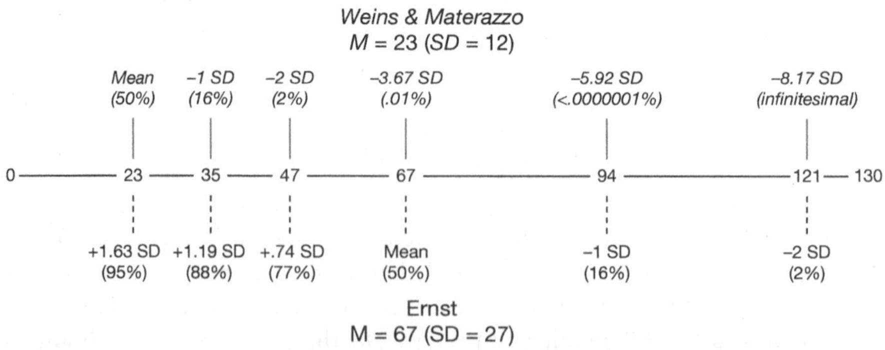

Figure 1.1 Impact of conflicting norms

Problem of Conflicting Indicators

	Norms A	Norms B
Sample Size	8	4
Recency	2	9
Methodologic Match	7	8
Sociodemographic Match	?	?

Figure 1.2 Problem of conflicting indicators

performance, such as age. However, in other cases the situation is much more like the circumstances displayed in Figure 1.2. Here, standing is represented on a scale of 1 (as poor as possible) to 10 (as good as possible). Norms A are clearly better than Norms B on one dimension, clearly inferior on another dimension, similar on a third dimension, and of uncertain status and comparative standing on a fourth dimension. It may also be the case that review of the literature on both normative data sets does not seem to yield anything obvious that helps much with choices.

Again, these are the kinds of complex and messy problems that can create the greatest and most important clinical challenges, and where true expertise is most required. Conflicting indicators are a common reality in many important choices that might be required in patient care: choosing to hospitalize or not hospitalize, selecting and designing possible alternative treatments, differentiating between conditions that can present in similar fashions and for which the evidence cuts both ways, choosing one possible consultant over another, or even selecting between competing theories. It is exactly these types of situations—in which one faces choices under high levels of potential uncertainty, and combining information effectively or optimally may place extreme strain on human judgmental capacity—that the science of decision making and the tools it brings can be of greatest potential value.

Ambiguous versus Definitive or Nearly Definitive Judgments and the Extreme Group Problem

(Authors' Note: Although we might not agree, some readers may consider this section on the extreme group problem esoteric, and they can skip forward to the next section, "Organization of This Book," without reducing comprehension of subsequent materials.)

For some cases or situations, conclusions are definitive or nearly definitive (D/ND). For example, D/ND predictions or conclusions might be possible when a series of potent indicators all point to sexual abuse (e.g., clear physical evidence, a confession, a trustworthy witness). Or, in a particular civil case, lengthy passages in a plaintiff's diary came to light that set out, well in advance, an elaborate plan to (a) falsify a medical injury, (b) feign psychotic symptoms supposedly resulting from the stress that injury caused, (c) bring a personal injury suit against the manufacturer of the device that supposedly caused the injury due to a design flaw, and (d) get back at a despised employer by also filing a Worker's Compensation claim against the facility at which he worked. The case had gotten all the way to trial, with decent prospects for success on all fronts, before the diary was discovered. One might argue that such surety is the rare exception, thereby explaining our use of the phrase or qualifier "definitive *or nearly* definitive". In contrast, other cases or judgment tasks are more difficult or ambiguous and create greater risk of error.

Various limitations and complications make it problematic to determine just how often D/ND cases occur across settings and clinical judgment tasks, and as knowledge advances, the frequency of D/ND cases can increase considerably. However, there is no need to split hairs here, and we suspect almost anyone would agree that some clinical decision tasks are easier or far easier than others. Various factors can increase the level of difficulty, such as restrictions in knowledge, limited cooperation from examinees, or changing presentations over time. One of the more common factors elevating difficulty is when the judgment in question does not involve separating clear-cut cases, such as between normal and abnormal presentations, but rather requires making subtler distinctions between individuals reasonably suspected of having a condition who do have the condition, and individuals reasonably suspected of having a condition who do not have the condition. For the "reasonably suspected" descriptor to apply, the basis for the suspicion must be validly associated with the condition in question. For example, one may suspect that an individual is feigning neuropsychological deficit because of a relatively high, but far from definitive, result on a measure with demonstrated value for appraising effort during testing. We use S+ (suspected of and has) and S− (suspected of but does not have) to refer to this type of situation. A variation on this theme is separating individuals suspected of having either Condition A (e.g., posttraumatic stress disorder) or Condition B (e.g., generalized anxiety disorder) who have Condition A, versus those who instead have Condition B, or perhaps have both Condition A and B.

Figure 1.3 shows differences that may occur in clinical versus research settings on a measure designed to evaluate effort on testing. Assume the measure is relatively new and in the early stages of development. Further assume that the middle point of the horizontal line for both graphs in Figure 1.3, as demarcated by the 0, reflects the mean number of errors for groups trying to perform to the best of their abilities, or equates to the 50th percentile (i.e., 0.0 SD). Again, this is the mean score for groups presumably exerting good effort. For the measure in question, keeping in mind that a greater number of errors reflects worse performance, we have aligned the graphs so that moving from left to right represents worse performance and potentially lower levels of effort. Consequently, because fewer errors reflect better performance, a score of -1.0 SD, for example, or a rate of error that falls 1 SD below the mean, reflects better than average performance, whereas

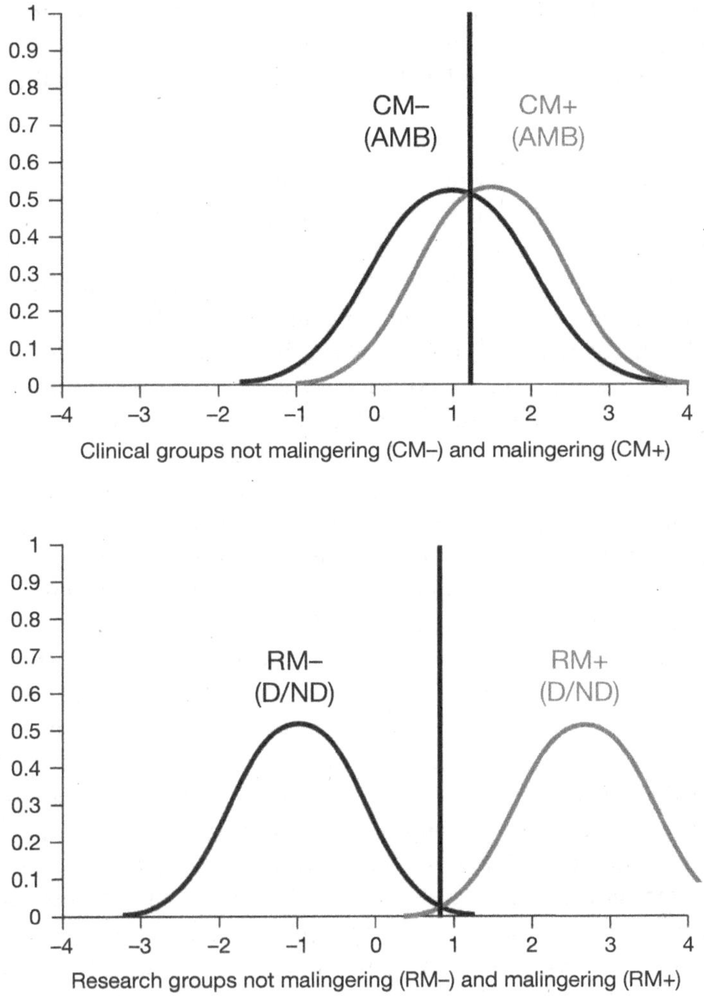

Figure 1.3 Illustration of the extreme group problem

a score of +1 SD reflects an error rate that falls 1 SD above the mean, or a greater than average number of errors.

The bottom half of Figure 1.3 depicts a research study in which the investigator has formed two groups: a good-effort group and a poor-effort group, in order to evaluate whether, or the extent to which, the groups perform differently on the effort test. As is commonly done, the investigator has labored to achieve accurate group assignments, that is, to exclude individuals who are not really trying their best from the good-effort group, and individuals who are trying their best from the poor-effort group. The concern is that if there are more than rare errors in group assignment, interpreting outcomes will become difficult or seriously compromised.

One approach to conducting such research is to start with cases in which individuals have completed multiple established effort measures, and to pare those individuals down into a group that obtains scores that easily surpass cutoffs for good effort across the measures (thereby becoming the good-effort group) and another group that falls well below cutoffs across most or all of the measures (thereby becoming the poor-effort group). Given these procedures, quite a few individuals might not qualify for either group and are excluded from the study. In some studies, a researcher might have to look through 200 case files or more to identify, say, 50 individuals for each group. The result is groups comprised of individuals who can be classified almost definitively, but who are extreme and quite possibly poorly representative of the original subject pool taken together. These groups are likely to be extreme because it is relatively unusual, even for individuals who generally exert good effort, to put forth excellent effort on all measures, and for individuals who generally exert poor effort to put forth very poor effort on most or all measures. Each group then completes the new measure, or perhaps the new measure was included in the overall battery of tests they completed originally but was not considered in the original group assignment to avoid confounded independent and dependent variables.

The bottom half of Figure 1.3 depicts the performance of two such groups on the new measure: a research group that is almost definitely exerting good effort or is not malingering (RM-), and a group that is almost definitely exerting poor effort or is malingering (RM+). With study designs of this type, which are relatively common, it would not be unusual to end up with groups whose mean performance differs by 3 to 4 SD, just as represented here (RM- group mean = -1 SD; RM+ group mean = ~ +2.75). Furthermore, considering that a score of 0.0 SD represents the mean level of effort for a normative sample, and that lower scores reflect greater effort, the RM- group's mean of -1 SD indicates better performance or effort than the normative group. Consequently, the optimal cutoff point between the RM- group and the RM+ group shifts to the left in comparison to the optimal cutoff point for the groups in the top half of Figure 1.3.

In contrast to the wide disparity between the groups in the research study, the situation in the clinic or in a forensic setting may often be quite different, at least with the more challenging cases. Generally, one is not particularly worried about the capacity to differentiate between insufficient effort when all valid indicators point to good effort and none point to poor effort, or when most or all valid indicators point to bad effort and none to good or optimal effort, because that is usually an easy undertaking. Rather, the cases of concern, and often the ones that come to attention or require expertise, are those for which there is a good basis to suspect poor effort, and one then has to try to distinguish between individuals who are suspected of malingering and are malingering versus those who are suspected of malingering and are not malingering. In Figure 1.3, these two groups are respectively identified as ambiguous clinical groups who are not malingering, CM-/(AMB), and ambiguous clinical groups who are malingering, CM+/(AMB). That differentiation can be much harder because valid indicators are not uniform, and one or more of the indicators can conflict with one another. Hence, rather than the groups' showing large differences, the differences are smaller, or more subtle, and the decision task is much harder.

In actuality, the effect size of about .50 depicted in the upper half of Figure 1.3 is moderate or relatively robust, and it is the formation of extreme groups in the study that can easily mislead us into thinking our methods are considerably more effective than their operational characteristics in many clinical settings and situations. In other publications, we have referred to the overrepresentation of effect sizes that can occur in studies as opposed to the levels commonly seen in clinical application as the *extreme group problem* (Faust et al., 2021). The extreme group problem also often shifts optimal cutoff scores in a way that increases the rate of either false-positive or false-negative errors. It can also lead us to rely on qualitative indicators that are effective in forming groups in the studies but that generalize poorly to the clinic, for if such qualitative features occurred regularly and had high validity, the clinical cases that are ambiguous would not be ambiguous but instead readily identifiable. Rather, the clinical cases are often ambiguous precisely because they do not show the features that make cases readily identifiable.

Some methods get considerable mileage by creating, often inadvertently, research conditions that exclude all but D/ND cases in group assignments. The end result is to generate what are frequently grossly inflated accuracy rates that generalize poorly to challenging clinical circumstances in which one must distinguish between those suspected (for good reason) of having a condition who have the condition, and those suspected of having a condition who do not have the condition. Cutoff scores emerging from such studies often increase false-positive or false-negative error rates, and qualitative indicators may lead to more errors than correct judgments, given their lack of generalization. The seemingly high accuracy rates will also tend to inflate confidence, which secondarily fosters multiple other, potentially serious problematic judgment practices, such as drawing premature conclusions or not attending sufficiently to potentially disconfirming evidence. Of additional concern, studies that are stronger methodologically, such as those dealing with group assignment in a manner that leads to more representative clinical cases, by virtue of having fewer extreme cases, will often produce lower accuracy rates than weaker studies that may largely restrict group assignment to extreme cases. Hence, the worse the methodology in group formation or the less representative the groups, the better the method may appear to be. Conversely, it is increasingly likely that a superior method tested with superior methodology will look worse than an inferior method tested with inferior methodology.

An analogy is a situation in which we are evaluating two training programs for potential baseball umpires. In the first program, when tested after program completion, the prospective umpires have to judge a series of plays in which runners are often safe or out by wide margins, and they have to achieve 95% accuracy. In the second program, when prospective umpires are tested, most of the plays are close or very close, because it is exactly this capacity that matters most—almost anyone can judge extreme plays correctly, but far fewer can judge very close plays accurately. When tested in this manner, the prospective umpires in the second program achieve an accuracy rate of 85%, or seemingly make three times more errors than do graduates of the first program. Even if the graduates from the second program developed considerably better skills than graduates from the first program, they might look considerably worse given the unevenness of appraisal methods, whereas the outcomes would be far different if the appraisals were equivalent. Unfortunately, in many studies in psychology comparing diagnostic methods, evaluations of accuracy are compromised or contaminated by the extreme group problem. Faust et al. (2021) provided guidelines for identifying the presence and degree of the extreme group problem, such as the percentage of individuals excluded during group formation, the number of exclusionary criteria, grossly inflated or unrealistically high effect sizes, and disparities in groups included in meta-analytic studies comparing assessment methods.

ORGANIZATION OF THIS BOOK

The materials in this book place primary emphasis on decision making practices and processes that impede versus enhance accuracy. The book is divided into three parts. Part I, which begins with this chapter, follows with a chapter that draws mainly from the authors' opportunities to conduct detailed reviews of mental health professionals' work, such as psychological and neuropsychological evaluations. This second chapter emphasizes common sources of error in clinical evaluations and decision making that are mainly linked to quality-control issues, such as drifting from important specifications for test administration. Such problems can often be attenuated or eliminated through diligent effort.

The remainder of the book draws heavily from decision research. In Part II, a number of chapters cover normative or advantageous decision practices that are commonly underused or disregarded. For example, Chapter 3 addresses departures from practices that are needed to appraise potential associations between variables accurately, such as whether a diagnostic sign or indicator of supposed value really is useful. This same chapter also addresses effective methods for analyzing such potential relationships, or for performing proper covariation analysis. Other chapters cover the tremendous advantages that can be realized by integrating frequency data or base rates into diagnosis and prediction (e.g., Chapter 6), and (Chapter 8) one of the most important questions in psychology and in many other fields: Which data integration strategy leads to more accurate predictions? Is it clinical judgment, which emphasizes subjective means of integrating and interpreting information, or statistical methods, which emphasize formal means of data combination?

Other chapters in Part II are devoted to common cognitive biases. These chapters emphasize what decision researchers often call *cold cognitive errors*. Cold cognitive errors are less a product of emotionally driven missteps and more a function of normal human cognitive processes that go astray in certain situations or problem domains. Such errors or problems are commonly underrecognized and thus may go uncorrected. For example, Chapter 4 covers the common tendency to test impressions or hypotheses by attending primarily to confirming evidence and less so to potential disconfirming evidence. Chapter 5 examines such biases as overestimating the predictability of outcomes once they are known, or in hindsight, as opposed to their actual predictability in foresight; and to common errors in appraising the likelihood that sequences of events or scenarios will occur. Such misappraisals can easily lead to reduced predictive accuracy and thereby compromise clinical effectiveness. Chapter 7 discusses the crucial topic of how to combine various pieces of predictive data and circumstances in which focusing mainly on holistic data integration may reduce, rather than enhance, judgmental accuracy.

Part II also includes two other chapters that address crucial issues in decision making in the mental health field. For both of these chapters, we have had the good fortune to recruit specialists to take lead roles: Ana Bridges for Chapter 9 and Gabriele Fariello for Chapter 10. Chapter 9 covers multicultural influences on decision making, such as judgmental biases that may diminish diagnostic and predictive accuracy when working with diverse groups. It also discusses parallels and contrasts between research on errors of cold cognition and research emphasizing the impact of racial and ethnic factors on clinical judgment, assessment methods, and diagnostic practices. Chapter 10 covers the use and influence of artificial intelligence and machine learning in clinical decision making, its current status, potential advantages and limitations, and its future prospects.

The last section of the book, Part III, is devoted to methods for improving diagnostic and predictive accuracy. As discussed in Chapter 11, some of the greatest obstacles to improvement are factors that, unfortunately, reduce awareness of our judgmental limits and the potential gains of adopting altered or supplemental practices. These factors stem from converging naturalistic conditions that make it difficult to avoid inflated confidence and to distinguish with sufficient consistency between situations in which experience is an effective teacher and those in which experiential learning often has critical limitations and drawbacks. In the final two chapters, we address such helpful steps as applying a successive hurdles approach for appraising the value of information, strategies for reducing confirmatory and hindsight bias, procedures for locating base rate information and established decision rules and interpretive procedures, and helpful assists for combining information, such as base rates with qualitative and quantitative indicators and diagnostic tests.

REFERENCES

American Psychiatric Association. (2013). *Diagnostic and statistical manual of mental disorders* (5th ed.). https://doi.org/10.1176/appi.books.9780890425596

Faust, D., Gaudet, C. E., Ahern, D. C., & Bridges, A. J. (2021). Assessment of malingering and falsification: Continuing to push the boundaries of knowledge in research and clinical practice. In A. M. Horton & C. R. Reynolds (Eds.), *Detection of malingering during head injury litigation* (3rd ed., pp. 1–156). Springer.

Reichenbach, H. (1938). *Experience and prediction: An analysis of the foundations and the structure of knowledge*. University of Chicago Press.

2

Avoiding Avoidable Error

Some factors limiting judgmental accuracy are easy to identify, but they may not be correctible, at least not immediately. For example, limits in knowledge and method, such as lacking precise ways to measure certain critical variables, can restrict judgmental accuracy. In other instances, research on decision making can help us reduce error and improve accuracy. For example, subsequent chapters address practical guidance based on research comparing the relative efficacy of various methods for collecting, integrating, and interpreting information. The research covers such topics as appraising the accuracy or predictive value of information, differentiating more and less useful information, combining or integrating information as effectively as possible, and the benefits of using helpful decision aids. Before getting to that literature and its pragmatic application, it is important to examine various sources of error or reduced accuracy that often can be attenuated or eliminated by simply maintaining systematic practices.

Given our consulting activities, we have had many opportunities to conduct detailed reviews of mental health professionals' work, especially psychological and neuropsychological evaluations. Our anecdotal experience accords with research showing that clerical or related errors are surprisingly common and account for many diagnostic and predictive mistakes (Allard et al., 1995; Allard & Faust, 2000; Charter et al., 2000; Slate et al., 1992). Errors, of course, are not unique to mental health professionals. For example, research shows that medical errors are a leading cause of morbidity and mortality in hospital settings (Graber et al., 2005). It is not easy to minimize error in light of the time pressure, needed levels of exactitude, and sheer number of appraisals and procedures that can be required in medical care or in a comprehensive psychological evaluation.

Errors may be understandable, but that does not lessen their harm. Given the frequency and human costs of error and the effectiveness of what are often relatively straightforward corrective steps, error reduction should be a high priority. Various potential corrective steps, such as the use of checklists, are discussed in Part III of this volume. The materials in the present chapter are intended to provide sobering examples of mistakes and lapses, and to highlight the importance of methodical work practices. Careful work habits can reduce both practitioners' malpractice risks, and, most importantly, negative outcomes in the first place. Our intent is not to make mental health professionals look bad, to question the general competency or dedication of mental health professionals, or to question the potential benefits of mental health services. We gladly acknowledge the voluminous literature that shows clearly that most individuals benefit substantially from therapy services (Huhn et al., 2014; McDermut et al., 2006; von Bronswijk et al., 2019).

Rather, our purpose is to illustrate the types of errors we have seen relatively often in our consultative work and that have been documented in the literature, errors we are all prone to make and that can require diligence and discipline to avoid or reduce. A brief list of such missteps includes:

- errors scoring and tallying results from psychological measures,
- unnecessary alterations in standard procedures that can distort outcomes (Lee et al., 2003),
- factual inaccuracies passed on from source to source,
- use of obsolete methods,
- failing to identify and gather information on the most predictive variables, and depending too heavily on indirect, inferential information, when more direct and trustworthy information is available,
- selecting inferior alternatives over stronger alternatives (e.g., giving insufficient consideration to the questions or populations for which tests or methods may be most useful, thereby treating validity as a global, not specific, quality)—and consequently selecting methods with weaker norms, weaker psychometric qualities, less informative research, or that fail to match the examinee as well as available alternatives,
- overemphasis on pathology and insufficient emphasis on positive qualities and strengths, and
- insufficient consideration of alternative causes.

The figures that follow illustrate many of these potential problems, some of which also relate to the decision literature that is discussed in subsequent chapters. Many of the figures are drawn from legal cases involving personal injury claims stemming from events such as motor vehicle accidents, falls, and possible exposure to damaging levels of toxins. Lest one think that various examples represent motivated "errors" designed to achieve intended aims, multiple figures originate from treating professionals who were not retained by lawyers representing one or the other side of a case. In addition, these errors were often observed in situations where much was at stake, and professionals therefore had good reason to believe their work would be closely scrutinized. Although most of the figures illustrate errors that, if undetected, would have favored plaintiffs' cases, other errors (see Figures 2.7 and 2.8) favored defendants and could have denied deserving individuals needed compensation. The figures have been de-identified, and any names that appear are fictitious.

SCORING ERRORS AND BREAKS IN STANDARDIZED PROCEDURES (FIGURES 2.1–2.4)

Scoring errors are apparently quite common in psychological assessment, as previously cited research indicates (e.g., Allard et al., 1995; Allard & Faust, 2000; Charter et al., 2000; Slate et al., 1992), and as we have observed time and again in case reviews.

Figures 2.1 and 2.2 demonstrate scoring errors and their potential significance. In the case from which these materials were drawn, the neuropsychologist described the two scores that fell toward the lower end of the average range (the 86 and 82) and the score in the borderline range (the 77) on composite indices as potential evidence of memory dysfunction, especially for an individual who tended to score higher in various other areas of testing. The composite indices measured such areas as immediate and delayed auditory memory (e.g., the capacity to remember the details of narrative passages). On a deposition (a session in which the opposing lawyer has the opportunity to ask the expert, under oath, about such matters as the underlying bases for conclusions), the expert indicated that scores that fell more than a standard deviation below the mean reflected impairment. The test in question has a mean of 100 and a standard deviation of 15. The expert placed particular emphasis on the scores of 82 and 77 as being most clearly reflective of abnormality, admitting that the 86 was equivocal. However, the expert made a number of scoring errors (e.g., counting up credits incorrectly), and when the scores were corrected, as seen in Figure 2.2, all scores fell within normal limits and undercut the expert's opinion.

Figure 2.3 illustrates the magnitude of some scoring errors. This result came from reversing a procedure for tallying scores (for some tests, one is supposed to

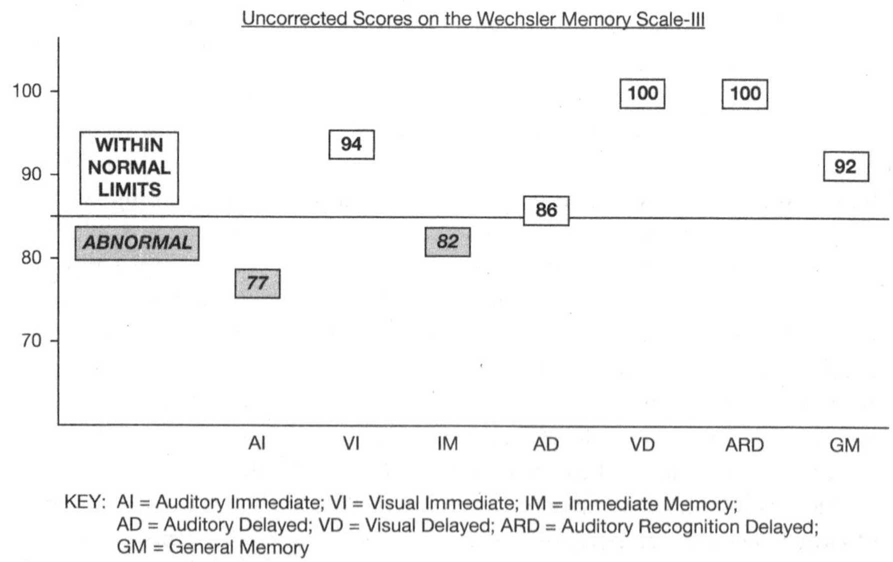

Figure 2.1 Uncorrected scores on the Wechsler Memory Scale

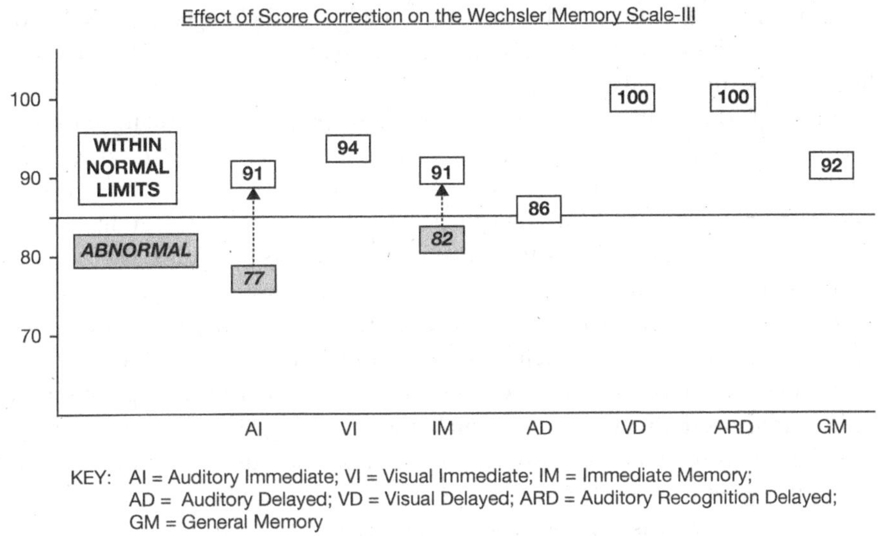

Figure 2.2 Effect of score correction on the Wechsler Memory Scale

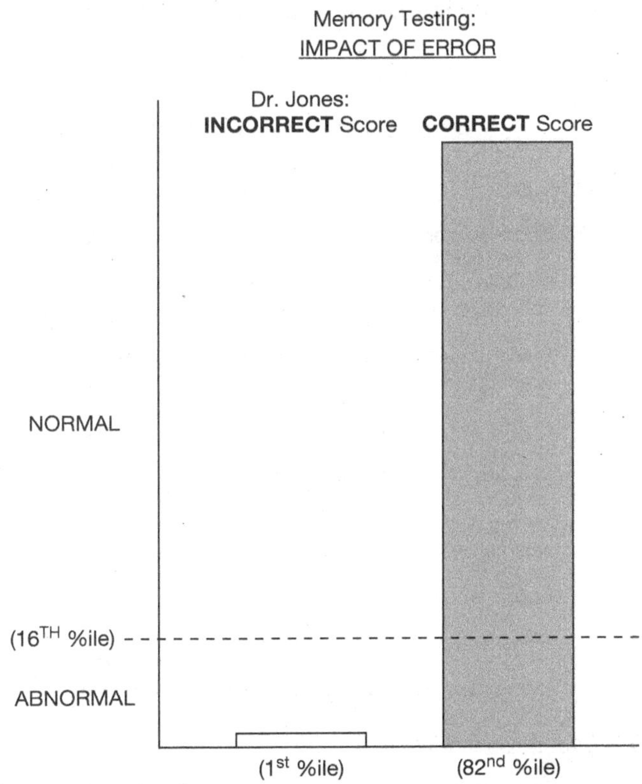

Figure 2.3 Impact of error on interpreting performance on memory testing

be subtracting rather than adding scores on items), and changed the result from a score worse than that of 99 of 100 individuals to an outcome better than that of about 8 in 10 individuals.

Figure 2.4 shows the first page of a series of pages summarizing dozens of scoring and procedural errors. For example, in numerous cases, the expert failed to follow standard procedures for test administration, which can have a sizeable impact on outcomes. For illustrative purposes, suppose a coach is timing someone in the 100-yard dash to see how that person's speed stacks up against that of others trying to make the track team. The other individuals have run on a level, asphalt track, without wind in their face. However, the person now being timed has to run uphill on a muddy track facing into the wind. Similarly, if a test is developed and normed under a certain set of conditions, the examiner must try to reproduce those conditions so that the comparison between the examinee and the normative or reference group is fair. Of course, there can be conditions in which standard procedures ought to be altered (e.g., perhaps an individual has a visual deficit that requires an increase in the size of the test materials), but these circumstances should be noted and greater caution typically exercised in interpreting test results.

The psychologist referenced in Figure 2.4, however, often violated administration and scoring procedures, either mistakenly or because she thought such alterations improved the measures (without background research testing or confirming her beliefs). For example, when test instructions indicated that the examinee should

Error/Problems in the Evaluation

WISC-III

Scoring errors

Mislabeled levels of performance (e.g., Digit Span = "borderline")

Discontinued prematurely or did not record procedures properly

Claims that improvement with extra time represents slowing without needed scientific basis (or in face of contrary literature)

Makes note of intra-subtest scatter contrary to scientific literature

Failure to record as per manual instructions

Altered standard procedures

Notes "calendar concepts" without scientific basis

Complex Figure Test

Erroneously concluded time to copy was excessive

Figure 2.4 Example of errors performing a neuropsychological evaluation

work as fast as possible *without making mistakes*, the psychologist skipped the last three words and then penalized the individual for each mistake made. One of the authors testified in the case and started to review these errors and missteps in a hearing before the judge in order to convey the tenuousness of the original psychologist's conclusions. After going over the first page of problems, the judge, who recognized the occurrence of many such errors after the original psychologist was cross-examined, wondered if the current expert planned to go over every one of them. That was not necessary. The judge subsequently excluded the original expert from testifying, an appeal was filed, and the exclusion upheld. A further appeal led to a reversal, based on the Court's ruling that scoring was not part of neuropsychological methodology and that only methodology was relevant to the admissibility decision. In any case, the lawyer who had retained the original expert decided not to use her and designated another expert instead.

Of interest, few of the errors in the Figures 2.1 to 2.3 could have been detected without accessing the experts' underlying test data. Psychologists may need to think twice before taking assessment results, in either a legal or a clinical case, at face value without reviewing the other psychologist's work. In legal cases, it is of course possible that some of the "errors" were motivated, but in many cases we have seen errors run in both directions and thus they probably did not serve an agenda.

OTHER SOURCES AND EXAMPLES OF ERROR AND PROBLEMATIC PRACTICES

The bar graph on the far left of Figure 2.5 illustrates the mean frequency with which normal individuals show relative weaknesses or "impairments" across a battery of cognitive or neuropsychological tests if one sets the cut-off at more than a standard deviation below the mean, as is commonly done. Stated differently, normal individuals show strengths and weaknesses, and consequently it is normal to be abnormal, but only up to a point. Additionally, tests have an error component, which can also contribute to dispersion in test results. Some neuropsychologists use batteries that generate 100 scores for various tests and subtests, resulting in many normal individuals obtaining somewhere between 10 and 20 low scores. Consequently, one can see how a focus on low scores could lead to false impressions. (See the discussion of confirmatory bias in Chapter 4.)

What made the current case remarkable was a complete reversal in the rate of normal versus abnormal results when the expert followed proper methodology (middle bar graph: 87% WNL/13% abnormal results) as opposed to when his methodology was flawed (far right bar graph: 13% WNL/87% abnormal results). His problematic methodology included, among other things, using inappropriate reference or normative groups, such as individuals with high levels of ability, as opposed to more typical or representative groups. This would be analogous to comparing a student who maintained a C average before a purported decline in neuropsychological functioning to a group of students who maintained

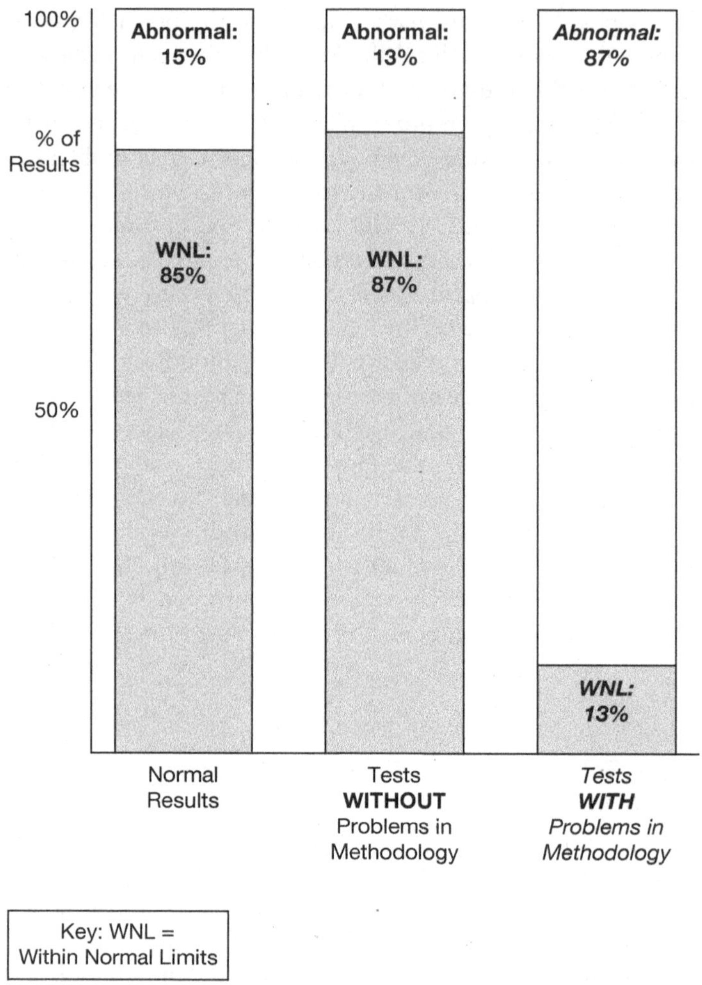

Figure 2.5 Effect of methodological errors on results of cognitive testing

an A average, and concluding that the individual's academic functioning had declined. Given such flaws in methodology, it seemed appropriate to disregard the results based on flawed methods and to limit the analysis to tests administered and scored properly.

Figure 2.6 addresses results from the Luria Nebraska Neuropsychological Battery (LNNB), which generates multiple test scores. The measure's developer suggested that in addition to test scores, qualitative features of test performance were also worth considering. For example, because test items might be missed for differing reasons, specific missteps in the examinee's reasoning processes might yield insights into the nature of cognitive weaknesses. The expert in this case, Dr. S., who diagnosed the individual he evaluated as having developed dementia after an accident and resultant brain injury, took this suggestion to a different level: He analyzed qualitative features exclusively, not even bothering to score test

Summary of Results on the LNNB

Measure	**Result**	**Did Dr: S. Discuss?**
Level of Intelligence	110 (at prior level)	NO
Presence of Brain Dysfunction		
Clinical Scales and S1	NORMAL	NO
Localization Scales	NORMAL	NO
Level of Compensation (S1)	NORMAL/ HIGH SCORE	NO
Localization of Dysfunction		
Left-Frontal	NORMAL	NO
Right-Frontal	NORMAL	NO
Left-Temporal	NORMAL	NO
Right-Temporal	NORMAL	NO

Figure 2.6 Summary of results on the Luria Nebraska Neuropsychological Battery

items and generate tallies. However, most research on the LNNB measure has examined quantitative results.

The middle column in Figure 2.6 ("Result") was generated by one of the present authors after obtaining a copy of the underlying test data and scoring the battery Dr. S. had administered. The end result was all normal scores. At the subsequent legal proceeding, Dr. S. testified first. Sadly, the plaintiff, who was present during the testimony, wept when Dr. S. described the plaintiff's supposed progressive dementia and, apparently finding the testimony intolerable, left before the cross-examination. In the cross-examination of Dr. S. the lawyer started by referencing the LNNB author's indication that the multiple quantitative scores formed the primary basis for evaluating test results. For each primary score that should have been generated, the lawyer then asked the expert whether he obtained a formal test score and whether the score was normal or not. Incidentally, the overall result (see the 110 under the first entry in the middle column) fell at almost the identical level the examinee had obtained before the accident on a measure designed to assess overall intellectual ability. The lawyer then asked the expert if he knew whether the multiple results represented in Figure 2.6 were correct, and if he wanted to check them himself to verify the outcome. The attorney's last question was whether it was true that in the LNNB manual, the LNNB author not only described the need to calculate scores for the various scales, but also whether the scores were the primary source of information for drawing overall conclusions. When the lawyer completed that question and the expert responded affirmatively (he had little choice because the manual was present in the courtroom, and the expert almost surely knew what it said about the matter), the expert asked if he could leave, was told he could, and made a hasty exit. Fortunately, his lawyer was a capable and honorable person and told the plaintiff what the expert had done and how it had misled all of them. The lawyer then dramatically changed his case presentation after this revelation of his expert's highly erroneous conclusion. (Despite his injuries, the plaintiff made a substantial recovery and went on to achieve at a high level in college, graduate school, and his chosen profession.)

Depending on circumstances, a psychologist may be less interested in comparing an examinee's results to members of the general population as opposed to results for a group that match the examinee more closely on factors that can influence test outcome. For example, a key issue may be whether an event or accident has diminished an individual's functioning. If that individual's pre-event functioning was unusually high or low, then comparison to the general population can be very misleading. For example, suppose an individual with 20 years of education has been exposed to levels of carbon monoxide (CO) that might, but also might not, cause a permanent reduction in intellectual capacities. Although education level is far from a perfect indicator of intellectual ability, individuals with much higher levels of education often obtain higher mean scores on certain measures than individuals with considerably lower levels of education. Given how often exceptions may occur, one should seek pre-event information. However, such information may not be available; therefore, comparing the examinee's test performance to the performance of individuals with comparable (versus lower or much lower) education levels improves the capacity to evaluate potential change.

In the present case, the expert lacked sufficient familiarity with guides provided in the pertinent manual for determining level of education, which is often a straightforward matter. Here, the expert made a gross error and underassigned level of education, which yielded the results displayed in Figure 2.7: all normal scores. When this error was corrected, as shown in Figure 2.8, the outcome looked

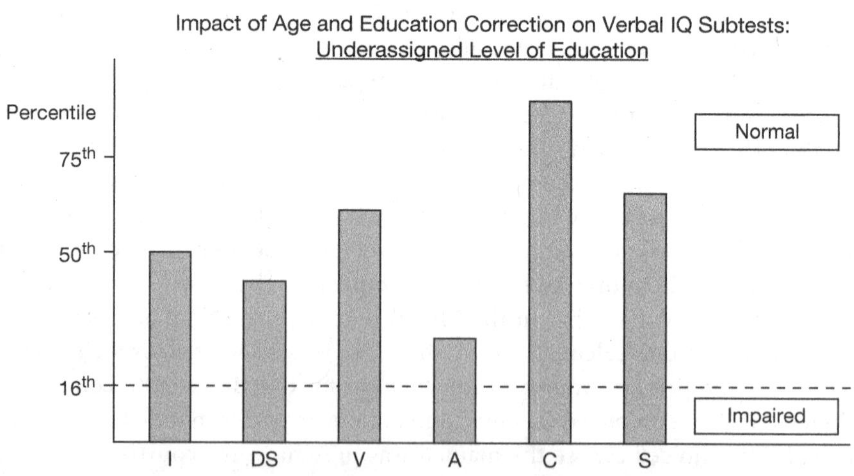

Figure 2.7 Impact of mistaken education adjustment on verbal IQ subtests

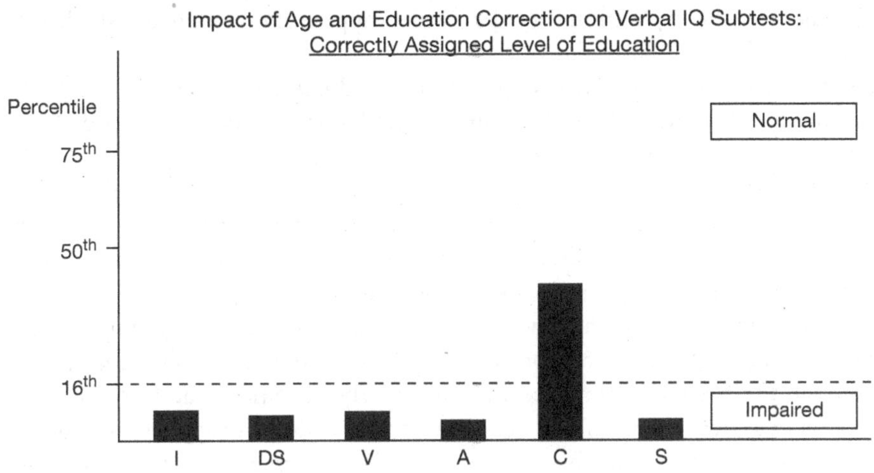

Figure 2.8 Results obtained after correcting education adjustment on verbal IQ subtests

very different, with scores falling within the abnormal range on five of the six tests and, along with other test outcomes, creating a strong basis for identifying cognitive loss.

Figure 2.9 comes from a case in which the psychologist had the examinee draw a 3-dimensional cube twice. The drawings appear on the top half of Figure 2.9. The cube to the left was drawn first, and is impossible, and hence the examinee was asked to try again. She then produced the cube to the right, which, according to the expert, was abnormal because two of the lines extended beyond the connecting point and thereby supposedly reflected perseveration (i.e., not stopping a behavior when appropriate). These were the only abnormalities the expert

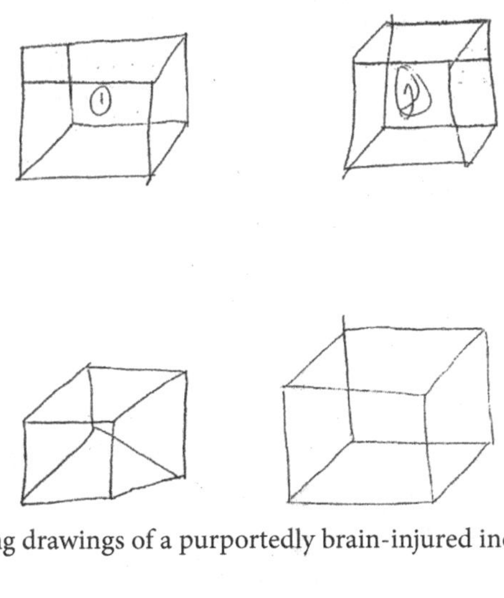

Figure 2.9 Comparing drawings of a purportedly brain-injured individual to drawings of normal individuals

identified on the evaluation, but they were supposedly enough to establish the presence of brain impairment.

One of the authors was teaching an undergraduate class at the time and asked for volunteers to draw the best 3-dimensional cube they possibly could. Two of the volunteers' drawings are reproduced on the bottom half of Figure 2.9, and they show features similar to those the purportedly brain-impaired plaintiff displayed. Obtaining a sample of drawings in this manner is not nearly as informative as comparing results across meticulously formed control and experimental groups; thus, this example is mainly intended to be illustrative.

As considerable research shows, the expectation of finding pathology can substantially alter the interpretation of clinical data (Temerlin & Trousdale, 1969), although the present example seems particularly extreme. In addition, it can be difficult to know what is normal versus abnormal without an appropriate comparison group, and if a mental health professional's work mainly involves individuals with maladies, almost anything commonly observed among clientele might come to be associated with pathology. However, such characteristics may be relatively or comparably common in normal groups of individuals as well. Thus, as described in Chapter 3, unless one knows how often a symptom or characteristic does and does not appear in groups of clients—the proportion of individuals who do and do not show that feature—and compares it to the proportion found in a group of normal individuals, one cannot determine if there is a true association between that characteristic and the condition of interest. In turn, without this information, one cannot determine whether the characteristic has any validity or diagnostic value for identifying the presence of the condition, as discussed in detail in Chapter 3.

Figure 2.10 shows a related example, in which an expert deemed that a set of test results for Ms. Clark were abnormal, based on a single low test score. However, a

Ms. Clark's Test Performance on the
2014 Neuropsychological Evaluation

Level	Number of Tests	Percentage of Test Scores at this Level
Superior or Very Superior	11	21%
Average Range	41	77%
Borderline	1	2%
Mild Impairment	0	0%
Moderate Impairment	0	0%
Severe Impairment	0	0%

Figure 2.10 Ms. Clark's performance on the 2014 neuropsychological evaluation

John's Self-Descriptions of His Prior Status
vs.
Pre-Accident Records

John's Self-Description:	Happy	Calm	Stable	Energetic	Easy-Going
vs.					
Pre-Accident Records:	*Distraught*	*Anxiety Attacks*	*Mood Swings*	*Fatigued*	*Agitated*

Figure 2.11 John's self-descriptions of his prior status vs. pre-accident records

more appropriate analysis would be to compare the performances of individuals with and without the condition. That analysis showed that Ms. Clark's results were unusual, but in the opposite direction from the expert's conclusion, because they demonstrated a greater rate of normality than the average normal individual!

As background for Figure 2.11 and covered in more detail in the text, memory is more a reconstructive process than a literal recording of prior events and experiences. For example, if initial impressions about a person gradually shift from negative to positive, our recollection of their prior behavior might shift as well. A prior behavior we viewed critically, such as that person's being late for a meeting and making up what we thought was an excuse, may subsequently be reframed. That seeming excuse—helping a motorist with a flat tire—may now be recalled as a legitimate delay due to an altruistic act.

There is even research suggesting that individuals can come to believe they have chronic deficits from very mild head injuries that actually have resolved, because they misremember their pre-injury functioning as being better than it was (a "good old days" effect; see Mittenberg et al., 1992). For example, a person who trips at the company picnic might believe she almost never showed such clumsy behavior before her head injury. Figure 2.11 illustrates this type of situation. Here, an individual reported an unremarkable pre-injury history, and for reasons not detailed here, such as ready willingness to provide pre-event records, it seemed likely his description was sincere. However, records for several pre-injury years showed almost the same problems as those reported to have started or worsened after the event. Interestingly, the initial evaluator accepted the individual's self-report as accurate and concluded that the event had caused a significant decline in functioning.

Figure 2.12 illustrates a related theme, although the sincerity of the initial report was more at issue here. A plaintiff in a legal case reported a number of serious, and what one would expect to be easily observable, problems, such as seizures and periods of unconsciousness. However, the plaintiff's wife, who independently completed a parallel form rating her partner's status, provided very different answers. The psychologist who conducted the original evaluation did not receive the spouse's ratings until weeks after seeing the plaintiff, and he was so convinced the plaintiff had major impairment that he rejected the spouse's report as invalid.

Responses to Dr. Smith's Questionnaire

	Ms. Jones	*Mr. Jones*
Faints sometimes	Not at all	*Very much so*
Has had scizurcs	A little bit	*Very much so*
Has been unconscious	Not at all	*Very much so*

Figure 2.12 Conflicting responses to a questionnaire

Self-report can be notoriously flawed, and different reporters rating the same individual, such as two parents, or parents and a teacher, commonly generate outcomes that deviate widely from one another. Correlations between raters may be in the .50s, .40s, .30s, or even lower, suggesting less shared variance than unique variation (see Conners, 2009; Reynolds & Kamphus, 2015). Additionally, because answers can be frankly contradictory (the child: frequently gets out of his chair in class; almost never gets out of his chair), psychologists may try to integrate information that cannot truly be aligned because one, or both, ratings might contain substantial error. Consequently, failing to gather key collateral information may lead to high error rates or considerable overconfidence in conclusions. Such conclusions may in turn become resistant to modification, even when change is warranted. The chapters that follow address such topics as the extent to which weak psychometric status compromises judgment accuracy, how the order in which information is reviewed can overly sway conclusions, tendencies to maintain initial impressions that should be overturned by later contrary evidence, the importance of prioritizing and at times narrowing focus to the most predictive variables, and considering alternative or supplemental interpretive strategies that place less emphasis on holistic approaches and subjective judgment.

Evaluators may be disproportionately influenced by salient and immediate information as opposed to information that may have equal or greater value but is less dramatic. Obviously, we ought to be swayed by information value, not presentation, but it can be difficult to separate one from the other or to manage how information is weighted. Figure 2.13 comes from a case in which a psychologist, renamed Dr. Smith for purposes of the figure, was convinced that an individual had severe deficits in such areas as attention and working memory. For those less familiar with the concept, *working memory* refers to the capacity to hold information in mind and perhaps perform mental operations on that information. For example, working memory might be required to keep a telephone number in mind for several seconds, or to calculate a restaurant tip in one's head. Dr. Smith's examination results directly clashed with the findings on multiple other examinations performed by various professionals, so either the examinee manifested these

Attention/Concentration

Healthcare Provider	Date	Provider's Impression
Jones	3-14-02	Attention Span Normal
Jones	3-28-02	Attention Span Normal
Johnson	1-17-03	Follows Complex Commands
Smith	***5-19-03***	***Digit Span less than 1%. Working Memory less than 1%. Conners Continuous Performance Test less than 1%***
Jones	5-20-03	Attention Normal
Smith	***5-22-03***	***Low Attention Scores on WMS-III***
Fisbee	6-10-04	Without Cognitive Deficits

Figure 2.13 Dr. Smith's vs. other healthcare providers' reported impressions of cognitive functioning

problems only in Dr. Smith's presence, which seemed highly unlikely, or some alternative explanation was in order. In any case, had Dr. Smith been aware of the other results, he may well have reconsidered his conclusions.

One of the authors served on an American Psychological Association (APA) Presidential Task Force charged with designing assessment curriculum. Numerous topics were suggested and then rated for importance by committee members. Ironically, obtaining collateral information, or information from sources beyond the psychologist's own assessment results, was rated by most members as an extremely low priority. This relative disregard of extra-office information seemed to be a potential blind spot, given the frequency with which these additional informational sources can play an essential role in supporting or disconfirming conclusions drawn from in-office sources, as several of the following figures illustrate.

Research suggests, for example, that individuals, even when motivated to be accurate, often mis-recall their prior school performance, details of occupations they held, their children's developmental milestones, the sequence of important life events, and various other items. Thus, when it is potentially important and feasible, there can be considerable value in obtaining direct sources of information in order to check on or cross-validate subjective reports. For example, depression may lead to overly negative self-appraisals. Consequently, depressed individuals may falsely believe their cognitive capacities are declining and become worried that they are developing dementia. In contrast, collateral information about performance at a challenging job might provide strong contrary evidence. In his classic article, "Why I Do Not Attend Case Conferences," Meehl (1973) described the matter of sometimes emphasizing indirect information over direct information as follows:

> "*Doing it the hard way.*" By this I mean employing some clinical instrument or procedure, such as a time-consuming . . . test, to ascertain something that documents in the patient's social record or an informant could tell one in a few minutes. . . . There are some types of cases in which such failure to look at the record may be especially misleading, such as the clever and ingratiating psychopath who can sometimes fool even a moderately experienced clinician. . . . In the differential diagnosis between an "unlucky" normal, an acting-out neurotic, a hard-core psychopath, and a solid-gold professional con man, the Rorschach, TAT, and MMPI . . . may be less illuminating than the school record, a social agency's file, or the police blotter. (p. 262)

Some of the terminology may have changed over time, but not Meehl's basic point.

Figure 2.14 presents results on two measures assessing speed of mental processing. On this testing (and on a number of other measures), Ms. J, a person in her twenties who had been in an accident, obtained scores that would be extremely low, even for individuals in their eighties. The figure is not meant to stereotype 80- to 89-year-olds, but considerable research shows that mental speed diminishes on many tasks by or before this age level, including the tests administered here. Based on these and other results, the neuropsychologist opined that Ms. J, who presumably was functioning normally before her accident, had suffered major cognitive losses.

Considering Ms. J's level of test performance and the importance of mental speed in many activities (e.g., driving), if she had really declined from normal functioning to a level worse than 99 of 100, or 999 of 1,000 80- to 89-year-olds, this behavioral change not only would be extreme, but also would be grossly out of proportion to the expected effect of the minor concussion in question. Nevertheless, due both to insufficient gathering of information about Ms. J's everyday activities, which likely would have proved highly revealing, and to the extent to which the psychologist's impressions were apparently affected by the salient and extreme test results, the testing outcomes were viewed as valid. Figure 2.15 starts with an extreme result on a different measure of mental speed drawn from another case. The figure also includes an expert's descriptions of some potential consequences of such an extreme deficit, but records detailing other examinations of Mr. Smith and his work performance directly contradicted the dire predictions.

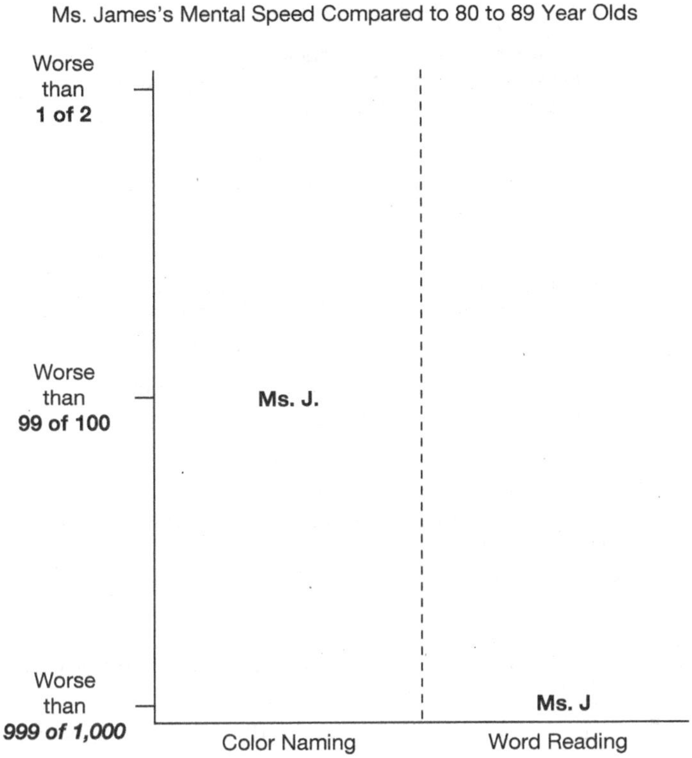

Figure 2.14 Ms. James's mental speed compared to 80- to 89-year-olds

Figures 2.16 to 2.18 are based on work records, which were requested after the expert described the deficits that could interfere with Mr. Franklin's work capacity. The expert's conclusions had been based on an interview, cognitive and psychological testing, and a narrow record review. The interview notes suggested

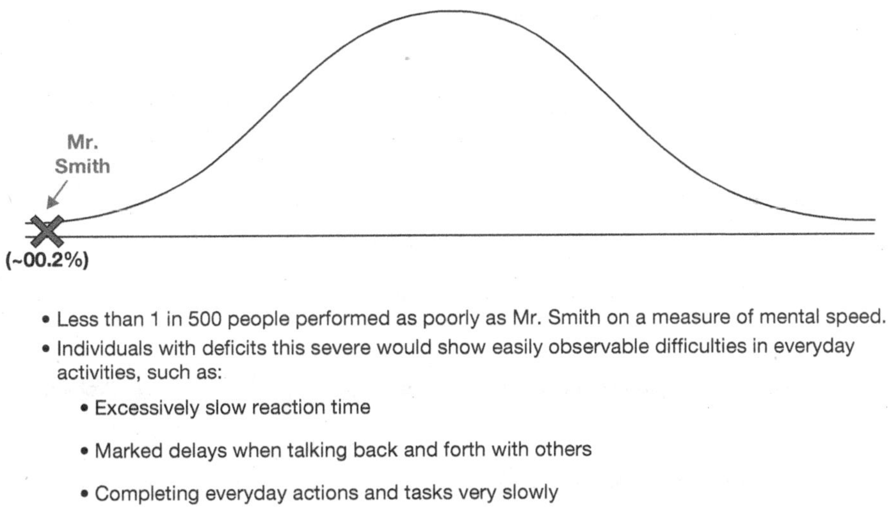

Figure 2.15 Mr. Smith's relative performance on a measure of mental speed

Mr. Franklin's Job Description

Preventive maintenance on equipment, such as heating and ventilating, pumps, fans, sterilizers, cage washers, boilers, chillers and refrigeration equipment.

General plumbing duties, pipe-fitting, installations, welding, brazing, and fabrication.

Provide calibration of pneumatic heating ventilation and air conditioning equipment, controls and instruments.

Maintain inventory of parts and supplies to complete projects.

Read and interpret documents such as safety rules, operating and maintenance instuctions, and procedure manuals.

Figure 2.16 Mr. Franklin's job description

that the expert's inquiry about work activities went into minimal specifics, barely extending beyond a job label.

The expert seemed confident about her predictions, based especially on the examinee's low scores on a number of cognitive measures. However, as is not unusual, the expert tended to view validity in overly global or general terms, as opposed to a more particularized quality with delineated boundaries and properties that can vary highly depending on the question and population in question.

Employment Evaluation: May 11, 20XX

Understands and follows safety guidelines	No Problem
Remembers work locations and procedures	No Problem
Works at an acceptable pace	No Problem
Understands and remembers detailed instructions	No Problem
Maintains attention and concentration on the job	No Problem
Requires extra supervision or attention	No Problem

Figure 2.17 Mr. Franklin's post-accident work evaluation

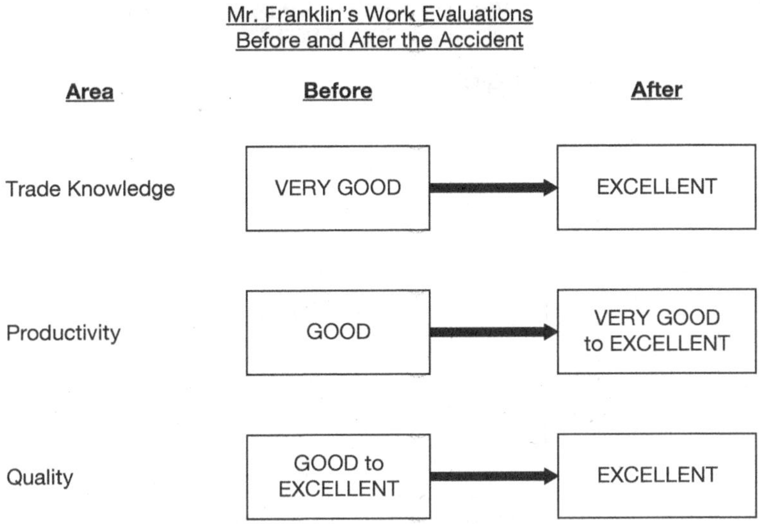

Figure 2.18 Comparing Mr. Franklin's work evaluations before and after the accident

Consequently, relatively low scores on, say, measures of memory and conceptual ability may be valuable for predicting performance on certain tasks or within certain work domains, yet in other areas that appear closely related these low scores may have minimal relevance. If one does not have in-depth knowledge of just what a job requires, even formulating an impression about how well assessment measures predict performance may be little more than an exercise in speculation.

In the present case, Mr. Franklin's seemingly simple job was far more involved than the psychologist assumed (see Figure 2.16), and job evaluations (see Figures 2.17–2.18) suggested that Mr. Franklin was performing at a highly effective level and did not show evidence of cognitive decline. Of course, if one is trying to evaluate work capacity, isn't it often better to seek out direct evidence, rather than depending primarily on inferences drawn from measures with questionable predictive utility for the outcome in question? Our intent here is not to question the potential value of inferential information or inferential reasoning, as both can prove extremely useful, or to question the potential value of cognitive and psychological assessment tools. Rather, it is to emphasize the propriety, all else being equal, of seeking out the most predictive information. In a surprising range of situations, obtaining information about the few most useful variables, and sometimes the single best variable, will produce accuracy rates that equal or exceed judgments based on far more extensive information, in particular if weak methods of data integration are used.

Figure 2.19 addresses the same theme, in this instance in a case involving an adolescent. Similar to the circumstances illustrated in Figures 2.16 to 2.18, indirect information was sought and valued over more direct information. Based on parental report and cognitive testing after the youth's possible mild concussion, the psychologist concluded that deficits were present and had caused reduced school performance. However, a comparison of the student's GPA from before and after

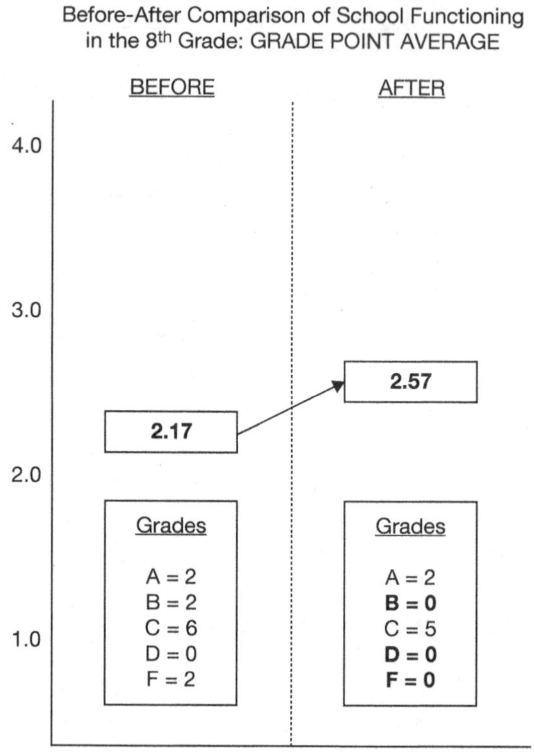

Figure 2.19 Before and after comparison of school functioning

the event suggested no drop in school grades. Of course, differences in teachers, curriculum, and other such factors might be of relevance as well, but a primary indicator of academic performance ran contrary to the psychologist's conclusions.

Figures 2.20 and 2.21 also address the potential value of information that may be contained in documents or sources that commonly fall outside mental health professionals' information-gathering practices. Here, a psychological expert concluded that the plaintiff's very low score on Part B of the Trail Making Test (TMT-B), shown on the left side of the figure, suggested serious shortcomings in mental speed and multitasking. On this test, one connects randomly arranged numbers and letters on a page in alternating sequence, as in 1→A→2→B→3→C, and so on. Often the major score of interest is time to complete the test, and because one must keep two dimensions in mind simultaneously and work as quickly as possible, the TMT-B emphasizes both speed of thinking and multitasking.

In light of the functions the TMT-B is designed to measure, it may be used to help inform decisions about driving capacity. Unbeknownst to the expert, an occupational therapist evaluating driving capacity also administered the TMT-B to the plaintiff in the same time period, but on this occasion outside the scope of the litigation (i.e., based on a clinical, not a legal, referral). The results of this second evaluation are represented on the right side of Figure 2.20. Thus, when the test was administered in the context of litigation, in which there was a potential

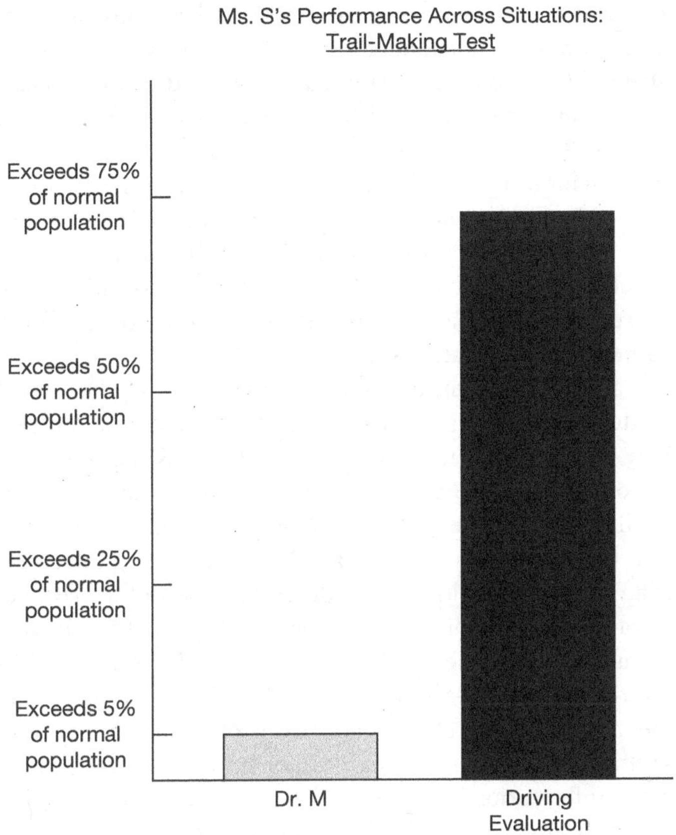

Figure 2.20 Shifting incentives and changes in test performance

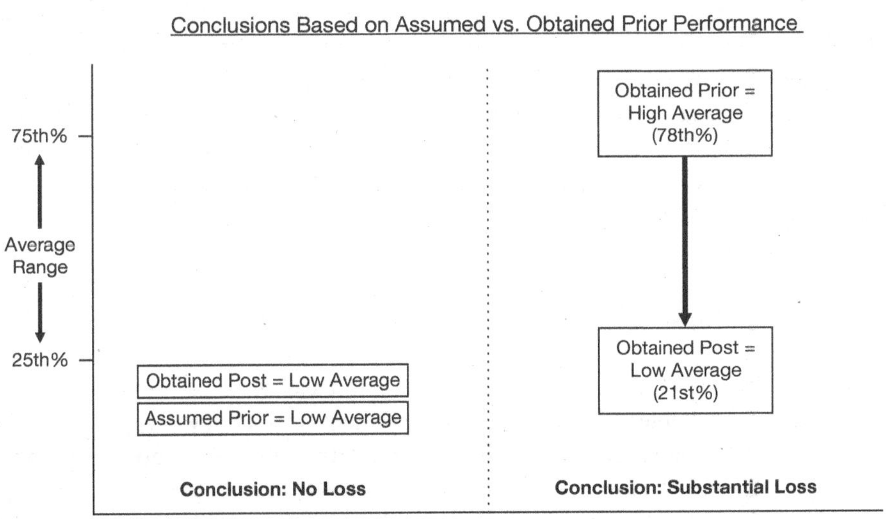

Figure 2.21 Conclusions based on assumed versus obtained prior performance

incentive to perform poorly for purposes of secondary gain, as opposed to the clinical context with the occupational therapist, which was aimed at determining whether the individual should be permitted to drive and hence created a potential incentive to perform well, dramatically different results were obtained. The expert psychologist's results on this and other tests and the additional information he had accessed convinced him that deficits were present, and apparently believing this, he prematurely terminated efforts to obtain thorough information. As seemingly occurred here, initial impressions can have a disproportionate influence on the data collection process and may lead to erroneous conclusions that are not sufficiently scrutinized or revised, even when they should be (for further discussion see Chapter 4, "Confirmation Bias").

Figure 2.21 also addresses insufficient data collection, or the tendency to formulate premature conclusions and thereby terminate information gathering too soon. In many psychological and psychiatric evaluations, a point of focus is possible diminution in functioning, because the presence or absence of change may be vital to a differential diagnosis. For example, in a legal case, adverse change might suggest that an accident caused psychological or cognitive loss, and in a clinical setting a decline could suggest the early stages of a neurodegenerative disorder or a progressive condition that is reversible, if caught early. Given the importance of evaluating possible change, it is prudent, whenever possible, to obtain the best information on level of prior functioning. However, this is far from universally done. At times the problem may be one of feasibility. For example, such information may be very difficult to access, or time urgency may not allow one to wait until the information becomes available. However, on other occasions, the effort could have been—but wasn't—made, perhaps because the practitioner was overconfident in the effectiveness of alternative methods. Although confidence is often extolled as a valuable quality, overconfidence is potentially dangerous when it interferes with more efficacious judgment practices.

Various methods for estimating prior or pre-event functioning, such as those that emphasize the use of current information for postdiction of earlier status, often generate sizeable errors. For example, one approach is to emphasize tests that have a strong association with overall intelligence (such as level of word knowledge) and that tend to be relatively unaffected by neurocognitive disorder unless it is relatively advanced. As depicted on the left side of Figure 2.21, a neuropsychologist used one such method, arrived at an estimate of low average prior intellectual functioning, found that it matched closely with the level of performance on a current intelligence test, and thus concluded that no loss in intellectual ability had occurred. However, as shown on the right side of this same figure, further searching turned up a prior intelligence test that had generated a much higher score than the estimate of prior intelligence the psychologist's method yielded. Thus, the best available information did not confirm consistency in capacities over time, but rather a large decline in functioning. Although one cannot always find a prior intelligence test, various sources of information are often available (e.g., records of academic achievement and aptitude testing) that are better predictors than methods extrapolating backward based on current test results. However, if a psychologist is overly confident and believes that the latter methods are considerably better than is truly the case, efforts to obtain better informational sources might not be pursued, at potentially great disadvantage to the patient or, in this case, the litigant.

A revised or updated test is not necessarily a better test, but in many cases studies that help to uncover the strengths and weaknesses of measures lead to improved versions. For example, some test items may become dated over time (e.g., an older version of the Wechsler Intelligence Scale that predated the policy of changing national holidays to Fridays or Mondays contained an item asking about the date of Washington's birthday). Alternatively, test norms may be refined or extended to more diverse groups, or components of tests that have deficient test-retest reliability may be eliminated or improved. Nevertheless, the authors have been involved in cases in which psychologists used versions of tests that had been replaced 5, 10, or even 25 years earlier, such as a case in which a psychologist used the first version of an intelligence test that had been revised and republished on three subsequent occasions. For some professionals, it is disconcerting to find that their date of graduation can be closely approximated by the versions of tests used, as was the case in Figure 2.22 with Dr. Jones. In addition to the WMS-R (Wechsler Memory Scale-Revised), Dr. Jones also used earlier versions of other tests that had been updated after Dr. Jones's graduation. The cross-examining attorney had Dr. Jones read passages from the updated manuals that described the need to revise the measures, problems in the older versions that were addressed, and potential advantages of the new versions.

Error secondary to the use of technology is another area of concern for mental health professionals. Even computerized scoring can generate error. Computerized scoring includes both commercially developed programs and self-designed programs. Typically, the programs function to sum raw scores, and in some instances, generate subscale raw scores or even transform a raw score to a standardized score. Computerized scoring programs typically yield fewer errors than hand-scoring (Allard et al., 1995). However, the source of computer-related error often precedes the automatized summation of scores and occurs instead during data entry (Luciana, 2003).

Many computerized scoring programs require the user to input responses obtained on paper-and-pencil tests into the program manually. In some cases, it

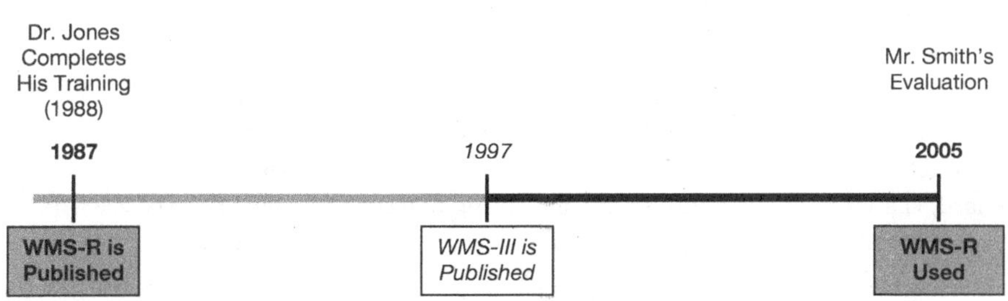

Figure 2.22 Example use of an outdated test battery

may be a simple binary response, indicated by typing a 0 or 1. In other instances, responses may include additional options. However, data entry may become more complex with measures that reverse-code several items. In reverse-coding, the examinee's response is input as the inverse when summing the scores. For example, using an illustrative scale measuring anxiety, in which higher scores indicate a greater level of anxiety, if the hypothetical item, "Are you rarely worried?" was reverse-coded, a response of No would be entered as 1 and a Yes response would be entered as 0 (whereas on items that are not reverse-coded, a Yes response corresponds to a 1 and No response to a 0). Hence, if the user is unsure about how responses to items that are reverse- coded should be entered into the scoring program, the risk of scoring error increases considerably.

A broad range of errors can arise from data entry. Consider the following scenario. A group clinical practice uses a homemade scoring program that is coded within Microsoft Excel. The spreadsheet is used to score the State-Trait Anxiety Inventory (STAI). One afternoon when manually entering responses from the STAI paper-and-pencil measure, a graduate-level trainee erroneously enters the response into cells that had been programmed to account for reverse-coding. Realizing the error, the trainee quickly deletes the erroneous input, but in so doing unknowingly also erases the embedded code. The trainee finishes scoring the measure and selects Save when closing the program. After that, each subsequent user will generate summed raw scores that fail to account for reverse-coding. This scenario highlights how a simple and unintentional mistake can result in an exponential increase in error. In other cases, due to errors, homemade scoring programs will systematically generate faulty scores. Especially for tests emphasizing relative elevations between scales as a major source for developing interpretive hypotheses (e.g., level of depression in comparison to level of activity), even minor errors can change scale relationships and alter clinical impressions substantially.

Other common sources of error include misappraising the value of information and problems combining or integrating information properly. Examples of the latter include being overly influenced by the salience of data as opposed to its informational value, or inadvertently being swayed by information of considerably lower value rather than by more valid information. In addition, the underutilization of helpful decision aids and guides can also contribute to errors.

REFERENCES

Allard, G., Butler, J., Faust, D., & Shea, M. T. (1995). Errors in hand scoring objective personality tests: The case of the Personality Diagnostic Questionnaire–Revised (PRDQ-R). *Professional Psychology: Research and Practice*, *26*(3), 304–308.

Allard, G., & Faust, D. (2000). Errors in scoring objective personality tests. *Assessment*, *7*(2), 119–129.

Charter, R. A., Walden, D. K., & Padilla, S. P. (2000). Too many simple clerical scoring errors: The Rey Figure as an example. *Journal of Clinical Psychology*, *56*(4), 571–574.

Conners, C. K. (2009). *Conners 3rd edition manual.* Multi-Health Systems.

Graber, M. L., Franklin, N., & Gordon, R. (2005). Diagnostic error in medicine. *Archives of Internal Medicine, 165*(13), 1493–1499.

Huhn, M., Tardy, M., Spineli, L. M., Kissling, W., Förstl, H., Pitschel-Walz, G., Leucht, C., Samara, M., Dold, M., Davis, J. M., & Leucht, S. (2014). Efficacy of pharmacotherapy and psychotherapy for adult psychiatric disorders: A systematic overview of meta-analyses. *JAMA Psychiatry, 71*(6), 706–715.

Lee, D., Reynolds, C. R., & Willson, V. L. (2003). Standardized test administration: Why bother? *Journal of Forensic Neuropsychology, 33*(3), 55–81.

Luciana, M. (2003). Practitioner review: Computerized assessment of neuropsychological function in children: Clinical and research applications of the Cambridge Neuropsychological Testing Automated Battery (CANTAB). *Journal of Child Psychology and Psychiatry, 44*(5), 649–663.

McDermut, W., Miller, I. W., & Brown, R. A. (2006). The efficacy of group psychotherapy for depression: A meta-analysis and review of the empirical research. *Clinical Psychology Science and Practice, 8*(1), 98–116.

Meehl, P. (1973). Why I do not attend case conferences. In P. Meehl, *Psychodiagnosis* (pp. 225–302). University of Minnesota Press.

Mittenberg, W., DiGiulio, D. V., & Bass, A. E. (1992). Symptoms following mild head injury: Expectation as aetiology. *Journal of Neurology, Neurosurgery, and Psychiatry, 55*(3), 200–204.

Reynolds, C. R., & Kamphaus, R. W. (2015). *Behavior assessment system for children* (3rd ed.). Pearson.

Slate, J. R., Jones, C. H., Coulter, C., & Covert, T. L. (1992). Practitioners' administration and scoring of the WISC-R: Evidence that we do err. *Journal of School Psychology, 30*(1), 77–82.

Temerlin, M. K., & Trousdale, W. W. (1969). The social psychology of clinical diagnosis. *Psychotherapy: Theory, Research & Practice, 6*(1), 24–29.

von Bronswijk, S., Moopen, N., Beijers, L., Ruhe, H. G., & Peeters, F. (2019). Effectiveness of psychotherapy for treatment-resistant depression: A meta-analysis and meta-regression. *Psychological Medicine, 49*, 366–379.

PART II

Gathering, Appraising, and Integrating Information

3

Assessing Whether Clinical Variables Are Related: The Important Task of Covariation Estimation

The reasons to administer psychological tests or to conduct other types of psychological assessment may include designing an intervention, enhancing understanding of an individual, diagnosing or categorizing a psychological condition or state, or predicting an outcome. For the moment, we focus on diagnosis and prediction. For example, the Violence Risk Appraisal Guide (VRAG) is used to help predict whether a person is likely to commit violence, and the Minnesota Multiphasic Personality Inventory-2 (MMPI-2) may be used to assist in diagnosis. At a fundamental level, the assumption is that a score on a psychological test covaries with some outcome. The same implicit or explicit assumption holds if one is using multiple scores, interview findings, or a combination of such variables, which is that such information will covary with outcomes of interest, where *covaries* means "is correlated with." For example, a person's high score on the VRAG is correlated with that person's likelihood of being violent in the future. Correlation is not the same as causation, of course. Scoring high on the VRAG does not cause a person to become violent, just as the rooster crowing does not cause the sun to rise. However, if two things are not correlated or associated, they cannot be causally linked: correlation is thus a necessary condition of causation.

A tumor in Broca's area can cause an aphasic condition that involves problems executing the sequential motor movements needed for fluent oral production of words (and often writing as well). The two conditions or occurrences—a tumor in Broca's area and the presence of aphasia—covary to a large extent with each other. Furthermore, one causes the other. It is proper to use covariation as a cue to possible causation, because a cause precedes its subsequent effect. Likewise, the absence of covariation can assist in ruling out a causal relationship.

The number of pigs in the United States in a given year covaries with the tons of pig-iron produced in that year. However births of pigs do not cause an increase in pig-iron production, nor does pig-iron production cause in increase in the birth of pigs. Nevertheless the two factors covary because both increase in times of economic growth and decrease in times of economic decline. Hence covariation does not establish causation. Two factors may covary because a third factor or other factors simultaneously cause both.

For a psychological test to be useful, or to possess any level of validity for its intended application, it is essential that the test results covary with some predicted outcome or diagnosis, and that the person interpreting the test results incorporate covariation analysis appropriately. How to perform and interpret covariation estimation is the topic of this chapter. Enhancing predictive accuracy and becoming a competent diagnostician require this knowledge.

WHAT'S SO DIFFICULT ABOUT COVARIATION ESTIMATION?

In this and other chapters, when presenting key concepts, we often start with basic examples and then build toward more complex ones. For example, we may start with a single test or test score, or a single condition or outcome. We recognize that, in practice, clinicians are often faced with problems involving multiple tests and test scores, multiple observations or other forms of information, and various intertwined outcomes and potential outcomes. However, starting with examples that might represent simplifications of what are often more involved matters means that concepts can be presented with greater clarity, thereby facilitating application to more complex circumstances.

Consider Table 3.1, in which a clinician renders a diagnosis, such as major depression, based on symptom X. Assume for the purposes of this example that the true diagnosis is known.

When we perform this demonstration in a classroom setting, we show class members 30 cards, one at a time. On the left half of each card is the presence or absence of a symptom (X or Not X) and on the right half of each card the presence or absence of a disorder (D or Not D). When college students are asked to estimate on a 0 to 100 scale what the relation is between the symptom and the disorder, the average estimate is around 70. However, the correct answer is 0.

Note that when symptom X is present, the disorder occurs 67% of the time (12/18). When symptom X is not present, the disorder occurs 67% of the time (8/12).

Table 3.1. Data Needed to Estimate the Covariation between a Symptom and a Disorder

		Disorder Present?	
		Yes	**No**
Symptom X Present?	**Yes**	12	6
	No	8	4

In other words, the presence of the symptom and the presence of the disorder are not related to each other. They do not covary. This same type of mis-estimation has been found among highly skilled professionals, such as nurses (Ganguly & Hammersley, 2009; Smedslund, 1963).

Assume that a clinician uses symptom X to render a diagnosis. Then Table 3.1 becomes Table 3.2.

To understand and describe diagnoses, we must introduce some very important terminology. In Table 3.2, the upper-left cell is called a *true positive*. A true positive occurs when the diagnosis is that the disorder is present, and the disorder actually is present. This diagnosis is accurate.

The upper-right cell of the table is called a *false positive*. Here a clinician makes a positive diagnosis (that the condition is present), but this diagnosis is incorrect.

The lower-left cell is called a *false negative*. A false negative occurs when a clinician makes a negative diagnosis (that the condition is absent), but the diagnosis is incorrect because the condition is present.

The lower-right cell is called a *true negative*. Here a clinician makes a negative diagnosis (that the condition is absent), and the condition is absent, so this diagnosis is accurate.

The data in Table 3.2 indicate that no matter what the diagnostician concludes, the disorder is twice as likely to be present as it is to be absent. Therefore, there is no point in asking this diagnostician to render a diagnosis. Using a 2 × 2 table, it is possible to ascertain the accuracy of a clinician's diagnoses. Covariation analysis is one of the methods, an especially important and fundamental one, for determining whether two variables are related, and it is not limited to ascertaining diagnostic value. One might also be interested in the association between an intervention and an outcome. For example, although a positive outcome may follow treatment in some cases, determining how often positive outcomes occur, and whether that rate equals or exceeds the rate of positive outcomes without treatment or with another treatment, also requires proper covariation analysis. An 80% success rate does not demonstrate treatment efficacy if one achieves the same level of positive outcomes without treatment. In some cases, one might even find a higher rate of positive outcomes with no treatment, because overall the treatment does more harm than good (something that is not that unusual a finding once experimental treatments are studied properly). Conversely, even if the rate of positive outcome is low, such as 20%, this result may still exceed the rate of positive outcomes without treatment.

Table 3.2. Data Needed to Estimate the Covariation between a Diagnosis and a Disorder

		Disorder Actually Present?	
		Yes	**No**
Diagnosis?	**Disorder Present**	12	6
	Disorder Absent	8	4

We now investigate difficulties that plague typical covariation estimation tasks. Most importantly, we discuss ways to overcome these difficulties.

Chapman and Chapman (1967)

Loren and Jean Chapman (1967) conducted perhaps the most famous study of the diagnostic process. In six experiments, they investigated the Draw-a-Person Test (DAP), based in part on their curiosity about the frequency with which highly capable individuals used this test method in the face of consistently negative research evidence on its predictive accuracy. Many clinicians had agreed that persons with various symptoms drew pictures of people characterized by specific features. For example, paranoid persons were said to draw pictures of people with large eyes, and persons concerned about their intelligence drew pictures of people with large heads. In other words, clinicians regularly perceived covariation between certain psychological problems and the pictures drawn by people with those problems, despite research yielding results contrary to such perceptions. What might be the cause of this widespread but inaccurate covariation estimation among these professionals?

In their first experiment, the Chapmans asked 108 undergraduates to examine 45 drawings of a person, purportedly done by different men. Beneath each drawing was a statement about the man who did the drawing, such as "He is worried about how manly he is." The Chapmans arranged the statements and drawings such that there was absolutely no correlation between them. Nevertheless, the persons in the experiment mistakenly perceived correlations that matched those supposedly "known" by professional clinicians. That is, the naïve subjects thought that paranoid men drew pictures of people with large eyes, men concerned about their intelligence drew pictures of people with large or emphasized heads, etc. The Chapmans then asked 45 undergraduates who had not participated in the prior experiment to rate how much each of the psychological problems "called to mind" each of several possible body parts. "Suspiciousness" called to mind the eyes more than any other body part, "intelligence" called to mind the head more than any other body part, etc. These results suggested that simple associative strength between problems and body parts was responsible for the illusory correlations that professional clinicians regularly misperceived, or that such associations fit with broadly shared cultural beliefs and stereotypes. These semantic associations distorted the clinicians' perception of the zero correlation that existed in the study. Although the Chapmans' research used undergraduates, the same general result has been found in studies of clinicians (Kurtz & Garfield, 1978; Lueger & Petzel, 1979).

STRATEGIES OF COVARIATION ESTIMATION

Assume that a diagnostician disregards all irrelevant associations and uses only appropriate or informative data. There is a second perverse influence on covariation

Table 3.3. Data Needed to Estimate the Covariation between Symptom X and a Disorder

		Disorder Present?	
		Yes	**No**
Symptom X Present?	**Yes**	Cell A (12)	Cell B (6)
	No	Cell C (8)	Cell D (4)

judgment: the use of suboptimal strategies in examining the relevant data. To explain this situation, we return to the 2 × 2 table introduced previously, but this time with the four cells labeled in a traditional manner (Table 3.3).

Why was the estimated covariation so high when the actual covariation was zero? The answer is the use of the Cell A heuristic. When Cell A has the largest number of entries compared to the other three cells, people note that when the symptom is present, the disorder is present a lot of the time, too. Therefore, they mistakenly conclude that the two factors—the symptom and the disorder—must covary. However, in this instance, the disorder occurs 2/3 of the time whether or not symptom X is present. Therefore, the two factors do not covary. This example shows that use of Cell A heuristic can lead to highly inaccurate covariation estimates. Use of this heuristic is enticing but seriously suboptimal.

Focus on Cell A is like a commercial with a testimonial. Dentist Smith says that Jones toothpaste has helped many patients. What we don't know, however, is how many patients it has not helped, or how the percentage of those who were helped versus not helped compares to the percentages for individuals who used another brand of toothpaste, or (dare we say) no toothpaste at all. This is similar to the assumption that persisted for centuries that bleeding sick individuals with leeches was helpful (which generally was not true except in a narrow subset of conditions). Given how many individuals were treated in this manner, by sheer numbers alone, quite a few recovered (leeches present–recovery present). When disproportionate attention was directed to Cell A, and insufficient attention to the numbers in the other cells, such as the percentage that did and did not get better if treated in another manner or who were not treated at all, false beliefs in the efficacy of the treatment were formed or maintained. Apparently, the "father" of modern psychiatry, Dr. Benjamin Rush, may well have contributed to the death of George Washington, the "father" of our country, by treating him with leeches, with Dr. Rush perhaps bemoaning at the end that President Washington died despite the treatment. The need to compare the ratio of positive to negative outcomes among those treated with a certain method versus those not treated is the rationale for a control group.

There are many examples in psychology in which primary focus on Cell A has fostered questionable or false conclusions, among both the public and professionals. For example, despite epidemiological evidence suggesting that the overall rate of violence is no greater among individuals with serious psychological disorders than it is among the general population (with isolated exceptions), many individuals assume major psychological disorders and violence are linked. Here, highly publicized and dramatic cases (e.g., Charles Manson, Jeffrey Dahmer), or instances that fall within Cell A (major pathology present–violence present), have fostered misperceptions or false associations.

Among many clinical psychologists, the belief that scatter or disparity in level of performance on intellectual or neuropsychological measures is an indicator of abnormality has persisted for decades. For example, if an individual achieves a high average or superior score in one area (e.g., mental speed) and a low score in another area (e.g., attention or concentration), it may be assumed that abnormality or brain disorder is present. However, research shows that disparities that are very common among normal individuals are commonly misjudged as pathological, and that greater than average levels of scatter can be associated with higher, rather than lower, levels of intellectual capacity (see Faust, 2012). In one widely read text, a level of disparity between intellectual subtests described as questionable or abnormal were obtained among almost 100% of the normative sample for the test. Again, focus on Cell A (scatter present–pathology present) was likely a major factor in this monumental error. Of course, some individuals with the described level of scatter do have pathology, so it is easy to find "positive" cases or seeming confirmation, but these cases are overwhelmed by false-positive diagnoses. How is it possible that such practices have persisted for decades? Some of this has to do with the ambiguity that may exist in determining a person's true status, and the exercise of what is essentially tautological reasoning. If a diagnostician assumes the presence of scatter is a strong or nearly sure sign of abnormality, cases that really don't fall within Cell A may nevertheless be judged as confirming instances of the association, blinding the practitioner to the occurrence of false-positive errors.

At other times, an individual may focus on an isolated cell to argue that some sort of general rule or finding is not legitimate, despite what might be strong overall evidence for the conclusion that is being challenged. For example, someone argues that seat belt use is not necessarily a good idea because their uncle Bob swerved off a road, wound up upside down in a lake, and would have drowned if he had been wearing a seat belt (failure to wear a seat belt, but positive outcome). Or, as we used to hear more commonly in the past, my Aunt Leticia smoked until very late in life and generally enjoyed excellent health, so smoking is not necessarily that bad. One even sometimes hears comparable arguments about highly effective medical tests or procedures because they missed some malignancy. Unless a method or relationship yields no exceptions (seat belts always protect against injury, or an MRI never fails to detect a tumor), then there will instances in which the less frequent event occurs. Furthermore, if one is looking at events that occur very frequently (e.g., car accidents), it will not be hard to gather many contrary instances or instances that fill any cell one selects, but what must be kept in mind is that it is not the number of instances one can cite for any of the cells, but the relative frequency across the cells that matters in evaluating covariation. Even if one can sadly pile up hundreds of instances in which individuals wearing seat belts died in accidents, if the relative rate of fatal outcomes is much lower among those who wear seat belts as opposed to those who do not (an analysis that cannot be conducted without examining data from all four cells, and which of course confirms that lower fatality rate), the argument that one is worse off using seat belts is revealed as fallacious. Given how often, purposely or inadvertently, individuals focus on a single cell and reach or foment questionable or erroneous conclusions, becoming cognizant of such error can be highly beneficial in evaluating evidence.

A slightly more sophisticated strategy is the A minus B heuristic. Users of this strategy compare Cell A with Cell B. The former comprises instances in which the symptom and disorder "go together." The latter comprises instances in which the symptom and disorder do not "go together." Hence if the former is greater than the latter, a positive covariation is assumed to be present. If the latter is greater than the former, then a negative covariation is assumed to be present. If the two cells are roughly equal in magnitude, then no covariation is assumed to be present. In Table 3.3, Cell A is twice the size of Cell B, so users of the A minus B heuristic mistakenly conclude that the data imply a positive covariation. Of course, this conclusion would be incorrect under the conditions present in Table 3.3.

In an applied setting, the A minus B heuristic may take the form of recognizing that a predictor is imperfect or not that strong, such as a potential marker of suicidal risk, but nevertheless believing it has value, when that indicator has essentially no value or even decreases predictive accuracy. For example, a clinician may believe a potential indicator of risk for self-harm is accurate only about 60% of the time, but that given the potential cost of error, it is worth using. However, if such a predictor is used in place of other predictors that have higher clinical utility, potentially tragic consequences may result.

A third strategy is the sum of diagonals heuristic. The diagnostician figures that the entries in Cells A and D both indicate that the symptom and disorder "go together." These entries confirm the covariation of the symptom and the disorder. Cells B and C disconfirm this covariation. So there are 16 confirming entries (12 + 4) and 14 disconfirming entries (8 + 6). Because these two sums are close, people correctly infer that there isn't any covariation between the symptom and the disorder. This strategy, the sum of diagonals, is better than the prior two grossly deficient strategies, because the sum of diagonals strategy uses the data in all four cells. However, this strategy is still deficient, as shown in Table 3.4.

In Table 3.4, the number of confirming entries is 26 (24 + 2), and the number of disconfirming cases is 14 (6 + 8). Because the number of confirming cases is almost twice as great as the number of disconfirming cases, a diagnostician might conclude that there is substantial covariation. However, the covariation is zero.

Table 3.4. Data Needed to Estimate the Covariation between Symptom X and a Disorder

		Disorder Present?	
		Yes	**No**
Symptom X Present?	**Yes**	24	6
	No	8	2

When the symptom is present, the person is four times as likely to have the disorder as not have it. However, when the symptom is absent, the person is still four times as likely to have the disorder as not. The presence of the symptom provides no information whatsoever about the likelihood of having the disorder.

Many other examples could be cited to illustrate the pernicious impact of failing to consider all four cells. For example, Dawes (1989) critiqued an article examining pet ownership among CEOs. The article noted that pet ownership was common among this group and argued that caring for a pet during childhood may have helped the CEOs develop greater maturity and thus contributed to their work accomplishments. What the article did not address was the comparative frequency with which individuals who were not CEOs cared for pets. Certainly, many individuals care for pets as children, and without knowing if there is any difference in frequency across the two groups, one is not in a position to appraise covariation or draw causal inferences.

Social psychologists have also pointed out that failure to perform proper covariation analysis may be an important factor in stereotyping (see Hamilton & Rose, 1980). For example, suppose 10% of individuals from various groups (e.g., young, middle-aged, sports fans, reality TV watchers, landscapers) show relatively low levels of motivation and drive. Now suppose further that someone grows up in a family that for some reason abhors landscapers, perhaps because a long-lost brother did extremely well in the business but failed to pay back other family members who had provided risky loans to give him his start. Individuals in an occupation like this might work on hot summer days with excessive sun exposure, and therefore need to rest occasionally. During family drives, the resentful parents are constantly pointing out occasions in which they see landscapers sitting idly (Cell A), reinforcing their own mistaken stereotypes and building false beliefs in their children. Almost all individuals have occasions on which they do not work hard, make careless mistakes, or could have been more considerate of others. If an observer focuses on those occasions in which such negative behaviors occur, they can build or maintain false conclusions about a person or groups stemming from insufficient attention to occasions on which such behaviors do not occur, and the frequency with which such behaviors are similar across individuals or groups. On the obverse side of the same coin, if a person idolizes another individual or group, they may selectively attend to instances of positive behavior and make the opposing error of elevating a person to near sainthood who does not really merit such a lofty appraisal.

The optimal strategy is the conditional probability strategy. Chi-square tests and phi coefficients employ this normative strategy in their calculation. The strategy is to merely compare the top row and the bottom row of the 2 × 2 table. If the conditional probability of having the disorder given that one has the symptom is the same as the conditional probability of having the disorder if one doesn't have the symptom, then there is no covariation. In Table 3.4, the probability of having the disorder is 80% if one has the symptom (24/30), and it is 80% if one doesn't have the symptom (8/10). So symptom X is not at all helpful in predicting whether the person has the disorder. There is no covariation between the two factors.

In order to perform accurate covariation estimates, one must use the data in all four cells. The conditional probability strategy does this. Two of the other three strategies do not. The third dysfunctional strategy—sum of diagonals—uses all four cells, but suboptimally.

Perverse Effects of Not Using the Data from All Four Cells

It is also essential that one has representative data for all four cells. For example, if data gathering is not performed properly and instances from one or another cell are overrepresented, then mistaken conclusions can result. Misrepresentative samples might occur, for example, when one seeks information about reactions to a particular service or product, and those with positive experiences are more likely to give feedback than those with negative experiences. Such an outcome might occur if sampling is done with visitors to a store, but individuals with less favorable reactions to that store are unlikely to return and, therefore, are underrepresented among the group of shoppers at any one time.

Sometimes it is difficult to obtain data for Cells C and D. For example, a friend of one of the authors was asked by a prominent football coach to give psychological tests to potential recruits to ascertain whether they had the attitude to be successful players. Those whom my friend deemed to be players that the coach should recruit would have their subsequent football prowess assessed by the coach in the coming years as they played for his team. The rows of the resulting 2 × 2 table were "Did well on the psychological tests" and "Did not do well on the psychological tests." The columns were "Played well" and "Did not play well." The coach was pleased that so many of the players my friend endorsed played well; Cell A had many more entries than did Cell B. However, players my friend rejected went to other colleges, and the coach at my friend's college didn't attempt to obtain any data on how the rejected players performed at the other colleges. Thus, there were no entries in Cells C and D. My friend was delighted that the coach didn't bother with data for Cells C and D, because my friend thought that the covariation between his assessment of the player's potential and the player's subsequent performance was probably very low. With no data for Cell C or D, the coach persisted in his completely unsubstantiated belief that my friend's diagnoses were outstanding. Had the coach been forced to play some of the recruits that my friend had rejected, the coach might have found out that Cell C exceeded Cell D by the same proportion that Cell A exceeded Cell B. This would have been devastating to the coach's opinion of my friend's clinical judgment.

Sometimes there is an opportunity to examine Cell C and D data, and such an examination can be extremely informative. Due to a court order, the University of Texas Medical School at Houston was required to enlarge its entering medical school class from 150 to 200 persons. The medical school had already accepted 150 students, who were drawn from the top 350 students among the 800 applicants. When the court order was issued, the medical school was forced to admit 50 students from the bottom 100 applicants. The top 150 students, who had been chosen by the admissions committee, were compared to the bottom 50 students, who were admitted due to the court order. The top students would comprise the top row of a 2 × 2 matrix. The bottom 50 would comprise the bottom row of the 2 × 2 matrix. The left column would be "Did well," and the right column would be "Did not do well." The two groups had the same performance at the end of their second year of training, fourth year of training, and first year of residency. The conclusion must be that the admissions committee had exhibited rather poor performance, because there was no covariation between their student selection and the students' medical school accomplishment (DeVaul et al., 1987).

Many people do not think that the data in Cells C and D are even relevant, so there is no need to try to obtain such data (Arkes & Harkness, 1983). For example, if one is testing whether a treatment has a salutary effect, the top row of a 2 × 2 matrix would be "Given the treatment," the bottom row would be "Not given the treatment" or "Given a placebo treatment." The left column might be "Improves," and the right column might be "Doesn't improve." Many people believe that the only relevant data are in Cells A and B: "If you are testing a treatment, why look at people who are not given the treatment?" However, Cells C and D comprise the control group. These data are needed, because it may be the case that those who are not given the treatment improve just as much as those who are given the treatment.

A central theme in this book is that the decision making literature can provide a significant edge in diagnosis and prediction, and examination of covariation analysis provides insight into some of the bases for this advantage. One such advantage relates to learning through direct experience versus other or supplemental means. We do not question whether personal experience is invaluable for certain learning, but it can also have some substantial disadvantages in a range of important situations. In the case of covariation analysis, we hope it is clear that one needs information from all four cells, and preferably information that is accurate and representative. Personal experience, however, may not, and often will not, provide such information. For example, if a therapist consistently implements a certain intervention for a certain problem or presentation, the therapist does not know what would happen had they acted differently. Thus, one might have information about the A and B cells (specific information about the percentage of individuals who do and do not do well), but not about the other two cells. It could be that the specific intervention has a higher success rate than all alternatives, but without comparative information (e.g., an alternative treatment group or a no-treatment group), how does one know if the best treatment approach has been selected, or even whether it has greater efficacy than no treatment? Similarly, if a neuropsychologist treats individuals with concussions, symptoms or behaviors seen commonly among such groups may be assumed to be associated with the condition. However, as it turns out, research shows that such assumptions are commonly incorrect or overperceived (Gunstad & Suhr, 2002; Leddy et al., 2015; Pulsipher et al., 2021). Not to make light of this, but both individuals who have and have not had concussions may forget where they park their cars, which is presumably the impetus for those signs, "Remember where you parked your car."

Yet, from the standpoint of experience alone, how could a therapist or neuropsychologist acquire information from all four cells in the course of practice? Individuals who are functioning well are unlikely, or at least considerably less likely, to seek clinical services in comparison to individuals who are experiencing difficulties. Furthermore, as noted, if the work involves intervention, the therapist does not know what would have happened had they used a different intervention from the one they selected. Hence, in such circumstances, science can provide considerable advantages over personal experience in acquiring the type and quality of information needed to discern possible associations among variables. With well-conducted research, one collects representative samples (e.g., of individuals who do and do not have a certain condition, or who are and are not in treatment), and information allowing one to compare frequencies across all four cells. In addition, steps can be taken to reduce potential biases in appraisal, such as double-blinding. How can even the most astute person compare relative frequencies in Cells A and B to relative frequencies in Cells C and D if that person has minimal and possibly nonrepresentative information from Cells C and D? This is in no way a negative commentary on the intellectual powers of mental health professionals. No matter how smart a person might be, if one is asking whether the ratio of A:B differs from the ratio of C:D, and a person lacks the latter information, intelligence will not make what is necessary unnecessary.

Without dogmatically elevating science above all other methods of knowing across all situations, it is important to recognize the varied circumstances in which science brings epistemological/methodological advantages that can elevate it above personal experience and aid greatly in extending the limits of personal observation. The potential advantages of science are sometimes presented with limited explanation, merely as something one should just take on authority. However, a careful look at what science can offer and how it compares to personal experience is not often explicated effectively. Covariation analysis provides a compelling example of the potential benefits gained by proper analysis of data and scientific methods.

Obtaining Data in All Four Cells

A common objection to the use of 2 × 2 tables to assess clinical judgment is that it is necessary to have a "gold standard." For example, Table 3.2's two columns are Disorder Actually Present—Yes and Disorder Actually Present—No. It is possible to do an autopsy to ascertain whether a deceased person did or did not have a particular disorder. This would enable a determination of whether a premortem diagnosis was accurate. However, what about a psychological test? What is the gold standard with regard to the indisputable presence or absence of a diagnosed condition? Table 3.2 requires correct placement of data into either the left or right column.

First, it is possible to correctly place many diagnoses. For example, in an early study, Werner et al. (1983) asked psychologists and psychiatrists to predict whether males admitted to an acute-care psychiatric unit would engage in assault during their first seven days on the unit. Merely observing whether an assault occurred during that period would provide all the data needed to complete Table 3.2.

Another common practice is to convene a panel of experts to decide on a diagnosis. If the panel members unanimously or nearly unanimously agree on the correct diagnosis, this becomes the basis for assignment to the left or right column of Table 3.2. In studies, it also may be possible to use much more thorough and involved (and more costly) approaches that are not feasible in everyday practice, such as extensive and repeated follow-up assessments to determine course over time.

Second, a failure to make an assignment to one of the columns of Table 3.2 is not merely a problem for the creation of a 2 × 2 table to assess clinical judgment. If a diagnostician cannot make such an assignment, one may be unable to ascertain if one's judgment or diagnosis is correct even if one does not use a 2 × 2 table. The table merely forces one to confront the fact that one needs an effective standard (although not always a gold one) to determine whether one's judgment or diagnosis is correct.

A gold standard may ultimately be necessary to determine definitively (or nearly definitively) whether a particular judgment is correct. However, as knowledge is developing, or in initial validation stages, silver or bronze standards may still help considerably in advancing knowledge. In fact, in many instances, if we already had gold standards for diagnosing or predicting, we might not need to do any research to improve diagnostic accuracy or prediction. The paradox here is that if one is demanding gold standards, one may have to know what one does not know in order to learn what one is trying to learn. It is very common at initial stages of knowledge development to use relatively valid but fallible indicators, as was done when initially validating measures of intellectual ability against teachers' judgments. If a method one is appraising has merit, it is likely to at least show an association with a valid but fallible indicator. For example, if one has a method that is correct 75% of the time in identifying the presence of some condition, then another method that agrees in most cases is probably on the right track. There are also ingenious methods that can help to correct for error in criterion groups, such as what has been labeled Mixed Group Validation (Dawes & Meehl, 1966; Jewsbury & Bowden, 2014).

TESTING TERMINOLOGY

Consider Table 3.5, which was taken from data reported by Torem, Gilbertson, and Light (1990), who examined the diagnosticity of the Draw-a-Tree Test. Torem et al. tested the hypothesis that certain features ("indicators") of a tree drawn by a person indicate whether that person had been physically, sexually, or verbally abused. Four questions can be asked about the value of this indicator of abuse.

When abuse has been reported or (presumably) actually occurred, how often does this test indicate that abuse has taken place? This is the sensitivity of the test,

Table 3.5. Data Reported by Torem et al. (1990)

	Abuse History	
	Yes	No
Tree Indicator Present	64	36
Tree Indicator Absent	74	97

which is 64/138 = 46%. This means that when abuse has occurred, the Draw-a-Tree test accurately detects that abuse slightly less than half of the time.

When abuse has not occurred, how often does the test indicate that abuse has not occurred? This is the specificity of the test, which is 97/133 = 73%.

When a positive test result occurs, how accurate is it? This is the positive predictive value (PPV) of the test, which is 64/100 = 64%.

When a negative test result occurs, how accurate is it? This is the negative predictive value (NPV) of the test, which is 97/171 = 57%.

Professional diagnosticians rely on these four characteristics to evaluate the worth of a diagnostic test. This particular test has a poor NPV, for example, and obtaining a negative test result would not provide convincing evidence that the person taking the test had not been abused. Professional diagnosticians need to know how to calculate such characteristics of any diagnostic tool in order to determine whether that tool should be utilized. In the case of this test, we must conclude that it would incur a very large number of classification errors if it were used to diagnose the presence of physical, sexual, or verbal abuse. In short, the covariation between this test's results and actual abuse is low. These four terms—sensitivity, specificity, positive predictive value, negative predictive value—comprise an excellent summary of a test's diagnostic properties. Note that the four terms do not describe statistical significance. A test might yield statistically significant classification performance, but it still may be insufficient as a basis for making a secure diagnosis. The data in Table 3.5 indicate that the test has correctly classified abuse status in only 59% of cases. Using a flip of a coin to diagnose abuse in this sample of persons would have achieved a classification almost as accurate as one would have achieved through use of the test. By considering the sensitivity, specificity, PPV, and NPV of the Draw-A-Tree Test, its serious shortcomings are unmasked. This is why diagnosticians must know how to calculate these factors, all of which are indicators of covariation.

Claims are sometimes made that a particular test has exceptional value for detecting conditions or problems that other tests miss far more often. This may seem like a compelling argument, especially when we are most concerned about avoiding false-negative errors, such as in the identification of abuse. However, such supposed value may be illusory because the seeming sensitivity may come at the cost of many false-positive errors. Suppose one identified a test that identified every single individual as having a serious psychological condition. Such a test, of course, would never miss a person with the disorder, but it would never identify a person without the disorder correctly, and thus is of absolutely no use. Conversely, if a test identified everyone as normal, it would miss every case of disorder, and likewise would be worthless. It is exactly for this reason that one cannot evaluate a test or diagnostic indicator without looking at both sensitivity and specificity, or better yet, without examining both PPV and NPV.

PPV and NPV: The Advanced Course

Consider the data in Table 3.6. The diagnostician gives a test whose positive result implicates the presence of a disorder, and whose negative result indicates the absence of a disorder.

Here is a case in which a positive test result for this infrequently occurring disorder is not very informative. Even if a positive test result occurs, the person has only a 26% probability of having the disorder. This PPV is rather low. However, if a negative test result occurs, the diagnostician can be 91% certain that the person does not have the disorder. This example shows that sometimes a test result can be helpful in ruling out a condition but not very helpful in ruling in a condition. The reverse is also possible. Thus it may be misleading to characterize a test as generally good or generally bad if the PPV and NPV differ substantially. The positive and negative test results may be differentially informative.

Another factor to consider is the cost of each type of error. Cells B and C contain the errors we call false positives and false negatives. Suppose that a false positive means that a benign treatment that is highly effective and has negligible side effects is temporarily administered to a person who does not have the serious disorder. This Cell B error has a small cost. However if a Cell C error means that a person who has the serious disorder is not given the treatment, a catastrophic result may occur; a Cell C error would be very costly. It may be advisable to use a test in a situation that results in many Cell B errors but results in hardly any Cell C errors. The relative costs of the errors will influence a decision to utilize a particular test. Another critical factor is the base rate of the condition one is trying to diagnose correctly. The base rate is the frequency of the condition in the population being tested. If, for example, the base rate for the condition of interest is very low, even a seemingly accurate method (under conditions of higher base rates) may make considerably more errors than correct identifications. The potentially sizeable influence of base rates deserves a chapter all its own (see Chapter 6).

Table 3.6. Data Needed to Estimate the Covariation between a Test Result and a Disorder

		Disorder Actually Present?	
		Yes	**No**
Test Result	**Positive**	18	50
	Negative	5	50

REFERENCES

Arkes, H. R., & Harkness, A. R. (1983). Estimates of contingency between two dichotomous variables. *Journal of Experimental Psychology: General, 112*, 117–135.

Chapman, L. J., & Chapman, J. P. (1967). Genesis of popular but erroneous psychodiagnostic observations. *Journal of Abnormal Psychology, 72*(3), 193–204.

Dawes, R. M. (1989). Experience and validity of clinical judgment: The illusory correlation. *Behavioral Sciences and the Law, 7*, 457–467.

Dawes, R. M., & Meehl P. E. (1966). Mixed group validation: A method for determining the validity of diagnostic signs with using criterion groups. *Psychological Bulletin, 66*(2), 63–67.

DeVaul, R. A., Jervey, F., Chappell, J. A., Caver, P., Short, B., & O'Keefe, S. (1987). Medical school performance of initially rejected students. *JAMA, 257*(1), 47–51.

Faust, D. (2012). *Ziskin's coping with psychiatric and psychological testimony* (6th ed.). Oxford University Press.

Ganguly, A. R., & Hammersley, J. S. (2009). Covariation estimates with costly information collection in audit planning: An experimental study. *Auditing: A Journal of Theory and Practice, 28*(1), 1–27.

Gunstad, J., & Suhr, J. A. (2002). Perception of illness: Nonspecificity of postconcussion syndrome symptom expectation. *Journal of the International Neuropsychological Society, 8*(1), 37–47.

Hamilton, D. L., & Rose, T. L. (1980). Illusory correlation and the maintenance of stereotypic beliefs. *Journal of Personality and Social Psychology, 39*(5), 832–845.

Jewsbury, P. A., & Bowden, S. C. (2014). A description of mixed group validation. *Assessment, 21*(2), 170–180.

Kurtz, R. M., & Garfield, S. L. (1978). Illusory correlation: A further exploration of Chapman's paradigm. *Journal of Consulting and Clinical Psychology, 46*(5), 1009–1015.

Leddy, J. J., Baker, J. G., Merchant, A., Picano, J., Gaile, D. Matuszak, J., & Willer, B. (2015). Brain or strain? Symptoms alone do not distinguish physiologic concussion from cervical/vestibular injury. *Clinical Journal of Sports Medicine, 25*(3), 237–242.

Lueger, R. J., & Petzel, T. P. (1979). Illusory correlation in clinical judgment: Effects of amount of information to be processed. *Journal of Consulting and Clinical Psychology, 47*(6), 1120–1121.

Pulsipher, D. T., Rettig, E. K., Krapf, E. M., & Stanford, L. D. (2021). A cross-sectional cohort study of post-concussive symptoms and their relationships with depressive symptoms in youth with and without concussion. *Brain Injury, 35*(8), 964–970.

Smedslund, J. (1963). The concept of correlation in adults. *Scandinavian Journal of Psychology, 4*(3), 165–173.

Torem, M. S., Gilbertson, A., & Light, V. (1990). Indications of physical, sexual, and verbal victimization in projective tree drawings. *Journal of Clinical Psychology, 46*(6), 900–906.

Werner, P. D., Rose, T. L., & Yesavage, J. A. (1983). Reliability, accuracy, and decision making strategy in clinical predictions of imminent dangerousness. *Journal of Consulting and Clinical Psychology, 51*(6), 815–825.

4

Confirmation Bias

Confirmation bias is defined as "the seeking or interpreting of evidence in ways that are partial to existing beliefs, expectations, or a hypothesis in hand" (Nickerson, 1998, p. 175). There is an enormous literature on this topic, because, as Nickerson (1998, p. 175) wrote, "If one were to attempt to identify a single problematic aspect of human reasoning that deserves attention above all others, the *confirmation bias* would have to be among the candidates for consideration." We have organized the voluminous body of research into four categories: unwarranted maintenance of hypotheses, biased testing of hypotheses, faulty memory for evidence, and distorted interpretation of evidence.

UNWARRANTED MAINTENANCE OF HYPOTHESES

The classic research in this category was done by Bruner and Potter (1964). A standardization group of participants was shown eight pictures in very poor focus. The clarity was gradually improved until each picture was correctly identified by 25% of the people. We call this the 25% point. The pictures included such familiar objects as a dog or silverware. The main experiment consisted of three groups of new participants. One group was shown very blurred (VB) versions of each of the items, another group was shown the items in medium blur (MB), and the third group in light blur (LB). The clarity of the images was improved gradually for each of the three groups until the focus was at the 25% point. Because the stopping point for each group was exactly the same, each of the three experimental groups should have been able to exhibit precisely the same level of correct recognition of the pictures at this point. However, the groups' performance differed markedly. The VB group was able to recognize 23% of the pictures, the MB group recognized 45%, and the LB recognized 60%. Why did the LB group recognize almost three times as many pictures as did the VB group?

If you were an unfortunate member of the VB group, the initial terrible focus of the picture probably led you to formulate an incorrect hypothesis about what that image actually depicted. As the focus improved, you were exposed to various aspects of the object's true identity. However, due to the fact that you had already formulated a hypothesis, you tended to interpret the new aspects in a biased way, perceiving them as potentially consistent with your initial incorrect hypothesis. This distortion of the incoming data thus retarded your ability to revise your hypothesis. The MB group was less likely to start with a worthless hypothesis, and the LB group's initial hypothesis was even less likely to be incorrect. The "stickiness" of the VB group's initial hypothesis was due to the participants' tendency to perceive the incoming information as confirming it. This is therefore a manifestation of confirmation bias.

A similar finding has been demonstrated in many clinical situations. Dailey (1952) asked two groups of sophomores to read a case history and then to make predictions about how a client answered a personality inventory. Because this was the case history of an actual client, the researchers did have the client's responses on the personality inventory. One group of students read the entire case history before making their predictions. The other group read half of the case history, made their predictions, read the second half of the case history, and then made their predictions again. The researchers examined the accuracy of the predictions that both groups made after reading the entire case. The people who made initial predictions after reading only half of the case history performed significantly more poorly on the predictions they made after reading the entire case compared to the group who made predictions only once after reading the entire case. The people in the former group were suffering from the fact that they had formulated a hypothesis about the client before they had read all of the relevant information. Being forced to make a premature conclusion about the client in order to formulate the initial predictions resulted in a hypothesis that was insufficiently altered in light of the subsequent information about the person. Instead, the premature conclusion resulted in ensuing data being seen as more supportive than it really was.

There are a number of ways in which a potentially biasing initial hypothesis can be instantiated. Hersh (1971) provided an early example. Graduate students who were experienced in testing each gave the Stanford-Binet Intelligence Scale to two children. The handwritten referral note accompanying one child was purportedly written by a teacher and stated that the child had high intellectual ability, social skills, and academic ability. The note accompanying the other child expressed the opposite characteristics (i.e., low intellectual ability, social skills, and academic ability). The former group of children scored 5.5 points higher than the latter group, even though the children were randomly assigned to each group. This result is often referred to as labeling bias, because a label can foster the generation of an initial hypothesis that can, in turn, result in a confirmation bias in the interpretation of test data.

Ross et al. (1977, Experiment 3) provide one of the most insidious examples of unwarranted hypothesis maintenance. Undergraduates were asked to read a case history of an actual patient and then rate how likely they thought each of five possible outcomes would be. The possible outcomes included the patient's making a financial contribution to Amnesty International, being a candidate for city council, plus three other possibilities. Some subjects in the experiment were first asked to explain what factors in the case history might explain why the patient would make a contribution to Amnesty International; others were asked what factors in the case history might explain why the person would run for city council. Half of the subjects in each of the two groups were explicitly told that the experimenter had no knowledge about whether any of the five possible outcomes actually occurred. Therefore, any explanations the subjects offered would pertain to a completely hypothetical event. Finally, the experimenter asked the people in the four subgroups to rate the likelihood of each of the five possible outcomes. A control group was asked to perform the ratings without first receiving any explanations. The results were that whatever outcome a person had been asked to explain, whether or not the experimenter stated that the outcome was hypothetical, was rated significantly more likely than the control group rated the outcome. Merely explaining something—anything—made it appear more likely! Generating a hypothesis about why a person might eventually do X is enough to boost the perceived probability of X. A hypothesis seems to take on a life of its own.

BIASED TESTING OF HYPOTHESES

In order to perform a proper evaluation of a hypothesis, one must perform an unbiased test of it. Many studies have shown that in clinical settings people selectively seek out information that tends to confirm the hypothesis currently under consideration and do not attend to information that would cast doubt on the current hypothesis.

One example is a study by Mendel et al. (2011). Psychiatrists and medical students were given a short vignette about a man who might be in the early stages of Alzheimer's disease or who might be experiencing a severe depressive episode. The evidence in the vignette was created in such a way that almost all of the participants selected the latter as the preliminary diagnosis even though the true diagnosis was Alzheimer's disease. All participants were given the opportunity to select 12 new pieces of information that had not been included in the original vignette. Six of the new items were consistent with each of the two potential diagnoses. Physicians could stop searching for new information and render a diagnosis at any point. A total of 13% of the psychiatrists and 25% of the students exhibited a confirmatory information search by asking to see more information consistent with the incorrect preliminary diagnosis than information consistent with the alternative diagnosis. Only 30% of the psychiatrists and 37% of the students who used a confirmatory search strategy eventually made the correct diagnosis, whereas 73% of the psychiatrists who used a disconfirmatory search strategy and 53% of the psychiatrists using a balanced search strategy made the correct diagnosis. In summary, if one only seeks information that would confirm what one has already hypothesized, the correct diagnosis is less likely to be made. Other studies that used therapists arrived at a similar conclusion: Confirmatory information is often more likely to be selected in arriving at a final diagnosis (see Strohmer & Shivy, 1994). As Mendel et al. (2011) showed, as long as potentially disconfirmatory information is shunned, the probability of arriving at a correct diagnosis is diminished.

Table 4.1. Confirmation Bias Example (Kern & Doherty, 1982)

	Disease A	Disease B
Fever	84%	46%
No Fever	16%	54%
Rash	73%	37%
No Rash	27%	63%

Kern and Doherty (1982) demonstrated a type of confirmation bias using an entirely different paradigm. Consider the situation depicted in Table 4.1. Senior medical students were told to imagine the situation in which they had to decide whether a patient had disease A or disease B. The medical students had been shown the pair of data in the upper-left cell of the table, namely that 84% of the people with disease A have a fever and 16% do not. The other three pairs of data were covered. The medical students were asked which one of the remaining three pairs of data they would uncover to help make the correct diagnosis. Bayes' Theorem (which is explained fully in Chapter 6) requires that to choose between disease A and disease B, one must consider this ratio: probability of symptom X given disease A/probability of symptom X given disease B, or $p(S_x|D_A)/p(S_x|D_B)$.

Hence the medical students should have chosen to examine the data pair in the upper-right cell of data, which would comprise the denominator of the ratio. Each of the 65 medical students was given two such cases. Only 11 of the 65 chose the upper-right pair for both cases; 45 failed to choose the appropriate pair in either case. Of these 45, 33 students chose the lower-left pair for both cases. It is impossible to compare the conditional probabilities of a symptom (fever) given each of two diseases if one seeks only information about one of the diseases! The misguided students who chose to examine the data in the lower left pair wanted to confirm a favored hypothesis, namely that the patient had disease A. So, they sought more information about the presence of a rash if the patient had disease A. To establish the relative likelihood of the two diseases, one must obtain the data in this ratio. What if the data in the upper-right pair had been 100%/0%? Then having a fever would have been more supportive of having disease B than disease A. The important ratio depicted above is called the likelihood ratio, and it is a good antidote to confirmation bias. It forces one to consider not only confirmatory information but also disconfirmatory information. One goes in the numerator, and the other goes in the denominator.

FAULTY MEMORY FOR RELEVANT DATA

Arkes and Harkness (1980) presented students in hearing and speech science with a list of four symptoms highly characteristic of Down's syndrome. The students were asked to render a diagnosis based on these symptoms; about half were able to do so. About two weeks later, the experimenters returned and presented 12 symptoms; four were the ones listed previously, four were related to Down's syndrome but were not presented previously, and four were unrelated to Down's syndrome and were not shown previously. The students were asked to rate each of the 12 symptoms on a 7-point scale where 1 meant "I'm absolutely sure it was shown two weeks ago" and 7 meant "I'm absolutely sure it was not shown two weeks ago." The students who had not been able to make a diagnosis during the first session were rather confident in the second session that the symptoms not shown previously were indeed new: The new symptoms related to Down's syndrome were rated 5.60, and those unrelated to Down's syndrome were rated 5.85. Those who had been able to make the diagnosis provided much different data. They were quite confident that the new symptoms unrelated to Down's syndrome had not been shown previously—giving a rating of 6.20. However, the new symptoms that were related to Down's syndrome were given a rating of 4.60, close to the middle of the scale, suggesting that these students were not sure whether or not they had seen these symptoms previously. Somehow, having made the diagnosis impaired their ability to correctly classify novel symptoms. One of us authors discussed this finding with a physician whom he had accompanied as the physician did rounds with a bevy of medical students, going from patient to patient explaining the medical situation of each patient to the students. I subsequently asked the physician if he could recall all of the symptoms upon which each patient's diagnosis was based. He said, "No, I can't recall all of the initial symptoms, but I can recall the diagnosis. That's cognitively more economical. I have to remember only one thing." As was the case with the hearing and speech students, once a tentative diagnosis is rendered, the data upon which the diagnosis was based tends to become less memorable. Worse yet, the diagnosis fosters the false recollection of confirmatory data, which in turn lends unwarranted support to the diagnosis.

Here's an example from cognitive psychology research. Baggett (1975) presented subjects with four slides showing four scenes in the following sequence: (1) a long-haired man in front of a barber shop, (2) the long-haired man walking into the barber shop, (3) the long-haired man getting his hair cut by the barber, (4) a now short-haired man leaving the barber shop. Both immediately and 72 hours later, the subjects were tested: they were asked to look at slides and to press as quickly as possible a button marked True or a button marked False depending on whether a presented slide "fits in with your understanding" of the events in the story. The subjects' reaction time to press the correct button was measured. One slide shown during the immediate and 72-hour tests was a picture of a long-haired man sitting in the barber chair but the man's hair had not yet been cut by the barber. This slide had not been shown in the original set of slides, but it depicted a scene that could be inferred from the original quartet of slides. When the test was immediate, the subjects' reaction times to the slides that were actually presented in the story were significantly quicker than the reaction time to the "implicit slide"—the one that had not been shown but which could have been inferred. After 72 hours, the reaction times to the presented slides and the implicit slides were nearly identical.

No longer could the subjects distinguish between what was actually presented and what was merely consistent with the story. This is an analogy to a diagnostic situation. Once the story or diagnosis is formed, a datum or symptom consistent with the diagnosis tends to be recalled as having been present even if it was not. An extra "consistent" but nonexistent piece of information helps to confirm the diagnosis.

In two experiments, Strohmer, Shivy, and Chiodo (1990) demonstrated this problem in a counseling setting. In the first experiment, professional counselors were presented with one of three different narratives of a bipolar individual. The narratives were constructed based on responses a person would endorse on the Sixteen Personality Factor Inventory (16PF). One description contained 12 descriptors from the 16PF that were consistent with the presence of self-control and eight consistent with its absence. A second narrative contained the reverse ratio of descriptors (8 vs. 12), and a third narrative contained 10 descriptors consistent with the presence, and 10 with the absence, of self-control. One week later, the professional counselors were asked to test the hypothesis that the person described in the narrative lacked self-control. They were also asked to list as many factors as they could recall that would be helpful in testing this hypothesis. There were two main results: (1) Regardless of which of the three narratives a counselor had read, more descriptors consistent with the lack of control were recalled. (2) The more descriptors recalled that were consistent with a lack of self-control, the more certain the counselors were about the hypothesis that the person lacked self-control. A second experiment by Strohmer et al. differed from the first in that (1) there was no time delay between reading the narrative and selecting descriptors to test the hypothesis that the person lacked self-control, and (2) the narrative was always available so that no memory was involved in testing the hypothesis. The results were the same as in the first experiment. Thus, the hypothesis that the person lacked self-control warped the recollection (Experiment 1) and selection (Experiment 2) of data so that the hypothesis enjoyed confirmation even when the number of disconfirmatory descriptors outnumbered the confirmatory ones!

DISTORTED INTERPRETATION OF EVIDENCE

Confirmation bias can pollute the interpretation of evidence. Filer (1952) provided a particularly troubling demonstration. After examining 156 case reports from 13 clinicians, Filer reported that there were several significant relationships between the personality of each clinician and the case reports of his or her patients. For example, "Examiners who stress hostility turned inward tend to be rated depressed and intropunitive" (p. 336). In a second study using a similar procedure, Filer reported, "The three most frequently mentioned defense mechanisms in reports are more characteristic of the clinicians than of their patients" (p. 336)! Apparently, the clinicians tended to warp their interpretation of the incoming data so that the data were to some extent a manifestation of each clinician's own personality.

This principle has been demonstrated experimentally by Anderson et al. (1977). The following is one of the stories used in their research:

> Rocky slowly got up from the mat, planning his escape. He hesitated a moment and thought. Things were not going well. What bothered him most was being held, especially since the charge against him had been weak. He considered his present situation. The lock that held him was strong but he thought he could break it. He knew, however, that his timing would have to be perfect. Rocky was aware that it was because of his early roughness that he had been penalized so severely—much too severely from his point of view. The situation was becoming frustrating: the pressure had been grinding on him for too long. He was being ridden unmercifully. Rocky was getting angry now. He felt he was ready to make his move. He knew that his success or failure would depend on what he did in the next few seconds.

Anderson and his colleagues used two groups of participants in the experiment. One was a group from an educational psychology course designed for persons planning a career in music education. The other group consisted of students enrolled in a weight-lifting class. Most people interpret the sample passage as an account of a prisoner planning his escape from a jail. This is how the educational psychology students interpreted it. However, based on the students' recall of the various aspects of the story, it was apparent that the majority of people in the weight-lifting class interpreted the story as a wrestler trying to escape from the grip of his opponent. The two groups interpreted the story quite differently depending on their experience and interests. It would not be appropriate to deem either group biased, because there is no normative right answer concerning how the story should be interpreted. The students' perspectives were understandably influenced by their own backgrounds. The therapists in Filer's study may also have had different training, backgrounds, or experience. In the clinical situation there is a normative answer—the correct diagnosis. If persons with different backgrounds cannot put them aside, the ability to arrive at the normatively appropriate diagnosis is jeopardized.

Another type of data distortion is particularly common. Once a decision maker "leans" toward a conclusion, subsequent data are interpreted in such a way that they tend to support the initial propensity. This is similar to the unwarranted maintenance of a hypothesis (the example that we began this chapter), but in this case the initial hypothesis is not yet completely formulated or endorsed. This phenomenon is therefore called *pre*decisional information distortion (DeKay, 2015; Russo et al., 1998). It is ubiquitous and has been demonstrated in medical diagnosis (Kostopoulou et al., 2012; Nurek et al., 2014; Rebitschek et al., 2015), legal decision making (Simon et al., 2001), and many other contexts. The general finding is that once a decision maker starts to favor one of multiple options, data supporting that option are distorted in a positive direction (proleader distortion), and data favoring other options are distorted in a negative direction (antitrailer distortion). These two processes consequently foster unwarranted confirmation of the tentative hypothesis.

COGNITIVE PSYCHOLOGY: HOT AND COLD COGNITION

When I (H.A.) was teaching an undergraduate course in cognitive psychology, I would present the following list of words for the students to recall: *blanket, sheet, bed, snooze, rest, dream, tired, pillow, snore, cot, nap*. Before they began their recall effort, I would ask the students first to count backward by 3s from the number 99 (99, 96, 93, etc.) for about 15 seconds. After this backward counting task, the students began their recall effort. Nearly every student was able to recall the word *sleep*. However, I never presented the word *sleep*. The word *sleep* is a close semantic associate to the 11 words I did present, and the 11 words I presented each activated its closest semantic neighbors in associative memory. Because *sleep* is a close associate to all the words I presented, its activation was particularly strong. Therefore, it was readily recalled. Arkes (1991) called such phenomena association-based errors.

Such errors are a strong influence in a large number of judgment pitfalls, among which is confirmation bias. If you are asked to consider the hypothesis "Pat is an angry person," memories of Pat's expressions of anger are activated more strongly than Pat's instances of placid behaviors. The differential search for, and recall of, activated supporting information rather than disconfirmatory information are quite biased (Snyder & Swann, 1978). As a result, the hypothesis that Pat is an angry person is "confirmed." Unfortunately, the differential activation of memories and information consistent with a hypothesis lends a false sense of coherence to the body of knowledge brought to bear upon a judgment (Morewedge & Kahneman, 2010).

We have included substantial cognitive psychology research in our discussion of confirmation bias in psychological testing because we believe that confirmation bias is a prime example of what cognitive psychologists refer to as a cold cognitive error. Such errors are not due to any motivated bias or prejudice but are instead due to the normal workings of the human information processing system. An example is the availability heuristic.

Kahneman and Tversky (1973) suggested that we judge probability and frequency by the ease with which relevant examples are brought to mind. For example, when one of us teaches an introductory psychology class, he presents to the students a list of the names of eight very famous women, interspersed with the names of nine very obscure men. When tested later, almost every student recalls more women's names than men's names, thus mistakenly concluding that there were more women than men on the list. The students are not prejudiced against men. They do not recall men's names at a lower rate due to antipathy toward males. (If this were the reason for the misestimation of the frequency of the names, this would be a hot cognitive error.) Instead, the women's names were simply easier to recall due to their notoriety. Their names were more available in memory, thus causing the false belief that their names were more numerous than the men's names on the list. Due to the lack of any motivation in making this mistake, it is considered a cold cognitive error. We suggest that confirmation bias and many other difficulties plaguing clinical judgment are due to cold cognitive errors. No one is to blame for such errors. Again, we emphasize that they are due to the normal working of the human information processing system.

We purposely juxtapose clinical psychology examples and cognitive psychology examples in our discussion of confirmation bias. To illustrate the former, we cite Dailey (1952), who showed that the predictions of a client's responses on a personality inventory were poor if the prognosticator had earlier made predictions after reading only half of the case history. The prognosticator did not use the subsequent information about the client to correct their earlier tentative predictions. Similarly, Bruner and Potter (1964) showed that when the focus of fuzzy pictures was greatly improved, people did not optimally use the new information to correct their earlier incorrect hypotheses. The subjects did not do poorly on the Bruner and Potter identification task because they couldn't think dispassionately about dogs and silverware: they made cold cognitive errors.

Arkes and Harkness (1980) showed that hearing and speech students misremembered symptoms that were consistent with their diagnosis. In their second experiment, the authors showed the same result when persons were trying to diagnose a plumbing problem. No one is motivated to misdiagnose plumbing problems, and no one has a prior "pet" plumbing hypothesis that they are trying to support in an unjustified manner. Biased recollection of symptoms consistent with a diagnosis represents a cold cognitive error. Merely telling people about cold cognitive errors and imploring people not to make them has generally not been a successful debiasing strategy (see Fischhoff, 1975). It is difficult to modify the normal way in which one processes information. Fortunately, there are ways to combat cold cognitive errors, and we discuss these techniques in subsequent chapters.

REFERENCES

Anderson, R. C., Reynolds, R. E., Schallert, D. L., & Goetz, E. T. (1977). Frameworks for comprehending discourse. *American Educational Research Journal, 14*(4), 367–381.

Arkes, H. R. (1991). The costs and benefits of judgment errors: Implications for debiasing. *Psychological Bulletin, 110*, 486–498.

Arkes, H. R., & Harkness, A. (1980). The effect of making a diagnosis on subsequent recognition of symptoms. *Journal of Experimental Psychology: Human Learning and Memory, 6*, 568–575.

Baggett, P. (1975). Memory for explicit and implicit information in picture stories. *Journal of Verbal Learning and Verbal Behavior, 14*, 538–548.

Bruner, J. S., & Potter, M. C. (1964). Interference in visual recognition. *Science, 144*(3617), 424–425.

Dailey, C. A. (1952). The effects of premature conclusions upon the acquisition of understanding of a person. *Journal of Psychology, 33*, 133–152.

DeKay, M. L. (2015). Predecisional information distortion and the self-fulfilling prophesy of early preferences in choice. *Current Directions in Psychological Science, 24*(5), 405–411. https://doi.10.1177/0963721415587876

Filer, R. N. (1952). The clinician's personality and his case reports. *American Psychologist, 7*, 336.

Fischhoff, B. (1975). Hindsight is not equal to foresight: The effect of outcome knowledge on judgment under uncertainty. *Journal of Experimental Psychology: Human Perception and Performance, 1*, 288–299.

Hersh, J. B. (1971). Effects of referral information on testers. *Journal of Consulting and Clinical Psychology, 37*, 116–122.

Kahneman, D., & Tversky, A. (1973). Availability: A heuristic for judging frequency and probability. *Cognitive Psychology, 5*, 207–232.

Kern, L., & Doherty, M. E. (1982). "Pseudodiagnosticity" in an idealized medical problem-solving environment. *Journal of Medical Education, 57*, 100–104.

Kostopoulou, O., Russo, J. E., Keenan, G., Delaney, B. C., & Douiri, A. (2012). Information distortion in physicians' diagnostic judgments. *Medical Decision Making, 32*, 831–839. https://doi.10.1177/0272989X12447241

Mendel, R., Traut-Mattausch, Jonas, E., Kane, J. M., Maino, K., & Kissling, W. (2011). Confirmatory bias: Why psychiatrists stick to wrong preliminary hypotheses. *Psychological Medicine, 41*, 2651–1659. https://doi.10.1017/S0033291711000808

Morewedge, C. K., & Kahneman, D. (2010). Associative processes in intuitive judgment. *Trends in Cognitive Science, 14*(10), 435–440. https://doi.10.1016/j/tics.2101.07.004

Nickerson, R. S. (1998). Confirmation bias: A ubiquitous phenomenon in many guises. *Review of General Psychology, 2*(2), 175–220.

Nurek, M., Kostopoulou, O., & Hagmayer, Y. (2014). Predecisional information in physicians' diagnostic judgments: Strengthening a leading hypothesis or weakening its competitor? *Judgment and Decision Making, 9*, 572–585.

Rebitschek, F. G., Bocklisch, F., Scholz, A., Krems, J. F., & Jahn, G. (2015). Biaased processing of ambiguous symptoms favors the initially leading hypothesis in sequential diagnostic reasoning. *Experimental Psychology, 62*(5), 287–305. https://doi.10.1027/1618-3169/a000298

Ross, L., Lepper, M. R., Strack, F., & Steinmetz, J. (1977). Social explanation and social expectation: Effects of real and hypothetical explanations on subjective likelihood. *Journal of Personality and Social Psychology, 35*(11), 817–829.

Russo, J. E., Meloy, M. G., & Medvec, V. H. (1998). Predecisional distortion of product information. *Journal of Marketing Research, 35*, 438–452. https://doi.10.2307/3152163

Simon, D., Pham, L. B., Le, Q. A., & Holyoak, K. J. (2001). The emergence of coherence over the course of decision making. *Journal of Experimental Psychology: Learning, Memory, and Cognition, 27*, 1250–1260. https://doi.10.1037/0278-7393.27.5.1250

Snyder, M., & Swann, W. B. (1978). Hypothesis testing processes in social interaction. *Journal of Personality and Social Psychology, 36*(11), 1202–1212.

Strohmer, D. C., & Shivy, V. A. (1994). Bias in counselor hypothesis testing: Testing the robustness of counselor confirmatory bias. *Journal of Counseling and Development, 73*, 191–197.

Strohmer, D. C., Shivy, V. A., & Chiodo, A. L. (1990). Information processing strategies in counselor hypothesis testing: The role of selective memory and expectancy. *Journal of Counseling Psychology, 17*(4), 465–472.

5

Impediments to Accurate Decision Making

There are a number of impediments to accurate clinical decision making. This chapter covers five of the more common ones. They are: hindsight bias, outcome bias, faulty conjunctive reasoning, the erratic effect of prior associations, and susceptibility to formatting.

HINDSIGHT BIAS AND OUTCOME BIAS

Consider the dramatic situation described in Dawson et al. (1988). At many hospitals, a clinicopathologic conference (CPC) is held in which all the medical staff attend in order to witness the presentation of a past case. As they enter the auditorium, the staff members are usually handed a sheet of paper summarizing the medical history, laboratory tests, and other information about the patient whose case will be described. The case has been studied very assiduously by the presenter—usually a young physician, because he or she will have to present it to the audience in great detail. Following the exposition of the case, the presenter suggests five or so possible diagnoses, announces what he or she thinks the correct diagnosis should be, and explains why that particular diagnosis is the one he or she favors. This person then sits down and awaits extremely anxiously as the pathologist who did the autopsy steps forward and announces the correct diagnosis.

Once the announcement of the correct diagnosis is made, many people in the audience covertly overestimate their likelihood of having been able to make that diagnosis beforehand without knowledge of the correct answer. This hindsight bias is defined as "the tendency for people considering a past event to overestimate their likelihood of having predicted its occurrence" (Arkes et al., 1988, p. 305). In several CPCs, Dawson et al. (1988) demonstrated this by asking half of the audience to estimate the probability of the five possible diagnoses before the pathologist revealed the true diagnosis. After the pathologist's announcement, Dawson and colleagues asked the other half of the audience to estimate the probability they would have assigned to the five possible diagnoses had they not just heard the correct diagnosis. These two groups were the foresight and hindsight groups, respectively. For three of four subgroups of medical staff, the hindsight respondents were about a dozen probability points "smarter" than the foresight respondents in estimating the probability of the correct diagnosis. The only group that did not succumb to the hindsight bias was the cohort of most senior physicians considering the most difficult cases. For example, in one of the CPCs used in Dawson et al.'s study, the presentation of a rare disease was highly atypical. Only the most experienced physicians would have had enough experience with that disease to know how unusual the disease's presentation was. Thus, only these veterans would have appreciated how unlikely they would have been to have made the correct diagnosis given how very well the disease was disguised. This subset of physicians considering the most unusual cases were the only ones who escaped hindsight bias.

One of the unfortunate consequences of hindsight bias is that it diminishes the educational value of the CPC. The audience members are supposed to learn from the presentation. The exercise is designed to teach audience members about a particular disease or condition. If the audience members think, "This case is not so difficult. I would have known it all along," they understandably feel that there is nothing new to be absorbed and understood.

Hindsight bias has also been demonstrated among psychiatrists (LeBourgeois et al., 2007) and neuropsychologists. In the latter research, Arkes et al. (1988) asked 102 neuropsychologists to consider the following:

> We would greatly appreciate your taking a few minutes to read the case below, which is part of an adjunct study on neuropsychological diagnosis. We would like you to decide what probability you would have assigned to each of three possible conditions had you been making the diagnosis.
>
> A 55-year-old man presents to an outpatient psychiatric clinic in a mildly confused and agitated state. He is oriented to person and place but is uncertain about the date, mis-stating it by about a week. He says he is having problems with his "nerves," and he exhibits a mild bilateral intention tremor.
>
> Review of background information indicates an unsteady work history with frequent job changes over the last three years. He has not even held undemanding jobs over the last two years due to poor work performance. The man's social network is limited to "a few drinking buddies." His wife reports that he has been drinking steadily for at least five years, averaging a six-pack or more a day, but that he stopped drinking one week ago when a close friend was killed while driving home from a bar. She also says that "he can't remember like he used to, his memory is getting worse and worse," and that "both of his parents got the same problem and went right downhill," when they were in their fifties. When questioned, she is not certain what condition the parents had but indicated they died in their early sixties and fears her husband will die similarly.
>
> Neurological exam is normal except for bilateral tremor. A CT scan is "equivocal but probably normal," although mild cortical atrophy cannot be ruled out. Neuropsychological testing indicates mild to moderate

dysfunction across most areas, with the greatest difficulties shown in attention, concentration, and higher level reasoning. For example, Digit Span is 4 (forward) and 3 (backward), and performance is poor on Trails (Part B) and Wisconsin Card Sorting Test.

Based on your consideration of the case, what is the probability you would assign to each of the diagnoses as the primary one? Assign a probability to each, making sure the probabilities add to 100%.

Alcohol withdrawal _____

Alzheimer's disease_____

Brain damage secondary to alcohol abuse______

These paragraphs comprised the instructions for the foresight group of participants. There were three hindsight groups, one for each of the three possible diagnoses. For each of these three groups, an extra sentence was inserted between the two sentences in the first paragraph of the instructions. The three sentences (one for each of the hindsight groups) were as follows: "This is the case of a man with a primary diagnosis of alcohol withdrawal." "This is the case of a man with a primary diagnosis of Alzheimer's disease." "This is the case of a man with a primary diagnosis of brain damage secondary to alcohol abuse." Table 5.1 contains the mean probability assigned to each diagnosis by each of the four groups.

Hindsight bias is manifested by the elevated probability assigned to the diagnosis purported to be the actual one compared to the probability assigned to that diagnosis by the foresight group. For every diagnosis, the people in the hindsight groups asserted they would have assigned a higher probability level to the "correct" diagnosis than the foresight group participants did.

Another negative consequence of hindsight bias is the potential for compromising the validity of a second opinion. If the person rendering the second opinion is aware of the first opinion, there is the danger that hindsight bias may make the second opinion less than an independent assessment.

Table 5.1. Estimated Probabilities for Each Diagnosis in the Study by Arkes et al. (1988)

Group	Outcome Provided	Outcome Explained		
		Alcohol Withdrawal (AW)	Alzheimer's Disease (AD)	Brain Damage/ Alcohol Abuse (BD)
Foresight	None	37	26	37
Hindsight	AW	**44**	24	33
Hindsight	AD	27	**34**	38
Hindsight	BD	22	28	**50**

Note: The estimates in boldface show the hindsight estimate for each diagnosis is larger than the corresponding foresight estimate for that diagnosis.

Outcome bias is very closely related to hindsight bias. In hindsight bias, the dependent variable is typically a probability estimate, such as "What is the probability you would have assigned had you not been aware of the correct diagnosis?" Outcome bias is generally assessed by queries concerning the performance of the decision maker, such as "To what extent do you think the psychiatrist was negligent?" or "Please rate the quality of the doctor's decision," or "Do you think the psychologist is liable for malpractice?" The cognitive challenge for the two biases is the same: A person who knows the outcome will find it very difficult to ignore that knowledge in assessing the behavior of a person who acted in foresight without the benefit of that knowledge. This has profound consequences in law, particularly in cases of alleged negligence. The jurors are told what has happened to the victim; they know the outcome. Can they fairly evaluate the behavior of a professional who acted in foresight before the outcome had occurred?

A study by LaBine and LaBine (1996) provides a discouraging answer to this question. This research was done in response to the *Tarasoff* decision in 1976, in which the court ruled that if a therapist determines that a patient may be dangerous, that therapist must also determine if there is an identifiable victim and take steps to protect that person. This requires that the therapist be accurate in determining if the patient is dangerous. The researchers presented 287 registered voters (potential jurors) with vignettes containing actual case material. The actions taken by the therapist in each of the six cases had previously been deemed to be reasonable care by a group of psychologists and psychiatrists. There were three versions of each case: (1) the patient eventually engaged in serious violent acts, (2) the patient did not engage in serious violent acts, and (3) the outcome of the case with regard to the patient's violent or nonviolent behavior was not mentioned. In all three versions, the patient was described identically, and the therapist's actions were described identically. Compared to their ratings of the therapist in the nonviolent vignette and the outcome-unspecified vignette, the subjects believed that in the violent vignette (1) the therapist's actions were less reasonable, (2) the therapist should have done more to prevent any violence from occurring, (3) the therapist's actions were less preventative of potential violence, (4) the violence was more predictable and foreseeable, and (5) the therapist was more negligent. Rating (4) is a typical hindsight result. The other results are typical outcome bias results. Result (5) would have grave consequences for the therapist in court. Remember: the therapist did exactly the same thing in all three versions of the vignettes.

There are many other studies in the medical field (see Caplan et al., 1991) and legal domain (see Casper et al., 1989; Hastie et al., 1999) in which analogous findings were obtained. The participants in the study by Caplan et al. (1991) were practicing physicians, so it is apparent that experts rating the behavior of other physicians can fall prey to outcome bias. As is often the case, the bias in the hindsight judgments in these studies was not due to low motivation, evil intent, or any other hot cognitive failing. The participants simply could not place themselves fully in the position of the person who had to confront the situation in foresight. This is another cold cognitive error due to the normal functioning of the human information processing system.

FAULTY CONJUNCTIVE REASONING

One of the authors presented this problem to his Ohio students:

Please rank the following three events according to how likely you think each one is to occur:

1. The Cleveland Indians will win the American League pennant this year.
2. The Cincinnati Reds will win the National League pennant this year.
3. The Cleveland Indians will win the American League pennant this year, and in addition, the Cincinnati Reds will win the National League pennant this year.

Every student ranked the third option as less likely to occur than either of the first two options. This makes perfect sense. The conjunction—both teams being victorious—requires that both of the components of the conjunction occur: The Reds must win, and also the Indians must win. It is more likely that one of them will win than it is that both of them will win. A conjunction cannot be more probable than either of its two components. It's mathematically impossible. All of the students rated the three events properly. (They did differ in their ordering of the first two options, of course.)

Here is a problem posed by Crupi et al. (2018, p. 758) to 82 physicians:

> A 40-year-old man . . . had a diagnosis of a herpes zoster infection. Please consider the following clinical conditions and rank them from the most to the least probable (ties are allowed):
>
> The patient has pain.
> The patient has pain and exhibits a typical rash.
> The patient does not have pain and exhibits a typical rash.
> The patient exhibits a typical rash.
> The patient has pain and does not exhibit a typical rash.

Eighty-one percent of the physicians ranked the conjunction (option 2) as more likely than one of its two constituents (option 1 or option 4). This is a conjunction error. A double conjunction error occurs when the conjunction is rated more likely than both of its two components. This occurred with 62% of the physicians.

What could explain this profound probability misestimation? Each of the two symptoms strongly support the diagnosis of herpes infection, and the two symptoms strongly support each other. They frequently but not always co-occur. Tversky and Kahneman (1983) explained conjunction errors as being due to the representative heuristic, in that both symptoms are representative of a typical herpes infection. Once the physicians were informed that this was a case of herpes, they considered the combination of the two frequent symptoms as very likely, even more likely than each of the two components separately. They endorsed a mathematical impossibility. In a much different medical context,

Arkes, Aberegg, and Arpin (2022) found that 78% of the physicians committed the conjunction fallacy. Apparently, committing this fallacy is a very common pitfall in the diagnostic process.

Faust (2003, p. 439) provided an example of how the faulty consideration of conjunctions may occur in a much different context. Suppose it is your professional duty to offer an opinion whether a person with a particular type of brain injury can be gainfully employed or the person instead should be provided with permanent disability payments. Following your examination of the person, you deem the probability of their being gainfully employed to be about 70%. However, gainful employment requires at least three steps: (1) The person has to actually seek employment. (2) The person has to be successful in obtaining employment. (3) The person has to be able to perform the job in a satisfactory manner. When asked to decompose your initial estimate into these three components, you now decide that each of the three steps has a 70% probability of occurring. This means that the conjunction of the three components has a probability of occurring of only $.7 \times .7 \times .7 = 34\%$. The initial estimate of 70% was far too optimistic. Decomposing a problem into its constituents can often lead to more accurate quantitative estimates (MacGregor et al., 1988).

ERRATIC EFFECT OF PRIOR ASSOCIATIONS

Gilovich (1981) asked newspaper sportswriters to rate various hypothetical college football players with regard to their potential of becoming professional football players. If a hypothetical player was said to have come from the same hometown as a current professional football player, that player was rated significantly more highly than if he came from a different hometown. Unless one thinks that a player's hometown comprises a substantial influence on his football talent, this would constitute a judgment bias. It is due to the association of the hypothetical player to the successful professional player on an irrelevant dimension. Note that the ability to quickly and easily associate related concepts is of enormous benefit. However, when close associations are based on information inappropriate to the task at hand, the association can have a detrimental influence. Arkes (1991) described such mistakes as association-based judgment errors.

We now turn to the task of diagnosis to illustrate an analogous finding. Many studies have shown that a recent case has a disproportionately large influence on a diagnostician's consideration of the current case (see Hatala et al., 1999; Mamede et al., 2010; Schmidt et al., 2014; Weber et al., 1993). For example, Schmidt et al. (2014) had physicians examine a set of cases in the first round of the study and then asked the physicians to examine new cases in a subsequent round. In some respects, the second round's cases were similar to the first round's cases, but the correct diagnoses of the paired cases were different. The physicians who had examined a similar case in the first round were less likely to make the correct diagnosis on the corresponding case in the second round. However, other studies have shown that if the earlier case is associated with the later case in a helpful way, the association-based influence can result in augmented accuracy (Allen et al., 1988; Brooks et al., 1991). The association between two cases can have either a positive or negative influence depending on the relation between the two cases' diagnoses.

Another way in which association-based errors can influence the accuracy of diagnoses and predictions is not due to the similarity of cases but due to the cuing of some extraneous factor that compromises accuracy. A sports example is provided by Hall et al. (2007). The task was to predict which team won a particular National Basketball Association (NBA) game during a prior season. All persons were provided with two excellent cues to make that prediction: (1) each team's won–loss record at the time of the game, and (2) which team was ahead at half-time. One of the two groups was also provided with the names of the two teams. This group's predictions were significantly worse than those of the group not given names of the two teams! Even though they did worse, the "names" group thought that the names of the teams helped their performance. The reason the names group did worse was that they relied less on the two excellent statistical cues than did the "no names" group. Instead, the names group relied to some extent on the familiarity of the teams' names. ("I know a lot about the Bulls. They were a dominant franchise for several years. I don't know much about the Timberwolves.") Unfortunately, familiarity with a team's name is not a good predictor of their performance in any one particular game, and it is not nearly as helpful a predictor as which team is ahead at half-time. Another result was that being provided with names increased the prediction confidence of participants who had watched a lot of basketball on television and were fans of the game. It did not increase their prediction accuracy. Indeed, there are many examples in which confidence and accuracy are not closely related.

This research has two major lessons to teach diagnosticians. First, as is explained further in Chapter 7, more information is not always better, particularly if the additional cues are poorly related to the to-be-predicted event.

Second, in a complex task in which there are multiple predictors that have a probabilistic relation to the to-be-predicted event, people are not adept at learning which cues are most helpful and which ones aren't. In another experiment by Hall et al. (2007), the participants received feedback after every game in which they made a prediction—who won and who lost. Furthermore, participants placed bets on each of their predictions. Even with this feedback and with financial consequences attached to their accuracy, the participants still relied on name familiarity too much and good statistical cues too little. The problem was that the name was associated with irrelevant information, such as prior franchise fame, a cue that was poorly related to the task at hand. The participants let this association influence their judgments. This is the same problem noted in the Chapman and Chapman (1967) study discussed in Chapter 3: "Paranoia makes me think of eyes, so I conclude that drawings with large eyes must be diagnostic of paranoia." Association-based errors are another example of cold cognition due to the normal functioning of the human information processing system.

SUSCEPTIBILITY TO FORMATTING

Professionals are called upon to render and communicate clinical judgments, and laypersons are called upon to understand clinical judgments. The data upon which the judgments are made can be presented in many different ways. The manner in which the data is collected and subsequently described can make a profound difference in its interpretation. This is what is meant by susceptibility to formatting.

As an example, we first consider studies by Slovic and Monahan (1995) and Slovic, Monahan, and MacGregor (2000). In the latter paper, the authors asked forensic psychologists and psychiatrists to examine the actual case histories of patients hospitalized with a mental disorder. The task for the professionals was to judge the likelihood that these patients would harm someone in the subsequent six months if the patient were to be released. The experimenters varied two main factors. The first was whether the professionals' estimates were to be made in terms of probability (e.g., 20%) or in terms of frequency (e.g., 20 out of 100). The second was whether the scale upon which the estimates were to be made had evenly spaced deciles (1%, 10%, 20%, 30%, 40%, 50%, 60%, 70%, 80%, 90%, 100%) or instead the lower end of the scale was more finely delineated, and the upper end was truncated (1%, 2%, 5%, 10%, 15%, 20%, 25%, 30%, 35%, 40%, > 40%). The two frequency scales were constructed in an analogous way—an evenly spaced version and one with finer delineation at the lower end plus truncation at the upper end. The first surprising result was that patients whose cases were rated with the scale having finer delineations at the low end were deemed by these professionals to have a lower probability of committing a harmful act than if the same cases were rated on the evenly spaced scale. The formatting of the scale made a significant difference in this important decision. The second surprising result was that in general the frequency scales led to lower likelihood judgments than did the probability scales. However, at a given likelihood (e.g., 20% vs. 20 out of 100) a patient was judged as having a higher risk if the judgment was made on the frequency scale. The authors hypothesized that this last result might be due to the fact that a frequency format leads one to think of an instance of a dangerous individual, but a probability format is more abstract and therefore is less likely to elicit such an affect-laden image. (Research by Blumenthal et al., 2010, and Pachur et al., 2012, lends some support to this hypothesis.) Whatever the cause of the formatting influences, ideally the important decision made by the professionals should not have been affected.

Another formatting issue that occurs in clinical/forensic contexts is the use of category labels. For example, when asked about the recidivism probability of an individual, professionals sometimes use scales with verbal labels, such as *high* or *medium*, rather than using probability estimates, such as 50%. Several studies have found that recidivism risk is judged to be higher when category labels are used as opposed to other means of risk communication (see Batastini et al., 2019; Krauss et al., 2018). Again, the format should not influence such important evaluations. Another problem with category labels is that a single label can be interpreted in a highly variable manner. For example, the average interpretation of the label *common* when it is referring to a symptom or side effect was interpreted by laypersons to mean anything from 34% to 71% (Andreadis et al., 2021).

A final example demonstrates attribute framing (Levin et al., 1998). Undergraduates were presented with six cases and were asked whether the person described in each case should be confined to a psychiatric facility for two weeks or should be released. Some subjects were informed that the person in one case had a 74% probability of no violence, and others were told that there was a 26% probability of violence. The latter resulted in more decisions to confine the person when the risk was either at high or at low levels, even though the two probabilities are functionally equivalent.

It should be noted that such studies generally do not provide a gold standard answer to the question about how risk information is most accurately measured and communicated. For example, which of the various groups in the Slovic et al. (2000) study provided violence estimates that most accurately corresponded to the true likelihood that persons committed any harmful acts in the subsequent six months? We know that the groups' estimates differed significantly depending on the format of the scale, but we don't know which scale format led to the best prediction performance. However, there have been studies in the nonforensic domain that have used informative dependent variables other than prediction accuracy. For example, Sinayev et al. (2015) presented adults with information about the side effects of hypothetical medications designed to lower elevated cholesterol levels. Four formats were compared: percentage plus risk label ("14% of people = very common"), percentage without risk label, frequency plus risk label ("14,000 out of 100,000 = very common"), and frequency without risk label. The percentage plus risk label resulted in the best comprehension as assessed by the number of correct answers to questions pertaining to the risk information that the adults had been provided. Of course, understanding the information is a very important dependent variable, but it doesn't directly answer the question about which format fosters the most accurate prediction performance in clinical cases.

This chapter on impediments to accurate clinical decision making does not discuss two important impediments: the improper use of base rates and the negative consequences of overconfidence. Both are important enough to be comprehensively covered in separate chapters, Chapter 6 for base rates and Chapter 11 for overconfidence.

REFERENCES

Allen, S. W., Brooks, L. R., Norman, G. R., & Rosenthal, D. (1988). Effect of prior examples on rule-based diagnostic performance. *Research in Medical Education, 27*, 9–14.

Andreadis, K., Chan, E., Park, M., Brenda, N. C., Sheema, M. M., Dematres, M., Delgado, D., Sigworth, E., Chen, Q., Liu, A., Liu, L. G., Sharko, M., Zikmund-Fisher, B. J., & Ancker, J. S. (2021). Imprecision and preferences in interpretation of verbal

probabilities in health: A systematic review. *Journal of General Internal Medicine, 36*(12), 3820–3829.
Arkes, H. R. (1991). The costs and benefits of judgment errors: Implications for debiasing. *Psychological Bulletin, 110*, 486–498.
Arkes, H. R., Aberegg, S., & Arpin, K. A. (2022). Physicians' probability estimates of a sequence of events. *JAMA Network Open*. https//:doi.org/10.1001/jamanetworkopen.2022.18804
Arkes, H. R., Faust, D., Guilmette, T. J., & Hart, K. (1988). Eliminating the hindsight bias. *Journal of Applied Psychology, 73*, 305–307.
Batastini, A. B., Vitacco, M. J., Coaker, L. C., & Lester, M. E. (2019). Communicating violence risk during testimony: Do different formats lead to different perceptions among jurors? *Psychology, Public Policy, and Law, 25*(2), 92–106.
Blumenthal, S., Huckle, C., Czornyj, R., Craissati, J., & Richardson, P. (2010). The role of affect in the estimation of risk. *Journal of Mental Health, 19*(5), 444–451.
Brooks, L. R., Norman, G. R., & Allen, S. W. (1991). Role of specific similarity in a medical diagnostic task. *Journal of Experimental Psychology: General, 120*, 278–287.
Caplan, R. A., Posner, K. L., & Cheney, F. W. (1991). Effect of outcome on physician judgments of appropriateness of care. *Journal of the American Medical Association, 265*(15), 1957–1960.
Casper, J. D., Benedict, K., & Perry, J. L. (1989). Juror decision making, attitudes, and the hindsight bias. *Law and Human Behavior, 13*(3), 291–310.
Chapman, L. J., & Chapman, J. P. (1967). Genesis of popular but erroneous psychodiagnostic observations. *Journal of Abnormal Psychology, 72*(3), 193–204.
Crupi, V., Elia, F., Apra, F., & Tentori, K. (2018). Double conjunction fallacies in physicians' probability judgment. *Medical Decision Making, 38*(6), 756–760.
Dawson, N. V., Arkes, H. R., Siciliano, C., Blinkhorn, R., Lakshmanan, M., & Petrelli, M. (1988). Hindsight bias: An impediment to accurate probability estimation in clinicopathologic conferences. *Medical Decision Making, 8*, 259–264.
Faust, D. (2003). Holistic thinking is not the whole story: Alternative or adjunct approaches for increasing the accuracy of legal evaluations. *Assessment, 10*(4), 428–441.
Gilovich, T. (1981). Seeing the past in the present: The effect of associations to familiar events on judgments and decisions. *Journal of Personality and Social Psychology, 40*(5), 797–808.
Hall, C. C., Ariss, L., & Todorov, A. (2007). The illusion of knowledge: When more information reduces accuracy and increases confidence. *Organizational Behavior and Human Decision Processes, 103*, 277–290.
Hastie, R., Schkade, D. A., & Payne, J. W. (1999). Juror judgments in civil cases: Hindsight effects on judgments of liability for punitive damages. *Law and Human Behavior, 23*(5), 597–614.
Hatala, R., Norman, G. R., & Brooks, L. R. (1999). Impact of a clinical scenario on accuracy of electrocardiogram interpretation. *Journal of General Internal Medicine, 14*, 126–129.
Krauss, D. A., Cook, G. I., & Klapatch, L. (2018). Risk assessment communication difficulties: An empirical examination of the effects of categorical versus probabilistic risk communication in sexually violent predator decisions. *Behavioral Sciences and the Law, 38*(SI,5), 532–553.

LaBine, S. J., & LaBine, G. (1996). Determinations of negligence and the hindsight bias. *Law and Human Behavior, 20*(3), 501–516.

LeBourgeois, H. I., Pinals, D. A., Williams, V., & Appelbaum, P. S. (2007). Hindsight bias among psychiatrists. *Journal of the American Academy of Psychiatry and the Law, 35*, 67–73.

Levin, I. P., Schneider, S. L., & Gaeth, G. J. (1998). All frames are not created equal: A typology and critical analysis of framing effects. *Organizational Behavior and Human Decision Processes, 76*(2), 149–188.

MacGregor, D., Lichtenstein, S., & Slovic, P. (1988). Structuring knowledge retrieval: An analysis of decomposed quantitative judgments. *Organizational Behavior and Human Decision Processes, 42*(3), 303–323.

Mamede, S., van Gog, T., van den Berge, K., Rikers, R. M., J., P., van Saase, J., L., C., M., van Guldeneer, C., & Schmidt, H. G. (2010). Effect of availability bias and reflective reasoning on diagnostic accuracy among internal medicine residents. *Journal of the American Medical Association, 304*, 1198–1203.

Pachur, T., Hertwig, R., & Steinmann, F. (2012). How do people judge risks: Availability heuristic, affect heuristic, or both? *Journal of Experimental Psychology: Applied, 18*(3), 314–330.

Schmidt, H. G., Mamede, S., van den Berge, K., van Gog, T., van Saase, J. L., & Rikers, R. M. (2014). Exposure to media information about a disease can cause doctors to misdiagnose similar-sounding clinical cases. *Academic Medicine, 89*, 285–291.

Sinayev, A., Peters, E., Tusler, M., & Fraenkel, L. (2015). Presenting numerical information with percentages and descriptive labels: A randomized trial. *Medical Decision Making, 35*(8), 937–947.

Slovic, P., & Monahan, J. (1995). Probability, danger, and coercion: A study of risk perception and decision making in mental health law. *Law and Human Behavior, 19*, 49–65.

Slovic, P., Monahan, J., & MacGregor, D. G. (2000). Violence risk assessment and risk communication: The effects of using actual cases, providing instruction, and employing probability versus frequency formats. *Law and Human Behavior, 24*(1), 271–296.

Tversky, A., & Kahneman, D. (1983). Extensional versus intuitive reasoning: The conjunction fallacy in probability judgment. *Psychological Review, 90*(4), 293–315.

Weber, E. U., Bockenholt, U., Hilton, D. J., & Wallace, B. (1993). Determinants of diagnostic hypothesis generation: Effects of information, base rates, and experience. *Journal of Experimental Psychology: Learning, Memory, and Cognition, 19*(5), 1151–1164.

6

Base Rates: One of the Diagnostician's and Prognosticator's Greatest Allies

If one were to identify perhaps the two or three things that could improve decision accuracy and prediction in applied psychology the most, almost surely one item on that list is proper use of base rates. It is a remarkable paradox that something so valuable is so often underutilized or neglected, perhaps partly because its surface appearance lacks bells and whistles. Something so substantive could hardly come in a more unassuming package.

A base rate is the frequency of occurrence, whether one is referring to bee stings, solar eclipses, or jaywalking on city streets. Base rates are often called prior probabilities. The term *prior probability* refers to the probability before any evidence is taken into account. For example, the base rate of a randomly selected person's blood type being AB is 4%.

Diagnostic and predictive accuracy hinge critically on base rates. In order to maximize accuracy, it is imperative to take into account the base rate of the to-be-predicted event. For example, it is easier to predict whether it will rain in Death Valley, California, on June 15 next year than it is to predict whether it will rain in Miami on that same date. It is doubtful that it has rained on June 15 in Death Valley in several centuries. The base rate of rain there on June 15 approaches 0%. Therefore, to be a highly accurate forecaster one merely has to estimate the probability of rain in Death Valley on any June 15 to be near 0%, thereby predicting that it will not rain. Here, one's accuracy rate over the years would approach 100%. In contrast, based on historical records, the base rate of rain in Miami on any June 15 is 55%. Therefore, if one predicted rain each June 15, one would achieve only a 55% accuracy rate overall. In order to predict accurately whether it will rain on June 15 in Miami next year, one would look toward other potential predictors, if available. Thus, the different base rates of rain in the two locations will allow the Death Valley forecaster to perform more accurately than the Miami forecaster. The same principle applies to clinical decision making. Using base rates by themselves, or combining them with other valid variables, can enhance the accuracy of diagnoses and predictions considerably, making base rates an essential or necessary aid to decision making. This chapter starts with fundamental applications of base rates and then proceeds to more complex situations.

PLAYING THE BASE RATES

Playing the base rates refers to always going with the more frequent outcome. For example, if one's adolescent child comes home past curfew 80% of the time, one always predicts a late return. Over multiple events (and assuming habits do not change), one would be right 80% of the time. Likewise, if a contractor comes in over budget 90% of the time, one would always predict excess charges, and here one would be right 90% of the time. Alternatively, if 1 in 10 individuals gets every word of the chorus to a semipopular song right, then if one always predicts an imperfect performance (or nonoccurrence of a perfect performance), one would also be right 90% of the time. Hence, one playing the base rates always predicts the most likely outcome, whether it is the occurrence or the nonoccurrence of some event or achievement. We are not necessarily suggesting such a strategy, because avoiding the more costly error (e.g., missing a condition) can be a greater concern than overall accuracy; rather, we're illustrating the principle under consideration.

If one starts with a dichotomous outcome (e.g., pregnant or not pregnant, continuation or termination from therapy after a certain number of sessions), then if one merely flips coins, the overall accuracy rate across a series of equally probable events should fall at about 50%. To the extent base rates exceed 50%, playing the base rates should result in a comparable increase in accuracy. For example, if a terrific quarterback completes 75% of passes and one always guesses a pass will be completed, one will be correct 75% of the time, or if a skilled surgeon achieves a good outcome with a certain procedure 95% of the time, one will achieve a 95% accuracy rate playing the base rates. Hence, the further the base rates exceed 50%, the more accurate one can be playing the base rates and the greater the extent to which one can improve upon chance predictions.

What might not be so obvious is that the same principle applies to the extent base rates fall below 50%. For example, if we move from the terrific quarterback to one who completes only 25% of passes, if we play the base rates and always predict a pass will not be completed, we will be correct 75% of the time. Similarly, if only 5% of individuals pick out lima beans from among a food array as their favorite, we will be right 95% of the time if we predict nonselection. Hence, the wider the variation from chance, whether it is upward or downward, the greater the level of accuracy achieved playing the base rates and the greater the improvement over chance.

The same fundamentals apply if there are more than two possible outcomes. For example, with three outcomes, random selection would achieve about 33% accuracy, so when the relative frequencies are lower or higher than 33% across these outcomes, playing the base rates should improve accuracy. However, unlike a 50–50 split, in which the base rates would have to exceed 50% to predict that an outcome will occur, with three possibilities they would now only have to exceed 33%; conversely, for one playing the base rates, a rate that falls below 50% is not sufficient to predict nonoccurrence but would have to fall below 33%. In this situation, as base rates increase for a single variable, there is considerable room for improvement over the 33% level of accuracy achieved by random guessing (e.g., one could conceivably improve from 33% to 100%, or achieve a threefold increase in accuracy).

In contrast, for purposes of illustration, suppose the base rate for one of the three possible outcomes in the setting of interest is 0%. That outcome can then be eliminated from consideration. Now, with two variables remaining, random selection should yield a 50% accuracy rate. The increase from about 33% accuracy through random selection to 50% represents a 17% improvement. Such a favorable change is considerably smaller than the magnitude of potential improvement as the base rate increases beyond 33%, and potentially reaches 100%. Nevertheless, using the base rates to increase accuracy from 33% to 50%, or to achieve a 17% improvement, still reduces error substantially.

Some base rates are so low or so high that exceptional levels of accuracy can be achieved playing the base rates. Take, for example, what are sometimes called Barnum statements, named after the circus showman who supposedly said there is a sucker born every minute. Barnum statements are true by virtue of being so common. Examples might be that you "can be sensitive to other's feelings," "sometimes work too hard," and "at times feel underappreciated." Perhaps 90% of individuals think one or more such things about themselves. Thus, if one is "reading" someone's palm and utters such descriptions, the base rates are so high that chances are excellent the person will endorse the accuracy of one or more of the statements and may even be impressed. One of the authors has a wife with some acting talent, who conducted palm readings at a charitable event. She presented Barnum statements with a dramatic flair, but all in fun and completely fabricated. Nevertheless, she was startled to see multiple sober nods and expressions of amazement! As the example shows, with high-frequency characteristics or occurrences, by merely playing the base rates one can achieve high accuracy rates, accuracy levels that may well surpass formal diagnostic indicators or test results.

Various phenomena in psychology are common or very common, or rare or very rare, examples of the latter being dissociative identity disorder and schizophrenia. This is certainly not to suggest we stop trying to identify such conditions. However, given the very high accuracy levels that may be achieved by playing the base rates (or in this circumstance by predicting nonoccurrence), betting against the base rates may result in a far lower level of accuracy than depending on tests or diagnostic indicators. To make matters worse, the lower levels of accuracy that can result from disregarding or underweighting base rates may not be evident to the decision maker. For example, as discussed subsequently in this chapter, a test that may seem to achieve a high level of success may be wrong far more often than it is right. For the moment, however, we present a last example of a low-frequency outcome and implications for playing the base rates.

Increased awareness of potential concussions and their impact, especially when they occur repeatedly, is a welcome development in neuropsychology and related fields, although concerns have been raised about certain diagnostic practices. For example, despite what may be claims or beliefs to the contrary, very-low-velocity car accidents are extremely unlikely to cause a clinically significant concussion, especially in an otherwise healthy individual. Hence, if one plays the base rates and assumes such an injury did not occur, one will be right in the great majority of instances. Again, this does not necessarily mean the possibility should always be dismissed in these circumstances, but very low base rates often increase the likelihood of a false-positive diagnosis considerably.

The use of performance validity tests (PVTs), which are designed to detect insufficient effort or invalid performance on cognitive measures, serves to illustrate increased risks of false-positive errors in low base rate conditions. When PVTs are used in circumstances in which base rates of poor effort may be relatively high, as may be the case in some legal settings when individuals are evaluated for cognitive decline, PVTs may prove effective. However, when used in clinical settings in which base rates for poor effort are likely to be low, things may change considerably. Assuming a 5% base rate of invalid test performance among older adults presenting for dementia evaluations and using the diagnosticity of various PVTs, Gaudet and colleagues (2023) found that the probability of a false-positive error (i.e., valid performance mistakenly identified as invalid) ranged from about 40% to over 90%! Using a PVT with low diagnosticity to detect a relatively rare event calls into serious question the use of some PVTs in dementia evaluations.

DOES A DIAGNOSTIC TEST OR INDICATOR HELP? IT DEPENDS ON THE BASE RATES

Suppose a study addresses possible indicators of a disorder or occurrence (e.g., posttraumatic stress disorder or parental neglect). As is common in psychology, suppose the study involves two equal-sized groups, one with the condition and a comparison group without the condition. The study shows that the diagnostic indicator, such as a psychological test score or the presence of a qualitative feature on interview, is accurate 75% of the time, and thus demonstrates a robust relationship with the disorder. Assume for the sake of this example that the 25% error rate is comprised of about half (~12.5%) false-positive identifications and about half (~12.5%) false-negative identifications. If the results of the study are trustworthy and hold up on replication, does this establish the utility of the diagnostic sign? The answer is maybe, and maybe not, depending on the base rates.

If half of the study participants have the condition and half do not, chance accuracy is 50%. The worst one can do playing base rates is chance level when the alternatives under consideration have exactly equal base rates. Consequently, although it is not the intent, by using equal-sized groups or groups with similar numbers, many studies create conditions that reduce or minimize the effectiveness of base rates. All else being equal, if the setting of application has base rates similar to the base rates in the background study (i.e., about a 50–50 split), study findings may generalize to that setting quite well. However, what happens if the base rates in those settings vary, or vary widely, from equal distributions?

If the base rate for the condition in the setting of application is 75%, then if one plays the base rates, one would achieve the same level of accuracy obtained in the background study when using the diagnostic indicator, which is accurate 75% of the time. If everyone is assumed to have the condition, then all mistakes would be false-positive errors. Such a decision policy might have similar, greater, or lesser negative consequences than the approximate 12.5% false-negative and 12.5% false-positive rates using the test or indicator, depending on the relative costs of the two error types. For purposes of this example, we assume that the diagnostic indicator is a test result. Certainly, in many clinical situations (e.g., risk of self-harm), false-negative errors can be worse or far worse than false-positive errors, so simply playing the base rate is likely a better option than testing and avoids needless time and expense. We understand that clinical decisions are usually based on far more than a test score, but again, we wish to begin with a base rate and a single indicator to elucidate fundamental principles, and will build toward greater complexity as we proceed.

As base rates deviate further from a 75% rate of occurrence, use of the base rates will start to outpace the test result, which has an accuracy of 75%. If, for example, the base rate is 90% and one always assumes the condition is present, accuracy will increase from 75% to 90%, or error will be reduced from 25% to 10%, a large improvement. This leads us to the following important guide:

- With dichotomous decisions, if the error rate of a diagnostic sign or indicator exceeds the error rate resulting from playing the base rates, use of the test will increase error relative to playing the base rates.

This guide is not solely applicable to situations in which base rates surpass 50% or chance level because, again, when a base rate is below 50% or chance level, the accuracy achieved by predicting nonoccurrence will also exceed chance. Thus, a 75% base rate and a 25% base rate, which both deviate from a 50–50 chance level equally, increase accuracy to an equal extent. However, with that said, knowing that the base rates increase overall accuracy may not be dispositive when deciding how to proceed, because there can be marked asymmetry between the costs of false-positive and false-negative errors. Nevertheless, all else being equal, the procedure that leads to greater accuracy is preferable.

IMPLICATIONS OF EXTREME BASE RATES

Even if false-positive and false-negative errors have unequal costs, extreme base rates may accelerate the error rate of diagnostic procedures or tests to such a degree that decision strategies may need to be reconsidered or reformulated. Years ago, one of the authors participated in a project involving a horrific problem. A large metropolitan hospital had averaged about three suicides a year among medical inpatients, and the hospital administration had asked the psychiatry department for assistance in identifying those at risk. The psychiatrists, psychologists, and other professionals convened, and one of the staff members presented a procedure with seemingly impressive accuracy rates, and only a 10% false-positive rate. The procedure was relatively time-consuming and costly, and in today's dollar value would likely have exceeded $300 per patient. This staff member also suggested that the procedure be used universally with all new admissions, assuming patients were physically well enough to participate. The hospital had about 100,000 patient admissions a year, making the base rate of completed suicide about 1/33,333 admissions. No one was debating whether the deaths were tragic and needed to be reduced if feasible.

The following explanation is by no means intended to reduce human life to dollars. Rather, it aims to examine the impact of extreme base rates, the extent to which they can alter the properties of tests and evaluative methods, and how the result might redirect intervention strategies. At a 10% false-positive rate, about 10,000 of the 100,000 patients would be misidentified as being likely suicide attempters for every three valid-positive identifications, or individuals identified correctly. The resultant ratio is three correct positive identifications over 10,003 (the three correct identifications plus the 10,000 incorrect identifications), or more than 3,300 errors for every correct identification, an error rate exceeding 99.9%. Thus, a test that performed well under study conditions with a 50–50 division of positive and negative cases, and which potentially seemed highly effective, was anything but effective in conditions with extreme base rates. The sheer magnitude of such potential impacts is one reason why use of base rates and the availability of base-rate information are so important. And it is not as if relatively extreme base rates are highly atypical in psychology, because they are not, nor are they in many other fields and circumstances. Various conditions and outcomes have high or low rates of occurrence, or extreme rates, and consequently base rates may be, far and away, the most helpful variable in predicting outcome.

Given the value of human life, one might willingly accept many errors in suicide prediction for even a few correct identifications. Even so, the price of such decision policies may cost more lives than they save when compared to other courses of action. In the present case, the original evaluations were projected to cost about $300 per patient times the 100,000 patients admitted annually. The resultant figures were about $30 million dollars annually, or $300 million more than a decade, even before adjusting for inflation. Perhaps the need for some of these evaluations could have been eliminated through some type of screening process, but the costs still would have been substantial. In addition, although certainly not as high a priority as preventing suicide, one might also consider the consequences of making about 10,000 false-positive errors. These include the fallout from documenting suicide risk in many patients' medical records despite almost always being wrong, and the impact this might have in the future, such as if the patient were applying for life insurance, as well as the cost of providing so much unnecessary service. Again, without reducing human life to a dollar value, taking the largely wasted

$300 million and redirecting it to providing critical medical services to individuals who might otherwise be unable to obtain such care, or to outreach programs that vaccinate individuals in order to reduce the spread of diseases to the general population, would almost certainly save many, many more lives.

One of the authors was present in the room when the initial proposal for suicide screening was advanced, and thus we can state from firsthand knowledge that the consequences of insufficient attention to extreme base rates were not appreciated for most of the meeting. Ultimately, one of the attendees, at professional risk given that person's status as a relative neophyte, put the numbers up on a board and proposed, alternatively, that the hospital purchase safety screens for the windows at all levels above the first floor. That option was not cheap, but it was vastly less expensive, was ultimately selected by the hospital, and proved highly effective. Recognition of base rates and their impact is not an abstract, ivory tower concern—it is a down-in-the-trenches, pragmatic tool for improving predictive accuracy and thereby human welfare.

APPLICATION OF BASE RATES IN CLINICAL DECISION MAKING AND PREDICTION

Some works in psychology age poorly, but others barely age at all. One of the most useful publications in applied psychology, Meehl and Rosen's (1955) classic article on the use of base rates, first appeared more than a half century ago. The foundations that Meehl and Rosen drew on actually date back much farther, to the genius of Reverend Thomas Bayes, an 18th-century mathematician. Although it took Meehl and Rosen to connect Bayes's work to psychology and to expand its implications, the principles, logic, and mathematics remain fundamentally unaltered, and hence retain their applied utility. In the discussion that follows, we start with the application of base rates in situations involving dichotomous choices.

Application of Base Rates to Dichotomous Choices

Framing the Problem

Some decisions involve dichotomous choices or judgments (e.g., treat or don't treat, refer or don't refer to a specialist, release or don't release from prison, or do or do not add medications to a psychotherapeutic intervention). Such decisions may be revised as situations change or feedback comes in about outcomes. Additionally, what appear to be dichotomous alternatives may obscure more nuanced or alternative possibilities. Nevertheless, in many situations, decisions or judgments need to be made that come down to two opposing alternatives. One cannot both drive and not drive across a road with rising flood water, and a therapist cannot both pursue and not pursue involuntary hospitalization, or continue and not continue working with a client who perhaps should be transferred to another professional.

Types of Variables

Discussions addressing decision making and contrasting alternatives can get bogged down if the nature of the variables under consideration is not clarified. At the risk of oversimplification, psychologists address three types of variables: physical entities (e.g., the human brain), events (e.g., one person striking another), and hypothetical constructs (e.g., anxiety). Rather than entering into conceptual fine points, such as more involved classification schemes or gray areas between one type of variable and another, we believe there is merit in treating these three classes of variables as potentially useful approximations.

Among the three classes of variables, the one perhaps needing further clarification is hypothetical constructs. By hypothetical constructs, we mean variables that are inferred and not directly reducible to observations, and that are embedded in a set of assumptions or theoretical networks. For example, anxiety, memory, motivation, and intelligence are inferred from observations and entail conceptualizations or theoretical networks that characterize their nature and manifestations. Theoretical networks addressing a hypothetical construct like anxiety may include physiological components, causative factors, triggering events, and impacts on perception and thinking. Psychologists may refer not only to hypothetical constructs, but also to all three classes of variables in the same sentence, as in, "Tim's increasing anger [hypothetical construct] led him to hit Rob in the face [an event] and cause brain damage [alteration of a physical entity]."

When discussing decision making or dichotomous possibilities, references to physical entities or events are often reasonably clear (e.g., hospitalize or do not hospitalize, pregnant or not pregnant, presence or absence of violent behavior), although some ambiguities may arise (e.g., whether a behavior should be classified as violent or not). With hypothetical constructs, matters can become blurred rather quickly (e.g., whether someone does or does not have mild problems in remote memory). We are not criticizing the use of hypothetical constructs, which are common in science in both more and less advanced fields. Hypothetical constructs can play a critical role in scientific advance, although they can become so speculative or loosely constructed that their accuracy and utility are doubtful. In order to reduce ambiguity when laying out fundamental principles of decision making, we often refer to physical entities and events, while recognizing that, justifiably, much of psychology addresses hypothetical constructs. However, for most of the decision making principles and procedures we describe, applicability should be similar across all three types of variables.

Selecting between a Base Rate and a Single Predictive Variable

Starting with a foundational situation, suppose in making a decision one has: (1) a single test score or diagnostic indicator (e.g., an elevated score on a post-concussion questionnaire, or seeming problems in immediate memory during an interview), and (2) a base rate (e.g., the likelihood of concussion following a motor vehicle accident with certain characteristics, such as moderate speed, airbag deployment, and a certain level of vehicle damage). The immediate decision is whether or not to diagnose a concussion.

For the moment, we will put aside the costs and benefits of correct and incorrect decisions. Hence, we will assume that our aim is to be as accurate as possible, because that will maximize benefit. If both the indicator and the base rate point in the same direction, there is no conflict and nothing to resolve. For example, if the test result and base rate both point toward a concussion, or against a concussion, there is no disparity, and we will decide accordingly. If we must make a dichotomous decision, but the diagnostic indicator and base rate conflict, then one must select one over the other. In making such choices, a bottom line question is which of the two informational sources is likely to be accurate.

Evaluating Predictive Variables Based on Merits, Not Appearance

There sometimes seems to be an odd bias in psychology to overweight or underweight certain classes of variables. What difference should it make, in and of itself, if a variable is a score on an objective test or a projective test, or a qualitative indicator, a bland statistic, or a base rate? One might rightfully argue that different classes of variables have different overall track records of success. Therefore, if one knew nothing about the operation of a specific variable, knowing the class it comes from might provide some information about the likelihood of utility. However, if variables in those classes have widely differing rates of accuracy, then underweighting or flat-out ignoring whole classes of variables seems counterproductive and akin to stereotyping. A specific variable or indicator in a class, even a class that has a weak track record overall, may still surpass an indicator in a class that has a considerably stronger overall track record. For example, even a variable with modest predictive validity will sometimes perform better than base rates, such as when the base rates for alternative choices both fall at 50% and hence offer no assistance. It is not as if we are always doing so well that we can overlook potentially helpful variables. Within the bounds of ethics and feasibility, it seems prudent to evaluate potential predictive variables by their demonstrated utility and not by the class in which they fall. Any advantage we can gain through proper analysis of possible predictors can translate into greater accuracy and human benefit.

As will be discussed in more detail later in this chapter in the section, "Psychological Reasearch on the Underutilization of Base Rates," unless individuals perceive some causal relationship between a predictive variable and an outcome, they tend to underweight or disregard it. The perception of a possible causal pathway or relationship (e.g., a high score on a measure of distorted thinking → presence of schizophrenia) may be one logical path to consider, but it is not necessarily the only one, and it may be weak or misleading. The idea that methods of measurement ought to contain some intuitive or apparent link to the outcome of interest can be plainly wrong, especially as measurement approaches become more sophisticated and knowledge advances. For example, it is hardly intuitive or obvious that measuring enzymes can help determine whether someone had a heart attack. Of course, once the link is explained to us, we often can see the connection, but when starting out, or absent more in-depth knowledge, the connection is anything but apparent. Along parallel lines, Goldberg (1965) found that an elevated score on the L (Lie) scale of the Minnesota Multiphasic Personality Inventory (MMPI) helped to identify major psychopathology, although that was never the scale's intended purpose. Rather, the L scale was initially developed to identify underreporting of personal shortcomings, not major psychopathology. The nonintuitive connection between elevated L scores and severe pathology may well have impeded acceptance of Goldberg's findings and the predictive method he developed.

Base rates often contain negligible theoretical or conceptual links to the outcomes we are trying to predict; nevertheless, they can often enhance accuracy considerably. Their predictive efficacy rests primarily on (1) the differential frequency of the to-be-predicted outcomes and (2) limitations in the diagnosticity of the predictive cues, not on conceptual ties to the outcomes we seek to identify or seeming links to potential causal pathways. The lack of apparent conceptual connection, however, does not justify underweighting or entirely disregarding base rates when they are useful, and sometimes outstanding, predictors. If we can move past overly broad judgments about classes of variables that rest on questionable or unsound foundations, we can focus primary on sound evaluative criteria for specific potential predictors, and in particular on well-conducted studies examining their effectiveness.

All Else Being Equal, Select the Stronger Predictor

When two variables conflict and a dichotomous choice is required, we cannot follow the common advice to integrate the information. Rather, one must elevate one predictor over the other, and whether the predictor is a test score, a clinical observation, or a base rate should not matter. What should matter is each variable's predictive utility. For example, suppose a test score achieves 70% accuracy, and a base rate, which points in the opposing direction, achieves 60% accuracy. Then, all else being equal, deferring to the test score is the better choice and, compared to the base rate, will reduce error from 40% to 30%. Note here that the base rate would improve accuracy relative to chance level, which given an equiprobable dichotomous choice is 50%. However, rather than integrating both sources of information, even when both have predictive validity, one selects the stronger predictor over the weaker predictor. This situation is hardly exceptional. There are many circumstances in which paring down the information that is used, including predictors that are valid but weaker than other predictors, improves accuracy. The nearly omnipresent adage that one should integrate all of the information is often mistaken, and sometimes decidedly so.

If the base rate, as opposed to the test, is a stronger predictor, then all else being equal, one would go with the base rate when the two conflict. The basis for the clause, *all else being equal,* is that, among other things, one may be willing to sacrifice overall accuracy in exchange for reducing either false-positive or false-negative errors if one or the other type of mistake has more serious potential consequences. For example, if parole decisions would be more accurate using a test, but using the pertinent base rate for reoffending reduces the chances of releasing dangerous individuals, a justifiable ethical and societal policy might be to go with the base rates. Such a policy might be especially preferable when there are viable prerelease interventions (e.g., addressing misuse of substances) that could reduce the risk of reoffending before release is reconsidered. Costs and benefits of accurate and inaccurate decisions may well be unequal, or even markedly skewed, and thus may be a critical factor in decision policies, as opposed to simply maximizing overall accuracy.

If the test result or the base rate is the stronger predictor, another option is to usually go with the stronger predictor, but to decide otherwise when a case seems exceptional in some respect and might justify a reversal of usual policy. Calling exceptions, or what might be referred to as *countervailing*, may seem to be an attractive option, because it leaves the decision maker with discretion. In addition, test scores, base rates, and other such bases for decision making are often far from perfect, and may result in fairly frequent error. For example, even with a base rate of, say, 85%, 15% of decisions will be wrong, and in other cases, base rates or diagnostic signs or indicators will have error rates that are twice as high or higher.

Although we delve more deeply into the issue of countervailing in Chapter 8 ("Comparing Clinical Judgment and Statistical Decision Methods"), the most immediate problem with such a strategy is devising a way to identify exceptions with sufficient accuracy. In order to do so at a level that corrects errors more often than it overturns correct decisions, one usually requires a method more accurate than any of the methods or predictive variables one has at hand. If such a procedure were available and feasible, one probably should have been using it in the first place. Thus, the problem with identifying exceptions is that it is hard to achieve the needed level of efficacy. Rather, such attempts to identify exceptions are often as, if not more, error-prone than the best available method. Hence, as discussed at length in Chapter 8, when attempts at identifying exceptions have an impact, the result is rarely to make things better, but far more often to make things worse.

To illustrate how accuracy can easily degrade when one calls exceptions, suppose a test yields an 80% accuracy rate (and 20% error rate), and a weaker method has a 60% accuracy rate (and 40% error rate). Unless one has an efficacious way of identifying exceptions, then each time one defers to the less accurate method because a new case seems to be an exception, one will likely increase the chances of error from 20% to 40%, or double the rate of overall error. We are not advocating, by any means, unquestioning adherence to one or another decision rule, because there can be strong reasons to question or reject the results of such methods. For example, a decision rule might become obsolete, be extended to groups for which it was not designed, or fail to take into account new and highly useful discoveries. However, we wish to emphasize that identifying exceptions is often far more difficult than decision makers might think, and that studies to date on this topic suggest almost uniformly that decision makers "identify" far too many exceptions and do not improve upon, and often diminish, the level of accuracy achieved by consistently adhering to the best overall decision procedures or variables (see Chapter 8). Thus, we should look, and look carefully, before we leap, especially if our actions rest more on subjective impressions than on trustworthy evidence.

Comparing Base Rates to Multiple versus Single Predictors

In contrast to the basic situation in which one must select between a base rate pointing in one direction and some other predictive variable pointing in an opposing direction, in many situations multiple potential predictive variables will be available for consideration. Although there is a tendency to overestimate the increment in accuracy when one combines predictive variables, there are numerous instances in which a combination of variables outperforms a single variable. (For example, when predicting whether violent acts will occur, one might examine such variables as social support and possible tendencies to misuse substances.) Assuming a situation in which one can collect information on a combination of variables and that combination outperforms any single component variable in isolation, the conceptual approach is no different than comparing the predictive accuracy of a base rate versus a single variable. All else being equal, one goes with the better predictor.

For example, assume: a base rate of 75%, that the single best variable achieves 65% accuracy, and that the best combination of variables achieves 85% accuracy. Assume further that the base rate points in the opposite direction of the best single indicator and the best combined indicators. Again, all else being equal, if one only has access to the base rate and the best single variable, one would go with the base rate because it is the stronger predictor. However, if one has access to the combination of variables, one goes with the combination because the combination is the better predictor. One essential qualification here is the need to know how well variables perform when combined, rather than having to guess about the impact of combining variables or simply assuming that more is necessarily better. If, for example, one guesses that the combination of variables under consideration achieves, say, 90% accuracy, but the actual level is 70% and the base rate is 80%, then one degrades accuracy by going with the combination over the base rate.

As we discuss in Chapter 7 ("The Integration of Information: Strengths and Limits"), it can be very difficult to intuit the outcome of combining variables. Adding a new variable may well increase overall accuracy. However, it is not unusual to find that adding a valid variable to the mix may not change overall accuracy at all, or can even decrease accuracy, especially when the other variables are stronger predictors than the variable being added. What often makes it so difficult to assess the precise impact of adding variables or the properties of combined variables using impressionistic judgment is that the outcome depends not only on the validity of the variables, but also on their degree of overlap. Adding a highly redundant variable often does little to change accuracy. For example, if one is evaluating health by measuring body weight with a highly accurate scale that reports results in kilograms, and then one adds another highly accurate scale that reports results in pounds, the second measurement will do nothing to enhance accuracy. In contrast, adding the measurement of blood pressure, despite its limitations, would likely enhance accuracy because blood pressure and weight capture some nonoverlapping information related to health status. Simultaneously and precisely accounting for the validity of predictors, their degree of redundancy, and the optimal way to combine them is far easier to achieve using formal methods as opposed to subjective judgment. Additionally, even modest differences in level of redundancy across variables, or the exact impact of adding valid but somewhat weaker variables to the mix, may entirely reverse optimal decision polices, such as whether to include a variable at all or to use the base rate rather than a combination of variables. The extensive literature discussed in Chapter 7 shows how hard subjective integration of such complex information can be and the advantages of various formal methods. Although the relative advantages of formal methods are sometimes bemoaned or rejected, they might better be seen as positive achievements, and not as a negative reflection of human ability. By improving predictive accuracy, formal methods can enhance client outcomes and serve as a source of pride for the field; psychologists and mental health experts have often demonstrated the intellectual prowess that extends, not limits, human capability.

DETERMINING THE LIKELIHOOD OF OUTCOMES, OR WHICH OUTCOME IS MOST LIKELY

In many situations, we are less interested in selecting between dichotomous choices and more interested in determining how likely an outcome might be (e.g., risk of reoffending, potential for success in one or another occupation, likelihood of benefiting from a certain intervention). Here, one is not so much concerned with choosing between a base rate pointing in one direction and a variable or variables pointing in another direction, but with combining base rates and other predictive variables to determine the odds of a particular outcome occurring. Keeping in mind that the accuracy of variables is a product of their level of validity and the base rates, we wish to combine the two sources of information to enhance our capacity to determine the likelihood of outcomes.

When combined with predictive variables, base rates can make a minimal, modest, large, or enormous impact on the likelihood of outcomes. To push this to the ultimate extreme for illustrative purposes, if one works in a setting in which the base rate for occurrence is zero, then one would not predict that outcome no matter what a test result or other variable indicates; conversely, if the base rate was 100%, one would always predict that outcome regardless of the test result or standing on other variables. Although the examples are extreme, it is not unusual in clinical settings for base rates to turn clinical predictions on their head or to change likelihoods up or down by twofold, fivefold, or tenfold or more.

If the performance of diagnostic or predictive methods is a joint property of their level of validity and the base rates, then the success methods achieve is not a constant but varies as the base rates vary. One could argue that there are few things more important in decision making than knowing just how well our methods perform. For example, if we underappraise a method's accuracy, we may fail to use it when it is superior to the alternatives we are considering. In many situations, overestimations of accuracy can be as, or more, harmful than underestimations, because overestimations can lead to risky decisions in situations with much to gain or lose. For example, being far too confident that an individual will not engage in violent behavior if discharged from the hospital can lead to insufficient safeguards and horrendous consequences. By properly integrating base rates and other predictors, we can often arrive at well-calibrated estimates of likelihood, such as how often predictions will be correct and incorrect.

Combining Base Rates and Diagnostic Indicators That Are Aligned

We will start with a conceptual approach to combining base rates and diagnostic signs and indicators, and then later present more precise, formal procedures that should be used whenever feasible. Again, we begin with a base rate and a single indictor and build complexity as we go. Suppose the question at issue is whether a person has posttraumatic stress disorder (PTSD). The base rate and the diagnostic indicator, such as a score on a questionnaire designed to screen for PTSD, may point in the same direction. For example, suppose that in a PTSD clinic, 65% of individuals presenting for evaluation have the condition. (We understand that many diagnostic categories themselves may be ambiguous, or may not be all that useful, but for the moment our intention is to illustrate fundamental principles.) Thus, the 65% base rate makes it more likely than not that a new patient has PTSD. Assume in addition that the new patient's score on a test that has been validated for identifying PTSD is elevated, and that 80% of individuals with such scores have PTSD. If these conditions hold (i.e., the base rate and the test align in favoring a certain outcome or condition), then the probability yielded by the combined base rate and diagnostic test exceeds the probability of the stronger indicator, which in this example is 80%.

As a rough rule of thumb, when the base rate and a diagnostic sign or indicator align, then the greater the disparity between the stronger indicator and the weaker indicator, the less the combined posterior probability will exceed the probability of the stronger indicator. For example, working with the 65% and 80% figures provided, and performing the formal calculations we will later describe, the combined probability is about 90%, an increase of 10% over the use of the test result alone. If the base rate still favored the outcome, but rather modestly—say it was 55%—the combined probability is about 86%, an increase of only 6% over the use of the test result alone. If the base rate is 75%, the combined probability is about 94%, an increase of 14% over the use of the test result alone. Thus, in order, when the disparity is 25% (base rate = 55% vs. test = 80%), accuracy increases 6%; when it is 15% (base rate = 65% vs. test = 80%), the increase is 10%; and when the disparity is 5% (base rate = 75% vs. test = 80%), the increase is 14%. To put this another way, when two indicators point in the same direction, and when the weaker of the two moves toward or approaches the strength of the stronger predictor, the greater the chances that the condition is present. None of this changes when one is combining the base rate with a combination of other signs and indicators, except one combines the base rate with the accuracy achieved by the amalgamation as opposed to the accuracy of a single variable.

Suppose again that a base rate and another indicator both point in the same direction, but in this case they both point in the negative direction. For example, suppose both the base rate and the test score indicate that PTSD most likely is not present. If both indicators point in the same direction, and the direction is negative, then the combined probabilities will be more extreme than the more extreme negative indicator. In this circumstance, the movement is in the downward direction, or toward a probability that is lower than the more extreme negative indicator.

To illustrate these impacts further, suppose the base rate for PTSD is 35%. Given a probability of less than 50%, the base rate favors the absence of a condition. Also assume that the test result indicates a 20% likelihood of PTSD. Here, the combined probability is 10%, or 10% less than the stronger indicator (i.e., the stronger indicator being the test result, which indicates only a 20% probability of PTSD). If the base rate is 45%, then the combined probability is about 14%, or 6% less than the stronger indicator; and if the base rate is 25%, the combined probability is about 6%, or about 14% less than the more extreme indicator. Again, the greater the disparity between the stronger indicator and the weaker indicator, the less accuracy improves relative to the stronger indicator: when the disparity is 25% (base rate = 45% vs. test = 20%), the accuracy improves 6%; when it is 15% (base rate = 35% vs. test = 20%), the change is 10%; and when the disparity is 5% (base rate = 15% vs. test = 20%), the change is 14%.

One might note that the changes and accuracy levels in the prior paragraph match exactly with the figures in the examples presented two paragraphs earlier (the paragraph that starts with, "As a rough rule of thumb . . . "). These parallel outcomes occur because the pairings of predictive accuracy for the various base rates and the test were identical, although for the first set of pairings both pointed in the positive direction, and for the latter pairings both pointed in the negative direction (i.e., indicated that the condition was absent). As a reminder, it is the extent of deviation from chance levels, regardless of whether they deviate in the positive or negative direction, that determines the magnitude of improvement that base rates achieve. Thus, for example, with a dichotomous choice, whether the base rate exceeds 50% by 30%, or falls below 50% by 30%, the same level of predictive accuracy is achieved by utilizing base rates in one's decision making. The only difference is that in the first instance (base rate = 80%), one playing the base rates always assumes the condition is present, and in the second instance (base rate = 20%), one playing the base rates always assumes the condition is absent. Finally, we would note that the principles we describe for combining a base rate with a single diagnostic sign or indicator that align with one another apply equally when combining a base rate with a compilation of signs or indicators that align with the base rate.

Combining Conflicting Base Rates and Diagnostic Signs and Indicators to Determine the Probability of Occurrence

In many situations, clinicians are faced with inconsistent or conflicting indicators. Here we focus on situations in which base rates and diagnostic signs and indictors are not aligned, or when a base rate points in one direction and a diagnostic sign points in the opposite direction. Suppose in a dementia clinic the base rate for neurodegenerative disorder is 60%. A patient performs well on a sophisticated cognitive screening test. In studies with equal-sized groups of individuals with and without dementia, a score at this magnitude identifies normal individuals 80% of the time, leaving a 20% probability that a dementia is present. Thus, the base rate and the test result conflict, and one wishes to combine them to obtain a more precise probability estimate.

When a base rate and a valid indicator conflict, then the probability of occurrence falls somewhere between the two respective probabilities. In the aforementioned example, the base rate indicates a 60% probability that the condition is present, and the test result indicates a 20% probability, leaving a combined probability somewhere between 60% and 20%. Again providing a rough rule of thumb, in such situations one shifts the probabilities in proportion to the relative strength of the indicators. Logically, to the extent one predictor is stronger than the other and the two conflict, the stronger predictor will have a greater influence than the weaker predictor when the two are combined. This circumstance is similar to a situation in which two observers are trying to determine if a dog in the distant shadows is a German Shepherd. The far better observer says that it is, and the much weaker observer says it is not. Generally, the much better observer should have a greater impact on our conclusions than the weaker observer.

Suppose that the base rate for the condition of interest is 90% (or falls 40% above chance level), and a test result indicates a 40% likelihood the condition is present (or falls 10% below chance level). Clearly, the base rate is a much stronger predictor than the test, and thus much of the shift when combining the variables should be toward the base rate as opposed to the test. If one converts both of these percentages to z scores (90% = a z score of about +1.18, and 40% = a z score of about -.25), and then finds the middle point (which is +1.28 + -.25 = +1.03), one can approximate the outcome obtained by using formal statistical methods (as described later in the chapter). As one can see, the stronger variable has the greater impact. Nevertheless, the stronger variable, which suggests the condition is present, is still adjusted downward to a modest extent. Thus, assuming the test is valid (which should be the case if it predicts more accurately than chance), when it generates an opposing result, it reduces the chances that the first predictor is correct.

What can be remarkable and perhaps counterintuitive is the extent to which a seemingly effective diagnostic sign or indicator can be negated or enfeebled by an extreme opposing base rate. Suppose, for example, one is trying to identify a very rare condition, which occurs in only 1 in 10,000 individuals, and one has a diagnostic test that achieves 95% accuracy, with a 0% false-negative error rate and a 5% false-positive error rate. Here, if one assumes no one has the condition, one will achieve a 99.99% accuracy rate. (We deal with the issue of missing all positive cases later in the chapter.) In turn, even given the test's 5% false-positive rate, the result will be 5% × 10,000 = 500 false-positive identifications, or about 500 errors for each case identified correctly. Thus, deviating from the base rates increases the rate of error nearly 500-fold (with the one valid-positive identification reducing the overall number of errors from 500 to 499). Even if the test had only a 1% false-positive rate, the outcome would still be about 100 errors for each case identified correctly.

Although shifts in accuracy rates or probabilities are rarely as great as the magnitude illustrated in the prior example, it still follows that the larger the deviation of base rates from chance level, the greater the potential impact on an opposing variable and the likelihood that using the base rate will increase accuracy. Less dramatic, yet still substantial, shifts in the accuracy of tests or diagnostic methods due to high or low base rates are common in psychology. For example, suppose an individual obtains an abnormal score on a post-concussion questionnaire that, with equal-sized comparison groups, achieves 80% accuracy, with a 10% rate of false-positive errors. Suppose that the individual completing the questionnaire had a very mild concussion, with the likelihood of, or base rate for, persistent symptoms falling at about 2%. Given this base rate, and despite the questionnaire result, the likelihood of this individual having long-term problems is less than 20%.

Again, the fundamental procedure remains the same whether one is combining a base rate with a single diagnostic sign or indicator or with a compilation of diagnostic signs and indicators. In many circumstances, base rates have a sizeable impact on the likelihood of outcomes, and tests that appear to be highly accurate, when yielding conflicting outcomes, may not change the overall or combined probabilities very much. Thus, base rates can be invaluable in maximizing predictive accuracy and avoiding being overly influenced, and sometimes potentially misled, by seemingly impressive tests and diagnostic signs or indicators.

USE OF BASE RATES IN DIFFERENTIAL DIAGNOSIS

Base rates can also prove very helpful in differential diagnosis. Suppose one is trying to distinguish between generalized anxiety disorder (GAD) and PTSD. Suppose in the setting of interest, cases of PTSD occur twice as often as cases of GAD, or at a ratio of 2:1. Starting again with a single diagnostic sign or test, that indicator may fall in the same direction as the base rate, or may conflict with the base rate. In the first instance, suppose the indicator, such as the result on a test appraising multiple possible anxiety disorders, favors PTSD over GAD by a ratio of 3:1. Thus, both the base rate and the test point in the same direction, with respective ratios of 2:1 and 3:1 both favoring PTSD over GAD. Clearly, all else being equal, we would select PTSD over GAD.

If, in addition, we wanted to determine the relative likelihood that PTSD is present as opposed to GAD, we can combine the base rate and diagnostic indicator. We have essentially the same type of situation presented earlier when one combines two consistent indicators. If we follow the rule of thumb described previously, the likelihood will be more extreme than the more extreme indicator. In this case, the test is the stronger indicator, with a ratio of 3:1 favoring PTSD over

GAD. Hence, when the base rates and test are combined, the chances that PTSD is present will exceed 3:1, and when calculated formally, will equal about 86%, leaving a 14% likelihood of GAD. To look at this from a slightly different angle, both the base rate and the test are consistent in pointing against the presence of GAD, and as such the odds of GAD will be lower than the more extreme of the two indicators, which is the 1 in 4 chance that GAD is present.[1] If one performs the formal calculation, and as must follow from the 86% likelihood of PTSD, the result is a 14% likelihood of GAD.

If the base rate and diagnostic indicator oppose one another, and if one has to make a dichotomous choice, then all else being equal, one goes with the stronger variable. For example, if the base rate is 80% for PTSD in the setting of interest and the test favors GAD 60% of the time, one goes with PTSD, and vice versa if the test is a stronger indicator than the base rate. If one is calculating relative probabilities, the outcome will fall in between the opposing probabilities, with the shifts becoming potentially substantial with extreme base rates. For example, even if a test favors dissociative identity disorder 80% of the time over an alternative condition, but the base rate for dissociative identity disorder in the setting of interest is about 1%, the combined odds will favor the alternative condition more than 25 to 1. Finally, the approach for making dichotomous choices or calculating probabilities is the same whether the base rates are being compared to a single diagnostic indicator or a composite of indicators, such as multiple tests, or tests and other diagnostic signs or symptoms.

All of the same principles can be applied when determining the likely outcome of an intervention, or one intervention versus another intervention. For example, in many situations, one has information about the general success of an intervention (e.g., that a certain type of therapy provided for a certain type of problem results in substantial improvement 70% of the time). In addition, there might also be information available about variables that can modify outcomes, such as motivation for treatment or social support. Here, one can combine the overall base rates with these other predictors, or one can apply the same type of analysis when predicting the relative likelihood of positive outcomes with alternative treatments. (More is said about these issues in Part III, "Corrective Methods and Strategies.")

FORMAL METHOD FOR COMBINING A BASE RATE WITH DIAGNOSTIC INFORMATION

As noted, using a formal method as opposed to rules of thumb provides greater accuracy and precision when determining the impact of combining base rates with other variables. We illustrate the use of this formal method with a problem one of the authors (Hal Arkes) faced when asked to investigate the funding for students with a learning disability (LD) in a community college system in the United States. The base rate for LD in students of the relevant age group was estimated to be around 3%. However, the guidance counselors in the particular state's community college system were diagnosing students with LD at a rate that was spectacularly higher than 3%. Something was seriously wrong with the diagnostic procedure.

Bayes' Theorem will illustrate the problem. The Theorem describes the proper way to update the base rate of an event given new information about the to-be-predicted event. The first term in Bayes' Theorem is the prior probability of an event. In this case, it is the assumed base rate of LD in this population, which was estimated to be about .03. We will use the "odds formula" for Bayes' Theorem, so the prior odds of LD in a sample of 100 persons is three persons with LD and 97 without LD. The prior odds are expressed as 3/97. This term has to be multiplied by the likelihood ratio, which is defined as the probability that a particular symptom occurs in a person with LD divided by the probability that this same symptom occurs in a person without LD, which is expressed as $p(\text{symptom}|\text{LD})/p(\text{symptom}|\text{not LD})$.

When the counselors were asked to name a symptom they used to diagnose LD, one they provided was "tight grip on a pencil." The counselors were then asked to indicate how much more likely it was that a student with LD would grip a pencil tightly than would a student without LD. Would it be 10 times more? (That would be a very diagnostic symptom indeed.) The group agreed that the 10:1 ratio seemed reasonable. Thus, the likelihood ratio, expressed in odds form, with the specific symptom of tight grip, becomes $p(\text{tight grip}|\text{LD})/p(\text{tight grip}|\text{not LD})$. This likelihood ratio represented the probability of having a tight grip given the person has LD divided by the probability of having a tight grip given the person does not have LD.

When the prior odds (3/97) are multiplied by the likelihood ratio (10), one obtains the posterior odds, which would be 30/97. (*Posterior* means after the piece of evidence—a tight grip–is considered.) We can convert the posterior odds to probability. To convert an odds formula to probability, the numerator should be divided by the numerator plus the denominator. For example, when a team has a 50–50 odds of winning, we don't mean that it will win all 50 of 50 games. We mean it will win 50 of 100 games. The numerator (50) is divided by the numerator plus the denominator (50 + 50 = 100) in order to convert to probability. Thus, the team's probability of winning any one game is 50% (50/100).

Similarly, when we say that the posterior odds of LD are 30/97, we mean that the numerator (30) should be divided by the numerator plus denominator (30 + 97 = 127). Thus, the posterior probability of LD given a person grips the pencil tightly is about 24%. This is the probability that the person has LD after the pencil-gripping symptom's "diagnosticity" is taken into account. That means that of all the students who are deemed to have LD because of their tight grip on the pencil, an alarming 76% will have been incorrectly diagnosed. This is a huge overestimation of LD in the community college system.

In actuality, the author was highly dubious that the likelihood ratio of gripping a pencil tightly was 10, but he allowed this high estimate to be used to make the point that even with this very generous estimate of 10, the counselors' LD diagnoses were likely to be wrong far more often than they were likely to be right.

This was shocking news to the counselors, but here there is no arguing with the mathematics of Bayes' Theorem. Exclusive use of the pencil-grip symptom would guarantee many incorrect diagnoses. The lesson to be learned from this example is that in order to correctly diagnose a rare event, one needs a symptom or test result with an extremely high likelihood ratio. Think of Bayes' Theorem as a contest between the prior probability and the likelihood ratio. If the prior probability makes a particular diagnosis unlikely, then the likelihood ratio needs to be extreme in order to make the posterior probability of that diagnosis high. If the prior probability is already elevated, then a more modest likelihood ratio is enough to make the posterior probability sufficiently high to facilitate diagnostic accuracy. For a prior probability of LD of only 3%, a tight grip on a pencil was not sufficiently diagnostic to foster accurate classification.

EFFECT OF BASE RATES ON POSITIVE AND NEGATIVE PREDICTIVE VALUES

A quick reminder: The positive predictive value (PPV) is the probability that a positive test is correct. The negative predictive value (NPV) is the probability that a negative test is correct.

To examine the effect of base rates on PPV and NPV, we'll use the example of a misguided faculty member in the English Department of a particular university who required every student in the class to take a psychological test. Let's assume that the base rate of major depression is around 7%. Let's also assume that the sensitivity and specificity of this psychological test in detecting major depression were both 70%. With 200 people in this faculty member's course, Table 6.1 depicts the situation after the administration of the psychological test:

The PPV of the test would be 10/66 = 15%. Not only was the administration of the test by the professor unethical, but the faculty member then compounded the problem by individually discussing the test result with each student. If each person who scored "depressed" on the psychological test was deemed depressed by the faculty member, this conclusion would be correct 15% of the time and incorrect 85% of the time. How can a test provide such poor performance and still be used? One likely reason is that individuals often do not recognize the degree of influence base rates can have on accuracy. One might also note that the negative predictive value (NPV) of the test was an impressive 97% (130/134).

Table 6.1. Data Needed to Calculate PPV and NPV When the Base Rate of Depression Is 7%

		Depression Actually Present?	
		Yes	**No**
Test Result	**Depressed**	10	56
	Not Depressed	4	130

Table 6.2. DATA NEEDED TO CALCULATE PPV AND NPV WHEN THE BASE RATE OF DEPRESSION IS 50%

		Depression Actually Present?	
		Yes	**No**
Test Result	**Depressed**	70	30
	Not Depressed	30	70

What if the test were now administered to 200 persons who complained of frequently being sad and who presented themselves at a psychological clinic for possible treatment? Let's assume that the same test is used, but the base rate of major depression is 50% among this group. Table 6.2 depicts this situation.

The PPV of the test would be 70%, almost five times greater than the PPV in the English class. The NPV would be 70%, somewhat lower than the NPV in the English class. The lesson to be drawn from this example is that the base rate can have a drastic effect on both the PPV and NPV. A test that might be very helpful in one sample might be entirely inappropriate to use in a different sample. The base rate of the condition must be considered in order to evaluate the suitability or efficacy of a psychological test, or how often in the setting of application it leads to accurate versus inaccurate outcomes.

This example illustrates what may happen when a test with a modest level of specificity is used as a screening measure. When the base rate is low, as is often the case when the general population is tested, the PPV will be very low, as was the case in the example in which the base rate of depression was only 7%. Given a low base rate, a large number of false positives will occur. These errors may result in the inappropriate provision of treatment for persons who need no treatment, and if the treatment carries risks, in potential harm. When a selected subset of the population is considered, such as when only those who present with certain symptoms comprise the base rate, then the PPV will be increased, and the proportion of false positives will be lowered. Thus, when selecting a base rate to "plug into" Bayes' Theorem, it is important to choose the most appropriate one.

SELECTING BASE RATES FOR USE; SOURCES OF BASE RATES

Various base rates have varying levels of applicability for different groups. For example, if one is trying to predict the likelihood of violent behavior, the base rates for the general population as opposed to individuals with a long history of violent behaviors are very different. Thus, if one uses base rates for the general population when evaluating a repeat violent offender, the probability of a further offense is likely to be underestimated; whereas using base rates for violent offenders will likely lead to an overestimation of probability for a member of the general population.

As a second example, base rates for exaggeration of psychological difficulties among individuals in civil litigation claiming PTSD are higher than base rates for individuals in treatment settings with no financial incentive to exaggerate. Here again, using the wrong base rate for the individual under consideration (litigant or nonlitigant) can lead to underestimates or overestimates of probability. Estimated base rates for exaggeration among litigants and nonlitigants are commonly assumed to fall at about 30% and 10%, respectively (Mittenberg et al., 2003). If one assumes that other information, such as scales designed to measure possible overreporting, point to about a 60% likelihood of exaggeration, one can see the impact when the differing base rates are entered into Bayes' Theorem (see Appendix 3).

A central guide for selecting base rates across many situations is to choose the narrowest base rate (assuming sufficient sample size and representativeness), with narrowness defined in this context by dimensions that influence the base rates and are relevant to the person in question. For example, suppose we are trying to determine the likelihood that a client will benefit from a certain treatment for major depression. The base rates for a positive outcome may vary considerably between those who have versus those who have not shown previous benefit from this same treatment or a related treatment, such as psychotherapy combined with a certain class of antidepressant medication. Thus, if the present client has undertaken the treatment of interest in the past, one would select the respective base rate applicable to the client's prior treatment response. This selection follows the first of the two enumerated considerations, which is to narrow down the selection along dimensions that influence the base rates, in this case prior treatment response. In the present example, other dimensions, such as age, might not alter the base rates for positive treatment response, and thus although potentially relevant to other diagnostic or predictive tasks, would not be relevant for this specific predictive undertaking.

Moving to the second consideration, dimensions that narrow base rates may not be pertinent to an individual. Returning to the last example, the treatment in question might not have been attempted previously with the client. Thus, although prior treatment response may influence base rates, this consideration cannot be applied to the current client. As another example, base rates for some type of disorder might vary across two types of treatment settings, but if a client is being seen in neither of those settings, that distinction is not relevant to the person in question.

Subsequent sections of this book address the use of base rates in clinical practice. Chapter 13 provides further general guides for applying base rates, Appendix 1 provides information on sources for base rates, Appendix 2 presents user-friendly methods for combining base rates with the diagnostic or predictive value of other variables (or for calculating Bayes' Theorem), and Appendix 3 contains examples and exemplars for combining base rates with other diagnostic signs, indicators, and test results.

PSYCHOLOGICAL RESEARCH ON THE UNDERUTILIZATION OF BASE RATES

Despite their potency in increasing the accuracy of decision making and prediction, substantial research suggests that people, clinicians in the mental health field included, often do not give adequate consideration to base rates. Although this problem was noted in a clinical psychology context by Meehl and Rosen in 1955, the problem was not more thoroughly investigated until 1972, when Kahneman and Tversky published their research on Jack the engineer or lawyer. A group of psychologists supposedly interviewed Jack, whose personality description follows:

> Jack is a 45-year-old man. He is married and has four children. He is generally conservative, careful, and ambitious. He shows no interest in political and social issues and spends most of his free time on his many hobbies, which include home carpentry, sailing, and mathematical puzzles.

One group of subjects was told that the description of Jack was randomly drawn from a sample of 100 persons that included 70 lawyers and 30 engineers. Another group was told that the description of Jack was randomly drawn from a sample of 100 persons that included 30 lawyers and 70 engineers. Thus the base rate of lawyers and engineers was reversed in the two groups. Both groups were asked to estimate the probability that Jack was an engineer. Of course, the base rate should have influenced the posterior probability that Jack was an engineer, and it did make a slight but statistically significant difference in the estimates of the two groups. However, the difference was not nearly as great as it should have been had the two groups used the base rate to the appropriate amount. This publication spurred a cottage industry of researchers investigating the underutilization of base rates.

Kennedy et al. (1997) showed that the addition of individuating clinical information, either relevant or irrelevant, resulted in a decrease in diagnostic accuracy among school psychologists compared to their accuracy when they were given only base-rate information. This study illustrates how critical the full consideration of base rates can be in enhancing diagnostic accuracy. As we mentioned earlier, just using base rates alone can sometimes surpass the accuracy achieved by trying to use other or additional information, and on occasion by a wide margin, especially when the base rates are extreme.

Casscells et al. (1978) provided the most famous demonstration of the underutilization of base rates. Physicians and fourth-year medical students at Harvard Medical School were given the following problem:

> If a test to detect a disease whose prevalence is 1/1,000 has a false-positive rate of 5%, what is the chance that a person found to have a positive result actually has the disease, assuming that you know nothing about the person's symptoms or signs?

This group of respondents most common answer was 95%. The correct answer is approximately 2%. Here is the solution according to Bayes' Theorem. The prior odds are 1/999; out of every 1,000 persons, 1 person has the disease and 999 do not. The likelihood ratio is *p*(positive test result|disease present)/*p*(positive test result|disease absent), which is 100/5. Everyone (100%) with the disease has a positive test result, but 5% of those who do not have the disease also have a positive test result. The posterior odds are 100/4,995, which is 0.02. The fact that the most common estimate was about 47 times too large suggests that the respondents were impressed with the high diagnosticity of the test (a decisive likelihood ratio) but were grossly deficient in the weight that they gave to the base rate.

It should be noted that minuscule likelihood ratios can be just as informative as large likelihood ratios. A test whose likelihood ratio has a tiny numerator and a large denominator converts the prior odds to much smaller posterior odds. A likelihood ratio of 1.0 means that the test or symptom is completely uninformative; it does not modify the prior odds at all. The more the likelihood ratio influences the prior odds in either direction from 1.0, the more useful the test or symptom will be.

Ajzen (1977) offered a major clue for the general underutilization of base rates. Ajzen hypothesized that a base rate was more likely to be used if it bore a causal relation to the to-be-predicted event. In the case of Jack, Jack's personality description contained information about his interests and motivations that would have had a strong causal influence on his choice of professions (lawyer or engineer). In contrast, the number of lawyers and engineers in the sample the psychologists interviewed would have had no causal bearing on Jack's choice of profession. Hence, the subjects in the experiment would have considered base-rate information much less relevant in making their estimates, even though it was statistically crucial.

To test this hypothesis, in the first of three experiments Ajzen presented data to subjects that indicated whether each of the following cues had a strong or weak relation to a student's grade point average (GPA): IQ score, hours spent studying, weekly income, and distance of home from campus. The first two factors would intuitively seem to bear a causal relation to GPA, but the latter two would not. Ajzen arranged the data so that for some groups of subjects the actual data reinforced the intuitive theory of what factors would or would not be causal, but for other subjects the data were reversed so that the latter two factors bore a strong relation to GPA whereas the first two factors did not. Ajzen found that when predicting GPA, the subjects gave significantly more weight to the factors that intuitively had an apparent causal relation to GPA than they gave to the factors that had an actual statistical relation to GPA.

Ajzen's second experiment provided more evidence that base rates are underutilized because they do not seem to bear a causal relation to the to-be-predicted event. One pair of groups read that a final exam was given at Yale University. One of these groups was told that about 75% of the students passed the exam, and the rest of the students presumably failed. A second group was told that about 75% failed the exam, and the rest presumably passed. Another group read that an educational psychologist was interested mainly in students who had passed the exam. Members of this third group were told that therefore 75% of the students in this psychologist's survey were chosen from those students who had passed the exam, the other 25% having failed. Members of a fourth group were told that the educational psychologist was interested mainly in students who had failed the exam. Members of this group read that therefore 75% of the students in this psychologist's survey were chosen from those students who had failed the exam, the other 25% presumably having passed. Everyone in all four groups then read a paragraph about Gary W and estimated whether Gary W had passed the exam. The base rate pertaining to the proportion of students who passed the exam had a powerful influence on subjects' estimate of how likely Gary W was to have passed the exam. However, the base rate pertaining to the psychologist's sampling of the students had only about a third as much influence. Apparently, the proportion that passed the exam had a strong causal influence on estimates of the ease or difficulty of the test. ("If 75% failed the exam, I guess that Gary wouldn't have been likely to do well.") In contrast, the sample the psychologist selected might not have seemed to be relevant. ("I don't see why the psychologist's sample would influence Gary's performance at all.") However, when one must decide whether Gary passed the exam, the 75/25 lopsided sample chosen by the psychologist is exactly as relevant as the proportion that passed or failed the exam. Base rates are very important whether or not they seem causal.

Besides their apparent lack of causal relevance, another reason base rates are underutilized is that they are pallid. They are abstract. Individuating information, such as Jack's hobbies, is vivid and concrete. This contrast between vivid and pallid information not only leads diagnosticians astray, but also influences patients. For example, Ubel et al. (2001) presented some adults with paragraphs containing the statistical data showing that bypass surgery cures angina (chest pains) in 75% of the people who undergo the procedure. Angioplasty (opening up an artery by inflating a balloon inside the blood vessel) has a 50% success rate in relieving angina. Also mentioned in the paragraphs was that hospitalization after angioplasty was much shorter than hospitalization after bypass surgery.

Ubel et al. used two groups of subjects in their experiment. Both groups of subjects read the prose descriptions of bypass and angioplasty, and the first group in addition read testimonials from four persons who had bypass surgery—three of whom had successful outcomes and one who did not—and from two persons who had angioplasty—one of whom had a successful outcome and one of whom did not. Thus, the testimonials were precisely proportional to the actual success rates of the two procedures, 75% for bypass and 50% for angioplasty. The second group of subjects read two testimonials from bypass patients and two from angioplasty patients, one successful and one unsuccessful for each of these two procedures. The statistical and other information was identical for the two groups. Nevertheless, the change in the content of the testimonials had a major impact on whether the subjects opted for bypass surgery. When the true success ratios were accurately reflected in the proportion of testimonials of successful outcomes, 44% of the subjects preferred bypass surgery. When there were the same number of successful and unsuccessful testimonials despite the identical information on the base rate of success, only 30% of the subjects chose bypass surgery. The testimonials served as vivid individuating information. Such information can significantly influence the impact of base-rate (statistical) information, even if the latter is based on a very large number of cases, far larger than the tiny number of testimonials.

Diagnosticians and patients who utilize base rates appropriately will enjoy a huge advantage in many situations over diagnosticians and patients who do not.

Ubiquity of Base-Rate Underutilization

Research by Meehl and Rosen (1955) and by Casscells et al. (1978) has shown that professional diagnosticians do not utilize base rates as much as they should. However, underutilization of base rates is also common in the reasoning of laypersons. Nisbett and Borgida (1975) provided an instructive example. In their first study, some subjects were shown the actual results of an earlier experiment in which people were tested on how strong a shock they would be willing to endure. The actual data were displayed in a histogram indicating that the modal response was to accept the highest of the four possible levels of shock. Very few people had refused to accept any shock or would accept only the very lowest level of shock. The remaining subjects in the Nisbett and Borgida (1975) study were not shown any of this true base-rate data from the prior shock experiment, but were asked to estimate how much shock the people in the prior study were willing to endure. Their estimate was that most subjects would accept the next-to-lowest level of shock and that very few people would be willing to endure the maximal shock. Thus, their intuitive base rate estimate departed radically from the true base-rate data. Nisbett and Borgida then presented either videotapes of interviews with three randomly chosen people from the prior shock experiment or written descriptions of these same three people to both the group that was informed about the actual prior shock data and the group that was not so informed. The interviews or written descriptions of the three people from the prior experiment provided relatively nondiagnostic information about their personality and some social characteristics. Among the dependent variables Nisbett and Borgida collected were predictions (actually postdictions) of how much shock each of these three people had been willing to endure. The result was that the postdictions for the group given the true base-rate information were extremely similar to the postdictions of the people who were not given the true base-rate information. Knowledge of the true base rate made no difference! The banal videotape or description of the interviewee simply overwhelmed any consideration of the base rate. Base-rate information given to the informed group that the modal choice by the subjects in the prior experiment had been maximal shock was completely ignored! As we conclude in our discussion of confirmation bias in Chapter 4, underutilization of base rates is not a judgment flaw limited to diagnosticians; we all are susceptible.

EXPERTS VERSUS STATISTICAL METHODS

"It seems obvious that neglect of base-rate information is the key to the relative weakness of experts, as compared to models" (Johnson, 1988, p. 225).

Although we discuss the impressive diagnostic accuracy of statistical models in Chapter 8, the above quote illustrates why we must mention their high level of performance in this chapter. Statistical models often incorporate base-rate information in rendering a prediction, and they do so properly. As we have seen, humans—even those who are experts—tend to underutilize this very important factor.

Grove et al. (2000) performed a meta-analysis showing that statistical models generally were equal to or often better at predictions and diagnoses than were unaided experts. Meehl (1954, pp. 24–25) suggested a way in which an expert might perform better than a model. Suppose a regression model was used to predict whether Professor Jones would attend a movie this Thursday. The predictors in the model might be Professor Jones' current workload, the day of the week, the popularity of the movie, and other relevant factors. However, a human judge might predict more accurately than the model if the judge knew that Professor Jones had just broken a leg and could not go anywhere this Thursday. Following Meehl, such cues, which might enable a judge's unaided performance to beat the model, have come to be known as "broken leg cues." Because human judges rarely perform better than a model, perhaps broken leg cues are rather uncommon, judges are not adept in using them when they exist, or judges think a cue is a broken leg cue when it actually is not. The general consensus is that judges are not accurate in identifying broken leg cues. As a result, judges often allow the presence of some errant cue to provide a rationale for ignoring the prediction of a model or a highly informative base rate.

Another reason people often underutilize base rates is that base rates are blatantly imperfect. If the team that is 35 points ahead at halftime wins 95% of the time, this means that 5% of the time, using only this base rate to predict the winner will result in an incorrect prediction. Many people think that perhaps that 5% error rate might be reduced if they could discern some subtle cue that other people have not noticed. Dietvorst and Bharti (2019) have shown that people believe that perfect prediction might occasionally be possible with use of their own unaided judgment strategy, but obviously this is not possible with the use of some statistical or mathematical strategy known to make errors. Einhorn (1986) summarized the situation very aptly: We have to accept some error to make less error. If using the base rate or some statistical strategy results in excellent but not perfect performance, the wise decision maker must accept this magnitude of error (at least until something better comes along) rather than use cues of questionable validity to try to achieve perfection. The latter approach will only result in more error—not perfection. Arkes, Dawes, and Christensen (1986) showed that when there was a financial incentive to render a correct judgment, the judges were less likely to use a helpful statistical decision rule compared to the situations in which there was no financial incentive. When we really want to be perfect, we apparently consider statistical rules, even those with low error rates, to be unacceptable. Under these circumstances, we are more likely not to accept a small amount of error in our quest for perfection, thus violating Einhorn's wise advice. Of course, many diagnostic situations contain very high stakes, so the temptation to ignore base rates or other statistical cues might be alluring. Diagnosticians who succumb to this temptation will perform worse than those who can resist.

REFERENCES

Ajzen, I. (1977). Intuitive theories of events and the effects of base-rate information on prediction. *Journal of Personality and Social Psychology*, *35*(5), 303–314.

Arkes, H. R., Dawes, R. M., & Christensen, C. (1986). Factors influencing the use of a decision rule in a probabilistic task. *Organizational Behavior and Human Decision Processes*, *37*, 93–110.

Casscells, W., Schoenberger, A., & Grayboys, T. (1978). Interpretation by physicians of clinical laboratory results. *New England Journal of Medicine*, *299*, 999–1000.

Dietvorst, B. J., & Bharti, S. (2019). People reject even the best possible algorithm in uncertain decision domains. https://ssrn.com/abstract=3424158

Einhorn, H. J. (1986). Accepting error to make less error. *Journal of Personality Assessment*, *50*(3), 387–395.

Gaudet, C. E., Gold, D., Casteluccio, B., McLaughlin, N. C. R., & Correia, S. (2023). Limitations of performance validity tests in dementia evaluations—The role of base rates. *Psychological Assessment*, *34*(11), 1074–1080.

Goldberg, L. (1965). Diagnosticians versus diagnostic signs: The diagnosis of psychosis versus neurosis from the MMPI. *Psychological Monographs*, *79*(9), 1–28.

Grove, W. M., Zald, D. H., Lebow, B. S., Snitz, B. E., & Nelson, C. (2000). Clinical versus mechanical prediction: A meta-analysis. *Psychological Assessment*, *12*(1), 19–30. https://doi.10.1037/1040-3590.12.1.9

Johnson, E. J. (1988). Expertise and decision under uncertainty: Performance and process. In M. T. H. Chi, R. Glaser, & M. J. Farr (Eds), *The nature of expertise* (pp. 209–228). Erlbaum.

Kahneman, D., & Tversky, A. (1972). On the psychology of prediction. *Psychological Review*, *80*, 237–251.

Kennedy, M. L., Willis, W. G., & Faust, D. (1997). The base-rate fallacy in school psychology. *Journal of Psychoeducational Assessment*, *15*(4), 292–307.

Meehl, P. E. (1954). *Clinical versus statistical prediction*. University of Minnesota Press.

Meehl, P. E., & Rosen, A. (1955). Antecedent probability and the efficiency of psychometric signs, patterns, or cutting scores. *Psychological Bulletin*, *52*(3), 194–216.

Mittenberg, W., Patton, C., Morgan, E. A., & Condit, D. C. (2003). Base rates of malingering and symptom exaggeration. *Journal of Clinical and Experimental Neuropsychology*, *24*(8), 1094–1102.

Nisbett, R. E., & Borgida, E. (1975). Attribution and the psychology of prediction. *Journal of Personality and Social Psychology*, *32*(5), 932–943.

Ubel, P. A., Jepson, C., & Baron, J. (2001). The inclusion of patient testimonials in decision aids: Effects on treatment choice. *Medical Decision Making*, *21*(1), 60–68.

7

The Integration of Information: Strengths and Limits

If one examines texts on psychological or neuropsychological assessment across decades, one often finds statements like the ones that follow, which are commonly presented as given. For example, in the first edition of Exner's widely read book on the Rorschach (1974), he stated:

> The meaningfulness of a particular class of responses is not simply determined by its presence or absence in a protocol but by its presence or absence in relation to the presence or absence of other classes of responses. . . . *Any interpretation of those responses requires* [emphasis added] a careful weighing of many other elements of the protocol, such as its length, location factors, form quality, organizational features, and the occurrence of other classes of responses, such as movement, form, and shading, before even the most tentative hypotheses can be formulated. (pp. 6–7)

In 1984, Exner further stated that:

> All of the formally developed approaches to the Rorschach test have included recommendations for a configural approach to the interpretation of the scoring of structural data. . . . *Any accurate assessment of a subject depends* [emphasis added] on interpreting the idiographic mixture of variables that appear in the records correctly. In other words, while the broader interpretive meaning of a variable does not change, its specific interpretive importance will vary considerably depending on the configuration of other variables. (p. 65)

In the second edition of her 1983 text, Muriel Lezak, a well-known neuropsychologist, stated that:

> For the examination to supply answers to many of the diagnostic questions and most of the treatment and planning questions *requires integration of all*

> *of the data* [emphasis added]—from tests, observations made in the course of the examination, and the history of the problem. (p. 162)

In the fifth edition of her text nearly 30 years later, Lezak did not change a word of this statement (Lezak et al., 2012, p. 177).

Matarazzo was a well-known psychologist, who assumed primary authorship of David Wechsler's classic text on intellectual assessment. In an article addressing the limits of computerized test interpretation (Matarazzo, 1986), he wrote:

> As I have repeatedly stated, even if today's computerized interpretations . . . were valid, the given product of a psychological test takes on *differential* meaning based on the unique characteristics and relevant context of the individual being assessed. This is an idea that most practicing psychologists take as a given. (p. 22)

Meyer et al. (2001) reviewed literature on the accuracy of psychological assessment. Most of the studies they covered generated positive or very positive results, although their method for selecting studies was not designed to achieve representativeness. Although we do not question the potential value of psychological assessment, one can achieve highly varying accuracy rates based on the studies one selects. In any case, when discussing studies that generated less impressive accuracy rates, they stated:

> To the extent that clinicians view all test data in a contextually differentiated fashion, the practical value of tests used in clinical assessment is likely greater than what is suggested by the research on their nomothetic associations. (p. 153)

They then suggested that conducting research examining this possibility is "incredibly complex" and approaches impossibility, which seems odd because there are many studies (which we discuss in Chapter 8) that have investigated just this issue and have not supported their supposition. Meyer et al. (2001) further stated:

> Our argument is not that clinical judgment will consistently surpass statistical decision rules in a head-to-head comparison. . . . Rather, it is that the practical validity of psychological assessment (i.e., the sophisticated integration of data from multiple tests and sources of contextual information) is probably greater than what is suggested by the validity coefficients found in the testing literature (i.e., scale data in which the many contextual factors affecting all observed scores are treated as error variance). Also, if this line of reasoning is extended, one should expect nomothetic validity coefficients for testing data to increase when researchers begin to differentially weigh scores to reflect individualized contextual influences. (p. 153)

In their valuable text on normative test data, Mitrushina et al. (2005) stated:

> Test data alone do not provide an adequate basis for making sound clinical judgments. . . . Interpretation of the data obtained from a neuropsychological examination *must* [emphasis added] take into account qualitative observations and the patient's history, background, present circumstances, motivation, attitudes, and expectations regarding self and the examination. . . . *All this information taken together provides a framework for an accurate understanding* [emphasis added]. . . . Failure to consider all aspects of the interpretive process will increase the probability of faulty inferences. (pp. 3–4, 6)

According to Barkley and Edwards (2006):

> The evaluation [of possible AHDH] *requires* [emphasis added] integrating information from multiple sources (parents, teachers, other caregivers, and professionals); using multiple means of collecting that information (semistructured and structured interviews, standardized behavior rating scales, the medical exam, and psychological testing as indicated); and surveying multiple domains of major life activities (family, peer, school, and community functioning, among others). (p. 365)

Finally, in their psychological assessment text, when describing an important step in test interpretation, Groth-Marnet and Wright (2016) stated:

> Phase 7 is a complicated phase *requiring the clinician to make sense of all of the data* [emphasis added] collected in a way that can be clearly communicated to the client and/or referral source. . . . Clinicians should create a dynamic understanding of how factors interact to explain what is happening for the client. To do this process well takes good training, supervision, and experience. (pp. 36–37)

Beliefs in the need to perform these feats of complex data integration and the ability of competent clinicians to do so are deeply embedded in the culture of applied psychology. One imagines that a graduate student asked to address strategies for interpreting clinical information during their oral comprehensive examination would likely be admonished (or worse) if responding with something so radically "deviant" as, "One would often be just as well off depending on one or a few data points and simply adding them up." Yet, one must ask: Would such a statement be warranted? How well do we integrate complex information? What are the potential consequences of pursuing complex data integration strategies?

An early, classic study highlighted the potential contrast between beliefs about our capacities to perform complex data integration mainly or solely through impressionistic judgment as opposed to practices incorporating methods that improve our powers of discernment. Werner et al. (1983) examined how well psychiatrists and psychologists integrated information to predict violent behavior among 40 men in a psychiatric intensive care unit. The 15 psychologists and 15 psychiatrists in the study averaged 15 and 17 years of experience, respectively. Each professional was given 19 pieces of information about each of the 40 male patients. Eighteen pieces of information were based on scaled scores from the Brief Psychiatric Rating Scale. The nineteenth variable was whether a violent act was the basis for each man's current hospitalization. The professionals' task was to predict whether each man would exhibit a violent or assaultive act during the 7 days post-admission.

The average validity for the 30 judges in predicting violent behavior was a discouragingly low .12. Perhaps one might entertain the hypothesis that this prediction task was so difficult that good performance could not be expected. However, a regression equation on the 19 cues revealed that their validity in predicting dangerousness was an extremely impressive .82. Thus, the cues were highly effective in predicting dangerousness, but the judges were unable to discern the relation between the 19 cues and the to-be-predicted event. This result is the crux of the discussion in this chapter: integration of multiple cues is a very difficult cognitive task. As Uhl (1966) showed, integrating as few as three simple cues may not be done well.

Table 7.1, which is adapted from Werner et al. (1983), shows why the professionals performed so poorly. Emotional withdrawal was the most informative cue; it

Table 7.1. Relationship of Predicted and Actual Assaults to Cues

Cue	Correlation of Cue with Judges' Prediction	Actual Correlation
Somatic concern	−.13	.00
Anxiety	.17	−.23
Emotional withdrawal	.10	−.42
Conceptual disorganization	−.38	.18
Guilt feelings	−.07	−.23
Tension	.36	−.17
Mannerisms and posturing	.38	.20
Grandiosity	.34	.15
Depressive mood	−.41	−.15
Hostility	.71	.30
Suspiciousness	.51	−.03
Hallucinatory behavior	.15	.37
Motor retardation	−.41	−.32
Uncooperativeness	.47	.03
Unusual thought content	.31	.14
Blunted affect	−.30	−.27
Excitement	.70	.18
Disorientation	.28	−.21
Assault led to admission	.48	.30

correlated -.42 with subsequent violent behavior. However, an analysis of the professionals' predictions revealed that they mistakenly thought that it correlated +.10 with subsequent violent behavior. The second most informative cue was hallucinatory behavior, which correlated +.37 with subsequent violent behavior. The professionals thought that the relation was only a rather paltry +.15. These highly experienced professionals thought that hostility and excitement were the most diagnostic cues, but neither of these cues bore a statistically significant relation to subsequent violent behavior. There are many tasks that professional diagnosticians can do very well, such as assessing each of the 19 cues that are used to make the predictions. In contrast, integrating the 19 cues is a task that diagnosticians do not perform well, despite their confidence that they can accomplish this undertaking at a very high level.

Of interest, Werner et al.'s study, and other studies like it on the prediction of violence, an area of vital concern, motivated tremendous efforts to do better. The efforts have gradually enhanced the capacity to predict violence considerably (see Zagar et al., 2009), although there is still much room for improvement, especially with long-term predictions. More broadly, the central aims of this chapter and Chapter 8 are to examine questions about data integration openly, to discuss methods and approaches that have made significant inroads in extending human capacity, and to work toward an understanding that can increase judgmental accuracy and improve client outcomes. Chapters 12 and 13 also provide extensive discussion of steps and strategies that can enhance data integration and decision accuracy.

CONCEPTUAL FRAMEWORK FOR EXAMINING CAPACITIES FOR COMPLEX DATA INTEGRATION

As noted, common guidance for clinical decision making is to gather comprehensive information and to then integrate much or all of the information, with particular attention paid to data patterns or configural relationships. The emphasis on patterns or configural relationships distinguishes the approach from more basic data integration, such as simply adding one piece of information with other pieces or conducting simple tallies. For example, when deciding whether or not to take a certain job, one might list the pros and cons and see which list is longer. One might also weight the entries, such as counting the weather in the job location as two times more important than the distance to the nearest airport. In either case, whether weighting all items the same or assigning differential weights, one is still adding the items and reaching a total, or using what has been deemed a linear strategy.

In contrast, examining patterns or configural relations among data points treats variables differently depending on their co-relationship with other variables. Hence, Variable A might be weighted differently depending on whether it co-occurs with another variable. For example, suppose we are considering the diagnosis of pneumonia. We could rate each symptom that is present as a 1, and assign a 0 if a symptom is absent. Thus, if a cough was present, and fever and lung congestion absent, we would generate a total pneumonia score of 1. Alternatively, we could use a decision procedure that discounts a cough if it does not co-occur with fever or lung congestion, and thus conclude that it is highly unlikely the person has pneumonia. With configural approaches, the importance of one or another symptom may be modified depending on whether it does or does not co-occur with other symptoms. At a foundational level, when the meaning or weight attached to a variable changes in relation to the status of other variables (e.g., their presence or absence, or their severity), one is taking into account configural relationships. Alternatively, one may frame such interpretive strategies as taking potential interaction effects into account. Pattern analysis is, for the most part, another variation on examining configural relationships.

In principle; the emphasis on configural relationships seems compelling across many situations that arise in psychology as well as other fields. Many things in nature almost surely show patterns or interaction effects. Consequently, when one can discern such phenomena accurately, one has often achieved a closer approximation to the true state of nature and may gain a vital predictive advantage. It is perhaps no coincidence that many of the most compelling examples in which deep knowledge of complex interrelationships and patterns have been realized come from hard sciences like physics and chemistry, and areas in medicine in which advanced knowledge has been achieved. For example, proper differentiation of various disease processes may lead to highly specific treatments with exceptional success rates. These developments often depend heavily on precise measuring tools, broad understanding of the major factors that influence outcomes, and advanced theories that rest on extensive scientific foundations.

However, where do we stand when we lack such advanced knowledge and such formidable tools as highly developed measurement methods and refined theories, and rather try to integrate complex information based primarily on subjective or impressionistic judgment? The exemplar statements at the beginning of this chapter call for the integration of numerous sources of information and suggest that our powers of information integration are almost unbounded. If one refers to integrating all the data and discerning interrelationships and patterns among the information, and one potentially has hundreds or even thousands of data points available (e.g., many single test responses, all manner of behavioral observations, many events in a person's life history), it is reasonable to ask just how well this can be performed. Additionally, it is more or less assumed that new members of the profession, or at least a portion of them, can be taught such skills.

In almost all cases, statements about such prolific data integration capacities come without citations to studies that demonstrate their existence. Rather, the fundamental basis often seems to be a deeply felt conviction that these activities have been, and can be, performed effectively, or the subjective sense that one has acquired the capacity to succeed in such efforts and that clinical experience and favorable outcomes confirm these beliefs. Without questioning the sincerity of such beliefs and the accomplished individuals who may articulate them, is that alone sufficient evidence to accept these assertions as givens, or might we be concerned with the lack of formal scientific support? In light of Meyer et al.'s (2001) statement that it would be extremely difficult or nearly impossible to study such proficiencies, one is led to consider that assertions about remarkable data integration capacities are being advanced despite the admission that scientific evidence to support them is lacking, and further, the presumption that such assertions might not even be subject to scientific study.

A field based on science is supposed to test its beliefs, and a central tenet of science, whether always followed or not, is that practitioners strive to avoid fooling themselves or anyone else. However, we do not have to depend on subjective impression or faith when it comes to the capacity to integrate complex information, because there is a sizeable body of literature that has examined human ability to perform such tasks. Ideally, of course, one hopes that such research shows a remarkable ability to regularly perform complex data integration, but, if it does not, we need to know how close we are coming and if or when supplemental methods might help us to approach or accomplish such aims. Before people learned to build bridges, thinking one could jump 35 feet between two cliffs may have seemed pleasing to some, but such mistakes can be bad ones, even if the alternatives are not ideal. Although the inability to jump long distances without help could deflate our self-image, finding successful means to do so is the greater accomplishment, especially when it serves to advance human welfare. For the many mental health professionals who devote their lives to improving human welfare, achieving that goal, even if it sometimes requires us to accept help and a bit of ego bruising, is a worthy trade-off.

RESEARCH ON THE CAPACITY TO INTEGRATE COMPLEX INFORMATION

At least three major lines of research have examined the human capacity to integrate information, which are covered in turn. They include studies examining whether, or the extent to which, decision makers enhance performance as the amount of information available to them increases; modeling or bootstrapping studies; and studies directly examining the capacity to solve problems requiring multidimensional analysis or cue use. In the materials that follow we emphasize human cognition, as opposed to perception. The human perceptual system is capable of rapidly and accurately integrating multidimensional information. However, many of the decision tasks that we face and are discussed in this book require a certain level of cognitive processing and capability, in part because perceptual processes alone will not suffice. Thus, although recognizing the demarcation is not exact, the focus here is on cognition and certain potential boundaries on cognitive capacities.

IMPACT OF ADDITIONAL INFORMATION ON DECISION ACCURACY

Often, beyond a surprisingly limited amount of information—perhaps as little as two or three of the best combined predictive variables—additional information often does little or nothing to enhance, and may even diminish, accuracy. Such an assertion directly contradicts the common edict to integrate all available or gathered information, but logic, mathematics, and research studies generally favor a more parsimonious approach. For example, Sawyer (1966) conducted a classic review of studies comparing the accuracy of clinical judgment based on interview results alone, test results alone, or both sources of information. (Given the era the review encompassed, all interviews were unstructured or flexible, and thus one cannot draw generalizations about structured interview methods.) The comparisons Sawyer examined generated similar levels of accuracy in a number of cases, but when differences occurred, judgments based on testing alone surpassed the accuracy of judgments based on testing and interview (both of which surpassed interviews alone). Thus, contrary to the notion that more is better, Sawyer found that less information (tests alone) was better than more information (when interviews were added).

How could such a seemingly strange outcome occur? The most fundamental explanation is that if that we start with relatively stronger predictors, then weaker or invalid information can move us further from the correct answer in comparison to ignoring such additional information entirely. If two accurate observers report that the car that struck a pedestrian was a dark blue Ford sedan, but a third, flawed observer states it was a brown Buick SUV, then the third observer's input cannot help matters and, to the extent it sways judgment, can only lead to error. The individual trying to piece together this information may not know just how accurate each observer is, and thus might give credence to the erroneous report, especially if that person provides the information in a confident manner. Here, the idea of integrating all the information is problematical, both because the information is directly contradictory and because some of the information is inaccurate or invalid. When decisions are not dichotomous but may be a matter of extent or degree, the same principles often still apply. Hence, for example, when attempting to estimate another individual's height, combining information from a less accurate source with information from a more accurate source, even if that less accurate source is not very far off, can still make things worse.

Decision making in psychology commonly provides potential access to multiple or many informational sources, and rarely are things so straightforward as one piece of information being definitely correct and another being definitely wrong. Again, however, the same principles operate. In particular, the accuracy or validity of different informational sources will likely vary, sometimes considerably, and some information may simply be invalid or inaccurate. Additionally, the accuracy of the information may be unknown or unfamiliar to the decision maker. Further, other key factors (see "Findings from Modeling Studies" below), such as relative redundancy across informational sources, may be exceedingly difficult to discern impressionistically, especially with a high degree of precision. Thus, in the clinical trenches, the problems described in the preceding paragraph are only likely to become more complex and challenging, not easier.

As noted, even valid information can diminish judgmental accuracy when combined with stronger information. Imagine one is facing a dichotomous determination, such as whether an individual will act on homicidal urges. Given the dichotomous nature of the task, blind guessing would result in 50% accuracy, so we will use this as a yardstick for comparison. (We realize that one may well still take a preventative course of action even if the risk is well below 50%, but for the moment we wish to focus primarily on predictive accuracy.) Further, for the sake of illustration, assume one has results from two tests, Test A, the best test available, which is 90% accurate, and Test B, which is 70% accurate. Both tests improve upon chance, with Test A reducing error from 50% to 10%, and Test B from 50% to 30%. At issue is the impact on accuracy if we include a second valid but weaker test (Test B) with another valid but stronger test (Test A).

If the two tests point to the same conclusion, there is no conflict to resolve. However, if the two tests produce different levels of accuracy, then there must be times they yield conflicting results. In general, each time we defer to Test B over Test A, we have increased the likelihood of error threefold, or from 10% to 30%. (In actuality, because they lead to different conclusions at least 20% of the time, it could even be the case that in every instance of disagreement, Test A is correct and Test B is wrong.) One possible response to the two tests' disagreement might be that a diagnostician would disregard Test A's superior accuracy occasionally based on some consideration, such as gut feeling. The problem is that in order to improve matters by selectively countervailing the prediction of Test A, one requires a method more accurate than Test A. If such a method exists, then if accessible or feasible, one ought to be using it instead of Test A. However, how can we expect to have a method available that is better than the best method we have available?

We are not suggesting that such decision making will typically be limited to two predictive variables, but starting with a fundamental situation can help illustrate the principles at issue. As the example shows, even valid information will not necessarily increase accuracy when added to other information, and thus the advice to use all information sources will have many exceptions. The same applies whether we are dealing with two variables or a considerably greater number of variables: valid but weaker predictors can decrease accuracy when added to stronger predictors. A better guide than using all available information is to prioritize *incremental validity*, or the impact resulting from adding additional information to the best information that is already available. Adding that additional information may: (1) increase accuracy, (2) not change accuracy (thus making its use ineffective and a potential waste of time and money), or (3) decrease accuracy. Unfortunately, the adage to integrate all of the information and the challenges of data integration all too often lead to the second or third outcome, as research indicates.

Various studies in applied psychology show that additional information may do little or nothing to improve judgmental accuracy or may even diminish performance levels (see Golden, 1964; Oskamp, 1965; Sines, 1959; Wedding, 1983). For example, Oskamp (1965) had psychologists and nonprofessionals review a detailed description of an individual and then try to predict that person's behavior from among a series of alternative choices. This person's actual behavior was known, thus providing a basis for appraising the study participants' predictive accuracy. The history was provided in four parts designed to contain an equivalent amount of information, and after each part was presented, the study participants made their predictions. As the amount of information increased, confidence increased, but not accuracy, dual findings that are common in such studies. In Wedding's (1983) study, judgments made on the basis of an abbreviated set of neuropsychological evaluation results were generally as accurate as judgments based on considerably more extensive information, although, again, confidence levels were higher when more information was available. Thus, an unwarranted increase in confidence without a concomitant increase in accuracy, as can easily occur as one collects additional information, leads to various pernicious results. For example, overconfident decision makers are prone to risky decisions, such as recommending hospital release for an individual with a history of violent behavior given a sense of near certainty they will not reoffend.

Much as Sawyer (1966) found in his comprehensive review, Dana et al.'s (2013) study also found that when interview information is added to other information, it may reduce accuracy. The authors asked undergraduates to interview a student in order to predict that student's grade-point average (GPA) for a particular semester. Interviewers were given information about the interviewee that included age, major, class standing, course schedule for the to-be-predicted semester, and current cumulative GPA. Interviewers were also told that the cumulative GPA was the best predictor. There were three types of interviews. In the accurate condition, the interviewer could ask only closed-ended questions (where answers were, for example, Yes vs. No or This vs. That), and the interviewee would answer accurately. In the random condition, the interviewee answered closed-ended questions accurately for the first half of the interview and randomly for the second half. In the natural condition, interviewers could ask any type of question and the interviewee would respond accurately. Then, in all conditions, the interviewers predicted the GPA for their interviewees. Another group of undergraduates were asked to predict the GPA of a student whom they did not interview, but whose age, major, class standing, course schedule for the to-be-predicted semester, and current cumulative GPA were all presented—exactly the same information that had been given to the interviewers. The interviewees in all groups were drawn from a panel of the same seven people.

The results were straightforward. Compared to the no-interview situation, the presence of any kind of interview information decreased the accuracy with which interviewers predicted GPA. In a second study by Dana et al. interviewers hearing only completely random responses from interviewees and those hearing only accurate responses equally thought that they were "able to infer a lot about this person given the amount of time we spent together" and believed that "I got information that was valuable in making a GPA prediction." Thus, the interviewers had a favorable impression of the interviews, but since predictive accuracy was the goal, the extra information provided by the interviews was entirely counterproductive.

Dana et al.'s study (2013) also illustrates other important guides and principles. First, as previously noted, a limited number or combination of the most valid predictors often approaches a ceiling in predictive accuracy. Consequently, if one starts with the best predictors or combination of predictors, then additional information will have weaker predictive value. The more information that is added, the greater the chance it will dilute the influence of the better predictors. Particularly in cases in which that additional, but weaker, information is salient or captures attention, such as information or impressions stemming from face-to-face interviews, then all else being equal, the greater the chance it will decrease the impact of the stronger predictors and increase the impact of the weaker predictors. The end result is diminished predictive accuracy.

Another example comes from the domain of finance. Slovic et al. (1972) performed an experiment with stockbrokers in which the brokers were presented with eight pieces of financial information about 64 companies and were asked to evaluate each firm with regard to its potential capital appreciation. In addition, the brokers were asked to distribute 100 points over the eight factors to indicate how much they used each factor in making the capital appreciation estimate. This subjective estimate of how much each factor was used correlated only +.34 with how much a regression analysis revealed that each factor was actually used. An important additional finding was that the more experienced a broker was, the lower their awareness of their actual use of each factor. It is as if the veteran brokers were "running on automatic," with lessened ability to reflect accurately on the impact the factors had on their judgment.

As mentioned in Chapter 6, one of the authors was asked to help school guidance counselors diagnose learning disability (LD) in community college students in a particular US state. In this state, the fraction of students diagnosed with LD was markedly greater than the proportion in any other state. To their credit, the counselors used standardized tests with known reliability and validity for their diagnostic judgments. Unfortunately, they also used additional cues, such as "tight grip on pencil" and "taps feet," to augment their diagnoses. These cues have very low diagnosticity in correctly identifying LD. Therefore, when added to the diagnostic process, these cues sabotaged the usefulness of the standardized tests.

MODELING/BOOTSTRAPPING

Creating Models

Lew Goldberg and collaborators were interested in studying the complexity of human data integration and interpretive strategies. In the course of their work, they examined whether models of decision makers could reproduce their judgments and, if so, how complex the models needed to be to do so successfully. In these studies, the term *judge* is often used, but this simply refers to the individual making a judgment, be it a layperson or a professional, such as a physician or psychologist.

In constructing models, one requires some basis for identifying cues or dimensions judges might use to reach conclusions. One source of information is to query the decision maker, such as asking psychiatrists what information they use to evaluate the possible presence and severity of depression. A mental health professional might respond by citing such factors as a sad facial expression, slowed motor movement (what is referred to as psychomotor retardation), flat affect, and self-reports of symptoms like melancholy, pessimism, low motivation, and sleep disturbance. These impressions about relevant information that may be taken into account in some decision task can be referred to as subjective cues, meaning that they are sources of information the professionals believe or report are influential in formulating judgments. The researcher may also decide to add certain cues or symptoms that other sources (e.g., articles on depression) suggest are essential to identifying depression, such as social isolation or thoughts of self-harm.

The professional might also be asked about interpretive strategies. Many professionals in many such situations report that they do not merely add up the potential cues, but also look at interrelationships or patterns among the data. The judge may indicate that some cues are more important than others, or that one or another cue may not be significant if it appears in isolation, but it can gain importance depending on the other symptoms that might also be present. For example, if a person describes sleep disorder but not sad mood, then the professional may report that the significance they attach to sleep problems as an indicator of depression may be reduced or minimized. In Goldberg's earlier research (1970), psychologists interpreting the Minnesota Multiphasic Personality Inventory (MMPI) often reported placing heavy emphasis on the pattern formed by relative elevations across results on clinical scales designed to capture varying psychological tendencies or mood states, or interrelationships among scale scores. For example, the score on a scale designed to measure relative levels of activation or energy might be said to reflect different processes or diagnostic possibilities if it co-occurred with another scale measuring characteristics like psychological distress or reduced impulse control.

Once cues are identified, cases are designed in which all information is held constant, except for the standing on one of the cues. For example, two cases might be identical except for the presence or extent of self-reported feelings of sadness. Hence, if this cue, which has been described subjectively (or impressionistically) as important in evaluating depression, really impacts judgment, then conclusions should differ when the standing on this cue differs. Proceeding in this manner, one can compare a judge's subjective impressions about the impact of a cue on his or her judgments with an objective measurement of impact, or what is referred to as a comparison of subjective versus objective cue utilization. One works through the cues one at a time, varying their standing across otherwise identical cases. Researchers also construct multiple case scenarios in which they alter cues in isolation so that measurement of cue use is based on a sufficiently large sample to draw more trustworthy conclusions. In addition, one can vary more than one cue at a time to examine possible interaction or configural effects. It could turn out that self-reports of sadness have a greater or lesser influence when they co-appear with other symptoms, such as decreased activity levels. A decision maker could increase the relative weight assigned to reported sadness when it co-occurs with reduced activity and de-emphasize reported sadness when decreased activities are not reported. By altering more than one cue simultaneously, a researcher can look at potential interactions or patterns among variables.

Goldberg was interested not only in comparing subjective and objective cue use, but also in using what was learned about an individual's or expert's cue use in attempting to build models that would duplicate their judgments. For example, analysis of a decision maker's cue use might show that certain variables did not influence judgments at all, and that other variables had a sizeable impact. Using such procedures and formal statistical analyses, one sets out to derive a formula or algorithm that captures a judge's cue use and thereby duplicates a judge's decisions. (At this point, information must be quantified in order to be processed mathematically, but even qualitative observations can usually be quantified, such as coding the presence or absence of unusual emotional reactions as 1 = present, 2 = absent.) After presenting a sufficient number of cases to build potentially effective models, one can have a judge review new cases and also have the model analyze that same information and predict what the judge will decide. It is common in such research to try to build individual models that duplicate the decisions of individual judges, although it is also possible to try to model group decisions.

Findings from Modeling Studies

To the extent a judge makes consistent decisions (e.g., the same information leads to the same conclusion), models can often succeed in reproducing that judge's decisions in most cases, such as 75% or 85% of the time, or even more often. Goldberg was particularly interested in how complex the models needed to become to duplicate decisions accurately. For example, would the models only need to add variables together, or would it also be necessary to account for patterns or configural relations (interactions) among variables? At the most basic level, a configural interpretive strategy does not examine standing on variables in isolation from one another. Rather, as noted, for one or more variables, standing on another variable or other variables can alter interpretation of the original variable. To return to a prior example, a doctor considering the diagnosis of pneumonia could count a cough as potential evidence for the disorder, but might discount that finding entirely if the patient has normal lungs and no fever. Hence, the use or relative impact of the first variable may be modified by status of other variables, and vice versa.

Modeling studies, which became a highly active area of research over time (see Armstrong, 2001), have produced a number of stunning results. Most germane to the current discussion was the finding that properly designed models often reproduce judges' decisions with a high level of accuracy, and often can do so by relying on just a few variables. For example, studies have shown that judgments that professionals believe require high levels of complex data integration and judgment, such as interpreting MMPI profiles (Goldberg, 1970), deciding whether to grant psychiatric inpatients temporary passes (Rorer et al., 1967), or differentiating between benign versus malignant stomach ulcers (Hoffman et al.,

1968), can often be reproduced by simple models that largely disregard configural judgments or interactions among variables. For example, a model's accuracy may not change at all if one includes procedures that account for configural analysis, or perhaps accuracy may increase by only a few percentage points. Thus, in contrast to the view that many decisions are highly complex and require the integration of numerous variables and careful consideration of data patterns and configurations, decisions can often be reproduced by simply adding up a few variables, or even just one or two.

Of further interest, one often finds marked divergence between subjective impressions of judgment practices and objective measures. For example: (1) although individuals tend to believe that they have accounted for numerous variables and integrated considerable information in reaching judgments, decisions are often based primarily on only a few variables; (2) variables that individuals believe have had a marked impact on their judgment have had minimal or negligible impact; and (3) variables believed to have minimal or no impact may have had considerable impact. Such findings are particularly important when we strive to focus our decision making on the best predictive variables and intend to disregard variables that should not be influencing our judgments, such as sociodemographic variables that do not predict relevant outcomes.

Consider a classic study by Holzman et al. (1984). Twenty-five gynecologists and 25 family physicians were presented with cases of postmenopausal women in order to ascertain what factors might lead the doctors to prescribe estrogen replacement therapy. Forty-six of the 50 doctors expressed the belief that estrogen reduces fracture risk. However, their actual estrogen-prescribing behavior was not consistent with this expressed belief. In other words, what the physicians said that they were doing and what they actually were doing were not closely related.

In neuropsychological assessments, in order to ascertain if a decline in mental ability has occurred due to an event, such as a motor vehicle accident that may have caused a mild traumatic brain injury, a clinician must estimate the level of pre-event or baseline functioning. The clinician may be unable to obtain pre-event information that will help much with this determination, and thus the need to estimate baseline capacities after the event has occurred makes the judgment task that much more difficult, but no less important. In many legal cases, the baseline estimate can have a major impact on judgments about the presence and degree of change, and thus can alter financial awards substantially, running into the hundreds of thousands of dollars, or more.

Kareken and Williams's (1994) study examined neuropsychological assessment and produced outcomes that aligned with Holzman et al.'s (1984) results. Kareken and Williams had 48 clinical neuropsychologists estimate Verbal IQ (VIQ) and Performance IQ (PIQ) based on protocols for five individuals. (Intelligence test indices have changed since the time of the study, but that would seem to be of minimal import in evaluating the outcome of Kareken and Williams's research.) The protocols included seven pieces of demographic information and the age-corrected Wechsler Adult Intelligence Scale-Revised Vocabulary scaled score (VOC) for each of the five individuals. The judges were also asked to specify the magnitude of the correlation between each of the eight predictors and the VIQ and PIQ, the two to-be-estimated factors. Finally, the judges were asked to specify their confidence in their estimates as each of the predictors was presented one at a time. This was done by asking the clinicians to specify a confidence interval around their VIQ and PIQ estimates such that they were 95% sure that their estimate fell within that interval.

There were several instructive results. Although the judges believed that VOC added no incremental validity to the prediction power of the demographic information, the judges' behavior indicated that they did attribute added validity to the VOC. In general, even predictors that the judges asserted were redundant tended to shrink the confidence intervals as they were included. Of course, if a predictor is truly and entirely redundant, it should not influence confidence intervals at all. For example, suppose one is appraising weight as a variable for predicting something about health status. If one used an extremely accurate scale to measure weight in pounds, and then added a second highly accurate scale to measure weight in kilograms, the second measurement would do nothing to increase judgmental accuracy or decrease error.

If someone is using a cue too much or too little, why not just instruct them to adjust their cue use? The value of such corrective information, however, is predicated on the diagnostician's awareness of the weights he or she places on various cues. Even with the best intentions, if we often lack insight into influential factors, then no matter how constructive and worthy our intent to improve our cue utilization, we probably will not reach our goals. As described in the discussion of decision aids and corrective approaches in Chapter 12, additional, more active steps that go beyond such self-instruction may well be required.

Perhaps the most remarkable finding in the modeling studies comes from instances in which the judge's decisions diverged from the model's output, that is, situations in which the judge generated one outcome and the model generated a different outcome, despite the model being built on the judge's own decisions. In instances of divergence, one may have a way to check on the accuracy of the two conflicting conclusions. For example, suppose the judge predicted that a psychiatric inpatient would not engage in aggressive physical behavior within a 72-hour period, whereas the model generated the alternative prediction. If records are available, the conflicting predictions can be checked to determine which one was accurate and which was erroneous. In studies in which the accuracy of divergent predictions can be checked, one finds that the models consistently perform as well, or better, than the judge. Thus, the models show an overall superiority because they either tie with the judges or, when there is a difference, most often exceed judges' performances.

That the models outperform the very judges upon whom they are based is sometimes referred to as Goldberg's paradox, and it explains one use of the term *bootstrapping*: the models are picking themselves up by the bootstraps, so to speak, which seemingly should not be possible. The models' relative overall superiority is likely explained mainly by their consistency. Given the same information, models produce uniform decisions. In contrast, human judges show some degree of random variation attributable to such factors as fatigue or distraction. To the extent decisions are based on valid variables, then consistency as opposed to fluctuation in cue use should result in higher overall accuracy rates.

What is one to make of these results, and why even bother with this research? First, as noted, modeling studies can provide insights into human decision making. Of note, the models are not necessarily intended to duplicate mental processes, but rather outputs or decisions that judges reach. For example, it is doubtful that individuals typically calculate interaction terms in their heads when evaluating the joint properties of variables. Rather, congruent with Goldberg's research aims, models provide important information about human judgment and limitations.

For example, judges commonly believe that they perform complex data analyses that are essential to reaching accurate judgments. However, if their decisions can often be reproduced by simple models that more or less add up results on a few variables (and sometimes do not even weight the variables differentially), then the configural or pattern analyses that individuals do perform do not seem to do much to augment decision accuracy. If these purportedly complex configural analyses were contributing substantially to decision making, then they ought to be regularly outperforming models that disregard patterns and interactions among variables, but that is not what occurs. Rather, if anything, the judges do not surpass the accuracy of the models, and when there is a difference, the models routinely come out on top.

A related side benefit to the modeling research is to demonstrate the viability of replicating certain human judgments, which can be of considerable benefit if we can locate proficient or leading decision makers and reproduce their conclusions. Once these models are created, they are explicit and available to almost anyone for application in settings of interest. At the same time, they do need to be monitored carefully and potentially changed or improved as circumstances and progression of knowledge call for alterations in procedures.

RESEARCH ON COMPLEX DATA INTEGRATION: LESSONS AND IMPLICATIONS

What are we to make of these various lines of evidence showing limits in the ability to integrate complex information? First, although the studies do reveal limits in certain aspects of human cognition under certain conditions, they should not be taken as general commentary on human intelligence or ingenuity, or viewed as intractable problems we cannot overcome. Rather, complex data integration can be extremely challenging, especially under conditions in which feedback is delayed, incomplete, and at times frankly misleading, conditions that are very common in clinical and naturalistic settings. However, human aptitude and sometimes outright genius have led to the development of various helpful approaches and methods that often go a long ways toward countering or overcoming the bounds of unaided human judgment (see Chapters 8, 12, and 13). Given such factors as overconfidence, the greatest challenge is getting decision makers to recognize the need for, and to adopt methods and strategies that bolster, judgmental accuracy.

Second, as noted, models of human judges are designed to duplicate decisions, but less so to mimic human judgment processes. Although on occasion individuals may simply go through a list of pros and cons to reach a decision, much like a linear model, human decision making is often more involved and influenced by a range of factors (e.g., intensity of emotional reaction to facets of a situation, subjective appraisal of risks and rewards, reference to past experiences or scenarios). Thus, it should not be assumed that the procedures used to create a model that duplicates decisions or judgments also match internal cognitive processes.

Third, the studies demonstrate limitations in the ability to perform complex or multidimensional problem solving. The studies show that our performance has upper bounds that do not begin to approach common assumptions about our capacities and presumed needs to integrate hundreds or thousands of data points at nearly optimal levels. However, falling short of such presumed abilities does not rule out the ability to perform configural judgments at all. In fact, studies show that individuals can and do perform configural judgments, although not nearly at the extraordinary levels of complexity and effectiveness often assumed (Ganzach, 1998). Rather, individuals may attend to, and be influenced by, interrelationships or interactions among two or three variables, although as dimensions are added, such decision making tasks often surpass demonstrated human capacity in the absence of decision aids. What is surprising, however, are the gaps between subjective impressions about the ability to integrate information and what studies show. The relevance of these gaps is that if individuals, mental health professionals included, chase strategies they believe are efficacious but are actually not nearly as helpful as they are assumed to be, they may bypass alternatives that are likely to achieve greater proficiency.

If decision makers were truly able to perform the types of extraordinary complex data analysis that are commonly described or assumed, they should routinely exceed the accuracy of simple models and linear statistical decision methods that do not incorporate patterns or interactions among data. Yet, such outcomes are highly unusual, and in the majority of cases, linear methods equal or exceed subjective judgments assumed to depend heavily on complex interrelationships among data (see Chapter 8). Thus, whatever our abilities might be for integrating complex information and identifying complicated patterns in data, these capacities generally do not seem to add much, if anything, to judgmental accuracy.

Rather than analyzing and integrating hundreds or thousands of variables proficiently, people often use considerably less complex strategies, taking perhaps just a few dimensions into account. Individuals apply such strategies to reduce cognitive strain or the level of mental processing that would otherwise be required. A number of the cognitive heuristics or biases we described in Chapters 3–6, such as confirmatory bias or incomplete covariation analysis, can be viewed as simplifying strategies that decrease information-processing demands. For example, primary focus on confirmatory evidence reduces cognitive burden by largely disregarding contrary evidence.

By reducing cognitive strain, simplifying strategies, or at least some of them, can sometimes improve decision making. For example, a strategy that can be surprisingly effective is to pick the single best predictive variable and depend on it entirely (Gigerenzer & Goldstein, 1996). Additionally, focusing on level of confirming evidence can have benefits because, all else being equal, an interpretation that is correct should generate more confirming evidence than an interpretation that is incorrect.

The problem with decision strategies that are too simple or that disregard too much information is that they can go far astray in the many situations in which the information that is being disregarded or underweighted makes a difference. In addition, in various circumstances, disconfirming evidence can be more powerful than confirming evidence. Take someone who tests a hypothesis by only performing confirmatory tests. To illustrate using a number series, suppose one has to determine an underlying concept and can use any single number or combination of numbers to perform tests of the concept. The individual starts by asking whether the sequence 1 → 2 is an example of the concept, and is told it is. The individual forms the hypothesis that the concept is ascending numbers. A person performing confirmatory tests could generate endless supportive results by inquiring, for example, whether 2 → 3 is an example of the concept, 3 → 4 is an example, 4 → 5 is, and so on. However, if the true concept is numbers that ascend or descend by 1, a single attempt to disconfirm the original hypothesis (5 → 4) should prove decisive if the feedback is correct. Furthermore, appraising the level of supportive evidence can be distorted by access or exposure to information, as may occur with TV viewers who prefer stations that tend to present events or descriptions congruent with their initial positions.

Conjunctive and disjunctive decision approaches provide examples of potentially helpful strategies that make use of interrelationships among information. Such strategies simplify decision making but are far from optimal. In a conjunctive strategy, one might require that a minimal standard be met across all variables that enter into a decision. For example, one might accept all job applicants who obtain a score of 6 or greater on a 10-point scale across all evaluative criteria, such as their (a) level of job experience, (b) letters of recommendation, (c) past ratings of job performance, and (d) presentation on interview. This strategy arguably considers interrelations among variables, because the way one treats the standing on one variable can be modified by the standing on other variables. For example, if an applicant obtains a 10 on the first dimension but a 4 on the second dimension, the top rating on the first dimension is overridden by the failure to meet the cutoff on the second dimension, thus leading to a no-hire decision.

Such a conjunctive strategy reduces cognitive strain because failure to meet any of the criteria is dispositive, and one does not need to consider whether all of the dimensions are equally important or should be weighted differently, whether the 1 to 10 scales across the dimensions are really comparable, and whether more complicated strategies may at times lead to different decisions. However, suppose two candidates line up as follows on the four dimensions:

Candidate 1: a = 10, b = 10, c = 10, d = 5 and Total = 35
Candidate 2: a = 6, b = 6, c = 6, d = 6 and Total = 24

The conjunctive strategy would lead one to reject Candidate 1 given the score on d that falls below 6 and to accept Candidate 2 given scores meeting the cutoff point on all criteria. However, is this the best choice? Unless dimension d is somehow far more important than the other variables and the difference between a rating of 5 versus 6 trumps the considerably larger advantages Candidate 1 has over Candidate 2 on the other three dimensions, Candidate 1 is the better choice. Although we have presented an extreme situation here, it illustrates the shortcomings of a conjunctive strategy of this type and its potential propensity for error. If one translates this into a clinical situation involving high stakes, such as whether to pursue involuntary hospitalization with a patient expressing suicidal or homicidal ideation, the vulnerability of such conjunctive strategies to error and the potential consequences gain greater immediacy.

Disjunctive strategies also account for interrelationships among variables, but they may focus on whether standing on any dimension exceeds a certain threshold. For example, suppose one is looking for individuals to fulfill certain roles on a research team, such as a statistician, a computer programmer, a writer, and a person with exceptional interpersonal skills who will serve as the face of the research team when interacting with the media and will also promote harmonious working relationships among research team members. In these circumstances, one may seek individuals with very high standings on any one of these dimensions. For example, the media relations person might be weak on three of the four dimensions, but exceptionally strong in public relations roles; another candidate might be a superb computer programmer but socially awkward, and so on. As long as a candidate possesses high-level skills on at least one of the dimensions (and a matching position for that person is open), lower standing on the other dimensions may be disregarded. Such a disjunctive strategy simplifies decision making and may lead to effective choices. However, situations could easily arise in which a better overall candidate is rejected over a weaker candidate, especially if a small difference on the relevant variable is more than offset by far greater strengths on other dimensions. For example, a person who is rated as a 9 out of 10 on statistical skills may still well exceed the job requirements, and another candidate with an even better 10 out of 10 rating on this one dimension may be so difficult interpersonally that the resultant disharmony will have broad adverse consequences for the research team's efforts.

OBSTACLES TO COMPLEX CONFIGURAL JUDGMENT AND DATA INTEGRATION

There are daunting obstacles to performing complex information integration mentally without the assistance of decision aids. Some may view our bounded capacities as reflecting negatively on human capacity. Such attributions may overlook the difficult challenges we encounter in these efforts, as well as the extent to which human ingenuity and penetrating intelligence have created tools that can greatly extend our efforts. Some of the challenges have already been described, such as limited insight into the factors affecting our judgment. Another obstacle is the potential difficulty of isolating the impact (if any) of multiple factors that may be influencing outcomes, as well as determining their relative levels of redundancy and their operation when combined or sorted in different ways.

By way of example, suppose a company wanted to ascertain if a new type of fertilizer would improve the growth of vegetables. The company should apply the new fertilizer to some plots and the usual type to other plots. Care should be taken to ensure that the two types of plots have the same amount of sunshine, water, and crop type. If every factor is held constant across the two plots, then any difference in vegetable growth could confidently be attributed to the difference in the fertilizer.

However, what if the two types of plots not only differed in which type of fertilizer was applied but also across 18 other factors, such as the type of crop, amount of water, amount of sunshine, frequency of weeding, presence of insects, etc.? Then the singular influence of the type of fertilizer would be nearly impossible to discern. Even persons with vast gardening experience would find it extremely difficult to ascertain the relation between any one of the 19 factors and plant growth.

This is the same situation that the professionals faced in the Werner et al. (1983) study on the prediction of violence, in which even professionals with extensive experience could not isolate the influence of each of the 19 variables and—worse yet—how they might interact with each other. For example, a particular fertilizer may augment plant growth in wet weather but "burn" the crops in dry weather. Similarly, anxiety may promote violence in some circumstances but inhibit it in others. A diagnostician is simply not capable of examining a stimulus with 19 varying factors and multiple possible interactions, appropriately integrating all of this information, and arriving at an accurate estimate of the influence of each one. More so, combining unknown—or possibly unknowable—levels of multiple factors makes data integration an exceedingly challenging task.

Other factors affecting our capacities for complex data integration include, for one, restrictions in working memory, which make it difficult for us to keep more than a relatively limited amount of information in mind simultaneously. Theories can provide major assistance in expanding our capacities to organize complex information into more manageable units and in analyzing and applying deep understanding of complex data sets. However such cognitive steps require a level of theoretical development that has not yet been achieved in many areas of psychology. As noted earlier, such capacities often depend heavily on factors like developing precise measuring tools and comprehensive understanding of the major factors that impact outcome. Given the complexities and challenges posed by the subject matter of our field, although excellent progress is being made in many areas, there remain few applied areas in which these conditions are truly satisfied.

However, none of this should be taken to suggest that there is little we can do to advance our decision making capacities and to improve the accuracy of our predictions. The chapters in Part III enumerate methods and strategies that can enhance decision making and thereby improve outcomes.

REFERENCES

Armstrong, J. S. (2001). Judgmental bootstrapping: Inferring experts = rules for forecasting. In J. S. Armstrong (Ed.), *Principles of forecasting: A handbook for researchers and practitioners* (pp. 171–192). Kluwer Academic Publishers.

Barkley, R. A., & Edwards, G. (2006). Diagnostic interview, behavior rating scales, and the medical examination. In R. A. Barkley (Ed.), *Attention-deficit hyperactivity disorder: A handbook for diagnosis and treatment* (3rd ed., pp. 337–368). Guilford Press.

Dana, J., Dawes, R., & Peterson, N. (2013). Belief in the unstructured interview: The persistence of an illusion. *Judgment and Decision Making, 8*(3), 512–520.

Exner, J. E. (1974). *The Rorschach: A comprehensive system*. John Wiley & Sons.

Ganzach, Y. (1998). Nonlinear models in decision making: The diagnosis of psychosis versus neurosis from the MMPI. *Organizational Behavior and Human Decision Processes, 74*(1), 53–61.

Gigerenzer, G., & Goldstein, D. G. (1996). Reasoning the fast and frugal way: Models of bounded rationality. *Psychological Review, 103*, 650–669.

Goldberg, L. R. (1970). Man versus model of man: Rationale, plus some evidence, for a method for improving on clinical inferences. *Psychological Bulletin, 73*(6), 422–432.

Golden, M. (1964). Some effects of combining psychological tests on clinical inferences. *Journal of Consulting Psychology, 28*(5), 440–446.

Groth-Marnet, G., & Wright, A. (2016). *The handbook of psychological assessment* (6th ed.). John Wiley & Sons.

Hoffman, P. J., Slovic, P., & Rorer, L. G. (1968). An analysis-of-variance model for assessment of configural cue utilization in clinical judgment. *Psychological Bulletin, 69*(5), 338–349.

Holzman, G. B., Ravitch, M. M., Metheny, W., Rothert, M. L., Holmes, M., & Hoppe, R. B. (1984). Physicians' judgments about estrogen replacement therapy for menopausal women. *Obstetrics & Gynecology, 63*(3), 303–311.

Kareken, D. A., & Williams, J. M. (1994). Human judgment and estimation of premorbid intellectual function. *Psychological Assessment, 6*(2), 83–91.

Lezak, M. D. (1983). *Neuropsychological assessment* (2nd ed.). Oxford University Press.

Lezak, M. D., Howieson, D. B., Bigler, E. D., & Tranel, D. (2012). *Neuropsychological assessment* (5th ed.). Oxford University Press.

Matarazzo, J. D. (1986). Computerized clinical psychological test interpretations: Unvalidated plus all means and no sigma. *American Psychologist, 41*, 14–24.

Meyer, G. J., Finn, S. E., Eyde, L. D., Kay, G. G., Moreland, K. L., Dies, R. R., Eisman, E. J., Kubiszyn, T. W., & Reed, G. M. (2001). Psychological testing and psychological assessment: A review of evidence and issues. *American Psychologist, 56*(2), 128–165.

Mitrushina, M., Boone, K. B., Razani, J., & D'Elia, L. F. (2005). *Handbook of normative data for neuropsychological assessment*. Oxford University Press.

Oskamp, S. (1965). Overconfidence in case-study judgments. *Journal of Consulting Psychology*, *29*, 261–265.

Rorer, L. G., Hoffman, P. J., Dickman, H. R., & Slovic, P. (1967). Configural judgments revealed. *American Psychologist*, *22*(7), 561.

Sawyer, J. (1966). Measurement and prediction, clinical and statistical. *Psychological Bulletin*, *66*(3), 178–200.

Sines, L. K. (1959). The relative contribution of four kinds of data to accuracy in personality assessment. *Journal of Consulting Psychology*, *23*(6), 483–492.

Slovic, P., Fleissner, D., & Bauman, W. S. (1972). Analyzing the use of information in investment decision making: A methodological proposal. *Journal of Business*, *45*, 283–301.

Uhl, C. N. (1966). Effects of multiple stimulus validity and criterion dispersion on learning of interval concepts. *Journal of Experimental Psychology*, *72*(4), 519–527.

Wedding, D. (1983). Clinical and statistical prediction in neuropsychology. *Clinical Neuropsychology*, *5*, 49–55.

Werner, P. D., Rose, T. R., & Yesavage, J. A. (1983). Reliability, accuracy, and decision making strategy in clinical predictions of imminent dangerousness. *Journal of Consulting and Clinical Psychology*, *51*(6), 815–825.

Zagar, R. J., Busch, K. G., Grove, W. M., & Hughes, J. R. (2009). Can violent (re)offense be predicted? A review of the role of the clinician and use of actuarial tests in light of new data. *Psychological Reports*, *104*, 247–277.

8

Comparing Clinical Judgment and Statistical Decision Methods

Suppose you had to make a critical decision, such as whether to have surgery for damage to your upper cervical vertebrae suffered in a fall off a ladder. The surgeon has indicated that without the surgery, a sudden blow or force to the head, as might occur in even a relatively minor car accident, could lead to permanent paralysis. However, the surgeon has also openly acknowledged that the procedure carries considerable risk and could lead to the very same outcome one is trying to prevent. The surgeon can only give you an imprecise estimate of the relative risks between undergoing or not undergoing the operation, leaving you in a deeply unsettling dilemma. Under such circumstances, if there was some way to attain a greater level of certainty or greater predictive accuracy, you would almost surely welcome the help. And if that help was a bland algorithm, but one that was tried and true and compellingly verified, it would probably be a poor move to disregard the assistance just because it did not come in the form of a chat with your doctor.

Oddly, we tend to accept help readily when it comes in certain forms or for certain purposes. We do not feel a sense of shame or inadequacy because, when time is of the essence, we choose to fly from New York to California rather than walk; because we use a calculator to divide a number like 23,719 into 1,227; because we use a phone to communicate with someone rather than shouting to them at their location three miles away; or because we take an antibiotic for a week to cure an infection that, if left untreated, might kill us. However, in many situations, perhaps most often due to miscalibrated confidence, we look askance at methods that can enhance our judgmental or predictive accuracy. Bypassing such assistance may be akin to rejecting the best decision method in situations like the example we provided of critical spinal surgery.

How best to predict human behavior and outcomes is a central question in psychology and one of great practical significance. It is also arguably the only one among the commonly cited great questions in the field for which the answer is known and the evidence overwhelming (and is very likely to remain so until other more powerful forms of decision aids or our applied theories of mind and behavior attain certain advanced characteristics). How best to predict human behavior preoccupied the mind of a young genius still relatively new to the field of psychology, Paul E. Meehl. Meehl had already been widely exposed to leading psychoanalytic thought, impressive clinical case studies, and anecdotal exemplars of clinical acumen, yet also to contrasting approaches or "dustbowl empiricism," with its commitment to rigorous scientific tests of knowledge and aversion to unrestrained speculation. How much did the theories and clinical judgments of such figures as Sigmund Freud and Karl Menninger have going for them in comparison to the Strong Interest Inventory or other similarly developed instruments that bypassed complex inferential judgments and instead emphasized relatively direct, empirically established relationships? Meehl had intense interest in applied clinical psychology, was impressed by differing approaches to predicting human behavior, realized the practical importance of the questions involved, and set out to determine what the limited research on the topic available at that time might show. This chapter starts where Paul Meehl's journey began, and then proceeds to the substantial body of literature, thought, and analysis that has developed since then.

FRAMING THE ISSUE

Defining and Categorizing the Two Methods

Certain misconceptions about clinical and statistical decision methods arise frequently, leading to unproductive counterpoints to supposed assertions that those holding one or another position did not actually take. Therefore, we will try to be as clear as possible. The central question addresses the comparative accuracy of different approaches for combining or integrating information when the differing methods are given access to the same information (i.e., when neither has an informational advantage). Starting with this central inquiry, one can move forward to other questions. We emphasize Meehl's conceptualizations, definitions, and framework because we believe they remain current. They are clear, cogent, and analytically sound and have served as the foundation for much of the research done on the issue over the years.

An important demarcation point is that Meehl's core inquiry addressed different methods for integrating or interpreting information, not the type of data or information being integrated. At odds with this core inquiry, one finds numerous comments in the literature about "actuarial" or "objective" data, with the writer perhaps suggesting that much of the issue involves the type of data that enters into decisions. We are not suggesting that type of information is unimportant, but simply that it does not pertain to the core issue we are considering here, which is methods for integrating or interpreting data. The data may be "objective" information, such as the scores on a test, but other sources of information, such as subjective impressions (e.g., a clinician's sense that someone comes across as odd) may also be among the information being considered, or even the sole source of information.

The two basic judgment methods being compared (with some additional variants to be discussed later) are clinical and statistical (or sometimes called actuarial) approaches. The word *clinical* is somewhat unfortunate because it does not necessarily refer to a clinician or healthcare provider. For example, a baseball scout may rely heavily on clinical judgment methods. Rather, clinical judgment refers to data integration in the head, or through subjective or impressionistic methods. In the case of a baseball scout, there may be varying sources of information, including detailed quantitative analyses, such as measurements of arm strength and running speed. Ultimately, however, the integration or interpretation of that and perhaps other information is reached through subjective data combination.

In the statistical method, as defined here or in the context of this issue, two conditions must be met. First, data combination must be fixed or prespecified, i.e., using the same data, the method always produces the same outcome. Once developed, the method for combining information does not depend in any way on clinical judgment. That does not mean one must unwaveringly accept the outcome, only that in the process of going from the data to the outcome, subjective judgment does not play a role.

Second, the conclusion or output must be based on empirically established relationships.[1] For example, if arm strength for a baseball player is being considered, then there must be an empirical basis that establishes a relationship between the standing on this variable and the outcome or outcomes being examined. When developing statistical decision methods, all sorts of variables one thinks might be useful may be examined, but if a variable under consideration turns out to lack predictive value, it should be excluded from the statistical decision procedure. In addition, because multivariate procedures, which are used frequently when developing statistical decision methods, can capitalize on chance and thereby yield inflated results on a first pass through the data, proper validation or cross-validation usually is needed before comparing their accuracy to clinical judgment methods.

Fulfilling one of the two conditions, but not both, is insufficient to meet the definition being used here for statistical decision methods. For example, many computerized interpretive programs are automated or unvarying, but they may be designed to mirror an expert's judgments. In turn, that particular expert's judgments may, or may not, be founded on empirically established relationships. Thus, statements like, "Computer-based test interpretations provide an example of the type of actuarial procedures Meehl had in mind," are not literally correct, and should these programs stray from empirically established relationships, then although they perhaps still retain the aura of statistical or actuarial judgment, they do not truly achieve that status. Various other judgment approaches may be proposed, such as attempts to blend clinical and statistical methods. We touch on such variations later, but for the moment we wish to concentrate on the two basic decision methods and conditions for a fair comparison.

1. Defined strictly, *empirical* means by observation, and is not a qualifier for something like *research* or *study*, as in, "Smith conducted an empirical study." To the best of our understanding, Meehl meant some formal method of data collection meeting reasonable standards of rigor, and not just casual observation.

Developing Statistical Decision Methods

It is sometimes stated that statistical decision methods are difficult and time-consuming to develop, or that they require large samples. This may or may not be true depending on particulars and aims, and thus some discussion of methods for developing statistical decision methods may be useful. Before proceeding, however, we note that despite another common assertion—that the availability and scope of statistical decision procedures are limited or sparse—there are numerous procedures already available for a broad range of clinical tasks (see further under the subsequent heading, "Statistical Decision Methods Are Difficult to Develop and Often Are Unavailable for the Decision Task at Hand"). Hence, one wishing to use statistical decision procedures does not have to start from scratch and often can simply pick from among already available methods.

For purposes of illustration, suppose there is a clinic with five mental health professionals and a couple of support staff. The clinic experiences a high demand for services, but it has limited resources and offers a treatment program that usually requires steadfast compliance and completion to achieve positive outcomes. When treatment compliance is satisfactory, about 80% of the clients experience substantial therapeutic gains. For example, a program for decreasing exceptionally high levels of digital technology use or gaming associated with seriously compromised adaptive functioning may require at least 15 sessions, as well as the involvement of multidisciplinary staff and familial and community resources to achieve lasting and meaningful impact. The clinic treats about 200 clients a year. To date, the clinic has experienced nearly a 40% drop-out rate, and thus a considerable proportion of their work is yielding minimal benefit. Understandably, other considerations might be weighed or prioritized in selecting clients for treatment, but for the sake of the current illustration, assume the clinic strives to maximize positive impact. All potential clients are initially screened in a staffing conference during which the professional team members examine information carefully, discuss their impressions about likely treatment compliance openly and cooperatively, and work toward consensus. In this way, the clinic hopes to improve on the modest predictive success the screening achieves.

In seeking improvement, the clinicians start by compiling a list of factors they believe might affect compliance (e.g., the availability of ready transportation, initial indications of high treatment motivation, and social support). As aids to developing the pool of potential predictive variables, they also examine studies and meta-analyses that have examined drop-out rates and predictors in related programs. Ultimately, 10 potential predictors are selected. Moving forward, at the time each new client is screened, participating staff follow their routine judgment practices and provide a global rating of likely compliance with treatment. After that is completed, they rate the 10 variables for each client on a scale of 1 to 5, ranging from the lowest to highest likelihood of compliance (e.g., 1 = low or very low, 2 = somewhat below average, 3 = average, 4 = somewhat above average, and 5 = high or very high). Some of the ratings may be based on objective or largely objective determinations (e.g., scores on a depression scale), and other ratings may rest on staff member's subjective impressions (e.g., seeming level of enthusiasm for treatment). Filling out these 10 items might require only two or three minutes per client.

Suppose the clinic normally accepts 60% of their potential clients after the screening is completed. If the clinic initially follows its usual procedures for screening clients, then among those accepted for treatment, the drop-out rate will likely remain at about 40%. Suppose that as the ratings are completed, one also finds a fair to large degree of variability on a number of items, and perhaps on total ratings as well. (If that does not occur, other steps can be taken.) Once, say, 100 clients who have been accepted for treatment get to an end point (do or do not finish treatment), one can perform a statistical analysis of the relation between treatment compliance and standing on each item and score totals. With modern computing power, especially if ratings have been entered into a spread sheet initially, such analyses could be conducted in a few minutes or less. One might find that some items had no predictive value, whereas other items or item combinations achieved varying degrees of predictive accuracy. One could then compare the predictive power of the staff members' usual global ratings to the predictive power that might be achieved using the best items or combination of items.

If one sees no trends in the data, then it might be time to reconstitute the list or end the trial run, but if the trends are positive, the clinic might go forward and cross-validate the original results on the next 100 clients and see if similar outcomes are obtained. Ideally, one might conduct a study in which nearly all applicants are accepted into treatment for a period of time because, depending on the efficacy of the routine screening procedures, it could well be that a certain percentage of individuals who would normally not be selected for treatment are equal or better treatment candidates than a certain percentage who are selected. However, in many circumstances, this might not be a practical or ethically justifiable strategy.

To reiterate, all that is required is compiling a list of candidate variables (which might be readily available in published studies), performing quick ratings on clients in the course of routine meetings, and conducting statistical analyses that examine and compare the accuracy of the usual predictive judgments with items and various combinations of items drawn from the initial item list. For example, we may find that six of the items each added something to predictive accuracy, and that if we simply weighted each item equally and tallied up a total score, we could improve predictive accuracy by 15%. If a similar outcome was obtained with a second sample, we would have developed a statistical decision procedure or rating scale that could likely be applied effectively to subsequent treatment candidates. Additionally, if the rating scale could also help us identify individuals at greater risk for ending treatment prematurely, we may be able to design brief interventions (e.g., motivational interviews) that would move them toward greater treatment commitment.

Many variations in procedure can be used to develop statistical decision rules, but they almost all involve data collection, followed by analysis of standing on the collected information and some type of condition, status, or outcome (e.g., clinical diagnosis or differential diagnosis; treatment responsiveness; or likelihood of engaging in some type of risky behavior). Some of these statistical decision procedures may be relatively simple and inexpensive to develop, and others may require protracted effort, especially to refine and improve them or to determine how level of accuracy relates to sociodemographic or cultural variables. Sometimes the efforts yield only negligible improvement or fail completely, and sometimes they improve things substantially and are well worth the resources they require. However, to argue that statistical decision methods necessarily require large expenditures of time and resources and sizeable samples to achieve anything worthwhile is a mistaken overgeneralization. Further, once quality statistical decision procedures are developed, they often save time moving forward (although they need to be monitored constantly and may well need to be updated over time), and unlike a particular clinician's subjective judgment, statistical decision rules can be made available for other professionals to use.

RESEARCH OUTCOMES

Early Analyses and Reviews

Meehl's Review

When Meehl (1954) published the first edition of his book on clinical and statistical prediction, only a relatively small body of research was available to inform his efforts. Although some have stereotyped Meehl as anti-clinician, such assumptions belie Meehl's personal history and the contents of his book. Meehl certainly brought a rigorous and deep analytic mind to his efforts. However, at the same time, he was an admirer of Freud (or at least the descriptive elements of Freud's work, but less so the overriding theory). He also openly endorsed the potential value of therapeutic treatment, including his own, and was a practicing therapist for many years. He assiduously considered and described potential advantages of clinical judgment over statistical methods, with almost half of his book addressing that topic. As Meehl stated in the book's preface:

> I do not honestly think that I am on either side of this debate. . . . When the major components of this long-standing controversy are teased apart by methodological analysis, I believe one can say some fairly definitive things about them individually. When such definite positions are taken in defiance of clichés, toes are stepped on. Perhaps the most I can hope for is that I have stepped on clinical and statistical toes without favoritism. (p. vii)

What were those "fairly definitive things"? The literature to date showed that although clinical and statistical methods achieved similar accuracy at times, when there was a difference, the statistical method consistently outperformed the clinical method, and thus was superior overall. In his book and for a considerable period of time after its publication, Meehl raised concerns about limitations of the research and presented various possible or hypothetical exceptions to research outcomes, such as situations in which highly skilled clinicians might discern patterns in data that were not captured by usual statistical methods. Others also raised concerns about such issues as the representativeness of the judgment tasks examined in some of the studies (e.g., prediction of students' GPA), which seemed removed from usual clinical concerns, the expertise of the participating clinicians, and the adequacy of the information with which study participants were provided. These were all legitimate issues requiring careful evaluation.

The hundreds of studies that have been conducted since Meehl's original publication have addressed these and other points, and although certain questions remain, the fundamental findings have been confirmed and even strengthened (Ægisdóttir et al., 2006; Grove et al., 2000). As more and more research evidence piled up that consistently ran counter to various possible exceptions Meehl had raised, he eventually concluded that the case for finding systematic exceptions to the overall superiority of statistical methods was increasingly untenable.

Before we begin a more detailed look at this body of research, its potential significance, and the ways it can be applied to improve prediction and consequently the quality of clinical services, we wish to emphasize the positive side of the outcomes. On the one hand, it may be unsettling to be equaled or outperformed on a professional decision task by an algorithm or statistical formula. (Who rooted for the steam drill over John Henry?) On the other hand, the effectiveness of statistical procedures is hardly a threat to most core activities clinicians perform, such as developing meaningful empathic connections with clients. Further, the development of statistical methods shines a favorable light on human proficiency and ingenuity, although some of the credit may need to be redirected. Finally, and perhaps most importantly, improved diagnostic and predictive accuracy can enhance human welfare.

Readjusting self-impressions about our relative proficiencies in certain domains is a small cost to pay for preventing an avoidable suicide or protecting society from a dangerous individual, especially when recognizing that naturalistic conditions make accurate appraisal of our judgmental accuracy very difficult. Furthermore, better overall methods are not distant, hoped-for developments, but often are readily available. One might put it this way. In an emergency in which a section of railroad tracks had to be repaired as quickly as possible to rescue an isolated group from likely starvation, we probably wouldn't consider it a blow to human self-esteem if we called in a steam drill. When there are human problems to solve and improved methods available that can be disseminated broadly, that is hardly a reason to hang our heads.

Sawyer's Review

Sawyer's (1966) update of Meehl's review yielded conclusions that have largely remained unchanged over time and that offer important insights. Sawyer identified nearly 50 studies that provided 75 comparisons between different methods for interpreting or integrating information. In addition to comparing the clinical and statistical methods, Sawyer also looked at different sources of information provided to the methods, which he referred to as *variable* and *fixed.* However, across the studies, all variable sources of information were unstructured interviews and all fixed sources were tests, and thus we simply refer to them directly as such. Studies were not available that compared clinical and statistical judgment methods when structured interviews were used, a topic we address after covering Sawyer's main findings.

Following Meehl's stated conditions for a fair comparison, Sawyer examined relative accuracy when informational source was held constant, the sources again being either unstructured interviews or tests. Sawyer also examined comparisons in which both sources of information were available. For studies using unstructured interviews as a data source, interview impressions had been coded. For example, qualitative impressions can be dichotomized (e.g., 1 = absent, 2 = present) or placed on a continuum (e.g., 1 = not at all, 2 = slightly, 3 = moderately, 4 = considerably, 5 = extremely). In addition, contrary to Meehl's specifications for a fair comparison, Sawyer also included studies in which the clinical and statistical methods did not have access to the same information, such as when, for example, the clinical method had access to both unstructured interviews and tests and the statistical method had access to only one or the other source. Consequently, Sawyer could also examine the potential impact when one or the other method was placed at a potential informational advantage or disadvantage. All in all, Sawyer was able to examine eight different conditions, although we only list the first six conditions initially because the great majority of research was limited to these six. The six conditions appear in Table 8.1.

Sawyer's review generated remarkably consistent results. Although a number of the comparisons yielded no statistically significant differences between methods, when a difference appeared, there were no instances in which the same type of comparison generated inconsistent or conflicting outcomes. For example, when a specific comparison favored one method over the other method (e.g., the

Table 8.1. Six of the Conditions Included in Sawyer's Review

	Type of Data	Interpretive Method
1.	Interview	Clinical
2.	Interview	Statistical
3.	Test(s)	Clinical
4.	Test(s)	Statistical
5.	Interview and Test(s)	Clinical
6.	Interview and Test(s)	Statistical

statistical method surpassed the clinical method when tests were the data source, or conditions 3 versus 4, respectively), no other comparison of the same interpretive methods and same type of data source generated a contrary result (i.e., condition 3 exceeding condition 4). Other studies examining the same comparison might show that the methods tied, but no case yielded a converse result. Obtaining this level of consistency in research outcomes in psychology across numerous comparisons seems strikingly unusual.

Starting with comparisons in which both methods had access to the same data (interviews only, tests only, or interviews and tests), that is, when meeting Meehl's conditions for a fair comparison, Sawyer found that the statistical method always equaled or exceeded the clinical method. From there, moving to comparisons in which data sources varied, Sawyer also found, perhaps surprisingly, that the statistical method always equaled or exceeded the clinical method, even when the statistical method was placed at an informational disadvantage. Thus, when statistical methods had access to interviews alone, they equaled or exceeded clinical judgments based on tests; when statistical methods had access to tests alone, they equaled or exceeded clinical judgments based on interviews alone; and when statistical methods had access to either interviews alone or tests alone, they still equaled or exceeded clinical judgments when the latter was based on both sources of information. All these findings have changed minimally across the large volume of literature generated in this area in subsequent years (see the following heading, "Updates to the Literature").

Sawyer's review permits a rank ordering of the six methods by level of overall accuracy, as shown in Table 8.2, which proceeds from top to bottom from most to least accurate.

Although we are not aware of an applicable survey on the topic, we hypothesize that frequency of use across clinical settings shows a negative association with level of overall accuracy, given, among other things, surveys indicating that statistical decision methods are markedly underutilized or undervalued (Furman, 2005; Meyers, 2015; Vrieze & Grove, 2009). That possibility is sobering, but it also illuminates a straightforward path to improving predictive accuracy, which is to increase the use of validated statistical decision or data-integration methods. As Chapter 7 details extensively, subjective methods of complex data integration pose extreme problems that are commonly underappreciated. Such problems can be substantially mitigated in many instances by increased use of formally developed decision aids.

Table 8.2. Sawyer's Review: Rank Order of the Six Conditions

Most accurate	• Statistical interpretation of tests and interviews
↓	• Statistical interpretation of tests
	• Statistical interpretation of interviews
	• Clinical interpretation of tests
	• Clinical interpretation of tests and interviews
Least accurate	• Clinical interpretation of interviews

Sawyer's rank ordering of overall accuracy has other important implications. Perhaps most counterintuitive given pervasive or commonly accepted thinking on the topic, clinical interpretation based on tests alone equaled or exceeded clinical interpretation based on tests and interview data, or to state this a bit differently, when provided with less, rather than more, information, clinicians were more accurate overall. In contrast, statistical interpretation was most accurate overall when based on both test data and interview data. What conclusion can be drawn from the contrast in level of accuracy across the clinical and statistical methods when varying levels of information are available?

The gain in overall accuracy when statistical methods are used and interview information is added to test data shows that interviews generate useful data that may not be elicited in other ways. Hence, the arch-critic who views interviews as a waste of time or worse is overgeneralizing and overlooking contrary evidence. Additionally, we wish to restate that Sawyer's review did not include structured interviews (which were far less developed at that time), and thus it could well have underestimated the utility of certain interview methods. However, it seems clear that when unstructured interviews are the main informational source and are interpreted impressionistically or using clinical judgment, the overall level of accuracy will often fall below that of other data integration methods, and perhaps short, or well short, of their commonly perceived utility. Further, when clinical judgment is used, one may do as well or better with test information alone. Adding unstructured interview data to test data, when it makes a difference, will generally move one in the wrong direction. The differing impact of adding interview data to test data when one relies on clinical versus statistical decision methods is of particular interest and raises important issues.

If adding interview data to test data decreases overall accuracy when clinical judgment is used but enhances accuracy when statistical methods are used, then clinical methods must not be utilizing interview data as effectively as statistical methods. More so, if adding interview data diminishes the overall accuracy of clinical judgments, then interview information is likely being misused more often than it is being properly utilized. This negative outcome again shows that what is often assumed or taken for granted—that additional information can only help—is extreme and subject to exceptions. Such a belief is not only flawed because some information can be invalid or worse than neutral, but also because information may not be used effectively. Here, the problem is not that interview data routinely lack value, but originates from the difficulties we often have separating truly valuable data from less useful or even invalid data, as discussed at length in Chapter 7. Research on topics like illusory correlation, covariation analysis, and clinical and statistical judgment is testament to the challenges involved in distinguishing stronger data from weaker or invalid data, and in integrating complex information using impressionistic or subjective judgment. Thus, for example, an interview impression of, say, flat affect may have considerable value. However, the value of that impression can be more than offset by impressions about other characteristics that have less predictive utility or that, given their salience, may sway judgment and override more accurate predictive variables.

At least two other points can be drawn from Sawyer's seminal review and from subsequent research on clinical and statistical decision methods. First, in various studies, even rudimentary statistical decision methods equaled or surpassed clinical judgment methods. For example, predictions based on just a few variables or even a single strong variable may equal or surpass the accuracy of subjective judgments. We do not relish making this point, but it has potentially critical ramifications for evaluating and developing statistical decision methods. In particular, before we reject a decision method because it seems too simplistic, we probably should check on literature to see how such methods compare to impressionistic or clinical judgments. Further, as discussed, a common objection to statistical decision methods is that they are very difficult to develop, and yet simple methods often can be created with limited resources and time and still may well provide advantages over unaided judgment.

Second, we can now consider the two other conditions that Sawyer examined and which we have not yet covered. In one of these conditions, which we refer to as *statistical synthesis,* conclusions based on clinical judgment were added as a potential variable or predictor for statistical decision methods. When one is developing statistical methods, one often enters multiple potential predictive variables that might have value or that one wants to examine, and then ascertains whether predictive accuracy has improved. In a properly developed statistical decision procedure, if analyses ultimately show that a variable is helpful, it is usually included in the predictive method (although not always, because, for example, it may produce little benefit, it may be resource intensive, or stronger predictors may be available). In contrast, if a variable adds nothing or diminishes accuracy, it is generally excluded.

Sawyer uncovered only a modest body of literature examining statistical synthesis. In no such comparison did adding clinical conclusions as a predictor significantly increase the accuracy of statistical decision methods over the level they achieved without this variable. Again, such outcomes do not negate the potential value of information that clinical interviews or observations can yield when included in statistical prediction methods. What the research does raise serious questions about is how much clinical judgments or conclusions contribute to accuracy beyond statistical prediction methods alone.

In the last condition Sawyer examined, which we refer to as *clinical synthesis,* researchers provided clinicians with the outcome of statistical decision procedures. The clinicians were free to use or not use that information as they saw fit. For example, on a dichotomous decision task, if the statistical decision method generated a conclusion that disagreed with the one they had reached through their clinical judgment, they could retain or revise their original conclusion. This condition and related variations have also been described as a clinical-actuarial approach, given the blend of the two interpretive methods.

Meehl referred to circumstances in which a clinician might or should reject a statistically based prediction as *broken leg* examples. He described a situation in which an individual regularly attended movies on Fridays, and thus one forecasting this individual's behavior for the next Friday would likely be correct by predicting attendance. (Base rates are often a core element of statistical prediction methods.) Of course, unusual or rare events can occur that are not accounted for by statistical methods. In Meehl's scenario, the individual breaks a leg not long before the upcoming Friday, which would probably result in an erroneous prediction if one follows the statistical method. Identifying possible exceptions is an important, if not crucial, concern. Even when statistical prediction exceeds clinical judgment, statistical methods may still make errors in a considerable percentage of cases. For example, clinical predictions might be correct 60% of the time and statistical predictions 70% of the time. Of course, there is benefit in reducing a 40% error rate to 30%, but 30% error, especially if one is dealing with potentially serious matters, such as a propensity for violent behavior, is far from desirable. Hence, it would be beneficial to have some way of identifying exceptions to statistical predictions, and thereby reduce the error rate as much as possible.

Sawyer found very limited research on broken leg examples, but what he did uncover suggested that clinicians defer to their own judgment over statistical decision methods too often, and consequently do not do better, and may do worse, than they would have had they uniformly followed statistical decision procedures. Since that time, the literature on possible broken legs has expanded, but it remains limited and mostly addresses a relatively narrow but important range of topics in psychology and law, such as the likelihood of violent behavior or reoffending.

Studies on countervailing suggest that decision makers with access to statistical decision methods countervail them in a considerable percentage of cases (e.g., 25% of the time or more), with one study (Schmidt et al., 2016) obtaining a rate of over 70%! Lower rates of countervailing may be found in settings in which doing so (especially more than occasionally) is strongly discouraged. Studies on countervailing conducted after Sawyer's review have also generally yielded negative results. The studies suggest that, at best, countervailing statistical decision methods (as opposed to strict adherence to statistical outcomes) does not improve accuracy, but at least does not decrease it. However, the usual impact is not neutral, but rather to degrade accuracy. The decline is sometimes small to modest, but it can be substantial, even dropping hit rates from relatively favorable levels to chance levels (Epperson & Gore, 2004; Girard, 1999; Girard & Wormith, 2004; Gore, 2008; Guay & Parent, 2018; Krauss, 2004; Schmidt et al., 2016; Storey et al., 2012; Wormith et al., 2012).

Beyond the studies directly examining the ability to identify exceptions, many of the numerous studies comparing clinical and statistical decision methods touch on the issue of countervailing. Assumedly, a significant number of clinicians in those studies who evaluated data sources like tests for which validated decision procedures were available would know the conclusions indicated by adherence to those methods. For example, for a test like the original Minnesota Multiphasic Personality Inventory (MMPI) and its updated versions, various statistical decision procedures are well known and easily applied (e.g., if one observes a score above a certain level on the F scale, then . . .). In such situations, clinicians could adopt the conclusion indicated by strict adherence to formally validated interpretive guidelines or instead countervail the conclusion. Not only Sawyer's review, but also the hundreds of subsequent studies in psychology on clinical versus statistical judgment have generated nearly uniform outcomes showing that the accuracy of statistical decision procedures almost always equals or exceeds that of clinical judgment methods. It is not even clear whether the percentage of studies in psychology that have generated potential exceptions to this general finding exceeds the expected Type 1 (false-positive) error rate (see Ægisdóttir et al., 2006; Dawes et al., 1989; Grove et al., 2000).

We are not advocating a decision policy in which one mindlessly defers to statistical decision rules, and the number of direct studies on countervailing is insufficient to draw precise conclusions or to thoroughly explore possible exceptions. Nonetheless, the available research on countervailing and the large volume of general studies comparing clinical and statistical judgment clearly suggest that clinicians countervail statistical decision procedures regularly or frequently. One might also consider that, to the extent clinicians' judgments and the statistical decision procedure agree, it is only in instances of disagreement that one can countervail. Thus, for example, if the two agree in, say, 60% of cases, and one finds a rate of countervailing that falls at something like 20% overall, the clinician is countervailing one of every two cases in which disagreement occurs. Keeping this consideration in mind, studies showing rates of countervailing that equal or well exceed 25% across cases as a whole may reflect decision policies in which clinical judgment is often, or almost nearly always, selected over statistically based outcomes.

Given the frequency with which countervailing occurs, it is of considerable importance to examine the ultimate impact of these practices. The research findings are clear. Countervailing rarely seems to bolster overall success and, contrary to the best intentions, is considerably more likely to decrease overall accuracy relative to levels achieved by relying on statistical decision rules with greater consistency. Thus, for every incorrect statistically based conclusion corrected by countervailing, there is at least one, and often more than one, correct statistically based decision that is spoiled or converted to error. This is not a "philosophical" point or position; it is merely a matter of math. If countervails were more often correct than incorrect, clinicians in the studies would be beating statistical decision rules regularly, but that is not what occurs.

Updates to the Literature

Various sources provide literature updates (Ægisdóttir et al., 2006; Dawes et al., 1989; Grove et al., 2000; Grove & Meehl, 1996; Meehl, 1996). Both Ægisdóttir et al. (2006) and Grove et al. (2000) performed extensive meta-analyses. The two meta-analyses overlap substantially, although Ægisdóttir and colleagues included literature from only the mental health field, whereas Grove at al. also included studies from medicine, the latter of which made up a minority of the overall body of literature they examined. A summary of accuracy rates appears in Table 8.3, which we created based on the two meta-analyses. Table 8.3 is limited to studies that provided hit rates. For the Grove et al. (2000) meta-analysis, we also eliminated medical studies and only included research addressing judgments in

Table 8.3. Summary of Accuracy Rates in Studies for Which Grove et al. (2000) and Ægisdóttir et al. (2006) Provided Hit Rates

Grove et al. (2000)		
	Percentage of Studies	
Level of Accuracy	Clinical Method	Statistical Method
.80–.99	6%	17%
.60–.79	60%	58%
.50–.59	19%	17%
.49 or lower	15%	8%
Ægisdóttir et al. (2006)		
	Percentage of Studies	
Level of Accuracy	Clinical Method	Statistical Method
.80–.99	3%	20%
.60–.79	60%	61%
.50–.59	29%	17%
.49 or lower	9%	2%

the mental health field. Consequently, the figures in Table 8.3 do not represent all the studies in the respective meta-analyses. However, a large percentage of the studies that addressed the mental health field are included, because most of them did report hit rates.

As one can see by examining Table 8.3, and consistent with Sawyer's review, the far larger volume of research that Grove et al. (2000) had available at the time of their work also demonstrated the overall superiority of the statistical method over the clinical method. Although ties between the methods occurred fairly often, when there was a difference in efficacy, the statistical method exceeded the clinical method in the great majority of instances. Grove et al. also found that when interview data were added to other data sources, the actuarial advantage over the clinical method increased, which again tends to rebut a common assertion that the clinicians in the comparative studies were disadvantaged by limiting their access to information.

Ægisdóttir et al.'s (2006) meta-analysis included more studies in the mental health field than Grove et al. given Ægisdóttir et al.'s later publication date. The studies cover a wide range of judgment tasks, such as diagnosis, prognosis, treatment length, and the prediction of suicide attempts. As shown in Table 8.3, Ægisdóttir et al.'s meta-analysis also demonstrated the overall superiority of the statistical method over the clinical method, with the Ægisdóttir et al. meta-analysis producing a slightly greater advantage than Grove et al. reported.

Ægisdóttir et al. also examined whether clinicians performed better when they had access to information gathered in their own practice settings. Just the opposite circumstance occurs in many judgment studies because clinicians are asked to evaluate information drawn from settings other than their own. One might hypothesize that using information from one's own setting would tap into the potential benefits of direct experience with similar individuals and local knowledge, and thereby improve clinical judgment and reduce or reverse the statistical advantage. However, the results did not support this possibility and, if anything, showed a trend toward decreased judgmental accuracy. One possible explanation is that increased familiarity with clientele may have increased tendencies to rely on subjective impressions and diminished tendencies to prioritize formally established relationships.

The relative advantage of statistical over clinical or impressionistic methods and the benefit of statistical methods in reducing error gain immediacy when examining Table 8.3. Across the two meta-analyses, if one considers the highest category for level of accuracy, the respective percentages for the statistical and clinical methods fall at 17% versus 6% and at 20% versus 3%. Thus, the frequency with which the statistical versus the clinical method achieves the highest level of accuracy is about three times greater in the Grove et al. (2000) meta-analysis and about seven times greater in the Ægisdóttir et al. (2006) meta-analysis. Although not included in Table 8.3, both meta-analyses showed that the statistical method generated a considerably greater percentage of outcomes falling within the .70 to .79 level of accuracy: 45% versus 30% in the Grove meta-analysis and 35% versus 18% in the Ægisdóttir et al. meta-analysis. Thus, taken together, the respective percentage of studies that fall at or above the .70 level for the statistical versus clinical methods is 62% versus 36% for the Grove meta-analysis and 55% versus 21% for the Ægisdóttir et al. meta-analysis.

Conversely, when one looks at the lowest level of accuracy (which for studies involving dichotomous choices falls below chance level), the respective percentages for the clinical method versus the statistical method are about twice higher in the Grove meta-analysis and about four times higher in the Ægisdóttir et al. meta-analysis. (Although these trends might seem clear, the relatively low number of outcomes falling within the lowest level of accuracy make these results rather tenuous.) Unlike Grove et al., whose figures were about equal, Ægisdóttir et al. also found that the clinical method generated almost 60% more outcomes falling within the second lowest level of accuracy, or at .50 to .59.

It is worth considering how these differences in accuracy might translate to practical consequences in applied settings. For example, assume that a statistical method reduces error by 10% to 15% compared to clinical judgment. Perhaps even a figure of 15% does not sound like all that much, but assume the clinical method produces a 70% accuracy rate and a 30% error rate. A 15% change would cut error from 30% to 15%, or in half. Over the course of a career, or across practitioners at a busy practice on an annual basis, this difference can translate into hundreds more correct decisions and hundreds fewer mistakes, or even thousands more correct decisions when one realizes one often must formulate multiple judgments for many clients. One can project the differences this might make in ultimate outcomes and human welfare when one is performing tasks like risk assessment or advising others how it should be performed, assisting in crucial treatment choices, or consulting regularly with a parole board. Taken together, the potential benefits accrued by the relatively simple step of using statistical decision methods more often would seem to make them attractive potential options that can help practitioners better fulfill their laudable goals of assisting others and enhancing human welfare.

Structured Professional Judgment

Before moving on to common concerns and misconceptions about statistical decision methods, we wish to briefly address what is usually referred to as *structured professional judgment* (SPJ). SPJ approaches emerged primarily from forensic psychology, and they are commonly aimed at improving judgments about such matters as risk for reoffending or violent behavior, and treatment selection and design. Descriptions and guidelines for SPJ vary, but the method primarily addresses the input end of decision making, or the variables to consider when formulating decisions, and less so the methods for combining or integrating information. Decision makers are provided with specified items, such as variables to consider when appraising level of risk. Procedures for identifying those variables differ across approaches, and they may rest primarily on research examining validity, or they could include some mix of the former as well as the developer's professional judgments or impressions about the utility of variables. Decision makers may also be encouraged to consider other variables they deem important, or to take into account contextual or dynamic factors, such as recent and immediate circumstances that might modify appraisals based on more static dimensions (e.g., a history of substance abuse or repeat offending). Often, rather than specifying a level of probability, decision makers place individuals into categories of risk, such as very low, low, medium, high, and very high. SPJ does not direct decision makers to use formal statistical procedures to reach conclusions or to integrate information. Rather, SPJ is commonly described as an alternative to such formal approaches, and it often encourages decision makers to consider modifying conclusions stemming from statistical decision methods, and perhaps to do so freely.

One can see certain appealing features of SPJ approaches and potential benefits. To the extent SPJ focuses decision makers on variables of established validity, it has the potential to improve judgments, especially when individuals might not be aware of such variables or do not consider them routinely. A body of literature, such as that reviewed by Grove et al. (2000), indicates that increasing the level of structure or uniformity in information gathering often enhances judgmental accuracy.

However, the SPJ approach frequently leaves much to individual discretion in deciding what information to gather or to consider beyond suggested variables, and sometimes it actively encourages decision makers to add variables as they deem fit. Leaving such decisions open or unstructured creates a clear possibility that weak or invalid variables will influence appraisals, and that the outcomes of statistical decision procedures will be disregarded or overturned too frequently, thereby decreasing accuracy. Research reviewed thus far, such as investigations of covariation analysis and Chapman and Chapman's (1969) classic studies on illusory correlation (see Chapter 3), has shown both how difficult it can be to appraise the presence or degree of association between variables and the susceptibility of even professional decision makers to drawing erroneous conclusions about the predictive power of variables. In addition, given the aforementioned poor track record in studies looking at countervailing statistically-based outcomes or trying to identify so-called broken legs, placing little or no boundaries on calling exceptions, or even encouraging it, is worrisome. Finally, negative reactions to formal statistical decision methods that are not hard to find in publications on SPJ can lead one to question whether some SPJ approaches emerged from resistance to the constraints of statistical decision procedures and the desire to maintain a certain level of autonomy.

Appraising SPJ approaches can be complex because of variations in prescribed procedures, common misunderstandings about statistical decision methods (e.g., the distinction between types of data and types of methods for data integration), and a substantial number of studies that do not provide the same information to the competing decision methods, or even the same case materials at all. For example, the accuracy of clinicians evaluating a series of cases using some variation of SPJ might be compared to the accuracy of another group of clinicians evaluating a different series of cases using an alternative decision method. Such complications notwithstanding, in studies comparing clinical judgment, SPJ, and statistical decision making, overall rankings from highest to lowest are as follows: statistical decision making, then SPJ, then clinical judgment (see Hanson & Morton-Bourgon, 2009; Mossman, 1994; Vogel et al., 2004). Also, as one commonly finds in the general literature comparing clinical and statistical decision methods, ties in accuracy are not unusual, but when there is a difference, it typically runs in the same direction.

In Vogel et al.'s (2004) study on the appraisal of general and violent reoffending, for example, SPJ and statistical decision methods achieved similar results, and both surpassed the clinical method. In contrast, in Hanson and Morton-Bourgon's extensive meta-analysis that combined the results of over 100 studies on recidivism risk among sexual offenders, they found that SPJ methods generally exceeded clinical methods, but that statistical methods had a clear advantage over SPJ. The effect sizes obtained for the three methods and three areas of appraisal are shown in Table 8.4. As is evident in the table, when compared to clinical judgment, SPJ obtained similar effectiveness in one category and exceeded the clinical method in two categories, but the statistical method was considerably stronger than SPJ, and especially clinical judgment, in all three categories. If one considers the importance of predicting recidivism, particularly in such areas as sexual and violent

Table 8.4. Comparative Effect Size for Clinical Judgment, Structured Professional Judgment, and the Statistical Method (Vogel et al., 2004)

Outcome Predicted	Category of Decision Method		
	Clinical	SPJ	Statistical
Repeated Sexual Offense	.42	.46	.67
Repeated Violent Offense	.22	.31	.51
Recidivism in General	.11	.26	.52

offenses, then examination of the last row is of particular relevance. An effect size of .11, as found with the clinical method, will likely result in poor judgment performance. An effect size of .26 is an improvement, but it will still probably lead to many errors. An effect size of .52, although still well below what we would like, will very likely achieve considerably greater success than an effect size of .26, and especially .11. It is not possible to calculate accuracy rates directly from these figures. However, when one progresses, for example, from an effect size of .11 to .52, error rate is likely to decrease substantially, including errors that can have dire consequences.

Given the benefits of maximizing accuracy, then, all else being equal, statistical decision making seems to be preferable to SPJ, and SPJ preferable to clinical judgment. The literature favoring statistical methods over clinical judgment is overwhelming, whereas the literature favoring statistical methods over SPJ is less extensive and arguably not as uniform. However, as the bulk of literature indicates an overall superiority for statistical methods over SPJ, it would seem that those advocating SPJ as the better method bear the burden of proof.

BASES FOR THE STATISTICAL METHOD'S OVERALL ADVANTAGE

When properly developed and applied, statistical decision methods represent a triumph in human prowess that enhances human welfare. Their advantage over subjective judgment methods can be traced to the amplification in unaided human judgment that properly designed decision methods offer. As is emphasized in Chapter 7, optimizing the integration of large or complex data sets subjectively is extremely challenging. Such integration requires one to determine as precisely as possible the strength of association between variables, the extent of overlap or redundancy across variables, and, in some cases, the weights to assign to predictive variables. Meehl's (1986) classic comment on this matter was:

> Surely we all know that the human brain is poor at weighting and computing. When you check out at the supermarket, you don't eyeball the heap of purchases and say to the clerk, "Well, it looks to me as if it's about $17.00 worth; what do you think?" The clerk adds it up. There are no strong arguments . . . from empirical studies . . . for believing that human beings can assign optimal weights to equations subjectively or that they apply their own weights optimally. (p. 372)

And as Dawes et al. (1989) later added:

> It might be objected that this analogy, offered not probatively but pedagogically, presupposes an additive model that a proponent of configural judgment will not accept. Suppose instead that the supermarket pricing rule were, "Whenever both beef and fresh vegetables are involved, multiply the

> logarithm of .78 of the meat price by the square root of twice the vegetable price." Would the clerk and customer eyeball that any better? Worse, almost certainly. When human judges perform poorly at estimating and applying the parameters of a simple or component mathematical function, they should not be expected to do better when required to weight a complex composite of these variables. (p. 1672)

These quotations also speak to the potential advantages of quantification and effective methods for combining and analyzing data. This is not to argue for the blind use of numbers, but surely in an array of situations, quantification (which can also accommodate qualitative information via coding) and formal methods for analyzing data can provide a substantial edge. If one is trying to determine such things as whether two variables interact across a large multi-dimensional data set, just how large an effect size a predictive variable might possess, or the level of redundancy across promising predictors—information commonly needed to build maximally effective decision procedures—formal data analytic methods are usually indispensable. And it seems specious to argue that the development of such methods reflects negatively on human capacity given the ingenuity and brain power needed to extend human reach through such innovations.

When properly developed, statistical decision methods include or exclude variables based on their demonstrated predictive utility and relation to the outcome of interest. For example, decision procedures based on multiple regression procedures are designed to weed out nonpredictive variables and retain valid predictors. Also, these methods often incorporate both the four cells of a covariation table (or use related approaches) when examining relations among variables, and base rates when analyzing the properties of predictive variables and potential combinations of predictive variables. For example, one can easily study the percentage of cases in which a potential sign or symptom occurs when a condition is present versus when it is absent. If it turns out that a true association exists, that variable may be incorporated into a statistical decision rule if it enhances the level of accuracy achieved without it or demonstrates incremental validity. As discussed previously, a valid but relatively weaker variable may diminish accuracy when added to stronger variables, which again can be very difficult to appraise using clinical or subjective judgment.

Finally, statistical decision procedures always yield the same outcome given the same set of data (unless some technical glitch occurs). We are not suggesting that these outcomes are perfectly accurate, which is often far from the case, or that potential exceptions should not be considered, but merely that the decision procedure itself is perfectly consistent. In contrast, human judges can exhibit random variation in decision making when factors like fatigue, momentary inattention, or order of case exposure sway judgment. To the extent that cues or variables possess validity, introducing noise or random fluctuations in judgment will decrease overall accuracy. For example, if a score on a valid test has a 75% chance of being correct but the test is mis-scored, than more often than not when that error changes judgment, a correct decision will be spoiled rather than an incorrect decision rectified.

CLEARING UP SOME COMMON MISUNDERSTANDINGS

Type of Data versus Type of Decision Method

Many writings on statistical or actuarial decision making (terms we are using interchangeably) conflate type of information with the type of method used to integrate information. Meehl's central focus was on the effectiveness of different methods for reaching decisions or integrating information, and not on the type of data being combined. However, some authors refer to actuarial or objective data, such as a test score, and believe that using such data qualifies a method as actuarial. Such practices can create confusion on multiple levels. Even if one is using objective data, one can still combine or integrate this information using either clinical judgment or statistical decision methods. For example, a neuropsychologist examining various scores on a test battery might combine them using clinical judgment, or, alternatively, using statistical decision methods.

Similarly, one can combine subjective data using clinical judgment or statistical methods (when available). For example, one might use a radiologist's impressions of x-ray features, code them as present or absent or using a Likert-type rating scale, and then incorporate them into a statistical decision procedure. In other situations, a combination of objective and subjective data might be used (as could be the case with the neuropsychologist referenced above), but that practice sets no constraint on the method used for integrating data (so long as subjective data is coded). Thus, (1) the type of information used and (2) the decision method used to combine information should be clearly distinguished from one another, and labeling a method as actuarial based on the former—the type of information used—often leads to confusion and questionable claims. For example, suppose someone claims a particular study demonstrates an actuarial advantage over clinical methods, but the only variable examined was type of data. Consequently, the study is really showing something else, at least if one is asserting something about different judgment methods or thinks one is addressing the core issue that Meehl raised. We are not contending that type of information is irrelevant or unimportant, only that type of information and type of method for combining information should not be confused with one another. This leads to the second common point of confusion, described next.

Fallacy: Statistical Decision Methods Address Only "Objective" Outcomes

In various situations, one is primarily interested in predicting subjective judgments or reactions, such as whether someone will like a certain wine, coworkers will like a new employee, or a young physician will have good bedside manner or typically make positive impressions on patients. Therefore, rather than predicting, for example, whether or not some event will occur, such as reoffending, one is trying to predict subjective reactions or impressions. We recognize that the boundaries between objective outcomes and subjective states or conditions can become blurry or take on varying degrees of ambiguity, as might be the case when trying to determine the presence or absence of an abnormal mood state. However, in many cases there is a meaningful and clear difference between objective and subjective outcomes, such as when one is evaluating whether palpating the skull led to an accurate identification of fracture (when compared to advanced imaging) as opposed to how often a physician strikes others as arrogant or how much a person likes yellow socks. Depending on one's focus, either objective or subjective outcomes may be of greatest interest. For example, if one is trying to design clothing that potential buyers find attractive, then an issue about the atomic structure of yellow socks versus red socks may be of far less interest than buyers' reactions.

Studies show that much like the overall edge statistical methods have in predicting objective outcomes, events, or conditions, statistical methods also do as well or better than clinical judgment in predicting subjective phenomena or reactions. An interesting example emerges from the vineyard and involves wine tasting or perceived wine quality. Once the process of producing wines is complete, one may find good consensus among experts about wine quality and pricing. However, if one can predict ultimate outcome or subjective appraisal of taste earlier in the process, a considerable financial advantage may result. As it turns out, the ability to make accurate predictions at earlier phases of production can be difficult and fraught with error, even for presumed wine experts. In contrast, statistical prediction based mainly on climate conditions during the growing season often outperforms experts (see Ashenfelter et al., 1995; Ashenfelter & Corsi, 2001). Studies reporting these outcomes led to vociferous protests. The *New York Times* (Passell, 1990) headline declared as the controversy unfolded, "Wine Equation Puts Some Noses out of Joint." As described in the article, one highly influential wine critic called the results "ludicrous and absurd," which, compared to some other reactions, might be considered reserved.

Fallacy: Statistical Decision Methods Always Exceed Clinical Judgment

Those who criticize statistical judgment sometimes make counterfactual claims about its relative effectiveness (e.g., that the combination of clinical and statistical methods is clearly superior), whereas those who advocate for statistical methods sometimes make obverse errors. For example, a proponent might claim that actuarial methods almost always exceed clinical methods, which is clearly false because in many of the studies the methods tie or do not show a statistically significant difference. The following is part of a memo that Meehl sent one of the authors. The second question mark that appears below (and was in the original memo), and which follows the phrase, "actuarial instruments," was placed there to reflect the failure to distinguish between types of information and methods for combining information, as we already discussed. Meehl (personal communication, 2000) stated:

> Does [an eminent professor who will go unnamed] send you all of his stuff? In [a publication], they assert that actuarial instruments (?) repeatedly shown more accurate than clinical judgment, instead of equal or greater. As bad as some of our students. Ouf! [It] bothers me not only by the scholarly carelessness shown, but from a "political" . . . standpoint. Makes it easy for muddlers to accuse the actuarial side of the debate of bias and shading the evidence. Do you think there's a way to cure him of this?

The frequency of ties, however, should not obscure the overall superiority of statistical prediction. When a difference appears between the methods, the statistical method almost always exceeds the clinical method, with some of the differences being sizeable, especially when concentrated effort has been directed toward further refining and improving statistical methods. However, to claim that the statistical method always outperforms the clinical method promulgates a falsehood and undercredits clinicians and clinical judgment. The latter error might be especially important in situations in which no statistical methods are available and one has to decide whether or not to go with clinical judgment.

Fallacy: Computer-Based Test Interpretation Necessarily Equals Statistical Prediction

As previously discussed, the two defining features of statistical prediction methods are: (1) the use of pre-specified or set interpretive methods that eliminate subjective judgment (such that the same data always lead to the same result), and (2) decision procedures based on established empirical relationships. Computer-based test interpretation (CBTI) often fails to meet the second condition. CBTI programs are set or unvarying (i.e., they meet the first condition), but they are usually based on an expert's (or experts') interpretive judgments. Although the interpretive procedures may draw extensively from scientific literature, they ultimately rest substantially on the expert's own reasoning or data integration. Thus, they may be based mainly on the expert's personal methods for integrating data or represent some hybrid of subjective judgment and statistically based methods. As such, they do not meet Meehl's definition of the statistical decision method.

When appraising CBTI in this context, one might consider the body of research indicating that when decision makers are free to accept or reject actuarial outcomes, their accuracy typically does not increase and, if anything, declines, when compared to outcomes achieved by strict adherence to statistically based decision methods. Given these research findings, it is hard to justify using CBTI that relies primarily on clinical judgment or some mixture of clinical and statistical methods over statistical methods alone, to the extent the latter are available. Additionally, CBTI often includes passages that encourage users to accept or reject interpretive statements as they see fit, adding another layer of subjective judgment. (Again, we definitely are not suggesting that statistical decision methods should never be questioned or rejected, only that countervailing such outcomes seems to occur too frequently and should be limited to unusual circumstances—see Chapter 13.) Furthermore, information provided by publishers about the extent to which CBTI programs rest on formal decision procedures as opposed to expert or subjective judgment may be far from sufficient, impeding attempts to evaluate the quality of their products.

SOME COMMON OBJECTIONS

Crummy Criteria

A sizeable minority of judgment studies have used methods for forming criterion groups or evaluating the accuracy of decisions that likely contain substantial error and thus make it hard to judge just how often clinicians' (i.e., study participants') conclusions or the output of statistical decision methods are right or wrong. For example, in a study comparing the accuracy of statistical and clinical decision methods for diagnosing depression, the separation of research participants into a depressed and a nondepressed group in the first place may itself be based on subjective appraisals of questionable accuracy. The result may well be to cast doubt on study outcomes. If the initial separation of individuals into groups is prone to error, how is one to know when or how often classifications generated by the statistical or clinical method are actually correct? For example, Dr. Psychologist, who has volunteered for the study, classifies the person from the first case as depressed and the person from the second case as not depressed, with the statistical method generating converse conclusions for both cases. How do we know how each method is doing if the original classification of cases is ambiguous or highly ambiguous? The level of uncertainty resulting from ambiguous benchmarks for correct and incorrect judgments in various studies comparing clinical and statistical decision methods has raised understandable concerns.

As so often seems to have been the case, after thoughtful concerns emerged during earlier phases of research on clinical and actuarial decision making, subsequent studies addressing these issues have not altered the original findings and, if anything, have tended to strengthen them. Over time, many studies have involved outcomes with reduced levels of ambiguity compared to various earlier studies, such as the occurrence of violent behavior in inpatient settings, the presence or absence of brain disorder as verified through advanced imaging methods, or, in the medical literature, length of survival following a specific diagnosis. Of course, even these outcomes may be subject to some degree of ambiguity or the influence of undetected or random factors, but they are often far less prone to error than what at times were vague and ever-changing psychiatric diagnoses. As shown in previously referenced reviews and meta-analyses (Ægisdóttir et al., 2006; Grove et al., 2000; Sawyer, 1966), studies incorporating less ambiguous criteria yield the same general outcomes (statistical methods almost always equaling or surpassing clinical judgment).

On a conceptual level, to the extent outcome criteria are uncertain or contain error, then so long as those errors do not systematically favor a certain outcome, they are likely to diminish the differences between a stronger method and a weaker method. Imagine a 100-yard dash in which each runner races separately. One runner is better than all of the other runners, but only by a small margin. If a stopwatch is faulty and can err by a few tenths of a second in either direction, with errors occurring in each direction with similar frequency, the chances it will misidentify a slower runner as the faster runner will be greater than would be the case with a more accurate stopwatch.

Likewise, suppose one is comparing how well clinical and statistical decision methods differentiate between individuals with and without posttraumatic stress disorder (PTSD). If the original assignments of individuals into a PTSD-present and a PTSD-absent group contain, say, 20% error in the first place, then the chances of detecting possible differences in judgmental accuracy across decision methods is diminished relative to the probability of assignments that contained minimal error. More specifically, as errors in original group assignment mount, there will likely be a corresponding increase in the number of times the stronger method generates a correct classification that is misidentified as an error, and the weaker method generates an incorrect classification that is misidentified as a correct classification. To illustrate this point, take the hypothetical extreme. Suppose the original classification into criterion groups contains 100% error. Further suppose that in actuality, a statistical decision method has an 80% accuracy rate and a clinical method a 60% accuracy rate. Given 100% misidentification in the criterion groups, every time either decision method produces a classification that is actually accurate, it will be identified as an error, and every time the methods produce a classification that is actually erroneous, it will be identified as accurate. The result will be a supposed 20% accuracy rate for the statistical method and a supposed 40% accuracy rate for the clinical method. As this extreme illustration shows, as error in original assignment to criterion groups increases, then so long as it is not systematic, it tends to work against uncovering true differences between methods. Thus, although criterion groups in various studies have contained more error than one would like, this tends to work against the stronger overall method, and studies in which more certain criteria have been used have not overturned the actuarial advantage.

Nonrepresentative Tasks

A number of early studies involved judgments outside the scope of clinicians' typical applied activities or areas of expertise, such as the prediction of grade point average or success in specific occupations. However, other early studies, and many studies since then, have examined important applied activities, such as intervention and treatment planning/response, forensic psychologists' predictions of reoffending or violent behaviors, and neuropsychologists' ability to identify cognitive dysfunction. Much like outcomes over time with studies using less ambiguous criteria, studies on activities of clear clinical relevance have not overturned earlier results. Additionally, in areas in which concentrated efforts have been directed toward improving statistical decision methods, such as the prediction of violent acts, the actuarial advantage has tended to increase over time (see in particular Ægisdóttir et al., 2006).

Nonrepresentative Decision Makers, or "It Doesn't Apply to Me"

Two related, common objections to the research on clinical versus statistical decision methods are: (1) that clinicians who participated in the studies must not have been particularly competent or skilled, and that a more representative sample of clinicians or better clinicians would have performed differently; and (2) that although the research may apply to others or some others, it does not apply to me. Two anecdotes illustrate both of these positions. One of the authors, while still a student, gave a talk on decision research to a large group of seasoned psychologists and psychiatrists. In the question-and-answer period that followed, a highly respected audience member, who happened to be one of the author's supervisors, "asked" whether different outcomes would have occurred if studies included clinicians who performed at a level equivalent to chess grandmasters. The author responded that this was possible, and expressed the hope that audience members would be willing to participate in a study that offered a chance to display such skills, which in turn might generate insights that could help others bolster their proficiency. No audience member, including the questioner, took up the offer, and the moment passed without too much long-term damage to the author's career prospects. (Ironically, unbeknownst to the author, Paul Meehl happened to also be in the audience, and he later offered the author encouragement.)

In another case, this same author presented a study on neuropsychologists' evaluation of cognitive deficit that, unfortunately, showed a disconcerting rate of judgment error, even among highly experienced practitioners. A prominent member of the audience responded by stating that the study was [a word for excrement], and that the participating clinicians were not representative of practitioners as a whole. The author referred back to statistics that had been presented earlier showing that the education, training, and other credentials of the sizeable group of participating clinicians closely mirrored national figures. The audience member responded that top-tier clinicians were not included. The author then indicated that, as had been shown in one of the other slides, we had conducted a subanalysis of individuals with elite credentials, and that they had performed no differently than the group in general. In no case did the audience member cite any contrary literature, and after pausing, simply pronounced that "no one who participated in your study could have been competent." Thus, a study outcome congruent with a larger body of literature was dismissed based on this individual's belief that the study should have come out differently and, because it did not, it had to be flawed. One of our former colleagues, Robyn Dawes, a major contributor to decision literature, called this sort of position an argument in a vacuum, that is, dismissing evidence that exists for hypothetical evidence one thinks would exist if a study were done to their standards (or came out they way they thought it should turn out based on their subjective impressions about how things were).

The large body of literature comparing clinical and statistical decision making has included a broad array of psychologists, psychiatrists, and other mental health professionals. Some of the studies include students, some professionals relatively early in their careers, and others highly credentialed individuals. For example, Goldberg's classic work on MMPI interpretation (Goldberg, 1965, 1968) included a number of preeminent psychologists and leading experts on the measure. Nevertheless, across these studies and a wide range of participants, results are remarkably consistent in showing the overall superiority of the statistical method. In Goldberg's (1965, 1968) work, none of the 29 participating psychologists, including the most highly credentialed ones, surpassed a linear composite of five variables that weighted each variable equally and did not take interactions or configural relationships into account. Such outcomes do not negate various advantages that can be accrued by quality education and training, but once again strongly suggest that the key to predictive accuracy lies, at present, in the development and proper application of statistical decision methods.

Various other studies on clinical judgment have included highly experienced and credentialed professionals. For example, in Heaton et al.'s (1978) study on detection of inadequate effort on neuropsychological testing, the group of participating professionals reads like a Who's Who of eminent neuropsychologists (the participants are listed in Footnote 2 on page 894 of the article). We do not doubt that some professionals are more accurate than others. However, considering the obstacles to learning from clinical experience in areas central to predictive accuracy, and the relatively small or modest advantage extensive experience might provide in these domains compared to meticulous adherence to the best validated decision procedures, we would once again state that the most accurate overall method for predicting human behavior is known and is very likely to equal or surpass even excellent clinicians who rely primarily on subjective or impressionistic judgment methods.

The counterclaim or belief that one is an exception to research outcomes could be accurate. However, given the extensive body of literature on clinical versus statistical judgment methods and the difficulty of finding exceptions, one must consider how the volume, quality, and consistency of this research evidence compare to the evidentiary basis for the self-claimed exemption to the research. On one side, there are hundreds of studies involving widely varying decision tasks and clinicians, and in many cases rigorous methodology, and which almost always produce the same general outcome, even when one examines judgmental accuracy on a clinician-by-clinician level. On the other side, the evidence for the counterclaim is almost always impressionistic. Such impressionistic evidence is unlikely to include representative samples, a formal comparison of the accuracy the one claiming to be an exception obtains versus statistical decision methods, protections against bias (such as blind assessment of outcomes), or, in many cases, even the feedback or follow-up information needed to determine whether the clinician's judgments were or were not correct.

Thus, it seems perfectly reasonable to ask two fundamental questions that are often pertinent to knowledge claims or hypotheses: What is the evidence? and What is the quality of the evidence? It would be exciting to find that certain professionals consistently beat well-developed statistical decision methods, because taking a close look at their practices might yield extraordinarily helpful information that can be passed on to others. In the meantime, searches for such outliers or positive exceptions across the large volume of research on clinical and statistical judgment methods, although far from complete, have generally proven unsuccessful. Instead, the most dependable way to enhance accuracy in many circumstances is to increase use of statistical decision methods.

Studies Did Not Provide Sufficient Information to the Clinicians

Judgment studies often provide less complete information than a clinician might prefer to have available. For example, a study on the interpretation of a psychological test may provide little or no information about sociodemographic variables, patient history, or interview responses. Objections about limited information are understandable given the usual high value placed on having comprehensive information, and certainly information that was not provided in various studies had the potential to increase judgmental accuracy. Consequently, in absolute terms, clinicians' level of accuracy may have sometimes underrepresented their performance in actual practice, or when they can gather the information as they see fit. That, however, overlooks the comparative question, because in many studies clinicians and statistical decision methods were provided with the same information, and thus to the extent the clinicians were disadvantaged, the same applied equally to actuarial methods. Therefore, the central question here is not necessarily absolute level of accuracy but comparative accuracy across the two methods, and the associated explicit or implicit assertion that the actuarial advantage would diminish, disappear, or be reversed, if information sources expanded or achieved greater fidelity with common clinical practices.

In examining the impact of available information on the comparative accuracy of statistical and clinical decision methods, it is important to recognize that assumptions about the value of extensive information do not necessarily align with research outcomes. As discussed in Chapter 7, beyond a surprisingly limited amount of high-quality information, additional information often does little or nothing to increase decision accuracy, and at times will diminish accuracy when less valuable information is combined with more valuable information. The discrepancy between common belief and common research outcomes provides a context for examining studies on clinical versus statistical methods that provide varying levels of information.

What is perhaps most instructive here is the differential impact one finds across the two methods as level of information increases. As discussed earlier when covering Sawyer's review, as the amount of information increased, or more specifically when unstructured interview data were added to test data, the overall accuracy of statistical decision methods either stayed the same or increased, thereby showing that additional information had a positive impact on overall accuracy. In contrast, with clinical judgment, when unstructured interview data were added to test data, accuracy either stayed the same or diminished, and thus had a negative impact on overall accuracy. The irony is that unstructured interviews may provide useful information, but when subjective judgment methods are used, that information is not processed productively overall, unlike when the statistical method is used.

Thus, the objection that clinicians are disadvantaged in the comparative studies by insufficient access to information runs contrary to the research findings; rather, the statistical method's edge over clinical judgment increases as studies provide greater amounts of information, or at least additional information sources. Much of the differential impact of additional information on clinical judgment versus statistical decision methods comes down to difficulties judging such matters as the relative strength and redundancy of information subjectively, in contrast to the properties of statistically based methods. Proper development of statistical decision methods dictates that only information found to be useful or that increases accuracy be included. In addition, statistical methods can easily take such factors as relative redundancy into account and examine various procedures for combining information and determining the impact of adding or excluding variables on overall accuracy.

"I Deal with Individuals, Not Numbers"

A common anti-statistical argument is that group data do not pertain to single events or individuals. Such a position contradicts fundamental principles of probability. Individual events or individuals certainly have unique features, but they also often share common characteristics that allow generalizations or tallied observations to attain varying degrees of predictive utility. For example, if only five in 100 individuals prefer liver over spaghetti, and one guesses that the next person who walks by will prefer spaghetti, one will likely be correct in that instance and, beyond that, correct in the great majority of cases. (And as might be apparent, this is little more than another application of base rates.) Of course, especially when generalizations have limited utility, we seek ways to do better or to augment their success, but in many cases trying to identify exceptions to generalizations or statistically based conclusions either fails to help or diminishes overall accuracy. In the mental health field, identifying exceptions to statistically based decisions with sufficient regularity or trustworthiness to bolster their accuracy often turns out to be more difficult than we imagine, and the ability to do so usually requires a more advanced method than we currently possess. If we had such an advanced method, we might well be using it over other alternatives in the first place.

Statistically based predictions often do take a number of individual characteristics into account. For example, an individual's standing on sociodemographic variables like gender and age, and that person's results on psychological and intellectual tests, could all enter into a prediction. If a clinician considers these or other individual variables and integrates them subjectively, and if a statistically based method integrates these same variables into decision making (and does so with greater overall proficiency), it is hard to see the basis for asserting that one method takes individual characteristics into account and the other does not.

Questions raised about integrating individual characteristics into decision making should be separated from the concern that one method is personal and the other impersonal and the impact that might have on intervention success. However, a clinician can be equally compassionate when applying either type of obtained information. Further, that same clinician will be in a better position to help when guided by more accurate information or predictive capacity. Is it more humane for a treater to provide inaccurate information in a kindly way that might have serious negative consequences (e.g., a false impression that assessment suggests a developing dementia), or to act with similar humanity but instead use a method that is more likely to produce a correct result? More accurate conclusions can bolster human welfare, and the compassion and care with which information is conveyed are often more a product of the way the clinician acts than whether the information emerges from clinical or statistically based methods.

"What Controversy? I Just Combine the Two Methods."

In a certain percentage of cases, and sometimes in a sizeable percentage, clinical and statistical decision methods generate contradictory outcomes (e.g., a person will or will not drop out of treatment before three sessions or will or will not make a suicide attempt). In such instances, one has to select between one or the other alternative and cannot combine the two. (We realize that if one is trying to determine the probability of some outcome or behavior, various approaches can be used to try to combine the information, but that is not the situation we are describing here when referencing contradictory outcomes.) Consequently, to suggest there is no potential conflict between the two methods or that no real issue exists seems to overlook a major potential dilemma or outcome, and sometimes the most essential choice point.

"I Know an Exception When I See One"

The broken leg problem is aligned with the immediately preceding issue of combining clinical and statistical approaches. Both issues often pertain to calling exceptions, or trying to identify, in instances of conflicting outcomes, which method is most likely to be correct. We have already covered this issue at some length, and to summarize succinctly, efforts to identify exceptions rarely seem to improve overall accuracy and far more often do not help or make things worse overall. With that said, however, in a range of situations, failing to ever call exceptions or adhering blindly to statistical decision methods no matter the circumstances can be dangerous and ill-advised. For example, a statistical decision method can become obsolete or may generalize poorly to certain groups. Thus, both extremes should usually be avoided (i.e., that one should freely overturn even a highly proficient and thoroughly validated actuarial method that provides a sizeable advantage over clinical judgment on matters of great importance, or that one should never countervail an actuarial method no matter how limited or questionable it may be). Rather, the dilemma is to formulate a rational and effective countervail policy.

Statistical decision methods are far from perfect, and thus from the start we know they will make errors, and perhaps relatively frequent errors. A method with a 67% hit rate will be wrong in one of three cases. Such errors can be very costly. Also, statistical methods may be casually extended to groups despite clear threats to generalization, such as individuals with major cultural differences who show stark contrasts with derivation samples. Further, the literature on identifying broken legs is less complete than we would like, and there is simply insufficient knowledge about when countervailing may be, or should be, indicated, or when existing statistical decision methods should not be extended beyond certain bounds without methodical pilot testing.

Many of the studies on clinical versus statistical decision making included tasks for which considerable research was available, and presumably some, if not many, of the clinicians in the studies were aware of decision procedures that they could have applied. Studies rarely set bounds on whether clinicians could or could not use statistical decision procedures known to them (and that could be applied under the study conditions). Thus, a subset of the overall body of research involved situations in which those who were aware of statistical decision procedures could have applied them to the clinical data they were analyzing and could have accepted or rejected the results of these decision procedures as they saw fit. It is uncertain just what percentage of study participants could have drawn on statistical decision methods, but here the consistency of research outcomes is helpful. If clinicians were able to distinguish effectively between situations in which they should or should not have followed statistical decision rules when they conflicted with their own conclusions, then various studies or at least subgroups of clinicians in studies should have beaten statistical methods regularly. Such outcomes, however, are rare (and do not even necessarily exceed frequencies expected by chance) both at a group level and in studies in which decision accuracy was examined for each clinician individually.

Hence, while recognizing the limits of the analyses and methods used in investigations thus far, a variety of studies and sources of evidence suggest that countervailing is more challenging than it might seem and that effective strategies for calling exceptions are not easy to develop or apply. Put simply, at least taken cumulatively, countervails are more likely to change a correct decision to an incorrect one than to correct an error. To the extent studied, it also appears that clinicians countervail too frequently and that the bases on which they select that option are not sufficiently valid to augment the level of decision accuracy that would otherwise be achieved. The frequency of countervailing and the unproductive or negative outcomes may be partly explained by subjective confidence levels. A major basis for countervailing would seem to be a subjective sense of confidence that one's clinically based judgment is more likely to be correct than the statistically based outcome. The literature showing the pervasiveness of overconfidence (see Chapter 11) and the limited association between confidence and accuracy raises major concerns about the soundness of basing countervails on such subjective states.

As we discuss in Chapter 13, for most decision makers, it would help if they decreased their number of countervails or proceeded conservatively. Ideally, one prefers to have strategies for determining when to countervail that are grounded in a compelling body of scientific literature. However, in the meantime, recognizing the potential danger of blind adherence to statistically based outcomes and the propensity of even strong statistically based methods to err, decisions to countervail or use alternative procedures might consider such issues as:

- The relative costs and benefits of correct and incorrect decisions (e.g., deciding a patient will not engage in self-harm using a statistically based procedure that is superior to clinical judgment but not particularly accurate may well be overly risky, and one should probably suppose that significant risk is present and take precautions).
- Whether serious concerns are warranted about the generalization of a statistical decision method to a group that differs in major ways from derivation samples, such as in their primary language or a range of sociocultural factors. Such concerns are heightened when alternative methods have been validated with those groups or at least clinical judgments can be directed toward variables with demonstrated value for the individual or individuals under consideration.
- Whether new variables, findings, or decision methods have become available since the development of the decision procedures under consideration and seem to be highly robust predictors. For example, a potent predictor may have been uncovered that is not included in the available actuarial method. Even a single robust predictor may outperform combinations of predictors that have limited or relatively low validity.

We discuss these and other considerations when weighting decisions to countervail in greater length in Chapter 13.

Statistical Decision Methods Are Difficult to Develop and Often Are Unavailable for the Decision Task at Hand

As noted, even simple statistical methods may equal or outperform clinical judgment and can be relatively easy to develop. If a criticism is that methods are based on insufficient sample sizes and that much larger numbers are needed, a simple question to ask is whether, even given these limits, the method outpredicts the alternative approach being proposed. Insufficient sample size can certainly be an issue and sometimes a fatal problem for statistical prediction methods, although the sample sizes on which clinical judgments are based may be no larger or even smaller, and also may have additional shortcomings that further compromise or negate their value. For example, in clinical practice, there may be minimal or no representation of one or more cells in a covariation table, such as those without a certain clinical indicator or those without the condition of interest. Even should such information be available, it may not have been analyzed formally to appraise such critical matters as relative frequency of occurrence. More broadly, it does not advance one's argument to point out the limitations of a method one is rejecting when the alternative one prefers shows equal or greater flaws on the same dimensions.

Although we have not finished a research project initiated by one of the authors and now spearheaded by Kathleen Monahan, we have already collected relatively extensive survey data on the frequency with which studies in major journals in applied psychology provide results that can be directly used as statistical decision procedures or used in this manner with some modification. As one would expect, studies in these journals contain numerous statistical analyses. Many of these analyses pertain to issues in applied psychology, such as expected outcomes following differing types and levels of head injury, findings that differentiate one disorder from another, base rates for various events or outcomes, and evaluation of potential predictive variables across a broad array of outcomes. In many cases, these analyses can be applied directly as statistical decision procedures, and in numerous other cases they can be converted into statistical decision procedures with relatively simple additional steps or analyses.

The number of studies directly comparing clinical and statistical judgment methods to one another runs into the low hundreds, and for specific clinical decisions there may not be any comparative studies available. However, the hundreds of comparative studies that are available overall show overwhelmingly that properly developed statistical decision methods in the mental health field almost always equal or exceed the accuracy of clinical judgment. In our survey of the literature, the preliminary evidence suggests strongly that there are thousands of studies examining the outcome of statistical analyses that can be applied directly as decision rules, or converted to such, covering many, many issues in applied psychology.

A major implication of the comparative studies seems clear. That literature shows that the odds of a properly developed statistical decision procedure equaling or exceeding the accuracy of clinical judgment are very good, and conversely, that a clinical judgment method has a very low probability of exceeding a statistical judgment method. Hence, these comparative studies provide clear guidance on what to expect when direct comparison studies are unavailable. Certainly, the odds are much higher that the statistical method will equal or exceed the clinical method as opposed to the clinical method proving to be superior. Hence, even when comparisons are lacking on a specific topic or area of judgment, it is a much better bet to predict that statistical methods will outperform the clinical method should there be a difference in accuracy, making the use of statistical decision procedures a sound choice (and a considerably sounder choice than selecting clinical judgment methods instead).

A distinction can be made between studies comparing clinical and statistical judgment as opposed to studies that generate statistical decisions procedures or outcomes but do not compare the two methods. For example, a study might examine variables that predict response to a certain form of psychotherapy, and in turn generate a predictive algorithm that can be applied to new therapy candidates. This study, however, may not compare the effectiveness of that algorithm to the accuracy of predictions that rely on clinical judgment. Nevertheless, even absent such a comparative study, if one considers the a priori odds of a statistical decision procedure equaling or surpassing clinical judgment, it is an excellent bet to go with the algorithm. There are thousands of studies in the mental health field involving a vast array of applied clinical decisions that have generated statistical formulae that can be used directly, or with some modifications, in diagnostic and predictive tasks. This turns the argument about the lack of available statistical predictive methods on its head. An abundance of statistical decision methods are available, and where they are available (and one has the alternative of instead using clinical judgment, which is almost always the case), there is a much sounder basis for increasing, rather than reducing, the use of statistical methods.

CONCLUSION

It is unfortunate that methods that can be so helpful in improving clinical practice and patient outcomes are often overlooked, undervalued, or viewed as professional or personal threats. Given the frequency with which highly questionable statements are made about actuarial or statistical decision methods, it is hard not to question the overall quality of didactic education and training on these matters. In one survey of doctoral level psychologists (Furman, 2005), only 2% of respondents agreed strongly with the statement, "Actuarial judgment is more accurate overall than clinical judgment," and over 60% disagreed with the statement to varying degrees. When asked to consider the statement, "Actuarial judgment and clinical judgment can be used in combination with each other and any argument about which is more accurate is pointless," less than 2% strongly disagreed, and 67% agreed with the statement to some degree or were neutral. And for the statement, "Any superiority in accuracy that actuarial judgment has over clinical judgment is mainly or solely due to the fact that actuarial judgment has access to information that is unavailable to the human judge," only about 5% strongly disagreed.

Undue confidence in clinical judgment may also lead to negative assumptions about the comparative effectiveness of statistical decision procedures. In addition, the laudable search for the highest possible level of accuracy may also lead to frequent countervailing that, ironically, more often diminishes, rather than enhances, accuracy overall. Understandably, when it comes to patient care, we want to make correct decisions as often as possible, but certain strategies for pursuing this worthy goal can have the opposite impact. Einhorn (1986) framed the issue memorably when describing the need in some circumstances to accept error to make less error. By this he did not mean we should cease striving to do better. However, given the current state of knowledge and the need to make decisions in the present or with the knowledge we have available at the time, an overall strategy that minimizes error, even if one knows the approach is far from infallible, is often the best alternative. Sometimes, discretion is the greater part of valor.

It is also sensible to ask where to direct research efforts to improve decision accuracy. It is instructive to examine trends in the accuracy of clinical versus statistical methods over the decades (Ægisdóttir et al., 2006; Faust & Ahern, 2012). Studies on the accuracy of clinical judgment do not seem to find much change over time. In contrast, where intensive efforts have been made to improve statistical methods, accuracy in various areas has tended to improve, sometimes dramatically, such as in the prediction of violent acts over relatively brief time periods (Zager et al., 2009). Dawes (see Dawes et al., 1993) referred to this as improving what works, or giving priority to methods that have an established track record of greater relative strength.

One of the most common refrains is that statistical decision methods threaten clinicians' job status or opportunities. We leave it to the reader to judge whether this is a compelling argument for using less effective overall methods that increase the potential for harm. But beyond that, it is hard to see how using statistical decision methods to assist in prediction narrows job opportunities. These methods need to be developed, monitored, and applied judiciously, thereby calling for, at minimum, the close involvement of individuals with the needed background and training to provide oversight. In many other cases, the use of methods that assist, for example, in making better intervention choices, does not eliminate or reduce the role of the treatment provider. Furthermore, there is much that mental health professionals do that is not threatened in any way by the use of decision aids, and if anything, given the serious undersupply of mental health services on a national and international level, it is worth finding ways to expand availability and reach more individuals in need.

To those who point to the limits of statistical decision procedures, we agree there are definite shortcomings, although the immediate question is how overall efficacy compares to available alternatives. In the meantime, statistical decision procedures can be seen as a way station to something better as knowledge advances. That movement forward can be frustratingly deliberate in a field dedicated to human welfare, and which faces many pressing unmet needs and a subject matter that often presents vexing problems and resists easy solutions. Thus, although at present we may often have to accept considerably more error than we would like to make fewer errors, over time, as knowledge grows, the level of error we have to accept should decrease substantially. Two of the best hopes for improvement are the development of more powerful theories and artificial intelligence. Chapter 10 address the current state of artificial intelligence and machine learning in the mental health field, warranted and unwarranted assertions about present accomplishments, and promising ongoing developments.

REFERENCES

Ægisdóttir, S., White, M. J., Spengler, P. M., Maugherman, A. S., Anderson, L. A., Cook, R. S., Nichols, C. N., Lampropoulos, G. K., Walker, B. S., Cohen, G., & Rush, J. D. (2006). The meta-analysis of clinical judgment project: Fifty-six years of accumulated research on clinical versus statistical prediction. *The Counseling Psychologist*, *34*(3), 341–382.

Ashenfelter, O., Ashmore, D., & Lalonde, R. (1995). Bordeaux wine vintage quality and the weather. *Chance*, *8*(4), 7–14.

Ashenfelter, O., & Corsi, A. (2001). Predicting Italian wine quality from weather data and expert's ratings. In M. Pitchery & M. Terraza (Eds.), *Oenometrie IX* (9th annual meeting of the Vineyard Quantification Society in Montpellier, Cahiers Scientific No. 4).

Chapman, L. J., & Chapman, J. P. (1969). Illusory correlation as an obstacle to the use of valid psychodiagnostic signs. *Journal of Abnormal Psychology*, *74*(3), 271–280.

Dawes, R. M., Faust, D., & Meehl, P. E. (1989). Clinical versus actuarial judgment. *Science*, *243*(4899), 1668–1674.

Dawes, R. M., Faust, D., & Meehl, P. E. (1993). Statistical prediction versus clinical prediction: Improving what works. In G. Keren & C. Lewis (Eds.), *A handbook for data analysis in the behavioral sciences: Methodological issues* (pp. 351–367). Psychology Press.

Einhorn, H. J. (1986). Accepting error to make less error. *Journal of Personality Assessment*, *50*(3), 387–395.

Epperson, D. L., & Gore, K. S. (2004, October). *Investigation of clinical overrides of the MnSOST-R and the resulting impact on predictive accuracy* [Paper presentation]. Research and Treatment Convention of the Association for the Treatment of Sexual Abusers, Albuquerque, NM.

Faust, D., & Ahern, D. C. (2012). Clinical judgment and prediction. In D. Faust (Ed.), *Coping with psychiatric and psychological testimony: Based on the original work by Jay Ziskin* (pp. 147–208). Oxford University Press.

Furman, A. L.-E. (2005). *Clinicians' knowledge and use of decision making research* [Unpublished master's thesis]. University of Rhode Island, Kingston, RI.

Girard, L. (1999). *The Level of Service Inventory–Ontario Revision: Risk/need assessment and recidivism* [Unpublished doctoral dissertation]. University of Ottawa, Ottawa, Canada.

Girard, L., & Wormith, J. S. (2004). The predictive validity of the Level of Service Inventory–Ontario Revision on general and violent recidivism among various offender groups. *Criminal Justice and Behavior*, *31*(2), 150–181.

Goldberg, L. R. (1965). Diagnosticians vs. diagnostic signs: The diagnosis of psychosis vs. neurosis from the MMPI. *Psychological Monographs: General and Applied*, *79*(9), 1–28.

Goldberg, L. R. (1968). Simple models or simple processes? Some research on clinical judgments. *American Psychologist*, *23*(7), 483–496.

Gore, K. S. (2008). Adjusted actuarial assessment of sex offenders: The impact of clinical overrides on predictive accuracy. *Dissertation Abstracts International: Section B: The Sciences and Engineering*, *68*(7-B), 4824.

Grove, W. M., & Meehl, P. E. (1996). Comparative efficiency of informal (subjective, impressionistic) and formal (mechanical, algorithmic) prediction procedures: The clinical–statistical controversy. *Psychology, Public Policy, and Law*, *2*(2), 293.

Grove, W. M., Zald, D. H., Lebow, B. S., Snitz, B. E., & Nelson, C. (2000). Clinical versus mechanical prediction: A meta-analysis. *Psychological Assessment*, *12*(1), 19–30.

Guay, J. P., & Parent, G. (2018). Broken legs, clinical overrides, and recidivism risk: An analysis of decisions to adjust risk levels with the LS/CMI. *Criminal Justice and Behavior*, *45*(1), 82–100.

Hanson, R. K., & Morton-Bourgon, K. E. (2009). The accuracy of recidivism risk assessments for sexual offenders: A meta-analysis of 118 prediction studies. *Psychological Assessment*, *21*(1), 1–21.

Heaton, R. K., Smith, H. H., Lehman, R. A., & Vogt, A. T. (1978). Prospects for faking believable deficits on neuropsychological testing. *Journal of Consulting and Clinical Psychology*, *46*(5), 892–900.

Krauss, D. A. (2004). Adjusting risk of recidivism: Do judicial departures worsen or improve recidivism prediction under the Federal Sentencing Guidelines?. *Behavioral Sciences & the Law*, *22*(6), 731–750.

Meehl, P. E. (1954). *Clinical versus statistical prediction: A theoretical analysis and a review of the evidence*. University of Minnesota Press.

Meehl, P. E. (1986). Causes and effects of my disturbing little book. *Journal of Personality Assessment*, *50*(3), 370–375.

Meehl, P. E. (1996). *Clinical versus statistical prediction: A theoretical analysis and a review of the evidence* (Revised ed. with new preface). Jason Aronson.

Meyers, J. F. (2015). *Development and psychometric evaluation of a clinical beliefs questionnaire for licensed psychologists* [Doctoral dissertation]. https://doi.org/10.23860/diss-meyer-joseph-2015

Mossman, D. (1994). Assessing predictions of violence: Being accurate about accuracy. *Journal of Consulting and Clinical Psychology*, *62*(4), 783–792.

Passell, P. (1990, March 4). Wine equation puts some noses out of joint. *New York Times*, p. 1.

Sawyer, J. (1966). Measurement and prediction, clinical and statistical. *Psychological Bulletin*, *66*(3), 178–200.

Schmidt, F., Sinclair, S. M., & Thomasdóttir, S. (2016). Predictive validity of the Youth Level of Service/Case Management Inventory with youth who have committed sexual and non-sexual offenses: The utility of professional override. *Criminal Justice and Behavior*, *43*(3), 413–430.

Storey, J. E., Watt, K. A., Jackson, K. J., & Hart, S. D. (2012). Utilization and implications of the Static-99 in practice. *Sexual Abuse*, *24*(3), 289–302.

Vogel, V. D., Ruiter, C. D., Hildebrand, M., Bos, B., & van de Ven, P. (2004). Type of discharge and risk of recidivism measured by the HCR-20: A retrospective study in a Dutch sample of treated forensic psychiatric patients. *International Journal of Forensic Mental Health*, *3*(2), 149–165.

Vrieze, S. I., & Grove, W. M. (2009). Survey on the use of clinical and mechanical prediction methods in clinical psychology. *Professional Psychology: Research and Practice*, *40*, 525–531.

Wormith, J. S., Hogg, S., & Guzzo, L. (2012). The predictive validity of a general risk/needs assessment inventory on sexual offender recidivism and an exploration of the professional override. *Criminal Justice and Behavior*, *39*(12), 1511–1538.

Zagar, R. J., Busch, K. G., Grove, W. M., & Hughes, J. R. (2009). Can violent (re)offense be predicted? A review of the role of the clinician and use of actuarial tests in light of new data. *Psychological Reports*, *104*, 247–277.

9

Research on Racial/Ethnic Bias and Professional Judgment: Errors in Cold Cognition, Hot Cognition, and Interconnections with Decision Research

Previous chapters focus primarily on two major topics: (1) cognitive biases, such as hindsight bias and confirmatory bias, and (2) normative principles and procedures that enhance judgment and decision making, such as covariation analysis and the use of base rates and statistical decision methods. When discussing both of these topics, we emphasized errors in "cold" cognition. Errors in cold cognition can be viewed as problematical information processing that occurs even when emotional factors play a limited role, or is minimally influenced or distorted by powerful emotions, such as fear or intense aversion. We also emphasized the extreme challenges one faces trying to integrate complex data using impressionistic or unaided judgment, limitations that again can be traced in substantial part to cognitive limitations as opposed to emotional factors. Fortunately, human creativity and aptitude have provided us with decision aids that offer invaluable help in extending boundaries in our ability to integrate complex data on our own. Resistance to decision literature may rest on factors other than cold cognition, but that is not pertinent to the immediate discussion.

The current chapter focuses on racial/ethnic bias and considerations of diversity and multiculturalism, topics of critical importance. We have waited until the fundamentals of decision research were introduced to provide the needed context and to assist in examining the relationship of work on racial/ethnic bias and cultural diversity to decision research. At least four points stand out in examining the interface between these two bodies of literature. First, there is little argument that racial and ethnic biases are often hot-button topics that stir strong emotions. It is hard to imagine that intense emotions and at times very superficial information processing foster optimal judgmental processes and decision making. Thus, one is dealing with not only errors in cold cognition, but also decision making that can be further compromised by the distorting influences of intense emotionality and inculcated perceptions and beliefs. Even individuals with the best intentions are susceptible not only to cognitive biases, but also to the emotionality that racial/ethnic issues can elicit. Mental health professionals are not immune to such emotional triggers, which can result from an intense commitment to avoid prejudicial practices, mixed in with worries about being perceived or labeled as racially biased and the consequences that might follow.

A second and related point is that it is highly improbable that strong emotionality somehow offsets cognitive biases and violations of normative decision procedures. Consequently, there are likely at least two layers and levels of potential interference with decision making, those mainly related to emotional factors and those mainly related to cognitive factors, and negating or attenuating the first source may do little or nothing to negate the second source.

Third, fundamental principles of effective decision making likely show good cross-situational application. In contrast, the specifics involved in applying these principles will likely often necessitate adjustment for diverse groups or individuals with sociocultural contrasts and should rest on a body of research examining cross-situational applicability. For example, principles involving the need for representative information for all four cells of a covariation table, or formal calculations for combining prior odds with diagnostic indicators to estimate the probabilities of various outcomes, should not change across populations or as racial/ethnic status shifts. However, various specifics, such as the variables that achieve the greatest predictive utility, the base rates that apply to different groups, or the tests that achieve the greatest level of accuracy and thus should be included in a statistical prediction method might change considerably.

Fourth, when trying to identify whether and what adjustments in specifics are needed in applied situations, one often encounters an insufficient research base. The same limitations also pertain to the available research examining the relationships between errors in cold cognition and errors rooted in the emotions that racial and ethnic issues commonly elicit, which are understandable. A long history of discrimination and mistreatment has often extracted a grave psychological and physical toll. Again, mental health professionals are not immune to emotional factors, no matter how good their intentions. In this chapter, we try to point out areas in which research on racial/ethnic bias and research on decision making intersect, and we highlight similarities, contrasts, and gaps in knowledge that clearly call for further study. Given limits in knowledge, many of our recommendations and reflections are more tentative than we would prefer.

In order, we start by highlighting the literature on racial and ethnic bias, and in particular the impact of such potential biases on the mental health field and professional judgment. We then address what seem to be certain key conceptual issues and assumptions, especially those involving shifts in judgment in relation to racial and ethnic characteristics that are more or less likely to serve as signposts for biases. We then proceed to areas in which the literature on racial/ethnic bias and the literature on decision making clearly or potentially intersect.

RACIAL/ETHNIC BIAS

There is increasing recognition that a significant portion of our scientific knowledge on mental health and related topics comes from research on WEIRD populations—populations in societies that are Western, educated, industrialized, rich, and democratic (Henrich et al., 2010). Even in these populations, disparities among subpopulations can wreak havoc on attempts to modify diagnostic and predictive methods. As the United States is becoming increasingly racially and ethnically diverse (U.S. Census Bureau, 2021), the need for clinicians to understand and address racial/ethnic bias is more pressing than ever.

Racial and ethnic biases are inclinations or predispositions we have about particular racial and ethnic groups (APA, 2021). These biases are not necessarily all positive or all negative—we often hold mixed biases about people. For instance, there are biases about people living in the U.S. South that assume Southerners are nice but not very smart. In contrast, biases about Northeasterners assume that they are bright but rude (see Fiske et al., 1999; Kinzler & DeJesus, 2013). These examples illustrate two important dimensions of racial/ethnic bias and biases about other sociocultural groups: warmth and competence (Cuddy et al., 2007; Dovidio & Fiske, 2012; Fiske et al., 1999).

Racial and ethnic biases are culturally acquired. Media, our families, friends, and peers, as well as our direct experiences with diverse others shape the development of bias (Hinton, 2017). The United States remains a highly segregated society; many people grow up in communities that are relatively homogeneous with respect to race/ethnicity, attend schools that are relatively segregated, and marry within their own racial/ethnic group (Bialik, 2017; Glasmeier & Farrigan, 2007; McGrew, 2019). This is unfortunate, because in the absence of direct experiences interacting with people of different races or ethnic backgrounds, the beliefs people have about groups with whom they do not regularly interact are formed from indirect sources, including parent and peer influences and media representations (see Fujioka, 1999). Media representations in particular are notoriously discriminatory against Black, Indigenous, and other people of color (Tukachinsky et al., 2015; Tyree, 2011).

Biases form the basis of stereotypes (Dovidio et al., 2010). Stereotypes are character attributions made about a particular group that are overextended or extreme, or just plain inaccurate. Stereotypes set expectations we hold, implicitly or explicitly, for group members. No matter one's personal beliefs and attitudes, people embedded in a given cultural context are aware of cultural stereotypes about different racial/ethnic groups (Devine, 1989). Stereotypes are automatically activated—meaning associations between a person of a particular racial/ethnic group and stereotypes about people of that group occur outside our conscious control, or without deliberate cognitive activity. In the case of clinical practice, for instance, we may expect an Asian client to perform at an above average level on a test of mathematical achievement (Cvencek et al., 2015), or our first-generation immigrant client who grew up in a household where Portuguese was spoken to score at a below average level on an English test of verbal intelligence (Spence et al., 1971). In these cases, we are drawing on cultural stereotypes about groups to set expectations for that individual's test performance.

People do not have to be conscious of their biases or stereotypes for them to influence judgments and behavior (Dovidio & Fiske, 2012). Priming studies show that cuing group membership (e.g., race) can prime trait stereotypes and subsequently influence behavior. For instance, a study of judgments about an actor's behavior revealed different interpretations of the behavior when the actor was Black versus White. In both cases, the actor engaged in an ambiguous action (bumping into someone). The behavior was more likely to be described as hostile or aggressive when the actor was Black than when the actor was White (Duncan, 1976; findings replicated by Sagar & Schofield, 1980). Research into explicit biases (biases or stereotypes that are within our conscious awareness) and implicit biases[1] (biases or stereotypes that are outside our conscious awareness) suggests that both predict discriminatory behavior (Latu et al., 2011; Rudman & Ashmore, 2007), although meta-analytic and replication studies highlight the inconsistent predictive utility of measures designed to detect implicit bias (see Blanton et al., 2009; Oswald et al., 2013). Nevertheless, it seems likely that stereotypes, whether we are aware of them or not, can influence clinical practice. For instance, therapists may hold implicit expectations that Black clients will be more hostile than White clients (Abreu, 1999). In addition, mental health professionals are more likely to dissuade Black and low-income potential clients from pursuing treatment compared to White and middle-class potential clients (Kugelmass, 2019; Shin et al., 2016). Further compounding potential biases is that clinicians rarely obtain systematic, representative feedback on the accuracy of their judgments and decisions—disgruntled patients rarely return to "correct the record"—reducing opportunities to learn from experience and alter mistaken beliefs.

Stereotypes not only set expectations for what people in a particular group will be like, they also set standards against which we then judge members of that group (Biernat et al., 1991, 2009; Eagly & Karau, 2002). When asked to appraise something or someone (such as how friendly a person is or how open they are to therapy), our resultant judgments are often influenced by the standards we hold for members of that group, rather than standards we hold for all people. This means that people from different social groups who perform identically on a test or who exhibit the same behavior may be judged differently. To illustrate, a Northerner and a Southerner in the United States who are identically friendly on some behaviorally specific measure may be rated differently on a subjective measure of friendliness if the rater views the two groups to which these people belong as different on friendliness. The Southerner may seem relatively unfriendly given the yardstick for comparison (Southerners in general), and the Northerner may seem relatively friendly given a contrasting yardstick for comparison (Northerners in general). Again, these alternations in judgment

[1] The research cited here is on implicit stereotypes and not implicit attitudes. Implicit stereotypes are measured by combining group membership words (e.g., Black, Asian, White, female, male) with adjectives that are stereotypically associated with that group (e.g., nurturing, dominant, athletic, smart). In contrast, implicit attitudes are measured by combining group membership words with affectively evaluative words (e.g., good, bad).

stemming from stereotypes may occur without us recognizing their occurrence, and are referred to as shifting standards.

Awareness of bias, prejudice, and discrimination, when present, can motivate people to intentionally change their behavior to respond in counter-stereotypical or nonprejudicial ways (Plant & Devine, 1998). Whether because of external pressures or internal motivation to treat people fairly, intentions to respond without prejudice can be powerful at shifting behavior. However, attempts to correct our behavior to counteract bias may also be ineffective (Lau et al., 2016; Wegener & Petty, 1997). When it comes to clinical judgment and decision making tasks where accuracy is paramount, efforts to self-correct bias can result in unpredictable and contradictory outcomes. Sometimes we might overcorrect (adjust our judgments too far, leading to inaccuracies in the opposite direction of what might be predicted based on the bias), correct in the wrong direction (exacerbating the bias), or correct when there is no need to do so (i.e., in a context where bias was not present in the first place).

RELATIONS BETWEEN BIASES AND SHIFTS IN JUDGMENT

Decades of research suggest that clients' race/ethnicity affects providers, or, at minimum, that it can. For example, multiple studies show that healthcare professionals' behavior, intentional or not, is different when interacting with clients of different races or ethnicities. For instance, on average, physicians collect less information and exhibit poorer communication when interacting with Black patients versus White patients (Street et al., 2007). Differences emerge in studies examining physicians' decisions to withhold treatment or to recommend invasive treatments in patients from different racial groups (Dovidio & Fiske, 2012), and in how much empathy counselors express toward a mock client who is Black as opposed to White (Burkard & Knox, 2004). In inpatient psychiatric settings, Black patients are more likely than White patients to be restrained, secluded, and medicated, and are discharged in fewer days, even when severity of psychiatric symptoms is controlled for (Flaherty & Meagher, 1980).

Studies of differences in healthcare providers' judgments/evaluations and diagnostic decisions suggest differences in relation to patients' racial/ethnic group membership. In a review of seven studies, Garb (1997) found evidence for more frequent diagnoses of psychosis in Black and Latinx clients (vs. White clients), even when measures of psychopathology did not support the presence of a psychotic disorder. Garb's review also showed that clinicians tend to overestimate risk of violence in Black (vs. White) patients hospitalized for psychiatric concerns and of Black and Native American (vs. White) people who were incarcerated. Other studies found mental health providers had a more pessimistic outlook about a mock client's treatment prognosis or potential for recovery when the client was described as Latinx or Black versus White (Arroyo, 1996; Rosenthal, 2004; Rosenthal & Berven, 1999) or of lower socioeconomic status (Thompson et al., 2019). Although there may be some element of truth to a pessimistic outlook given the impact of discrimination and other disadvantages these groups commonly face, attributions may nevertheless focus on individual as opposed to social factors (we return to this point later).

In contrast to the studies cited above, which tend to show greater pathologizing of minoritized patients, some studies find racial/ethnic minority groups are judged to be less impaired than their White counterparts or are less likely to be diagnosed with psychiatric disorders. For instance, in a vignette study, researchers presented mental health professionals with identical case descriptions except for varying race. Clinicians rated the client as less impaired when they were described as Black versus White or East Asian (Gushue et al., 2021). In medicine, physicians' ratings of pain in Black patients were lower than their pain ratings for White patients (Hoffman et al., 2016). Black women are significantly less likely to be diagnosed with posttraumatic stress disorder than are White women, despite comparable rates of hospitalizations for sexual assault and interpersonal violence victimization (Seng et al., 2005). In his review of eleven studies, Garb (1997) found that most studies on racial differences in ratings of clients' emotional disturbance or maladjustment obtain null effects; however, when differences are detected, clinicians tended to rate Black clients as less impaired than White clients.

A recent review of decisions made by healthcare professionals and trainees (most of whom were psychologists) found evidence of disparate clinical decisions in 77% of the 149 studies examined (Featherston et al., 2020). Differences included clinical decisions related to screening, assessment, diagnosis, treatment, and prognosis made during hypothetical clinical scenarios. The hypothetical scenarios involved identical case descriptions with the exception of modified key sociodemographic information (e.g., patient race). A critical assumption many studies make, and which we turn to in a moment, is that difference is equivalent to bias. But first, we briefly consider the possible reasons for observed differences in healthcare providers' judgments.

TYPES OF ERRORS IN JUDGMENT SHIFTS

Broadly speaking, the research we have discussed suggests that healthcare providers at times adjust their behavior, decisions, and judgments based on a patient's race or ethnicity. However, the studies also illustrate that these adjustments are not always in one direction (such as seeing greater pathology in minoritized patients versus majority White patients). Indeed, the literature can be summarized as showing that sometimes clinicians overdiagnose/overestimate pathology, sometimes they underdiagnose/underestimate pathology, and sometimes there is no observed difference. Despite what may seem like a muddle, these contradictory findings may be comprehensible.

Adjustments to clinical judgments and decisions may occur for various reasons, such as lack of cultural knowledge and implicit or explicit biases, which are central concerns in this chapter. However, some reasons are likely valid and important, indeed critical, to consider and should be the basis of adjusting clinical judgments and decisions (e.g., different base rates for conditions). Conceptually, at least five situations seem to merit attention: (1) adjusting clinical decisions when there are valid reasons to do so; (2) not adjusting clinical decisions when there is no need to do so; (3) adjusting clinical decisions when there are invalid reasons to do so, such as on the basis of inaccurate stereotypes or racial biases; (4) adjusting clinical decisions in an attempt to counteract a bias or stereotype, but the correction is greater than it should be (i.e., overcorrecting); and (5) failing to adjust when there are valid reasons to do so. It is clear that it is only in the first situation that proper adjustments should consistently increase the accuracy of clinical judgments and decisions. In the fourth situation, adjustments might or might not do more harm than good because over-correction may be better or worse than no correction at all. In the other three situations, adjustments or their failures will result in increased error. We consider each situation in turn.

Situation #1: Valid Adjustments

To the extent our judgments are correctly altered for sociocultural subgroups, we will increase our decision making accuracy. There are certainly instances in which group membership does alter base rates or frequencies of conditions or characteristics. Lower optimism about positive outcomes in Black and Latinx versus White clients, for example, may have some elements of truth given the impact of discrimination and other systemic disadvantages these groups commonly face. (That is not to say, of course, that the situation is fair or desirable, only that one trying to make as accurate a prediction as possible or to adjust intervention approaches in an effort to offset a more negative prognosis may be able to provide greater assistance given a more accurate appraisal of the situation.)

As another example, imagine a patient presents to a physician for concerns about frequent headaches, nausea, and trouble maintaining balance. What is the probability that the patient has a brain tumor? In such cases, an important consideration for determining the likelihood of a brain tumor is the patient's age. Nearly all brain tumors occur in people over the age of 20 (McKinney, 2004). If the patient is a pediatric patient, the likelihood that the set of symptoms indicates a brain tumor is much lower than if the patient were older (in a pediatric patient, one might suspect bacterial meningitis instead, which is much more common among children than adults; CDC, 2019). The change in expectation for brain tumor as age advances is not an example of ageism; rather, it reflects true alterations in base rates, or a change in the prior odds (see Chapter 6, which addresses base rates).

Situation #2: Valid Lack of Adjustments

In many cases, race and ethnicity should not shift a clinician's judgment because these factors are not predictive of the outcome of interest. For example, although there are well-documented differences by race and ethnicity for who is likely to contract COVID, mortality among patients who are hospitalized with COVID is similar across racial and ethnic groups (Mackey et al., 2021). Recurrence of major depressive disorder among patients who discontinued antidepressant medication was similar across racial and ethnic groups (Trinh et al., 2011). Across multiple clinical trials of psychotherapy for substance use disorders, researchers found no significant differences in primary outcomes of interest (quantity and frequency of substance use) between Black and White patients (Lowman & Le Fauve, 2003). In these kinds of circumstances, making decisions about clinical interventions that differ by patient race/ethnicity could lead to varying and potentially inequitable outcomes for one or another group.[2]

Situation #3: Invalid Adjustments

Adjustments in clinical judgments and decisions resulting from inaccurate stereotypes (i.e., changes that are not backed by the best evidence we have available, or alterations that exceed true shifts in frequency) will likely introduce racial/ethnic bias into clinical decision making. Racial/ethnic bias may lead us to overlook factors that are relevant to judgmental accuracy and attend instead to factors that decrease accuracy. For instance, a belief that alcohol use in adolescence is normative in some cultures may lead a clinician to overlook true signs of a substance use problem in a Latina high school client who drinks. As previously referenced, media tend to offer stereotypic portrayals of racial and ethnic group members (Tukachinsky et al., 2015; Tyree, 2011). If a clinician has relatively little experience interacting with people of diverse backgrounds, these media messages may be very influential in the types of associations the clinician forms when encountering a minoritized client in clinical practice. For instance, the trope of the angry Black woman, someone who is sassy, ill-mannered, and illogical, may be readily and automatically called to mind when a clinician is first meeting a Black female client. This representation leads the practitioner to expect an angry and ill-mannered client. Perhaps this is why women with Black-sounding names are significantly less likely to be offered mental health appointments than those with more White-sounding names (Shin et al., 2016). Likewise, if a clinician has seen only one or two Latinx men in therapy, both of whom expressed some machista beliefs about the subservient role women should take in a relationship, the clinician may markedly overestimate the degree to which sexism is going to be present in future Latinx male clients.

There is a tendency to associate shifts in judgment related to racial or ethnic characteristics, changes in obtained base rates for one or another disorder, or differences in evaluative results as prima-facie evidence of bias. Certainly, in many cases, that is exactly the case. However, as noted, there are other circumstances in which group membership does shift base rates or the frequency of various outcomes, and those differences are not merely a product of bias (Reynolds & Suzuki, 2012). A previous example addressed the relation between age and the likelihood of brain tumor. Similarly, if individuals' safety is at greater risk, as

[2] Here, we will not delve into a possible alternative, which is that treatments could be more potent or beneficial across racial/ethnic groups and that a comparable outcome might be evidence of bias. Conceptually, we are only interested in illustrating the case where there are no group differences and the clinician does not use group membership to adjust his or her clinical judgment or decision.

might be the case with many minoritized groups, and if a measure of anxiety generates higher scores for that group as opposed to scores obtained for a group with considerably less reason to be worried, should we automatically conclude that the measure is flawed?

When frequencies and outcomes truly vary across groups, the main explanation may trace back to inequities, but those that originate in systemic or societal factors may still be misattributed to inherent individual differences. For example, if minority members are issued loans with higher interest rates than Whites and are underpaid for the same work activities, their rate of default may be higher, yet such differential frequencies could diminish if inequities in pay were eliminated. Misattribution and faulty analysis of causal relationships can cause a host of problems. For example, concluding that a group has some form of personal weakness or flaw, as opposed to recognizing the impact of inequitable social conditions and prejudices, shifts needs and intervention strategies in a very different direction.

Situation #4: Overcorrections

Ironically, an emphasis on explicit stereotypes and cultural sensitivity may lead mental health professionals to overcorrect or to make judgments about minoritized clients from a relative (i.e., within-group) perspective and consequently to see minoritized clients as less impaired than is merited or their White counterparts (see Abreu, 1999; Cheng et al., 2017; Gushue, 2004; Gushue et al., 2008). Perhaps due to professionals' desire to be nonprejudiced, true impairment in minoritized clients may be explained away as perfectly understandable given the circumstances. The desire to avoid pathologizing difficulties in functioning, especially when a savvy clinician recognizes systems of inequity that negatively impact the client, can have the unintended consequence of missing true problems that could be reduced or resolved through therapeutic intervention.

Situation #5: Failures to Adjust When Necessary

Lack of knowledge about how conditions may express themselves in diverse racial and ethnic groups can lead to inaccurate and even fatal judgments. For instance, early in the COVID-19 pandemic, the Centers for Disease Control and Prevention noted that symptoms of serious, life-threatening infection included blue lips and low blood-oxygen levels, as measured by pulse oximetry. However, discoloration of the lips and face is less evident in Black patients and pulse oximetry readings are less trustworthy in Black patients (Sjoding et al., 2020). The lack of appropriate race-specific guidelines on how COVID manifests in different groups has had deadly consequences (Tien, 2020).

Sometimes diagnostic errors result from a failure to consider the context of the client and to make situational, rather than dispositional, attributions for symptoms (the *fundamental attribution error*). Bridges and colleagues (2012) found rates of generalized anxiety disorder in Latinx immigrants to be nearly six times higher than estimates in the general population. However, qualitative probing revealed this extreme rate was likely due to anxiety about genuine external stressors faced by undocumented participants and not because of an excessive worry that was disproportionate to the reality of the situations they faced. Failing to consider contextual factors can lead to erroneous judgments in the clinical context (e.g., an improper and unwarranted clinical diagnosis) and perhaps misdirected or unhelpful treatments (e.g., assigning worry exposure or trying to change the patient's thoughts rather than acknowledging and addressing the real external stressors the patient is facing).

DETERMINING VALID VERSUS BIASED ADJUSTMENTS

Unfortunately, in the mental health field, we often lack a yardstick with sufficient scientific status to determine whether we are making accurate adjustments based on valid data or inaccurate adjustments based on stereotypes, overcorrecting to counteract stereotypes, or failing to adjust when adjustments are warranted. In addition, determining the potential racial/ethnic bias in our instruments or statistical decision procedures is similarly vexing. Given differential costs and a long history of harm caused by racial prejudice, bias is a possibility that merits the utmost scrutiny. In the case of tests and other assessment methods (e.g., questionnaires and structured and unstructured interviews), bias can arise from multiple sources. For example, test bias can originate from factors related to the development of assessment methods (e.g., inappropriate test content or inappropriate standardization samples), factors associated with the use of clinical procedures (e.g., language or communication differences between clinicians and clients, inequitable social consequences or outcomes of test performance), or factors associated with the variables we are trying to assess (e.g., intelligence or depression, which are culturally defined to at least some degree; Reynolds & Suzuki, 2012).

Consider Table 9.1, which illustrates ways clinical judgments, tests, and statistical decision tools can be biased. Test bias may well be present when the outcome of the test or decision tool mismatches the true state of things in a systematic

Table 9.1. Defining Test Bias According to True State of Nature and Test Conclusions

		True State of Nature	
		Real differences among groups exist	**Groups are not different**
Test Results	**Test shows group differences**	Accurate test or decision tool	Bias
	Test shows no group differences	Bias	Accurate test or decision tool

(versus random) fashion (Reynolds & Suzuki, 2012). Consequently, for an ability test, for example, it is not only group differences in scores when true differences do not exist that shows bias, but also when a test fails to capture group differences when differences actually do exist. Determining whether there are true differences, differences due to test bias, or some mix of the two can be very challenging, but there is a benefit to at least proceeding with conceptual clarity as opposed to mindsets that will almost inevitably lead to serious misinterpretations.

Although knowledge of the true state of nature is a normative ideal for clinical decisions, in many cases we use tests, diagnoses, or other judgments to predict something else—an outcome that is often more important than the test or diagnosis itself. For instance, we may use a diagnostic interview to try to identify the treatment that is likely to be most effective for the client. We may use a statistical decision tool to determine whether someone is a good candidate for surgery, or if someone poses little risk to the public and therefore is eligible for parole. If we could see into the future in these cases, we would much prefer to have knowledge of the actual outcome we are trying to predict (treatment responsiveness, surgical success, criminal recidivism) than to know the outcome of the test. This means that for many of our applied clinical purposes, we are most interested in what Reynolds and Suzuki (2012) called differential predictive validity.

Differential predictive validity refers to situations in which a test or statistical decision tool predicts an important outcome better in one social group than in another. Take the example of the Correctional Offender Management Profiling for Alternative Sanctions (COMPAS), a decision tool to predict criminal recidivism in adults awaiting trial (Larson et al., 2016). COMPAS showed differential predictive validity because it was more accurate at predicting recidivism in majority White defendants than in Black defendants. In another example, Bridges and colleagues (2019) found that a common screening measure for major depression had a 75% accuracy rate (and thus a 25% error rate) in English-speaking Latinx individuals but only a 67% accuracy rate (and thus a 33% error rate) in Spanish-speaking Latinx individuals. Hence, the same test showed differential accuracy in predicting depression in one group compared to another group.

In summary, to the extent a factor relates to a test result but not the outcome of interest, that factor likely demonstrates test bias; whereas to the extent a factor is associated with the test result and the outcome of interest, the factor demonstrates predictive validity. For example, and illustrated in somewhat extreme terms, if age impacts a test assessing health, but status on that health variable has negligible or no true relation to age, then age is a biasing factor; in contrast, if age is related to the score and also shows a strong relation to the health variable, then it is not a biasing factor but rather is capturing something else or legitimate variance. (In actual practice, such relations may be less extreme, such as age impacting the test and showing a weak association with health, as opposed to age impacting the test and showing at least a moderate association with health.) Thus, assessing test bias is not just a matter of looking for average differences between groups on a test or other metrics, but also of looking at whether legitimate group differences, especially those of clinical relevance, are detected accurately. A test, for example, that fails to detect differences in levels of risk for self-harm across groups because results are skewed by sociodemographic factors nonpredictive of risk is not operating effectively and certainly should not be embraced as minimizing bias.

Unfortunately, if the criterion variable (or outcome of interest) used to validate a test or statistical decision tool is also fraught with test bias, it may create the false impression that the test is unbiased. For instance, if factors that create racial and ethnic inequities in COMPAS risk scores also impact scores on criminal recidivism, then the COMPAS may look unbiased when it is biased. Indeed, this was shown to be the case with the COMPAS. The risk of criminal recidivism initially appeared equal across risk levels between racial groups; however, majority Black neighborhoods are policed more than majority White neighborhoods and Black defendants are more likely to be arrested and prosecuted for petty, nonviolent crimes than their White counterparts. When risk of only violent criminal recidivism (ostensibly what the COMPAS diagnostic tool is designed to assess, in the service of keeping communities safe) was examined, the bias in risk scores across racial groups emerged (Larson et al., 2016). In summary, attention to potential bias in the criterion variable is just as important as attention to bias in test scores and statistical decision tools. Such impacts are common but may be subtle, and thus can be easily missed despite the level of harm to human lives that can result. (For additional information on this topic, including the contamination of both independent and dependent variables and the manner in which biasing factors can creep into artificial intelligence and machine learning programs, see Chapter 10.)

Other challenges create additional complications. A test may not be biased insofar as it reflects true differences among groups (Table 9.1), but if the conditions that create those differences originate from systemic racial injustice, they still create problems for us and especially for the group faced with these inequities. For instance, the Examination for Professional Practice in Psychology (the EPPP) has recently been scrutinized for racial bias (Sharpless, 2019) because psychologists of color have a lower pass rate than non-Hispanic White psychologists. However, there may be biases that well predate the EPPP that in fact suggest these differences may partly reflect the impact of social inequities and not solely flaws in the test.

To illustrate, differences in graduate school admissions procedures may result in graduate students of color attending less prestigious graduate programs that do not do as well preparing their students to take the EPPP (indeed, Yu et al., 1997, found that quality and competitive attributes of graduate programs predicted EPPP scores). And before that, differences in the colleges and high schools that these groups attended, differences in resources, access to advanced placement or college preparatory classes, cost of attendance, and the need to work to afford tuition and housing may mean that students were not as competitive for more prestigious schools that would better prepare future psychologists for graduate school admissions and the EPPP. Public school funding from property taxes may create educational inequities among people of different racial and ethnic backgrounds that ripple through their entire educational trajectory.

In the end, a test like the EPPP may be detecting differences in educational preparation among different groups accurately, or at least in part. These differences, however, may arise less from test bias and more from systemic factors and inequities that combine to reduce test performance. The conclusion that the test is biased may lead us to miss out on the opportunity to move "upstream" and address the original conditions that produced such inequities in the first place. Part of the problem is that attributing differences to test bias or, usually far worse, to different levels of human potential, often misidentifies fundamental causes, can demean individuals, encourage unfair or biased treatment, and interfere with recognizing and correcting the true sources of inequity. As this example further illustrates, we should not limit ourselves to investigating social determinants of biases in clinical judgment and decision making, but also look at structural variables that create the social determinants of inequities.

Summary

In summary, psychological processes both within and outside of our awareness can influence our interactions with, and judgments about, people of diverse racial and ethnic backgrounds. There is only a limited literature directly examining the link between these psychological processes and mental health professionals' clinical judgment, and the studies that do exist often conflict. Older studies suggest Black clients are more often diagnosed with psychotic disorders than White and Asian clients, possibly because of a tendency to misconstrue cultural expressions of distress. Despite a possible propensity for clinicians to diagnose serious mental illness more often in Black clients, judgments about relative impairment tend to operate in reverse: racial and ethnic minoritized clients are often judged as less impaired than their White counterparts, perhaps reflecting a shifting standard (i.e., tendencies to judge these clients as functioning relatively well in comparison to clinicians' expectations for the client's group). Studies of racial/ethnic differences in clinical judgment rarely focus on the psychological processes that may be operating. Furthermore, these judgments may well be influenced by emotions (negative and positive) and multiple processes may be operating simultaneously, making it highly challenging at times to determine if clinical judgments and adjustments are valid or biased. Even the best intended clinicians are likely to be influenced by these processes and may overcorrect to counteract stereotypes. Although it is likely that processes related to racial/ethnic bias on the whole will negatively impact judgmental accuracy, the literature is not sufficiently developed for us to know how. However, we are confident that in mental health care, like in medicine, we do not need perfect awareness and full knowledge to reduce inaccuracies stemming from racial/ethnic bias.

RACIAL/ETHNIC DEBIASING STRATEGIES

Approaches to countering racial/ethnic biases as opposed to reducing cognitive biases and underuse or misuse of normative methods, may overlap at times, but also diverge in important respects. In this section, we focus on research and strategies for countering racial and ethnic biases, and especially potential points of divergence with the extensive materials on debiasing and implementation of normative methods covered in Chapters 12 and 13. When there are commonalities, in order to avoid redundancy, we generally refer the reader to these two chapters. It is not until the next section of the present chapter that we discuss how the specifics of normative procedures and their application may need to be modified when used across diverse groups. Throughout this discussion, the focus is on the use of debiasing strategies and related corrective procedures with mental health professionals, while recognizing that many mental health professionals have increasingly received extensive training in multiculturalism and diversity, although not necessarily on the intersection with decision literature. Additionally, focusing on mental health professionals is not intended to suggest in any way that racial/ethnic biases among members of the general population is of secondary importance.

A fundamental point of departure between many racial/ethnic debiasing strategies and those designed to counter cognitive biases and underuse of decision aids and procedures (e.g., statistical decision methods) relates to views on the potential benefits and limits of insight into problem judgment practices. At the risk of overgeneralizing, approaches to racial/ethnic biases tend to assume that increased self-insight potentially achieves significant change (although certainly not comprehensive solutions). With racial/ethnic biases, societal factors that promulgate inequities remain a large part of the overall problem, and although gaining greater self-insight and motivation to alter biases on the part of individuals might help at a broader level, insight alone will not necessarily do much to achieve widespread social and political change.

Approaches to cognitive biases and insufficient implementation of decision aids often view insight into problematical judgment practices as a potentially helpful beginning, but as accomplishing very little by itself. Rather, active steps and enhanced capabilities are needed, especially when it comes to normative practices. For example, realizing one may not be performing proper covariation analysis does little good unless one learns the skills needed to execute the reasoning and procedural steps required. In other cases, given factors described in Chapter 12 and Chapter 13, realizing one has cognitive biases and instructing oneself not to be influenced by them also seems to accomplish little, unless active corrective steps are taken.

If errors in hot cognition and lack of self-awareness are often embedded in racial/ethnic biases, then interventions aimed at reducing emotionality and increasing self-insight and empathy, as will be described, may activate productive change. However, even if errors of hot cognition are diminished, this is likely to do little or nothing to address errors of cold cognition. Hence, a two-tiered corrective strategy for racial/ethnic biases might be needed. These corrective approaches might first be directed toward factors leading to errors of hot cognition (e.g., anger, resentment, problems taking the other's role). To the extent progress is made, one might then supplement these approaches with interventions aimed at cognitive biases, as well as insufficient knowledge and use of normative decision methods and decision aids.

We would note that boundaries between errors of hot and cold cognition are not as distinctive as sometimes suggested, and it is unrealistic to think that such problematic practices as confirmatory bias or steadfast resistance to statistical decision methods are devoid of emotionality. People may feel strongly about proving that they are right and therefore be especially attuned to confirmatory evidence, and practitioners with lifetime devotion to helping troubled individuals and perhaps inflated confidence in their clinical judgment will not necessarily be dispassionate when presented with evidence about the overall superiority of statistical judgment methods. Nevertheless, it is doubtful that these sorts of issues and investments elicit the same level and frequency of emotionality as issues and conflicts surrounding racial/ethnic bias. Clinicians would not be expected to face social ostracism or potential serious threats to their physical well-being because they were resistant to using actuarial judgment, whereas the stakes and consequences involved in racial/ethnic issues can often be life-changing, and highly destructive at that. Thus, issues related to racial and ethnic biases, and test bias, often elicit strong emotional reactions (e.g., pity, resentment, disdain, or anger). Increased potential for strong affective components brings us back to the two-layer view of errors in hot cognition adding to, or compounding, errors in cold cognition or cognitive biases.

To the extent a clinician is either failing to make appropriate adjustments to clinical decisions and judgments or making counterproductive adjustments, attention to racial and ethnic debiasing techniques is worthwhile. Conceptually, and differing in ways from common approaches to reducing errors of cold cognition, strategies for reducing racial/ethnic biases often start with efforts to increase clinicians' self-awareness of their biases and their knowledge about stereotypes. Greater awareness can raise motivation to respond in an unbiased way, and increased motivation may serve as an effective springboard for positive change. Considerable social psychology literature shows that conscious effort can reduce biased behavior and decisions. A recent meta-analysis on interventions to reduce prejudice finds the interventions are effective at improving attitudes toward minoritized groups in the real world (i.e., interventions in applied vs. laboratory settings; Hsieh et al., 2021). A comprehensive review of strategies similarly found small but positive effects for many types of racial prejudice reduction interventions, although long-term impacts are often unknown (Paluck et al., 2021). We describe the nature of these efforts, but caution the reader that little of this work has been applied to the arena of clinical care (Ricks et al., 2021).

Depending on the background of mental health professionals, racial/ethnic debiasing strategies might start with psychoeducation about racial/ethnic bias. Similarly, some psychoeducation about the historical context of racism, especially as it relates to health service provision, may well be useful. Increasing awareness of bias and racism itself will do little to mitigate inaccuracies in clinical judgment on the basis of race/ethnicity, but lack of awareness can certainly lead to biased judgments to the extent that a clinician unthinkingly relies on stereotypes and false beliefs and assumptions. Awareness is also critical to enhancing internal motivations to respond without prejudice (Plant & Devine, 1998), which can be essential because effective racial debiasing often requires conscious cognitive control.

An important aspect of psychoeducation/raising awareness about bias is understanding that everyone has biases. We are cultural beings, embedded in a society that provides us with messages about group membership. Even if we categorically reject stereotypes and are highly motivated to respond in a fair and equitable manner, learned cultural stereotypes will automatically be activated as we interact with people from diverse backgrounds. That we have learned these stereotypes is not a matter of personal shame, nor contrary to a sincere quest for justice. It simply means we have been socialized in a particular way. Psychoeducation about pervasive bias can reduce personal shame and guilt and increase an openness to engaging in racial debiasing strategies. It is critical we understand that no one is inoculated against potential biases.

An understanding of bias and an awareness that we all engage in automatic stereotyping to some extent, coupled with a commitment to acting in a just and fair manner, leads us to the second evidence-based component of racial debiasing. Approaches to racial debiasaing with scientific support can be broadly categorized as cognitive, affective, and behavioral. Cognitive racial debiasing strategies include generating counter-stereotypic examples (Blair et al., 2001; Devine, 1989; Devine et al., 2012), individuation (Brewer, 1988; Fiske & Neuberg, 1990), and taking the perspective of stigmatized others (Galinsky & Moskowitz, 2000). Stereotypes are primed easily when encountering someone of a different race or ethnic background, and thus an intentional effort to generate examples of people from that background who run counter to the stereotype can reduce bias.

For example, to counter a stereotype of a blue-collar Latinx worker, a person may think of specific examples of Latinx professionals (such as Justice Sotomayor). Yao Ming, a 7′6″ Chinese professional basketball player who played for the Houston Rockets, might serve as a counter-stereotypic example of an Asian man (or of a professional basketball player). Lumping many or most everyone from a social group into a single category diminishes the large within-group variability that exists. There will be few things that all social group members share. Therefore, it can be helpful to use individuating strategies—which consider explicitly how this person is an individual rather than a member of a particular group. Perspective-taking can increase compassion for others and reduce bias by putting oneself in someone else's shoes, or imagining how someone else is experiencing a situation.

On the affective side, Burgess and colleagues (2007) suggest clinicians should be trained in emotional regulation skills. However, the research on emotion regulation interventions is just emerging and most studies fail to demonstrate long-term effectiveness. Nevertheless, some research shows positive emotional states can reduce racial categorization and enhance attention and openness to seeking new information in a clinical encounter, at least in the short term (see Stell & Farsides, 2016).

On the behavioral side, clinicians may want to consult with trusted colleagues or supervisors and increase opportunities for intergroup contact. It can be helpful to seek feedback from trusted others about one's racial/ethnic and judgment "blind spots." Although every person has biases, in many circumstances group decisions tend to be more accurate than individual decisions (Bahrami et al., 2010). Research outcomes suggest, for instance, that forming "adversarial" research collaborations (collaborations between two or more people with opposing views) helps to combat biases and to conduct more accurate, reproducible science (Cowan et al., 2020). In the clinical context, having clinical care decisions reviewed or discussed by diverse teams may help uncover and potentially offset individual biases.

Increasing contact with diverse others can decrease stereotypes and biased behavior (Pettigrew, 1998; Pettigrew & Tropp, 2006). The more contact and positive encounters we have with people who are different from us, the less stigma and prejudice we tend to hold (Devine et al., 2012; Sparkman et al., 2016). Greater contact with diverse groups gives people opportunities to learn how people are similar and to de-emphasize differences, which can enhance a sense of empathy and clinical rapport. Stigma reduction is also associated with greater perspective-taking—the ability to see things from another person's point of view.

RELATIONSHIPS BETWEEN DEBIASING RACIAL/ETHNIC BIASES, COGNITIVE BIASES, AND SHORT-COMINGS IN IMPLEMENTING NORMATIVE DECISION PROCEDURES

So far, we have described ways that racial and ethnic biases can influence clinical judgments and decisions above and beyond the existing challenges created by cognitive biases in general, and strategies for reducing racial/ethnic bias and discrimination. We have described racial/ethnic bias as often involving errors in hot cognition because biases tend to evoke strong affective reactions—even and perhaps especially among people committed to justice and fairness. It remains to connect judgmental traps and shortcomings related to racial/ethnic biases, and intervention strategies that often emphasize errors in hot cognition, to the broader literature emphasizing errors in cold cognition, such as cognitive heuristics and underuse of normative methods. Specific ways that racial/ethnic bias and stereotypes might interact with cognitive biases (e.g., in clinical assessment tools like tests, questionnaires, and structured and unstructured interviews) and with underuse of normative procedures is a seriously understudied area. Of particular interest is the extent to which or how the general body of decision literature applies to racial/ethnic biases, and how application might vary as a function of patient sociodemographic characteristics.

Potential Linkages with Cognitive Biases

Racial/ethnic bias may reinforce or activate numerous cognitive biases, although specifics have generally not been articulated in the literature. Therefore, we offer a few hypothetical examples of how racial/ethnic bias and cognitive biases may be linked. Confirmation bias (see Chapter 4) covers a number of related decision habits, including the tendency to seek out information to support what one already believes and to ignore or discount information that fails to fit with preconceived notions. Stereotypes can be powerful automatic associations that could lead clinicians to fall prey to confirmation bias. For instance, if someone believes the stereotype that all Middle Eastern people are Muslim and therefore abstain from alcohol, they may fail to ask questions about alcohol and substance use at an intake appointment (perhaps out of a well-meaning desire not to be offensive). In contrast, perhaps a clinician subscribes to the stereotype that Native Americans as a group struggle with alcohol problems, so in an intake with a Native client, the clinician may ask about alcohol use multiple times, in multiple ways, and even assume that whatever alcohol use the client reports (e.g., 2–3 drinks per occasion) underestimates the true amount the person consumes.

Hindsight bias (see Chapter 5) describes the tendency to believe, once the outcome of an event is known, that the outcome was more predictable than was actually the case, or in foresight. For instance, a clinician may hold the stereotype that dishonoring the family is especially shameful for Asian adolescents. If the clinician is working with a depressed Chinese boy whose parents recently expressed their disappointment in him, and the boy subsequently dies by suicide, the clinician may feel this was a predictable outcome and experience terrible guilt that they did not do enough to intervene to prevent the boy's death. However, it is likely that the clinician did not see suicide as a significant risk for the client during their last session, because parents often tell their children they are disappointed in them and in nearly all cases such a tragic outcome is not the result.

An illusory correlation (see Chapter 3) is certainly potentiated by stereotypes. An inaccurate stereotype about a particular racial or ethnic group can create a sense that a certain trait is typical of the group. If a clinician further seeks to confirm their prior belief and discounts contrary evidence, the illusory correlation or inaccurate stereotype will prevail.

Technology and checklists can be leveraged to reduce the interaction between racial/ethnic bias and cognitive biases (see Appendix 6). Including even a single question or two within electronic health records that ask clinicians to note what specific behaviors they observed that led to specific judgments about a client can be enough to disrupt bias (Eberhardt, 2019). A prompt to focus on potential contrary evidence to a particular clinical judgment (e.g., inclusion of potential "rule outs") can be especially effective to counteract stereotypes. Structured (vs. unstructured) diagnostic tools and interviews can reduce bias by ensuring that clinicians cover essential areas rather than relying on their (perhaps automatic and unconscious) biases to lead the conversation. With that said, interview strategies and topics may also need to be tailored in certain ways to avoid content that might be considered taboo by some groups and to extend coverage to areas of inquiry that would likely be irrelevant for other groups (e.g., if time was spent in refugee camps and under what conditions).

Potential Impacts on, and Implications for, Normative Procedures

Normative procedures, such as covariation analysis, adjustments in base rates, and statistical decision tools, remain important strategies to overcome inaccuracies in clinical judgment and decision making. As noted at the beginning of this chapter, these procedures remain important in the context of working with diverse clients. What may shift, however, are the specific estimates or variables that are included in the procedures.

In terms of covariation analysis, Chapter 3 highlighted the importance of having adequate representation in all cells of a covariation table. For instance, if as a clinician I know of only a handful of people who are Marshallese and none have depression and all are very close to their family members, I may underestimate the likelihood of depression in Marshallese populations (indeed, I may even be so brazen as to suspect that Marshallese are happy people because they have strong kinship bonds and therefore are buffered from depression). However, if I know dozens or even hundreds of Marshallese people, including some who have strained family relationships and some with depression, then my ability to assess covariation between ethnicity and depression is at least in principle enhanced.

Often we simply lack adequate normative data from diverse populations to estimate proper base rates. Considerable effort is being directed toward enhancing diversity of normative data for tests and research (for instance, greater representation is a requirement for federally funded clinical trials), so one hopes that normative procedures will benefit from this increased knowledge. Even when single studies lack sufficient diversity, combining small subsamples across multiple studies can yield important insights (Lowman & Le Fauve, 2003).

Statistical decision methods can be especially helpful in increasing the accuracy of clinical judgments. However, these tools may be racially biased if they are developed on largely White samples (Lee, 2018; Vyas et al., 2020) or if they use inappropriate variables (Obermeyer et al., 2019; Vyas et al., 2020) (see Chapter 10). Some variables may predict an outcome of interest in one group, but fail to predict (or fail to predict as well) the outcome of interest in another group. For instance, Obermeyer and colleagues (2019) found bias in an algorithm designed to identify people with complex health needs who could be targeted for managed care programs. In particular, at the same health risk score, Black patients were objectively sicker than White patients (i.e., had more chronic health conditions and worse lab ratings on biomarkers of health). The authors found that this disparity in risk score was based on the amount of healthcare dollars the patient was costing insurance companies. If Black patients tend to delay seeking care and struggle to access care, their healthcare dollars can underestimate their health problems. In the criminal justice system, the opposite happens: Black defendants are assessed as having higher risk for re-offending than are White defendants on a statistical prediction tool (COMPAS) and are therefore less likely to be released while awaiting trial (Vyas et al., 2020), despite prospective studies showing COMPAS scores are not as accurate in Black as in White defendants (Larson et al., 2016). It is therefore imperative that when identifying samples on which algorithms are developed for statistical prediction, those involved in generating the tools are diverse (or at least highly informed about diversity considerations), that the variables used to generate predictions are meaningful and operate similarly across groups, and that the impact of algorithms is continuously evaluated once they are deployed (Lee, 2018; Obermeyer et al., 2019). In sum, statistical decision tools remain important to address bias, but the specific inputs and procedures that these tools use may need to be modified for different racial/ethnic groups.

Statistical decision tools can include a patient's race or ethnicity if estimates suggest a difference in the base rate of a particular condition or treatment response in one group versus another. However, race, by itself, is rarely an appropriate variable to include in such analyses. Ideally, clinicians and researchers would consider alternatives to race/ethnicity in statistical models. Perhaps there are more proximal predictors (e.g., consequences of being minoritized, the effects of poverty, acculturation level) that should form a basis for judgment rather than the person's race or ethnicity (Lee, 2018; Vyas et al., 2020). Scientific research may not yet permit such a leap; therefore, it is essential that scholars deliberately incorporate these factors into their work (Churchwell et al., 2020). We should remain mindful, however, that this is a temporary solution to a complex problem.

CONCLUSIONS AND FUTURE DIRECTIONS

It is a commitment to improving accuracy in our judgments and decisions that motivates us to consider and address racial and ethnic biases. Setting the causes of racial/ethnic differences aside for the moment, mental health professionals have a responsibility to address bias in their work. Fortunately, many tools developed to combat other types of biases can be leveraged to combat racial/ethnic bias, too. There are larger systemic and organizational level changes that will take time but are important for improving accuracy and reducing racial/ethnic bias in the long term. These include recruiting, retaining, and graduating more diverse students in the health service professions; establishing a commitment to diversity, equity, and inclusion among organizational leaders; conducting studies with more racially/ethnically diverse samples; including healthcare outcomes, not just patient satisfaction, in studies of culturally competent interventions and bias; conducting more comparative studies, especially within social groups; leveraging electronic medical records to alert clinicians when they are deviating from standard practice; and developing statistical tools on more diverse populations. Awareness of racial/ethnic bias in judgment and decision making is increasing and, as in so many other areas of healthcare and clinical practice, we are optimistic that the next decade will bring about important improvements in this arena.

REFERENCES

Abreu, J. M. (1999). Conscious and nonconscious African American stereotypes: Impact on first impression and diagnostic ratings by therapists. *Journal of Consulting and Clinical Psychology, 67*, 387–393.

American Psychological Association. (2021). *APA dictionary of psychology*. dictionary.apa.org

Arroyo, J. A. (1996). Psychologist bias with Hispanics: An analog study. *Hispanic Journal of Behavioral Sciences, 18*, 21–28.

Bahrami, B., Olsen, K., Latham, P. E., Roepstorff, A., Rees, G., & Frith, C. D. (2010). Optimally interacting minds. *Science, 329*, 1081–1085.

Bialik, K. (2017). *Key facts about race and marriage, 50 years after* Loving v. Virginia. Pew Research Center. pewresearch.org/fact-tank/2017/06/12/key-facts-about-race-and-marriage-50-years-after-loving-v-virginia/

Biernat, M., Collins, E. C., Katzarska-Miller, I., & Thompson, E. R. (2009). Race-based shifting standards and racial discrimination. *Personality and Social Psychology Bulletin, 35*, 16–28.

Biernat, M., Manis, M., & Nelson, T. E. (1991). Stereotypes and standards of judgment. *Journal of Personality and Social Psychology, 60*, 485–499.

Blair, I. V., Ma, J. E., & Lenton, A. P. (2001). Imagining stereotypes away: The moderation of implicit stereotypes through mental imagery. *Journal of Personality and Social Psychology, 81*, 828–841.

Blanton, H., Jaccard, J., Klick, J., Mellers, B., Mitchell, G., & Tetlock, P. E. (2009). Strong claims and weak evidence: Reassessing the predictive validity of the IAT. *Journal of Applied Psychology, 94*, 567–582.

Brewer, M. (1988). A dual-process model of impression formation. In T. Srull & R. Wyer (Eds.), *Advances in social cognition* (pp. 1–36). Erlbaum Associates.

Bridges, A. J., Andrews, A. R., & Deen, T. L. (2012). Mental health needs and service utilization by Hispanic immigrants residing in mid-Southern United States. *Journal of Transcultural Nursing, 23*, 359–368.

Bridges, A. J., Dueweke, A. R., Anastasia, E. A., & Hernandez Rodriguez, J. (2019). The positive predictive value of the PHQ-2 as a screener for depression in Spanish-speaking Latinx, English-speaking Latinx, and non-Latinx White primary care patients. *Journal of Latinx Psychology, 7*, 184–194.

Burgess, D., van Ryn, M., Dovidio, J., & Saha, S. (2007). Reducing racial bias among health care providers: Lessons from social-cognitive psychology. *Journal of General Internal Medicine, 22*, 882–887.

Burkard, A. W., & Knox, S. (2004). Effect of therapist color-blindness on empathy and attributions in cross-cultural counseling. *Journal of Counseling Psychology, 51*, 387–397.

Centers for Disease Control and Prevention (CDC). (2019). *Meningococcal disease: Age as a risk factor*. cdc.gov/meningococcal/about/risk-age.html

Cheng, A. W., Chang, J., O'Brien, J., Budgazad, M. S., & Tsai, J. (2017). Model minority stereotype: Influence on perceived mental health needs of Asian Americans. *Journal of Immigrant and Minority Health, 19*, 572–581.

Churchwell, K., Elkind, M. S. V., Benjamin, R. M., Carson, A. P., Chang, E. K., Lawrence, W., Mills, A., Odom, T. M., Rodriguez, C. J., Rodriguez, F., Sanchez, E., Sharrief, A.,

Sims, M., & Williams, O. (2020). Call to action: Structural racism as a fundamental driver of health disparities. *Circulation, 142*, e454–e468.

Cowan, N., Belletier, C., Doherty, J. M., Jaroslawska, A. J., Rhodes, S., Forsberg, A., Naveh-Benjamin, M., Barrouillet, P., Camos, V., & Logie, R. H. (2020). How do scientific views change? Notes from an extended adversarial collaboration. *Perspectives on Psychological Science, 15*, 1011–1025. https://doi.org/10.1177/1745691620906415

Cuddy, A. J. C., Fiske, S. T., & Glick, P. (2007). The BIAS map: Behaviors from intergroup affect and stereotypes. *Journal of Personality and Social Psychology, 92*, 631–648.

Cvencek, D., Nasir, N. S., O'Connor, K., Wischnia, S., & Meltzoff, A. N. (2015). The development of math-race stereotypes: "They say Chinese people are the best at math." *Journal of Research on Adolescence, 25*, 630–637. https://doi.org/10.1111/jora.12151

Devine, P. G. (1989). Stereotypes and prejudice: Their automatic and controlled components. *Journal of Personality and Social Psychology, 56*, 5–18.

Devine, P. G., Forscher, P. S., Austin, A. J., & Cox, W. T. L. (2012). Long-term reduction in implicit race bias: A prejudice habit-breaking intervention. *Journal of Experimental Social Psychology, 48*, 1267–1278.

Dovidio, J. F., & Fiske, S. T. (2012). Under the radar: How unexamined biases in decision making processes in clinical interactions can contribute to health care disparities. *American Journal of Public Health, 102*, 945–952.

Dovidio, J. F., Hewstone, M., Glick, P., & Esses, V. M. (2010). Prejudice, stereotyping and discrimination: Theoretical and empirical overview. In J. F. Dovidio, M. Hewstone, P. Glick, & V. M. Esses (Eds.), *The SAGE handbook of prejudice, stereotyping and discrimination* (pp. 3–28). SAGE.

Duncan, B. L. (1976). Differential social perception and attribution of intergroup violence: Testing the lower limits of stereotyping of Blacks. *Journal of Personality and Social Psychology, 34*, 590–598.

Eagly, A. H., & Karau, S. J. (2002). Role congruity theory of prejudice toward female leaders. *Psychological Review, 109*, 573–598.

Eberhardt, J. L. (2019). *Biased: Uncovering the hidden prejudice that shapes what we see, think, and do*. Viking.

Featherston, R., Downie, L. E., Vogel, A. P., & Galvin, K. L. (2020). Decision making biases in the allied health professions: A systematic scoping review. *PLOS One, 15*, e0240716.

Fiske, S. T., & Neuberg, S. L. (1990). A continuum of impression formation, from category-based to individuating processes: Influences of information and motivation on attention and interpretation. In M. P. Zanna (Ed.), *Advances in experimental social psychology*, Vol. 23 (pp. 141–208).

Fiske, S. T., Xu, J., Cuddy, A. C., & Glick, P. (1999). (Dis)respecting versus (dis) liking: Status and interdependence predict ambivalent stereotypes of competence and warmth. *Journal of Social Issues, 55*, 473–489.

Flaherty, J. A., & Meagher, R. (1980). Measuring racial bias in inpatient treatment. *American Journal of Psychiatry, 137*, 679–682.

Fujioka, Y. (1999). Television portrayals and African-American stereotypes: Examination of television effects when direct contact is lacking. *Journalism and Mass Communication Quarterly, 76*, 52–75.

Galinsky, A. D., & Moskowitz, G. B. (2000). Perspective-taking: Decreasing stereotype expression, stereotype accessibility, and in-group favoritism. *Journal of Personality and Social Psychology, 78*, 708–724.

Garb, H. N. (1997). Race bias, social class bias, and gender bias in clinical judgment. *Clinical Psychology: Science and Practice, 4*, 99–120.

Glasmeier, A. K., & Farrigan, T. L. (2007). Landscapes of inequality: Spatial segregation, economic isolation, and contingent residential locations. *Economic Geography, 83*, 221–229.

Gushue, G. V. (2004). Race, color-blind attitudes, and judgments about mental health: A shifting standards perspective. *Journal of Counseling Psychology, 51*, 398–407.

Gushue, G. V., Constantine, M. G., & Sciarra, D. T. (2008). The influence of culture, self-reported multicultural counseling competence, and shifting standards of judgment on perceptions of family functioning of White family counselors. *Journal of Counseling & Development, 86*, 85–94.

Gushue, G. V., Lee, T. R., & Kim, J. E. (2021). Racial triangulation and shifting standards in mental health assessments. *Journal of Counseling and Development.*

Henrich, J., Heine, S. J., & Norenzayan, A. (2010). The weirdest people in the world? *Behavioral and Brain Sciences, 33*, 61–83.

Hinton, P. (2017). Implicit stereotypes and the predictive brain: Cognition and culture in "biased" person perception. *Palgrave Communications, 3*, 17086.

Hoffman, K. M., Trawalter, S., Axt, J. R., & Oliver, M. N. (2016). Racial bias in pain assessment and treatment recommendations, and false beliefs about biological differences between Blacks and Whites. *Proceedings of the National Academy of Sciences of the United States of America (PNAS), 113*, 4296–4301.

Kinzler, K. D., & DeJesus, J. M. (2013). Northern = smart and Southern = nice: The development of accent attitudes in the United States. *Quarterly Journal of Experimental Psychology, 66*, 1146–1158.

Kugelmass, H. (2019). "Just the type with whom I like to work": Two correspondence field experiments in an online mental health care market. *Society and Mental Health, 9*, 350–365.

Larson, J., Mattu, S., Kirchner, L., & Angwin, J. (2016). *How we analyzed the COMPAS recidivism algorithm.* propublica.org/article/hot-we-analyzed-the-compas-recidivism-algorithm

Latu, I. M., Stewart, T. L., Myers, A. C., Lisco, C. G., Estes, S. B., & Donahue, D. K. (2011). What we "say" and what we "think" about female managers: Explicit versus implicit associations of women with success. *Psychology of Women Quarterly, 35*, 252–266.

Lau, T., Morewedge, C. K., & Cikara, M. (2016). Overcorrection for social-categorization information moderates impact bias in affective forecasting. *Psychological Science, 27*, 1340–1351.

Lee, N. T. (2018). Detecting racial bias in algorithms and machine learning. *Journal of Information, Communication and Ethics in Society, 16*, 252–260.

Lowman, C., & Le Fauve, C. E. (2003). Health disparities and the relationship between race, ethnicity, and substance abuse treatment outcomes. *Alcoholism: Clinical and Experimental Research, 27*, 1324–1326.

Mackey, K., Ayers, C. K., Kondo, K. K., Saha, S., Advani, S. M., Young, S., Spencer, H., Rusek, M., Anderson, J., Veazie, S. Smith, M., & Kansagara, D. (2021). Racial and ethnic disparities in COVID-19-related infections, hospitalizations, and deaths: A systematic review. *Annals of Internal Medicine, 174*, 362–373.

McGrew, W. (2019). *U.S. school segregation in the 21st century: Causes, consequences, and solutions*. Washington Center for Equitable Growth. equitablegrowth.org/research-paper/u-s-school-segregation-in-the-21st-century/

McKinney, P. A. (2004). Brain tumours: Incidence, survival, and aetiology. *Journal of Neurology, Neurosurgery, & Psychiatry, 75*, ii12–ii17.

Obermeyer, Z., Powers, B., Vogeli, C., & Mullainathan, S. (2019). Dissecting racial bias in an algorithm used to manage the health of populations. *Science, 366*, 447–453.

Oswald, F. L., Mitchell, G., Blanton, H., Jaccard, J., & Tetlock, P. E. (2013). Predicting ethnic and racial discrimination: A meta-analysis of IAT criterion studies. *Journal of Personality and Social Psychology, 105*, 171–192.

Paluck, E. L., Porat, R., Clark, C. S., & Green, D. P. (2021). Prejudice reduction: Progress and challenges. *Annual Review of Psychology, 72*, 533–560.

Pettigrew, T. F. (1998). Intergroup contact theory. *Annual Review of Psychology, 49*, 65–85.

Pettigrew, T. F., & Tropp, L. R. (2006). A meta-analytic test of intergroup contact theory. *Journal of Personality and Social Psychology, 90*, 751–783.

Plant, E. A., & Devine, P. G. (1998). Internal and external motivation to respond without prejudice. *Journal of Personality and Social Psychology, 75*, 811–832.

Reynolds, C. R., & Suzuki, L. A. (2012). Bias in psychological assessment: An empirical review and recommendations. In I. B. Weiner (Ed.), *Handbook of psychology* (2nd ed., pp. 82–113). John Wiley & Sons.

Ricks, T. N., Abbyad, C., & Polinard, E. (2021). Undoing racism and mitigating bias among healthcare professionals: Lessons learned during a systematic review. *Journal of Racial and Ethnic Disparities, 3*, 1–11.

Rosenthal, D. A. (2004). Effects of client race on clinical judgment of practicing European American vocational rehabilitation counselors. *Rehabilitation Counseling Bulletin, 47*, 131–141.

Rosenthal, D. A., & Berven, N. L. (1999). Effects of client race on clinical judgment. *Rehabilitation Counseling Bulletin, 42*, 243–265.

Rudman, L. A., & Ashmore, R. D. (2007). Discrimination and the Implicit Association Test. *Group Processes and Intergroup Relations, 10*, 359–372.

Sagar, H. A., & Schofield, J. W. (1980). Racial and behavioral cues in Black and White children's perceptions of ambiguously aggressive acts. *Journal of Personality and Social Psychology, 39*, 590–598.

Seng, J. S., Kohn-Wood, L. P., & Odera, L. A. (2005). Exploring racial disparity in posttraumatic stress disorder diagnosis: Implications for care of African American women. *Journal of Obstetric, Gynecologic, & Neonatal Nursing, 34*, 521–530.

Sharpless, B. A. (2019). Are demographic variables associated with performance on the Examination for Professional Practice in Psychology (EPPP)? *Journal of Psychology, 153*, 161–172.

Shin, R. Q., Smith, L. C., Wejch, J. C., & Ezeofor, I. (2016). Is Allison more likely than Lakisha to receive a callback from counseling professionals? A racism audit study. *The Counseling Psychologist, 44*, 1187–1211.

Sjoding, M. W., Dickson, R. P., Iwashyna, T. J., Gay, S. E., & Valley, T. S. (2020). Racial bias in pulse oximetry measurement. *New England Journal of Medicine, 383*, 2477–2478.

Sparkman, D. J., Eidelman, S., & Blanchar, J. C. (2016). Multicultural experiences reduce prejudice through personality shifts in openness to experience. *European Journal of Social Psychology*, *46*, 840–853.

Spence, A. G., Mishra, S. P., & Ghozeil, S. (1971). Home language and performance on standardized tests. *Elementary School Journal*, *71*, 309–313.

Stell, A. J., & Farsides, T. (2016). Brief loving-kindness meditation reduces racial bias, mediated by positive other-regarding emotions. *Motivation and Emotion*, *40*, 140–147.

Street, R. L., Gordon, H., & Haidet, P. (2007). Physicians' communication and perceptions of patients: Is it how they look, how they talk, or is it just the doctor? *Social Science & Medicine*, *65*, 586–598.

Thompson, M. N., Chin, M. Y., & Kring, M. (2019). Examining mental health practitioners' perceptions of clients based on social class and sexual orientation. *Psychotherapy*, *56*, 217–228.

Tien, C. (2020). *COVID-19 symptom lists and detection tools may exhibit racial bias.* verywellhealth.com/covid-symptom-detection-racial-bias-5093649

Trinh, N. T., Shyu, I., McGrath, P. J., Clain, A., Baer, L., Fava, M., & Yeung, A. (2011). Examining the role of race and ethnicity in relapse rates of major depressive disorder. *Comprehensive Psychiatry*, *52*, 151–155.

Tukachinsky, R., Mastro, D., & Yarchi, M. (2015). Documenting portrayals of race/ethnicity on primetime television over a 20-year span and their association with national-level racial/ethnic attitudes. *Journal of Social Issues*, *71*, 17–38.

Tyree, T. (2011). African American stereotypes in reality television. *Howard Journal of Communications*, *22*, 394–413.

U.S. Census Bureau. (2021). *2020 U.S. population more racially and ethnically diverse than measured in 2010.* census.gov/library/stories/2021/08/2020-united-states-population-more-racially-ethnically-diverse-than-2010.html

Vyas, D. A., Eisenstein, L. G., & Jones, D. S. (2020). Hidden in plain sight: Reconsidering the use of race correction in clinical algorithms. *New England Journal of Medicine*, *383*, 874–882.

Wegener, D. T., & Petty, R. E. (1997). The flexible correction model: The role of naïve theories of bias in bias correction. In M. P. Zanna (Ed.), *Advances in experimental social psychology* (Vol. 29, pp. 141–208).

Yu, L. M., Rinaldi, S. A., Templer, D. I., Colbert, L. A., Siscoe, K., & Van Patten, K. (1997). Score on the Examination for Professional Practice in Psychology as a function of attributes of clinical psychology graduate programs. *Psychological Science*, *8*, 347–350.

10

Machine Learning and Artificial Intelligence: Promise, Prospects, Cautions, and Application to Decision Making in Mental Health

On a day in 1966, a young woman in Cambridge, Massachusetts, began a conversation with a therapist:

> Young Woman: "Men are all alike."
> Therapist: "In what way?"
> Young Woman: "They're always bugging us about something or other"
> Therapist: "Can you think of a specific example?"
> Young Woman: "Well, my boyfriend made me come here."
> Therapist: "Your boyfriend made you come here?"
> Young Woman: "He says I'm depressed much of the time"
> Therapist: "I am sorry to hear that you are depressed."

This seemingly unremarkable conversation was, in fact, not between a young woman and her therapist, but between a young woman and one of the most famous artificial intelligence (AI) programs of all time, created by Joseph Weizenbaum at the Massachusetts Institute of Technology and published in the seminal paper "ELIZA: A Computer Program for the Study of Natural Language Communication Between Man and Machine" (Weizenbaum, 1966). More than five decades later, we have come far in many ways and yet, in some ways, not far at all. Despite Henry Markram's assertions that we would have a "detailed, functional artificial human brain" by 2019 (Fildes, 2009) or ubiquitous AI-based chatbots in areas like customer service, a robust virtual companion, let alone a psychologist, remains elusive. Nevertheless, machine learning (ML) and AI are, and will remain for the foreseeable future, important tools for the practicing clinician and neuroscientist.

Since the first conference on AI at Dartmouth in 1956, the promise of AI has seemed to be "just around the corner." It is easy to become cynical and dismissive of the progress that has been made over the years, but in contemporary society, ML and AI have become an important and pervasive presence, influencing personal choices, business strategies, military action, medical interventions, and indeed the science and clinical application of psychology, psychiatry, and neuroscience fields in general. As can be seen in Figure 10.1, the number of Google Scholar search results has increased exponentially in the past 30 years. Given the aim of the present book, the current state of the art and potential immediate benefits, promise, and various limitations of ML and AI as they apply to decision making in psychology are likely to be of considerable interest.

Although noteworthy distinctions can be made between ML and AI, for the purpose of this chapter and simplicity, we use the terms largely interchangeably and may use the term *algorithm* to refer to either. It is sometimes said that one can start a religious war by attempting to define either ML or AI at a conference on ML or AI, but suffice it to say that we consider AI to be (mostly) a form of ML,[1] while many forms of ML are not considered AI. Furthermore, many ML algorithms exhibit properties similar to those of modern neural networks with respect to several of the topics covered in this chapter. In instances where distinctions may be relevant, we endeavor to underscore the types of ML or AI algorithms to which the statements apply.

This chapter covers how ML and AI algorithms can be powerful tools for augmenting, supplementing, and sometimes replacing human decision making

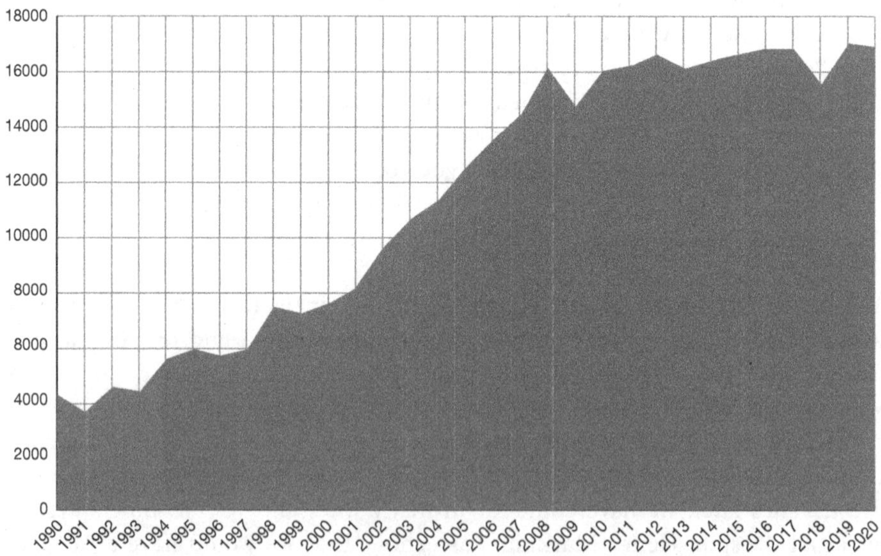

Figure 10.1 Number of Google Scholar results for (psychology OR psychiatry OR psychotherapy) AND ("machine learning" OR "artificial intelligence")

[1] For example, many in the field consider expert systems to be a form of AI but not a form of ML; however, the pedantic distinction is not likely to be of much interest to most readers.

in general and in psychology specifically. We discuss several of their limitations, some caveats, and other lingering questions they raise. We highlight some common misconceptions and popular red herrings. We provide a brief comparison of artificial neural networks to natural ones and allude to some similarities with human cognition as well as underscore some stark contrasts. Without question, AI is here for the long haul and, when used judiciously with the appropriate level of understanding, it confers significant advantages to those who can harness its power. We therefore consider how it is currently being used in clinical research and practice in the mental health field.

Recent discussions by prominent researchers tend to favor augmenting clinical assessments and interventions using AI, even while highlighting some of the concerns (Bickman, 2020; Fiske et al., 2019; Horn & Weisz, 2020). It is possible, even likely, that AI's most significant near-term contributions will rest on its predictive value rather than its ability to form causal inferences (Yarkoni & Westfall, 2017). Although psychologists often endeavor to discover the reason behind human psychological and cognitive differences and similarities, AI currently does not provide insight into causative relationships. However, AI does provide significant predictive and correlational insights that are useful in assessment and intervention or as guides for further investigation of underlying causes. Causal inference, even with the advent of big data, remains notoriously challenging (Hasan et al., 2010), and the ability to explain the implied conclusions of AI, particularly in the clinical realm, remains an active area of research that would require its own discussion (Miller, 2019).

In recent years, research into "explainable AI" has gained considerable traction; the objective is to create ML and AI algorithms that can "explain themselves" or, more reasonably, so that a knowledgeable person can accurately infer the reasons the algorithm arrived at its conclusion, decision, or output. What exactly constitutes a good or reasonable explanation is still debated (Miller, 2019); however, it is important that clinicians not refrain from methods shown to be effective simply because they lack an intuitive understanding of how or why they work. Empirically sound analytical methods should be preferred whenever possible.

The number of publications addressing ML and AI in the mental health field increased sharply from the early 1990s through 2007, and since then, more than 10,000 publications have been indexed by Google Scholar annually (see Figure 10.1). An increasing number of promising applications may well be of interest to clinicians; however, the sheer volume can be daunting. Although some claims about AI's superiority are exaggerated (Levingston, 2015; Tieu, 2015), research shows that well-trained and monitored algorithms can outperform clinical judgment on a number of important tasks, and hence can help mental health professionals improve diagnostic and predictive accuracy. We later highlight a few of the items that seem most promising. ML and AI approaches have demonstrated a promising ability to outperform other current clinical decision making approaches for some time (Bennett & Hauser, 2013; Youyou et al., 2015), with increasing promise in a wide range of areas. Appendix 4 provides examples of recent research in using ML and AI to understand, diagnose, treat, and assess outcomes in five areas of clinical practice.

OVERVIEW OF ARTIFICIAL NEURAL NETWORKS

The following several sections cover some topics of interest for those seeking to better understand artificial neural networks and how they compare to, and contrast with, natural neural networks, such as those found in the human brain. Readers who prefer to skip these sections may feel free to move ahead to the section "Understanding and Interpreting AI and ML Decision Making Research in Psychology" (on page 212).

Although there are numerous types of ML and AI algorithms in decision sciences, psychology, and neuroscience, we would be remiss in not reviewing artificial neural networks, since they present some interesting and striking similarities to natural neural networks as well as some notable stark contrasts. The artificial neuron in its various permutations borrows from the natural neuron but is many orders of magnitude less complex (much as two drawn stick figures might relate to Michelangelo's *La Pietà*) and has spatiotemporal limitations not present in its natural distant cousins. Nevertheless, these simplified neurons, when aggregated into networks, exhibit surprisingly complex capabilities and equally interesting parallels to those observed in natural neural networks, as well as some rudimentary aspects of human cognition. (We leave to the reader the fascinating line of inquiry that attempts to determine if artificial neural networks will ever fully mimic all aspects of human cognition or gain "consciousness.")

Artificial neurons and artificial neural networks have existed for a surprisingly long time. McCulloch and Pitts (1943) first postulated a mechanism to create an artificial neuron in 1943, while noted psychologist Frank Rosenblatt published the Perceptron in 1958, which is widely heralded as the first working computer code for artificial neurons and, when these artificial neurons were tied together, the first working neural network.[2] Although modern variants differ in some critical aspects that improve either efficiency or utility, many aspects of their designs remain substantially similar to original artificial neural networks. We therefore briefly discuss the original binary-output (either 0 or 1) and continuous output (any decimal value between 0.0 and 1.0) versions of the Perceptron. Modern implementations add interesting variants and complexity,[3] but they are not material to this current broad overview.

The first implementation of the Perceptron outputted either a 0 or a 1, representing the rough equivalent of a natural neuron firing or not firing. Figure 10.2 depicts the approximate equivalence of different parts of the Perceptron and natural neurons.

In a Perceptron network, the inputs represented as x_1 through x_n are numeric values with any range and are somewhat equivalent to stimuli received by a neuron. The bias weight and input, w_0 and x_0 respectively, represent the "excitability" of the Perceptron, which varies from Perceptron to Perceptron. The weights (w_1 to w_m) are multipliers for the inputs. When the previous input of a Perceptron is

[2] Rosenblatt wrote a Cornell Aeronautical Laboratory report (number 85-460-1) titled "The Perceptron—A Perceiving and Recognizing Automaton (Project Para)" in January of 1957, but the peer-reviewed publication came a year later.

[3] For example, we briefly mention simple transformation functions, but the history of, efficacy of, and counterintuitive nature of the rectified linear activation function (ReLU) and other modern derivatives (e.g., Leaky and Parametric ReLU), all popular transformation function variants, are a fascinating read for those so inclined.

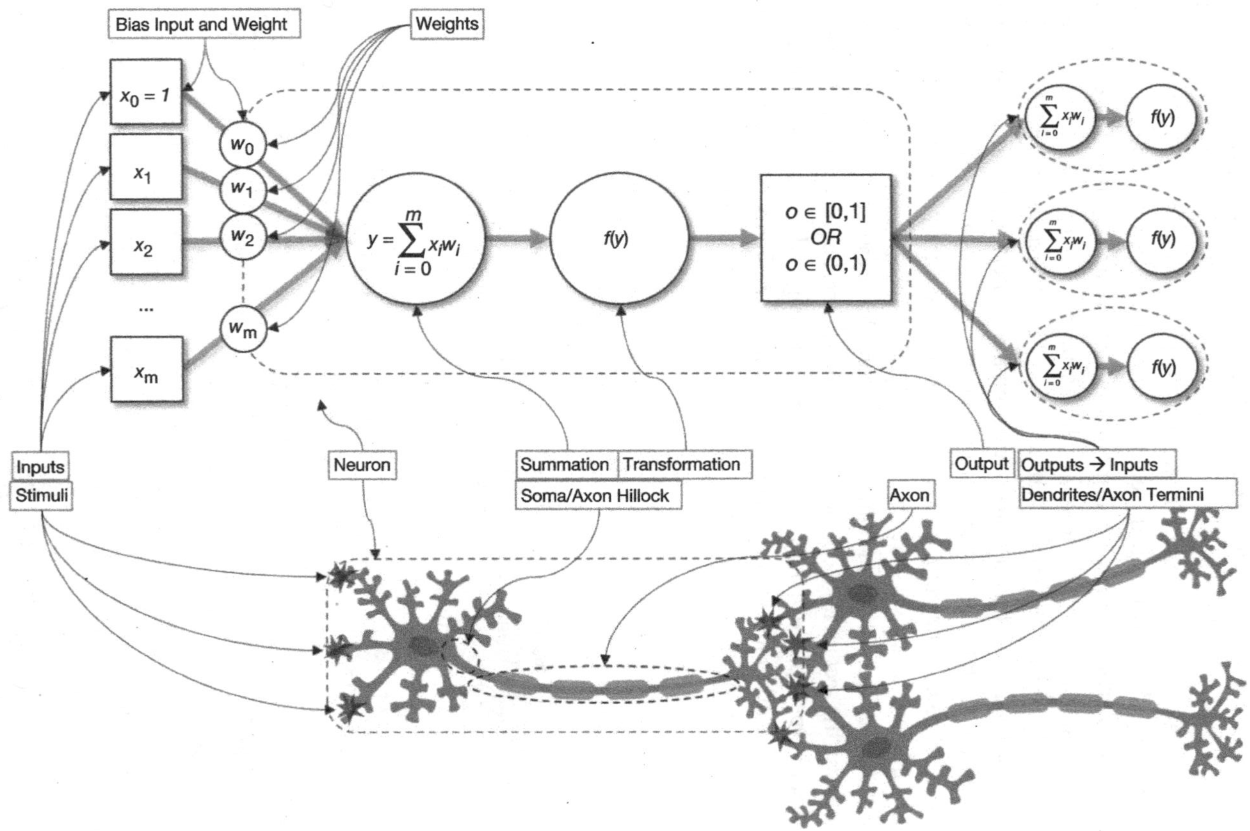

Figure 10.2 The artificial and natural neurons

another Perceptron, each Perceptron-to-Perceptron communication has its own independent weight. The inner workings of the Perceptron can be approximated with two functions, one of which adds all the inputs multiplied by their respective weights, referred to as the summation function, and one of which takes that result, the sum, and transforms it in the case of a binary output Perceptron into either a 1 or a 0 by applying a threshold or step function, usually referred to as the transformation function or activation function. This approximates the natural neuron's activation threshold, where if the equivalent of the sum of the input stimuli sufficiently depolarizes the neuronal membrane, the neuron "fires." If we represent each artificial neuron as a circle and each interneuron connection as a line, we can schematically represent a somewhat complex "deep learning" neural network (in this case a small, feed-forward deep learning neural network) as in Figure 10.3.

In Figure 10.3, the left-most collection of neurons, also referred to as nodes, are the neurons that receive the input from the data, while the right-most layer is the output layer. In this example, if we were trying to detect if an image contains a cat, a dog, or a horse, then the topmost node might provide a confidence estimate for the image being that of a cat, the second for a dog, and the last for a horse. For binary output networks, one would expect to see 1, 0, 0 as outputs for a cat image, whereas for the more commonly used continuous output it might be 0.87, 0.63, 0.38 for the same cat image, with the system "choosing" cat and providing a confidence estimate of 0.87.

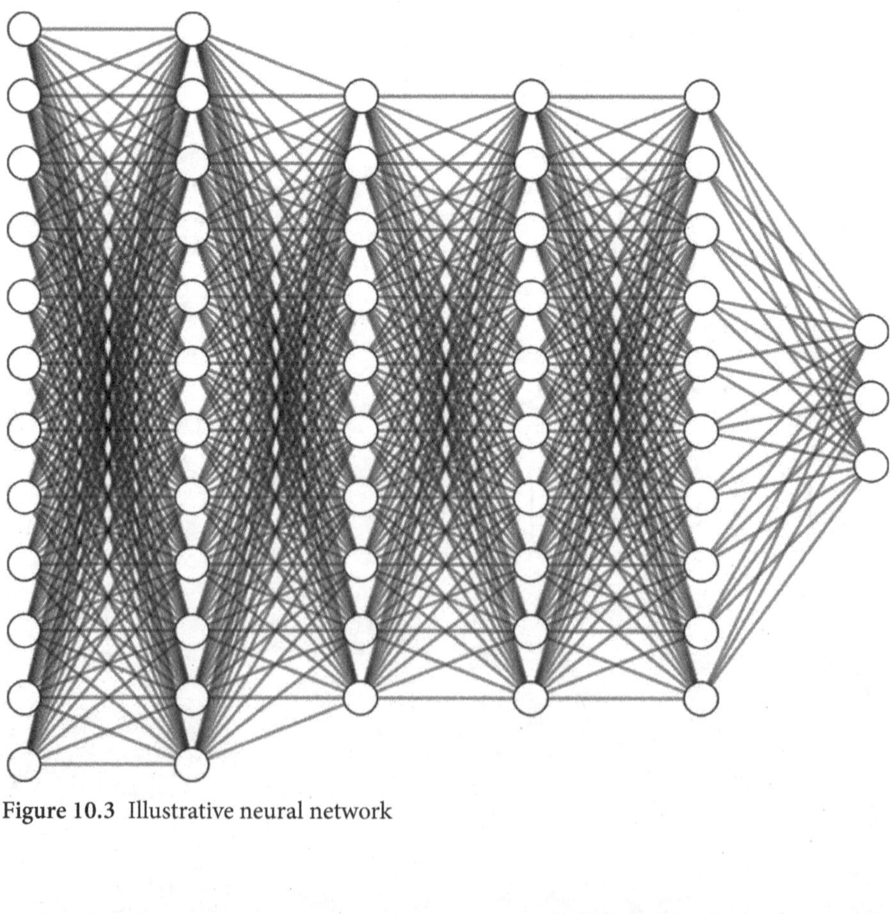

Figure 10.3 Illustrative neural network

For a well-trained neural network that attempts to gauge the likelihood that a patient may develop symptoms of major depressive disorder, the system may output 0.87 based on training data and the data provided on the specific individual. Although this is often interpreted as a probability, it is not. As with the cat example above, it is the confidence estimate, which often has more in common with asking a person, "What do you think is the probability that John Doe will develop MDD?" than it does with a traditional statistical estimate. A score of 0.87 should be considered not as a specific 87% chance, but as a general "likely" chance. It is important to stress that this is true only for well-trained neural networks that were trained on sufficiently complete data (enough features) that were reasonably unbiased and representative of the population on which the algorithm is to be used and when run against reliable data on the person. Poorly trained neural networks or input data that differ substantially from the data used to train the neural network will output untrustworthy estimates and should not be used. Additionally, most well-trained modern neural networks will have confidence estimates that approach probabilities based on the input data, but it is often difficult to ascertain this, particularly with commercially available "black boxes." In contrast, at least for now, models produced in a more open-source manner with peer-reviewed publications may be more trustworthy since they are "open box" and can be evaluated effectively by others. It is therefore recommended that for black-box AI that purports to provide good predictive value, the reader should use such systems cautiously unless those systems were clinically validated by third parties. When independent evidence is scarce or not accessible, the cautious clinician may wish to augment the diagnosis with other more traditional assessment methods.

BIAS, FAIRNESS, CONVERGENCE, AND DIVERGENCE

Unfortunately, the term *bias* can mean several things in ML and AI. The bias of an artificial neuron generally refers to the amount added to the neuron's inputs during the summation (through the bias input and bias weight in the example above) and is sometimes referred to as the intercept bias or intercept term. The bias of an algorithm can refer to statistical bias, or how different the expected value is from the produced value. However, when referring to algorithmic bias or bias in AI, we are usually referring to the tendency for an ML or AI algorithm to exhibit the equivalent of prejudices, often reflected in the training data generated by humans. When the bias of a system or algorithm is reduced over time, it is said to converge on fairness, whereas when it increases over time, it is said to diverge from fairness.

Most ML algorithms suffer from biases, much as humans do, which the reader would do well to keep in mind. It may be useful to explain how some of these biases may come about. Let us assume that you have a well-trained model that, based on several cognitive tests and genetic tests, assesses whether a specific treatment for schizophrenia will be effective for an individual. The system finds that the treatment is less effective for some people based on their genes, which happen to include genes that are more prevalent in African Americans. Although it is possible that these genes have a direct causative effect on treatment, it should be considered less likely than an alternative explanation—that the treatments have been less effective for other "fairness" reasons, namely that people are treated differently based on the color of their skin. We have several decades of research that suggest that physicians and clinicians explain treatment less rigorously to people of color, impart less of a sense of import or urgency with respect to the need to be compliant with medication and other interventions to them, are less likely to follow up with them, and have a tendency to evaluate subjective assessments, including severity, compliance, and impact, differently than with other groups (Bowser, 2001; Doescher et al., 2000; Hagiwara et al., 2013; Murray-García et al., 2000; Saha et al., 1999). Since the above factors affect the outcome and are related to the visible phenotypes of the patient rather than any fundamental efficacy of treatment, any well-trained algorithm trained on genetic data will discover that genes linked with African American phenotypes affect outcomes. Unfortunately, if an algorithm suggests to a clinician that a certain intervention will be less effective for a particular group, such as African Americans, that clinician may be less aggressive in suggesting rigorous adherence to the treatment schedule, less inclined to follow up, and impart less of a sense of import to the patient. All these things tend to degrade outcomes further, which, when fed back into the algorithm's training, will further exacerbate the algorithm's bias and further reduce the likelihood that African Americans will receive effective treatment. This is an example of a system or algorithm that diverges from fairness, and which would have significant negative impact on a subpopulation.

Not all algorithms diverge. For example, Correctional Offender Management Profiling for Alternative Sanctions (COMPAS) is a commercially available solution that attempts to assess if a defendant is likely to commit another crime. In other words, the system attempts to assess the defendant's likelihood of recidivism. Some studies have claimed that COMPAS did significantly overestimate recidivism rates for Black and Hispanic defendants while underestimating rates for Caucasian defendants (Larson et al., 2016; Rudin et al., 2020; Skeem & Lowenkamp, 2016). Although this is abhorrent, another study reported that approximately the same level of bias was exhibited by human adjudicators (Dressel & Farid, 2018). However, one of the advantages of COMPAS is that, presumably, as additional information is entered into the system, the system will become better at predicting recidivism rates for Blacks and Whites alike. If true, this would be an example of an algorithm that over time will converge on fairness and could well exhibit less bias than various human decision makers. The output of such programs might also serve as a check on human judgment, or even an approach for calibrating the tendencies of decision makers. Whether or not this will happen at a sufficiently rapid rate is another question, however.

Functional Similarities between Natural and Artificial Neural Networks

In this section we take an interesting sidetrack that, although not directly applicable to clinical interventions, shows that the emergent topography and functionality of artificial neural networks can converge on some of the same features as those present in nature. In that vein, we note that artificial neural networks sometimes exhibit surprising similarities to natural neural networks and at times they have provided insights into the inner workings of the human brain. We cover two striking similarities below and suggest to curious readers that they explore the growing use of artificial neural network structures to provide insights on how natural neural networks form and work as well.

Similarities with the Visual Cortex

In 1959, while at Johns Hopkins University, David Hubel and Torsten Wiesel demonstrated that the visual cortex of cats contained single neurons that responded to the presence of lines oriented in certain directions. Electrodes detected elevated activity in certain neurons only when a line on the screen was oriented in a specific direction, as shown in Figure 10.4. These findings, along with Hubel and Wiesel's invention of the single-neuron tungsten electrode, were largely credited for their both winning the Nobel Prize in Physiology or Medicine in 1981. Subsequent research demonstrated that similar sets of neurons were present in many animals and in all mammals. This research indicated that these neurons appear to be sensitive to specific orientations of light and dark bands.

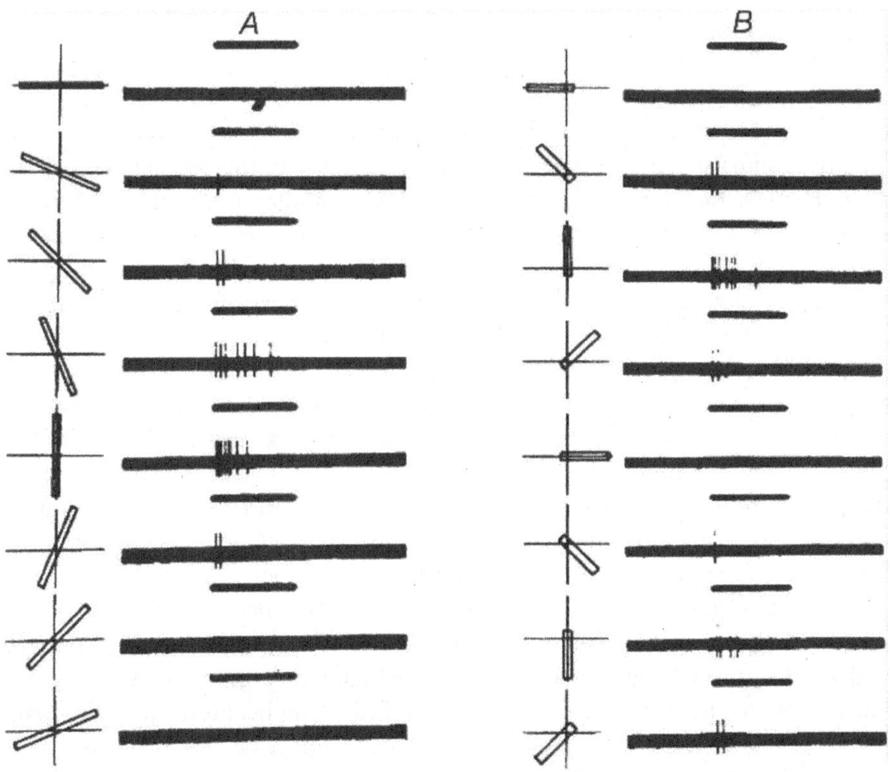

Figure 10.4 Visual cortex neuronal activity of two different neurons (Hubel & Wiesel, 1959)

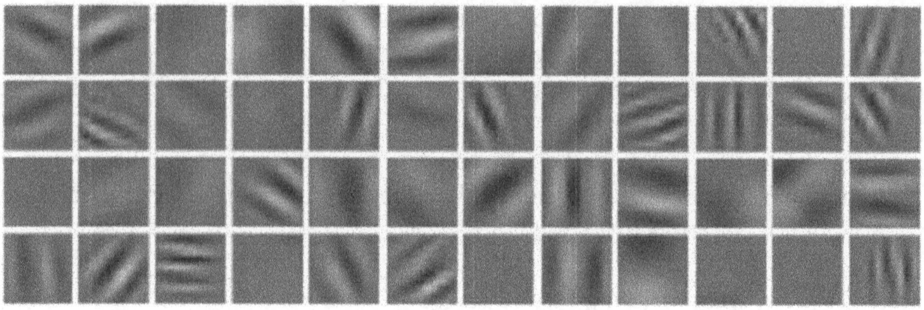

Figure 10.5 Example of the first layer of convolutional neural network (CNN) activation

These neurons are generally posterior to the optic chiasm and merge visual input in the striate cortex (V1) and correspond approximately to the first layer of a computer vision convolutional neural network (CNN), the most common type of neural network used in computer vision. When we look at the first layer's activation sensitivity in CNNs that are high performing, the majority learn activation patterns substantially similar to those of the neurons of the visual cortex, which are sensitive to oriented bands of light and dark. The CNNs were not "programmed" to be sensitive to these features, the CNNs "learned" them. Figure 10.5 shows a typical visual representation, albeit partial, of the first layer activation in a computer vision CNN where the various orientations of bands of light and dark can be seen.

Superstition in the Machine

ML and AI systems can exhibit the equivalent of two interrelated human qualities—affirmation bias and superstition. As used in the present chapter, *affirmation bias*, the preferred term in AI and ML, is similar in meaning to the term *confirmation bias,* as used in decision research and the present book in general (see Chapter 4). With general affirmation bias, the analogy is rather straightforward. Items that a neural network learns early are easily reinforced with new data but require considerably more contrary information to unlearn. Similarly, AI can internalize some superstitious "beliefs," figuratively speaking, since AI is not conscious, at least not yet. If an artificial neural network "learns" that two events are correlated, even if they are not (such as the case of black cats and bad luck), that belief can persist within the system even after some significant attempts to "teach" the system differently. This can be observed comically in AI that has trained ostensibly to win at some video games (Bontrager et al., 2019). Although many of the effects of errant learning can be comical, it is important to remember that ML and AI are generally effective when applied to data that are substantially similar to the data on which they were trained, and they may become less reliable, and at times unpredictable, when the data are highly divergent from training sets. Fortunately for the future of ML and AI in clinical applications, there are many tools that help detect and correct bias, two feats that have been more vexing when attempted in humans.

Other Caveats

With the increasing acceptance of algorithmically assisted psychology, the challenge for many lay people is to understand the difference between clinically validated and scientifically sound algorithms and those that at best overpromise and underdeliver and at worst are unequivocal snake oil. There are countless numbers of online quizzes and a proliferation of apps for phones and computers that purport to use AI or ML to provide the user with ostensible clinical evaluations. Although surprisingly effective and simple differential diagnostic tools have been available for quite some time, there is, of this writing, none approved to provide a replacement for proper human-led clinical assessment and care. The U.S. Food and Drug Administration (FDA) just recently began tentatively approving some AI-augmented or AI-based systems, but this remains uncharted territory and, because the protection of intellectual property based on ML and AI is still in question, most commercial providers prefer to keep their systems and services locked in a secure black box. The regulatory landscape is expected to change rapidly in North America, Western Europe, and much of the world. Until such a time as these systems can be rigorously assessed by agencies like the FDA or the European Union's EMA, part of the burden will be on the clinician to help their patients navigate the onslaught of unregulated apps, tools, and interventions.

Keeping all that we have covered so far in mind, there are several promising tools already available or well under development for diagnosis and assessment of interventions. Unfortunately, many commercially available tools and phone-based apps maintain a trade-secret approach to their algorithms, which, although understandable given the uncertainty surrounding the intellectual property of ML and AI algorithms, presents a problem when attempting to assess the validity and efficacy of their claims. Furthermore, the FDA is, as of this writing, just beginning to approve ML- and AI-based tools, with the European EMA following close behind. However, due to the inherent nature of ML and AI algorithms, the traditional and strict software validation requirements for embedded software cannot be applied in the same manner, presenting regulators and clinicians with some uncertainty.

THE STATUS AND PROMISE OF ML AND AI

Despite the nascent nature and shortcomings of the current state of the art of ML and AI in clinical psychology, they are already powerful tools that can help the practitioner make better decisions and help their clients realize improved outcomes. It seems likely, though by no means assured, that AI-based algorithms will drastically improve the diagnostic capabilities of practicing clinicians and help disentangle some of the more complex psychological disorders, which are often interrelated. Some of the research cited in this chapter demonstrates algorithms that already outperform the average subjective assessment considerably. Results of a meta-analysis suggest that by combining clinical and neuroimaging variables, ML models are able to predict responders and nonresponders to cognitive-behavioral therapy with nearly 75% accuracy (Vieira et al., 2022). With active research on integrating audiovisual analysis of patients as well as more recent comprehensive AI-assisted genome-wide association studies that help, among other things, predict the efficacy of pharmacological and other interventions, we can expect to see considerable research and development activities in this area.

Understanding and Interpreting ML and AI Decision Making Research in Psychology

Methodological training in clinical psychology has often been grounded in null hypothesis significance testing (NHST). Applied clinical research frequently attempts to "test" models that may include 100 or fewer cases to determine the extent to which a variable, or combination of variables, differentiates between those with and without a condition of interest, or those who do or do not experience a certain outcome, or the degree to which a condition or outcome of interest is present (e.g., mild, moderate, or severe). In so doing, researchers must select from a given set of limited variables to preserve adequate statistical power to detect group differences. If resultant statistical procedures are then adopted for clinical use, the evolution of statistical procedures often falls behind conceptual advances, which, in the absence of methodological refinement, often hinders clinical advancements.

ML addresses the shortcomings of NHST. ML often draws on large data sets, and an a priori hypothesis is not a prerequisite to conducting an analysis. Rather, by using repeating mathematical formulas, ML will identify relations among variables. Consequently, researchers are then positioned to translate ML results to inform clinical decision making and to better approximate data-driven solutions. Perhaps ML's primary advantage relative to NHST is its ability to continuously revise and update the underlying relationships among data through "training" (for a succinct description, see Schultebraucks & Galatzer-Levy, 2019, pp. 217–218). In short, researchers select a set of variables with discriminative utility, such as self-ratings on four scales to differentiate between individuals with and without posttraumatic stress disorder (PTSD). Researchers, blinded to participants' standing on the outcome of interest (e.g., PTSD), collect a second data set that includes the same variables in order to cross-validate and refine their models. The models undergo optimization, which then allows researchers to determine the most appropriate model for their intended purpose. Last, researchers collect a third data set, which has not yet been subjected to the model, to assess the generalizability of the model and thus its applicability to different populations. As may be inferred, large data sets are typically required for this approach; however, ML is not as prone to error stemming from human bias. Rather, ML aims to identify and refine an optimal combination of predictors. The following sections highlight case examples illustrating positive contributions and areas for growth as ML research continues to proliferate within clinical psychology.

ML Success in Psychology: Prediction of PTSD

PTSD is associated not only with personal suffering and diminished adaptive functioning, but also with increased use of health and other social services that incur considerable economic burdens on individuals and society. Not surprisingly, relative to the general population, individuals who serve in the military are at increased risk for developing PTSD (Wisco et al., 2014). Consequently, identifying approaches to mitigate the prevalence of PTSD in this population is likely to have a significant personal and societal impact. To this end, ML has been applied in identifying novel predeployment factors that predict deployment-related PTSD and that might aid in its prevention (Schultebraucks et al., 2020).

In a sample of 473 active-duty U.S. Armed Forces personnel, Schultebraucks and colleagues (2020) examined predeployment polygenic, epigenetic, metabolomic (i.e., small molecules or metabolites), endocrine, inflammatory, and routine clinical lab markers (referred to as "features" in ML parlance) to determine which best predicted postdeployment PTSD status at 90 to 180 days after deployment. In alignment with ML's "inner loop" approach to model development, 75% of the sample were randomly selected to partake in training the models using random forest (RF) ensembles of decision trees; the remaining 25% were reserved for model testing or validation using support vector machine (SVM) classifiers. The ML models predicted PTSD with a high degree of accuracy, as evidenced by sensitivities and specificities ranging from 0.78 to 0.89 and 0.71 to 0.79, respectively. The models also provided a rank ordering of features shown to be most predictive of PTSD development, which included self-report ratings of sleep quality, anxiety, depressive symptomatology, and attention.

Relative to the translational application, these results illustrate how ML might enhance efficiency in clinical practice and accuracy in decision making when working with military personnel. Namely, prior to deployment, sleep quality, anxiety, and depressive symptomatology, all of which are readily measurable in clinical settings, showed high predictive utility in personnel at risk for developing PTSD. In contrast, alcohol use, which is widely believed to increase an individual's risk for PTSD, did not display predictive utility and was not included in final predictive models. Taken together, these results highlight the "real-world" application of ML procedures (e.g., in informing deployment decisions, and in making determinations regarding access to predeployment interventions) and their lack of susceptibility to inclusion of extraneous predictor variables in the absence of supportive data (e.g., alcohol use).

Support for the use of ML approaches to inform PTSD management is rapidly growing (Schultebraucks & Galatzer-Levy, 2019). ML has yielded insights regarding predictors of risk for PTSD and associated trajectories (i.e., a remitting versus nonremitting course) through seemingly readily available information ranging from social media use (Reece et al., 2017) to traumatic event and injury information (Galatzer-Levy et al., 2014). Specifically, Reece and colleagues (2017) extracted statistical features from 43,950 participant Instagram photos and developed models that detected the presence of depression more accurately than general practitioners. The researchers relied on continuously training ML models with differing subsamples, in contrast to deriving a static statistical rule from the full sample. The results underscore a key distinction between statistical decision making, which relies on statistically supported decision making rules, and ML, which involves a process of continuous refinement through testing, optimizing, and validating models on new cases. Stated simply, ML relies on more adaptive processes than statistical decision making uses. As applied in clinical settings, ML has shown promise in the prediction of PTSD through its capacity to distill the most salient predictors from a broad pool of variables.

ML Room for Growth in Psychology: Suicide Prediction

Although ML has shown promise in multiple domains of clinical psychology, it is not without shortcomings. Namely, a recent simulation/empirical study revealed a significant risk for overestimating prediction accuracy when inappropriate models are selected (Jacobucci et al., 2021). The authors applied ML to data from the National Comorbidity Survey to model the association between suicide ideation and suicide attempts in a sample of 885 individuals. The model included demographic variables, psychiatric diagnoses, negative life events (e.g., childhood neglect), personality variables, and a history of suicidal behaviors (e.g., suicide ideation age of onset). The analysis revealed that specific combinations of ML training and validation procedures were prone to overestimate the classification accuracy of these variables as measured by the area under the curve (AUC). Specifically, when the optimism-corrected bootstrap procedure was combined with the gradient booting machine and random forests procedures, AUC values increased by more than 0.10, and in some instances more than 0.15. As can be seen, ML methods are fallible and subject to flaws in model selection. In the setting of a critical undertaking, such as the prediction of suicide attempts, systematic errors in accuracy, even if relatively modest, can result in tragic consequences. As discussed in detail in Chapter 11 ("Overconfidence and the Limits of Experience") and in Chapter 12 on debiasing and corrective procedures, overconfidence in decision accuracy can lead to unnecessarily risky decisions and is associated with a series of problem practices. It can be exceedingly helpful to know how uncertain one should be. Although critical shortcomings persist with respect to the clinical utility of ML in suicide prediction, ML has shown promise in detecting increased risk for suicidal behavior over time (Nordin et al., 2022).

Moreover, it is important to acknowledge that ML will not offset psychometric shortcomings of the measures from which data have been collected (Jacobucci & Grimm, 2020), but it may attenuate them to some extent. Jacobucci and Grimm (2020) examined how altering the reliability of underlying variables used in an ML procedure affected model interpretation (i.e., using values of 0.3, 0.6, and 0.9). Their simulations revealed that the likelihood of researchers' inferring inaccurate relationships among the data was inversely related to reliability, such that poor reliability of underlying indicators was associated with inaccurate inferences. As illustrated in preceding chapters, and upheld in relation to ML, measurement error can be remarkably difficult to overcome. Unfortunately, numerous variables used in the mental health field, such as results on various tests or subtests and impressionistic judgments about standing on important variables, have poor measurement properties and yet may be popular choices (Rabin et al., 2016).

ML as a Relative Upgrade? Substance Use Treatment Response

Substance use disorders have a high global prevalence and account for significant disability; alcohol use disorder is the most common by a wide margin (Degenhardt et al., 2018). Improving clinicians' ability to predict treatment response represents a worthy aim with potential for substantial societal impact. To what extent, then, might ML offer utility in advancing existing protocols for predicting treatment response in individuals with alcohol use disorders?

This research question has undergone preliminary investigation in Australia. Symons and colleagues (2019) assessed the extent to which ML models outperformed clinical staff (i.e., physicians, nurses, social workers, and clinical psychologists) in predicting alcohol dependence treatment outcome following a course of behavior therapy. Specifically, researchers defined treatment outcome as the completion of an entire treatment protocol and sustained abstinence from alcohol. Both clinicians and ML models received the same data inputs; however, the ML models were "trained" on an initial data set of 780 cases, and the test set for both samples consisted of 50 additional cases. Results revealed relatively comparable accuracy between the 10 most accurate clinicians (overall accuracy, 56.1%; sensitivity, 56.9%; specificity, 53.9%) and the 10 most accurate ML models (overall accuracy, 61.4%; sensitivity, 22.3%; specificity, 75.1%), with notable divergences in sensitivity and specificity rates.

Symons and colleagues (2020) implemented a similar study design using a larger set of cases for "training" (1,016) and test cases (220). Additionally, the researchers also assessed the predictive utility of a traditional binary logistic regression model. Similar to the prior results, the ML models trended toward a higher rate of overall accuracy (63.1%) relative to clinicians (56.3%); however, the logistic regression model exceeded both aggregate groupings, achieving 70% overall accuracy. In the context of research described throughout this book, these results appear to underscore the potential benefit of reliance on statistical methods; however, they also highlight the remaining challenges faced by ML methods in demonstrating significant value added above and beyond existing methods.

THE VALUE ADDED BY ML IN DECISION MAKING IN PSYCHOLOGY

ML is still in its early stages, and its applications in decision making and clinical psychology are rapidly advancing. As described above, ML has displayed promise in some domains but remains subject to potentially serious or fatal flaws in others. As has been discussed in preceding chapters, much psychological research is devoted to uncovering causal explanations for behavioral phenomena and is less focused on predicting behavioral phenomena. Yarkoni and Westfall (2017) contended that ML represents a pathway toward rebalancing the distribution of research effort in psychology to foster a greater emphasis on predictive pursuits. The authors leave the readers with the following regarding the future of ML in psychology, and the benefit of focusing on prediction:

> Ultimately, the new machine learning approaches working their way into psychology should be seen as opportunities, not threats. . . . There is no denying that in many cases, a focus on prediction will reveal major holes in an otherwise elegant explanatory story, and many well-known findings—some with seemingly large effect sizes—will likely fail to survive rigorous cross-validated analysis in large samples. But those explanatory models that successfully capture important aspects of human psychology should be much more likely to survive such tests—and will emerge with stronger empirical support as a result. What we will hopefully then be left with are models that can demonstrably do something foundational to the study of psychology: reliably predict human behavior. (Yarkoni & Westfall, 2017, p. 1118)

REFERENCES

Bennett, C. C., & Hauser, K. (2013). Artificial intelligence framework for simulating clinical decision making: A Markov decision process approach. *Artificial Intelligence in Medicine*, *57*(1), 9–19. https://doi.org/10.1016/j.artmed.2012.12.003

Bickman, L. (2020). Improving mental health services: A 50-year journey from randomized experiments to artificial intelligence and precision mental health. *Administration and Policy in Mental Health*, *47*(5), 795–843. https://doi.org/10.1007/s10488-020-01065-8

Bontrager, P., Khalifa, A., Anderson, D., Stephenson, M., Salge, C., & Togelius, J. (2019). Superstition in the network: Deep reinforcement learning plays deceptive games. http://arxiv.org/abs/1908.04436

Bowser, R. (2001). Racial bias in medical treatment. *Dickinson Law Review*, *105*(3), 365–383. https://www.ncbi.nlm.nih.gov/pubmed/16523590

Doescher, M. P., Saver, B. G., Franks, P., & Fiscella, K. (2000). Racial and ethnic disparities in perceptions of physician style and trust. *Archives of Family Medicine*, *9*(10), 1156–1163. https://doi.org/10.1001/archfami.9.10.1156

Dressel, J., & Farid, H. (2018). The accuracy, fairness, and limits of predicting recidivism. *Science Advances*, *4*(1), eaao5580. https://doi.org/10.1126/sciadv.aao5580

Fildes, J. (2009, July 22). *BBC news*. http://news.bbc.co.uk/2/hi/technology/8164060.stm

Fiske, A., Henningsen, P., & Buyx, A. (2019). Your robot therapist will see you now: Ethical implications of embodied artificial intelligence in psychiatry, psychology, and psychotherapy. *Journal of Medical Internet Research*, *21*(5), e13216. https://doi.org/10.2196/13216

Galatzer-Levy, I. R., Karstoft, K. I., Statnikov, A., & Shalev, A. Y. (2014). Quantitative forecasting of PTSD from early trauma responses: A machine learning application. *Journal of Psychiatric Research*, *59*, 68–76.

GBD 2016 Alcohol and Drug Use Collaborators (2018). The global burden of disease attributable to alcohol and drug use in 195 countries and territories, 1990–2016: A systematic analysis for the Global Burden of Disease Study 2016. *The Lancet Psychiatry*, *5*(12), 987–1012. https://doi.org/10.1016/S2215-0366(18)30337-7

Hagiwara, N., Penner, L. A., Gonzalez, R., Eggly, S., Dovidio, J. F., Gaertner, S. L., West, T., & Albrecht, T. L. (2013). Racial attitudes, physician-patient talk time ratio, and adherence in racially discordant medical interactions. *Social Science & Medicine* (*1982*), *87*, 123–131. https://doi.org/10.1016/j.socscimed.2013.03.016

Hasan, O., Meltzer, D. O., Shaykevich, S. A., Bell, C. M., Kaboli, P. J., Auerbach, A. D., Wetterneck, T. B., Arora, V. M., Zhang, J., & Schnipper, J. L. (2010). Hospital readmission in general medicine patients: a prediction model. *Journal of General Internal Medicine*, *25*(3), 211–219. https://doi.org/10.1007/s11606-009-1196-1

Horn, R. L., & Weisz, J. R. (2020). Can artificial intelligence improve psychotherapy research and practice? *Administration and Policy in Mental Health*, *47*(5), 852–855. https://doi.org/10.1007/s10488-020-01056-9

Jacobucci, R., & Grimm, K. J. (2020). Machine learning and psychological research: The unexplored effect of measurement. *Perspectives on Psychological Science*, *15*(3), 809–816.

Jacobucci, R., Littlefield, A. K., Millner, A. J., Kleiman, E. M., & Steinley, D. (2021). Evidence of inflated prediction performance: A commentary on machine learning and suicide research. *Clinical Psychological Science*, *9*(1), 129–134.

Larson, J., Angwin, J., Kirchner, L., & Mattu, S. (2016, May 23). *How we analyzed the COMPAS recidivism algorithm*. https://www.propublica.org/article/how-we-analyzed-the-compas-recidivism-algorithm

Levingston, S. A. (2015, July 13). So, be honest. Have you lied to your doctor? *The Washington Post*. https://www.washingtonpost.com/national/health-science/so-be-honest-have-you-lied-to-your-doctor/2015/07/13/be1ad134-f35b-11e4-b2f3-af5479e6bbdd_story.html

McCulloch, W. S., & Pitts, W. (1943). A logical calculus of the ideas immanent in nervous activity. *The Bulletin of Mathematical Biophysics*, *5*(4), 115–133. https://doi.org/10.1007/BF02478259

Miller, T. (2019). Explanation in artificial intelligence: Insights from the social sciences. *Artificial Intelligence*, *267*, 1–38. https://doi.org/10.1016/j.artint.2018.07.007

Murray-García, J. L., Selby, J. V., Schmittdiel, J., Grumbach, K., & Quesenberry, C. P., Jr. (2000). Racial and ethnic differences in a patient survey: Patients' values, ratings, and reports regarding physician primary care performance in a large health maintenance organization. *Medical Care*, *38*(3), 300–310. https://doi.org/10.1097/00005650-200003000-00007

Nordin, N., Zainol, Z., Mohd Noor, M. H., & Chan, L. F. (2022). Suicidal behaviour prediction models using machine learning techniques: A systematic review. *Artificial Intelligence in Medicine*, *132*, 102395.

Rabin, L. A., Paolillo, E., & Barr, W. B. (2016). Stability in test-usage practices of clinical neuropsychologists in the United States and Canada over a 10-year period: A follow-up survey of INS and NAN members. *Archives of Clinical Neuropsychology, 31*(3), 206–230.

Reece, A. G., Reagan, A. J., Lix, K. L. M., Dodds, P. S., Danforth, C. M., & Langer, E. J. (2017). Forecasting the onset and course of mental illness with Twitter data. *Scientific Reports, 7*. https://doi.org/10.1038/s41598-017-12961-9

Rosenblatt, F. (1958). The Perceptron: A probabilistic model for information storage and organization in the brain. *Psychological Review, 65*(6), 386–408. https://doi.org/10.1037/h0042519

Rudin, C., Wang, C., & Coker, B. (2020). The age of secrecy and unfairness in recidivism prediction., *Harvard Data Science Review, 2*(1). https://doi.org/10.1162/99608f92.6ed64b30

Saha, S., Komaromy, M., Koepsell, T. D., & Bindman, A. B. (1999). Patient–physician racial concordance and the perceived quality and use of health care. *Archives of Internal Medicine, 159*(9), 997–1004. https://doi.org/10.1001/archinte.159.9.997

Schultebraucks, K., & Galatzer-Levy, I. R. (2019). Machine learning for prediction of posttraumatic stress and resilience following trauma: An overview of basic concepts and recent advances. *Journal of Traumatic Stress, 32*, 215–225.

Schultebraucks, K., Qian, M., Abu-Amara, D., Dean, K., Laska, E., Siegel, C., Gautam, A., Guffanti, G., Hammamieh, R., Misganaw, B., Mellon, S. H., Wolkowitz, O. M., Blessing, E. M., Etkin, A., Ressler, K. J., Doyle, F. J., 3rd, Jett, M., & Marmar, C. R. (2021). Pre-deployment risk factors for PTSD in active-duty personnel deployed to Afghanistan: A machine-learning approach for analyzing multivariate predictors. *Molecular Psychiatry, 26*(9), 5011–5022. https://doi.org/10.1038/s41380-020-0789-2

Skeem, J. L., & Lowenkamp, C. (2016). *Risk, race, & recidivism: Predictive bias and disparate impact*. https://doi.org/10.2139/ssrn.2687339

Symons, M., Feeney, G. F. X., Gallagher, M. R., Young, R. M., & Connor, J. P. (2019). Machine learning vs. addiction therapists: A pilot study predicting alcohol dependence treatment outcome from patient data in behavior therapy with adjunctive medication. *Journal of Substance Abuse Treatment, 99*, 156–162.

Symons, M., Feeney, G. F. X., Gallagher, M. R., Young, R. M., & Connor, J. P. (2020). Predicting alcohol dependence treatment outcomes: A prospective comparative study of clinical psychologists versus 'trained' machine learning models. *Addiction, 115*, 2164–2175.

Tieu, A. (2015, July 16). *We now have an AI therapist, and she's doing her job better than humans can*. https://futurism.com/uscs-new-ai-ellie-has-more-success-than-actual-therapists

Vieira, S., Liang, X., Guiomar, R., & Mechelli, A. (2022). Can we predict who will benefit from cognitive-behavioural therapy? A systematic review and meta-analysis of machine learning studies. *Clinical Psychology Review, 97*, 102193.

Weizenbaum, J. (1966). ELIZA—A computer program for the study of natural language communication between man and machine. *Communications of the ACM, 9*(1), 36–45. https://doi.org/10.1145/365153.365168

Wisco, B. E., Marx, B. P., Wolf, E. J., Miller, M. W., Southwick, S. M., & Pietrzak, R. H. (2014). Posttraumatic stress disorder in the US veteran population: Results from the National Health and Resilience in Veterans Study. *Journal of Clinical Psychiatry, 75*, 1338–1346.

Yarkoni, T., & Westfall, J. (2017). Choosing prediction over explanation in psychology: Lessons from machine learning. *Perspectives on Psychological Science, 12*(6), 1100–1122. https://doi.org/10.1177/1745691617693393

Youyou, W., Kosinski, M., & Stillwell, D. (2015). Computer-based personality judgments are more accurate than those made by humans. *Proceedings of the National Academy of Sciences of the United States of America, 112*(4), 1036–1040. https://doi.org/10.1073/pnas.1418680112

PART III

Corrective Methods and Strategies

Part III of the book covers methods and strategies for increasing diagnostic and predictive accuracy. Chapter 11 address overconfidence and boundaries in learning from experience in clinical settings. These two factors can hinder recognition of benefits gained by increasing the use of strategies and steps to help attenuate cognitive biases and to enhance the evaluation and integration of information. Chapter 12 emphasizes debiasing strategies, and Chapter 13 covers an array of approaches that can improve effectiveness in gathering, apprising, and integrating clinical information. We also wish to call the reader's attention to Appendix 6, which provides both a detailed and condensed summary of guides and steps for increasing the accuracy of clinical judgment and decision making that appear throughout this book. Either of these summaries might serve as a checklist for clinical practices.

11

Overconfidence and the Limits of Experience

In Chapter 1 we make the point that mental health professionals are in the business of prediction. Will this patient be a danger to himself or others? Will this therapy client be better served with exposure therapy as opposed to less distressing approaches? A vast literature leads one to the conclusion that professionals who predict often do not perform as accurately as they (or others) would like, findings not limited to the mental health field. For example, Goldman (2018) reported that autopsies have revealed that "Class 1 errors," defined as principal causes of death that were missed and would have affected patient survival had they been identified, occur in approximately 10% of cases. The performance of forensic examiners in generating accurate criminal risk assessments has been very disappointing (Rettenberger & Eher, 2016). Tetlock (2005) has found that experts making predictions about sociopolitical events often do no better than chance! Rather than presenting a litany of embarrassing data, we turn instead to our primary tasks of (1) explaining why, even when prediction performance is weak, (2) professionals nevertheless often have high levels of confidence.

COMPLETE FEEDBACK IS OFTEN LACKING

As mentioned in Chapter 3, one of the authors has a psychologist colleague who consults with a major college football team. The head coach asks him to examine the data for each potential recruit and to provide a psychological assessment of that player's potential. The coach is very pleased with the psychologist's track record. A large fraction of the blue-chip recruits whom the psychologist has endorsed have played well. Therefore, the coach thinks that this colleague's predictions are very accurate. The coach is happy that Cell A of Table 11.1 greatly exceeds Cell B. It is important to note that the coach does not keep track of the players whom the psychologist has rejected. Those football players are not offered an athletic scholarship, and presumably they seek other opportunities.

Table 11.1. THE FOUR CELLS OF DATA NEEDED TO COMPUTE THE RELATION BETWEEN A PREDICTION AND AN OUTCOME

		Plays Well?	
		Yes	No
Colleague's	**Positive**	Cell A	Cell B
Prediction	**Negative**	Cell C	Cell D

The psychologist hopes that the coach does not investigate the performance of the players who have gone elsewhere, because those blue-chip recruits may be playing extremely well 2,000 miles away in a different athletic conference. What if the fraction of the rejected players who are playing well elsewhere exceeds the fraction of the endorsed players who are playing well for the team that has hired our colleague? Cells C and D contain the data that would destroy our colleague's good standing with the coach. By considering only the data in Cells A and B, the coach's feedback is woefully incomplete and potentially very misleading. This coach will never learn the true accuracy of the psychologist's judgments with such incomplete feedback. Perhaps we cannot blame the coach for not collecting the data in Cells C and D. To do so would require detective work to ascertain where the rejected players eventually enrolled. Then it would be necessary to observe their performance against teams different than the ones that play against the coach's team. This would be a difficult and time-consuming chore. So our psychologist colleague's job is pretty secure, thanks to the coach's inadequate feedback.

There are many instances in which the bottom row of Table 11.1 is absent. For example, anyone in a human resources department responsible for hiring will probably not know the fate of the people not hired. Another common example of this situation occurs when some intervention is instituted to improve people's performance. The top row of Table 11.1 represents people to whom the new program is administered. Cell A represents program participants who have improved. Cell B represents those who have not improved. A charlatan we read about designed a grossly unorthodox program designed to improve reading among adolescents. The director of this program announced that among those in the top row of Table 11.1, the proportion of adolescents in Cell A exceeded those in Cell B. However, there were no data whatsoever in Cells C and D, which would have contained the results of a control group that received sham or placebo training or a comparison group that received an alternative intervention. With no control group, we cannot know if the grossly unorthodox program, whose data would be depicted in the top row, resulted in poorer outcomes than the people not enrolled in the program, whose data would be depicted in the bottom row, or individuals receiving a different treatment program. Many people don't think a control group is necessary: "If I want to evaluate an intervention, why do I need a group of people who don't get the intervention?" Such an attitude will guarantee incomplete feedback. People with this attitude are in a poor position to learn from their experience, or more accurately, they may mis-learn from their experience. Smith and Dumont (1997, pp. 341–342) highlighted the importance of training diagnosticians on the implications of the cells within a 2 × 2 table like the one depicted in Table 11.1.

Therapists who employ Strategy X with clients may be pleased with the frequency of successful outcomes. However, without trying Strategy Y, they may never find out that it would have been much more effective. The real world does not always supply control groups or comparison groups.

Another reason why feedback is incomplete is that the outcome of a prediction may be unknown. If a client does not return, should the diagnostician conclude that the intervention has been successful? Perhaps the client does not return because he or she has concluded that the intervention was worthless or that the diagnosis was incorrect. For judgmental accuracy to improve, the more complete, nonambiguous, and veridical the feedback the better, and to the extent feedback falls short, learning may be impeded or completely enfeebled (Schiff, 2008).

THERE MUST BE A RESPONSE TO WHICH FEEDBACK OCCURS

Dawson et al. (1993) studied physicians' accuracy and confidence in predicting the hemodynamic status (blood flow characteristics) of patients who would undergo right-heart catheterization. Before the catheter was inserted into each patient, each of 198 physicians was asked to estimate three different measures of hemodynamic status and to express their confidence in each estimate. Then the catheter was inserted, and the three measurements were made. We might expect two different results of this study: (1) Physicians would be more accurate in an estimate in those instances in which they were more confident in the estimate; or (2) the more experienced physicians would be more accurate in their estimates, because they would have learned from their greater experience with right-heart catheterization. With regard to the first expected result, there was no significant relation between confidence in an estimate and its accuracy. With regard to the second expected result, the correlations between level of training (postgraduate year of the physician) and accuracy for the three measures of hemodynamic status were +.03, -.01, and -.05, all disappointingly low and not reliably different from zero. However there was a statistically significant correlation between level of training and confidence (+.28). The experienced physicians were not more accurate than their less experienced colleagues, but they were significantly more confident. How could this be?

When the physicians were requested to estimate hemodynamic functioning before they inserted the catheter, this request represented the first time they had ever been asked to provide such a judgment. In the past, after each physician had observed the catheter's data, they likely concluded that the data were pretty much what they would have predicted. Thus, their confidence in their predictive accuracy was enhanced the more times this bogus confirmation occurred. This does not represent feedback. This represents hindsight bias. After the hemodynamic status is known, the tendency is to mistakenly believe that one "knew it all along." However, in the research study, the estimates were made by each physician before the catheter was inserted. Thus, the physicians came to realize that they didn't "know it all along." This was their first learning experience. In order for true feedback to occur, one must first make a response. If there is no explicit response before the feedback is obtained, the response accuracy obviously cannot be improved. The physician participants were first forced to make a response. The catheter then provided the feedback. This is how one can learn from experience. Only when true learning occurs may an increase in confidence be warranted.

TREATMENT EFFECTS

Consider the job of a program officer at the National Science Foundation (NSF). This highly responsible job requires many decisions about which research proposals should be awarded taxpayer money. Suppose the NSF director wanted to assess how well program officer Jones was rendering those decisions. The director might note that the investigators to whom Jones awarded funds were more productive than those who were not funded. Wouldn't that be solid evidence that Jones could predict who would do successful research? In fact, it would not be good evidence, because the persons who were awarded money could buy excellent equipment and hire talented assistants. Those who were denied funds could not do such things. The success of the former researchers over the latter could be due entirely to the consequence of the funding decision, not to the accuracy of Jones' judgment. In this context, a *treatment effect* is defined as an effect of the judgment on a dependent variable or outcome. The greater research success of the person who received the NSF grant may have resulted from receiving the grant and not because Jones had accurately judged that person's proposed research to be better than the research of other applicants.

Treatment effects can result in high levels of unwarranted confidence in the accuracy of one's judgment. For example, if a school psychologist decides that a child belongs in the talented-and-gifted (TAG) program, the placement of that child in the TAG curriculum may have very positive educational benefits, even if the psychologist's evaluation was incorrect, but the outcome will tend to increase the psychologist's confidence in his or her judgmental accuracy.

THE UBIQUITY OF OVERCONFIDENCE

Only 1% of drivers rate their driving skill as below average (Reason, 1990). Approximately 94% of academics rate themselves in the top half of their profession (Mele, 1997). To say the least, such self-evaluations are highly suspect. How well do psychologists think they perform? A recent survey found that the average psychologist thought that he or she performed at the eightieth percentile in terms of patient outcomes. A quarter of the clinicians thought that they performed at the ninetieth percentile (Walfish et al., 2012). Absolutely no one thought that they performed below the fiftieth percentile. As these survey results suggest, psychologists are generally overconfident in their therapeutic effectiveness and diagnostic judgments (see Faust et al., 1988; Huss & Zeiss, 2004; Odeh, 2006; Oskamp, 1965; Wedding, 1983), with a lack of correlation between confidence and accuracy also documented (see Desmarais et al., 2010; Goldberg, 1959; Nadler et al, 1994). A meta-analysis of the relation between confidence and judgment accuracy in clinical decision making found a "small but statistically significant" correlation between the two (Miller et al., 2015, p. 553), but it is important to note that a small positive correlation can be consistent with systematic overconfidence.

The same trend toward overconfidence has been found among physicians. We have already presented the results of Dawson et al.'s investigation (1993), in which veteran physicians estimating hemodynamic functioning were more confident but not more accurate than their less experienced colleagues. Risucci et al. (1989) asked surgical residents to rate themselves on ten areas of performance. They were also rated on these same areas by their supervisors and peers. The surgical residents also took an objective test, the American Board of Surgery In-Training Examination. On seven of the ten areas, the residents rated themselves higher than the supervisors did. The correlation between the self-ratings and the objective test scores was zero. Barnsley et al. (2004) asked 30 medical officers in their first postgraduate year to rate their confidence in performing each of seven important medical procedures. Their tutors also rated the officers' competence in performing the procedures. In every case, the medical officers' confidence exceeded their supervisors' rating of competence. In addition, there "was no correlation between the . . . self-ratings of confidence and their measured competencies" (p. 358). A meta-analysis (Davis et al., 2006) performed on the relation between self-assessed versus observed measures of competence among physicians concluded: "A number of studies found the worst accuracy in self-assessment among physicians who were the least skilled and those who were the most confident. These results are consistent with those found in other professions" (p. 1094).

The three factors we have discussed already—incomplete feedback, no explicit response, and treatment effects—are not just reasons why diagnosticians do not always learn from experience: these factors also foster overconfidence. If a diagnostician notes only that Cell A is larger than Cell B, that incomplete feedback will likely foster overconfidence in their diagnostic ability. If one does not make an explicit response and instead relies on what one thinks one would have predicted, hindsight bias can doom a fair assessment of one's predictive accuracy. If one does not take treatment effects into account, one will mistakenly conclude that one's judgment is better than it actually is. However, there are additional pitfalls that foster overconfidence.

The first is the overgeneralization of expertise. Consider the following study by Bradley (1981, Experiment 1). Undergraduates were asked to rank their expertise in 12 areas of knowledge, such as science, history, food, etc. They were asked three true–false questions in each of the 12 areas. One of the three questions within each of the these areas was impossibly difficult, because it pertained to an extraordinarily obscure fact, so no one would know whether it was true or false. On the first pass through the 36 questions, only the options "true" and "false" were available, but the students were then asked to go through the list again, this time with a third option available—"I don't know." Of course, on their first pass through the list, the students were correct about 50% of the time on the impossibly difficult true–false questions in all 12 categories. The most important data were obtained from the second pass through the list. As a student's self-assessed level of expertise in a category increased, the student became less likely to admit that they did not know the answer and became more likely to persist in their initial random answer! In other words, if a category was deemed to be one about which the student was knowledgeable, ignorance was less likely to be admitted, and the answer about which the student had no knowledge whatsoever was more likely to be maintained. Apparently, if one thinks one knows a lot about a topic, one also thinks that one is knowledgeable about anything on that topic. Lack of willingness to admit lack of knowledge will foster overconfidence. Analogous results have been reported by Trafimow and Sniezek (1994).

A second additional pitfall fostering overconfidence has been called the Kruger-Dunning Effect (1999). Those who are unskilled in an area are the ones least likely to have the tools required to evaluate their own performance. For example, Haun et al. (2000) administered an objective test to medical laboratory personnel. The test assessed their knowledge of the clinical relevance of tests, their knowledge of medical terminology, and their problem-solving ability. In all three areas, those who scored lowest on the objective test were the most overconfident about their own performance. If one doesn't have the skills to do well in a domain, how can one accurately assess one's skills in that domain? Without such assessment skills, overconfidence is likely. The wife of a famous professional tennis player was once asked if she was "any good" at tennis. She replied, "I'm good enough to know that I'm not any good." According to the Kruger-Dunning Effect, if she had been a bit less good, she wouldn't have known that she wasn't any good.

WHAT'S SO BAD ABOUT BEING OVERCONFIDENT?

Overconfidence has some serious disadvantages. A considerable proportion of the research on overconfidence involves physicians, including psychiatrists in some studies, although studies with psychologists tend to yield similar outcomes (e.g., Desmarais et al., 2010; Faust et al., 1988; Huss & Ziess, 2004; Odeh, 2006; Oskamp, 1965; Wedding, 1983). First, highly confident physicians are less likely to request additional diagnostic tests (Friedman et al., 2005; Kovacs et al., 2020; Meyer et al., 2013). Of course, when additional diagnostic tests are needed but not ordered, physicians are less likely to make the correct diagnosis. Indeed, Kovacs et al. (2020) showed that overconfident healthcare workers provided lower-quality care than their less confident colleagues. Baumann et al. (1991) suggested that overconfidence may make clinicians less receptive to quality assurance programs. If one is confident that he or she is already delivering high-quality outcomes, why bother with a quality assurance program? Berner and Graber (2008) hypothesized that one reason that physicians are reluctant to comply with clinical guidelines is that many clinicians are inappropriately confident that they don't need them.

In a survey of psychologists, Wade and Baker (1977) found that a large fraction of clinicians eschew adherence to standardized testing methods, instead modifying them in idiosyncratic ways. The resulting modified tests have unknown validity and reliability. Despite deficient evidence to support such modifications, the psychologists are apparently confident that these alterations will somehow enhance reliability and validity.

Premature closure refers to tendencies to draw conclusions too soon, before sufficient information has been gathered, and to maintain those beliefs even when subsequent contrary evidence should be decisive. Overconfidence fosters *premature closure* as hypotheses are being considered and—worse—not being considered. For example, Voytovich and Rippey (1982) calculated a "realism score" for each of 83 medical students, which reflected an awareness of what one knows and doesn't know about a case. Those with a higher realism score were less likely to have premature closure on the case in question.

A third issue is that overconfident physicians are less likely to recognize when they have made an error (Brezis et al. 2019). Mistakes are less likely to be rectified if one will not acknowledge that they have occurred.

A common theme in this book is that the judgment and decision making shortcomings we document are not maladies specific to diagnosticians. They are problems for all of us. For example, Arkes et al. (1986) asked baseball experts and persons with moderate knowledge of baseball to decide which of three players won the Most Valuable Player Award in the National League for each of 19 years. A very helpful decision aid was available to both groups of decision makers. The people with moderate knowledge performed better than the experts on this task, because the experts were less likely to use the helpful decision aid. As is frequently the case, the experts were seriously overconfident. The people with moderate knowledge were much less confident, so they were more willing to use the aid, and therefore did better. This result is similar to the findings discussed earlier that the most confident physicians were less likely to order additional diagnostic tests.

PSYCHOLOGICAL PROCESSES AND OVERCONFIDENCE

Confirmation Bias

Confirmation bias refers to a set of related tendencies which, at their core, give undue favor to the beliefs we hold versus contrary possibilities (see Chapter 4). Such tendencies include (a) primarily or exclusively searching for evidence supporting a tentative hypothesis (versus searching sufficiently for contrary evidence as well), and (b) over-interpreting or weighting evidence as supporting a tentative hypothesis. Mendel et al. (2011) found that those who sought mainly confirmatory information for their initial hypothesis were much less likely to arrive at the correct diagnosis than were those who adopted a disconfirmatory strategy. Of course, differentially seeking evidence supportive of one's viewpoint is a sure way to increase confidence in it, whether or not the enhanced confidence is warranted.

Lord et al. (1979) conducted a classic study on interpreting evidence. The authors presented opponents and proponents of capital punishment with the results of two studies, one of which supported the effectiveness of capital punishment and one that arrived at the opposite conclusion. Both proponents and opponents rated this mixed evidence as supportive of their point of view. As a result, the polarization of their attitudes increased following their biased interpretation of the equivocal evidence. Increased confidence in one's original opinion is the hallmark of confirmation bias.

A particular methodology illustrating confirmation bias is based on distortion of multiple incoming cues in a manner that supports an emerging belief. Kostopoulou et al. (2012) provided a prototypical example. Physicians read three scenarios, each of which depicted a patient with two possible diagnoses. The initial information in each scenario favored one of the two diagnoses. Next, some neutral cues were presented; they favored neither of the two competing diagnoses. In one of the three scenarios, the neutral cues were followed by cues favoring the alternative hypotheses. The neutral plus the conflicting cues were insufficient to reverse the adherence to the initial hypothesis for the majority of the physicians. There were two other results of interest. The amount of distortion of the cues toward favoring the initial diagnosis was greater if the belief in the initial diagnosis was greater. Second, the distortion was reduced in physicians who had more than 10 years of experience. Studies of this type offer examples of the predecisional distortion paradigm, which in this case refers to physicians interpreting nonsupportive cues as being more supportive of an emerging diagnosis, whereas a control group whose members were not primed with an initial hypothesis evaluated the nonsupportive cues more objectively (DeKay, 2015; Russo et al., 1996). Of course, information distortion in favor of the initial diagnosis increases one's confidence in it.

The "Explanation Effect"

It's always possible to generate an explanation for one's prediction or diagnosis, and merely doing so increases one's confidence in the event's occurrence (Koehler, 1991). Ross et al. (1977, Experiment 3) conducted a classic study on this topic. Some subjects were asked to explain how being involved in a hit-and-run accident might have happened to a psychiatric patient. Others were asked how that person might have decided to run for city council. All subjects were asked to rate the likelihood of these two events plus three others. Half of each group was told that the target event (city council candidacy or traffic accident) was purely hypothetical, the other half of each group was not told this. Compared to control groups, who were not asked to explain the occurrence of either event, those who explained the possible occurrence of either target event rated its likelihood significantly higher, whether or not the event was deemed hypothetical. Merely explaining an event increased its rated likelihood. This phenomenon may be one reason why experts sometimes have greater overconfidence than less experienced diagnosticians. With more expertise, one has a greater amount of data to draw upon to concoct a richer explanation, thus strengthening the "explanation effect."

The Influence of Power

Physicians and mental health professionals are often in an influential or powerful role in their interactions with clients. For example, in clinical and forensic settings, mental health professionals who perform assessments or consult to 3rd parties or agencies can greatly influence a person's life or the outcome of critical decisions. Several studies have shown that persons assuming a powerful role are prone to overconfidence (See et al., 2011). A closely related finding is that persons is such roles are less likely to accept advice from others (Van Swol et al., 2019), which mirrors the finding that overconfident healthcare providers (versus those with more appropriate levels of confidence) are less likely to seek or heed the guidance of a decision aid. Given the small but positive correlation between confidence and diagnostic accuracy (Miller et al., 2015), confident diagnosticians are generally more accurate, but unfortunately they are also frequently overconfident (see Klayman et al., 1999).

The Attitude and Needs of the Client

Patients like healthcare providers who express certainty (Johnson et al., 1988). People in general like decision makers who are more confident (Price & Stone, 2004). Because patient satisfaction is a worthy goal, a diagnostician might be tempted to express overconfidence despite the disadvantages we've enumerated. In fact, the United States Supreme Court, in the *Neil v. Biggers* decision, stipulated that jurors can use the confidence with which a witness testifies as a basis for assessing a witness' credibility. Appearing credible would generally seem to be a worthy goal, too.

However, there is a difference between being confident and being overconfident. If the client's needs are primary and the diagnostician's needs are secondary, then the justification for overconfidence is diminished.

THE PROBLEM OF SELF-INSIGHT

A factor contributing to overconfidence that deserves special consideration is self-insight. In the present context, self-insight refers to a decision maker's ability to express the bases for his or her decision accurately. One reason a mental health professional might be overconfident is that they are not aware of how they go about rendering any particular diagnosis or prediction. They confidently express how they are doing it, but a simple mathematical analysis of their behavior often reveals that what a clinician says is not what that practitioner is actually doing. We want to emphasize that this discrepancy is not due to deceit on the part of the decision maker. The person is trying to be truthful, but their lack of awareness of the bases for their decision prevents accurate expression of those bases.

Here's a typical and very early example. Oskamp (1967) asked clinical psychologists to examine a person's MMPI (Minnesota Multiphasic Personality Inventory) results and to judge whether the person was medically or psychiatrically hospitalized. As a group, the clinicians thought that the amount of weight they placed on the various scales was as follows: Sc scale—13%; F, K, Hs, D, Pa, and Pt scales—8% to 9%; L, Hy, and Pd scales—6%. A simple regression equation revealed the amount of weight the clinicians actually placed on each scale as they made their decisions: Sc scale—36%; Pt scale—16%; D scale—8%, F, K, and Pd scales—5% to 6%. The correspondence between what the clinicians reported were the bases for their decisions and the true bases was very weak. Our point here is not whether their decisions were accurate. We are just interested in whether the clinicians could accurately articulate how they were rendering their decisions. They could not. The use of the Sc scale was almost triple what they claimed, and their use of the Pt scale was about double what they claimed. They also claimed to be using much more information than they really did utilize.

We repeat: This judgment flaw is common to many professionals. For example, Holzman et al. (1984) asked 25 gynecologists and 25 family physicians to state what their policy was for prescribing estrogen to postmenopausal women. A regression analysis showed that the factors that the physicians said were important in rendering their decision were actually not the factors that they used in rendering their decision. Dhami and Ayton (2001) investigated the bail versus jail decisions of 81 magistrates in the United Kingdom. The magistrates' stated bases for their decisions corresponded poorly with the mathematical analysis that indicated the true bases. Klein (1998) investigated the decisions made by many professionals, such as nurses and firefighters, and concluded that they could not accurately articulate the bases for their decisions. This does not imply that their decisions were poor. It does mean that if they were told that they could improve their accuracy, thereby making it more consistent with their high confidence, if only they would modify the weight they placed on Factor X, they probably wouldn't know how much weight they currently placed on Factor X. They might not know that they were even using Factor X!

What makes the lack of self-insight so pernicious is that it appears to get worse as one becomes more experienced in performing tasks. We've previously mentioned a study by Slovic et al. (1972), who asked 18 stockbrokers and five graduate students in business to examine 64 stocks using eight factors highly pertinent to the likelihood of capital appreciation. With a simple statistical analysis, the authors were able to ascertain the actual weight each participant gave to each of the eight factors. The authors also asked each person to divide up 100 points among the eight factors to indicate the subjective weight each person thought he or she had assigned to each factor in rendering a capital appreciation judgment. There was a correlation of -.43 between experience and the accuracy of the subjective weight assignments! Slovic et al. hypothesized that as one is learning how to perform a judgment task, one has to consciously utilize each potential cue (according, one hopes, to some approved strategy). However, as one becomes more practiced, the task can be done more "automatically." The bases for each decision thus become less accessible to conscious reflection. This has troubling implications for education. For example, if the veteran gynecologists in the Holzman et al. study were asked to instruct students on their policy for prescribing estrogen to postmenopausal women, the policy these experts would confidently recommend would likely not be the one that they actually use. If we make the generous assumption that the policy that they actually use is optimal, then the different one that they express to the students is not.

ONE OBVIOUS ANTIDOTE FOR OVERCONFIDENCE

Although overconfidence is widespread, small groups of people seem to be immune. Expert bridge players (Keren, 1987), horse race handicappers (Phillips, 1987), and weather forecasters (Murphy & Winkler, 1984) exhibit confidence that is relatively well tuned to their accuracy level. *Calibration* is the term used to describe the relation between confidence and accuracy. A diagnostician is well calibrated if 90% of the diagnoses to which he or she assigns 90% confidence are correct. A person is well calibrated if the group of predictions or diagnoses to which X% confidence is assigned are correct X% of the time. Note that all three of these groups of professionals get incontrovertible immediate feedback. For example, if during a year a weather forecaster assigns 100% probability of rain to 60 of the 365 days, job security would be enhanced if it rained on those 60 days. And at midnight each day there would be no doubt whether it had rained that day, so that feedback would be extremely helpful in fostering appropriate calibration of confidence and accuracy. In our coverage of debiasing techniques, we discuss additional ways of improving the calibration of confidence and accuracy.

REFERENCES

Arkes, H. R., Dawes, R. M., & Christensen, C. (1986). Factors influencing the use of a decision rule in a probabilistic task. *Organizational Behavior and Human Decision Processes*, *37*, 93–110.

Barnsley, L., Lyon, P. M., Ralston, S. J., Hibbert, E. J., Cunningham, I., Gordon, F. C., & Field, M. J. (2004). Clinical skills in junior medical officers: A comparison of self-reported confidence and observed competence. *Medical Education*, *38*, 358–367.

Baumann, A. O., Deber, R. B., & Thompson, G. G. (1991). Overconfidence among physicians and nurses: The micro-certainty, macro-uncertainty phenomenon. *Social Science & Medicine*, *32*(2), 167–174. https://doi.org/10.1016/0277-9536(91)09957-J

Berner, E. S., & Graber, M. L. (2008). Overconfidence as a cause of diagnostic error in medicine. *The American Journal of Medicine, 131*(5A), S2–S23. https://doi.org/10.1016/j.amjmed.2008.01.001

Bradley, J. V. (1981). Overconfidence in ignorant experts. *Bulletin of the Psychonomic Society, 17*(2), 82–84.

Brezis, M., Orkin-Bedolach, Y., Fink, D., & Kiderman, A. (2019). Does physician's training induce overconfidence that hampers disclosing errors? *Journal of Patient Safety, 15*(4), 296–298. https://doi.org/10.1097/PTS.0000000000000255

Davis, D. A., Mazmanian, P. E., Fordis, M., Harison, M. V., Thorpe, M. V., & Perrier, L. (2006). Accuracy of physician self-assessment compared with observed measures of competence. *JAMA, 296*(9), 1094–1102.

Dawson, N. V., Connors, A. F., Jr., Speroff, T., Kemke, A., Shaw, P., & Arkes, H. R. (1993). Hemodynamic assessment in managing the critically ill: Is physician confidence warranted? *Medical Decision Making, 13*, 258–266.

DeKay, M. L. (2015). Predecisional information distortion and the self-fulfilling prophecy of early preferences in choice. *Current Directions in Psychological Science, 24*(5), 405–411.

Desmarais, S. L., Nicholls, T. L., Read, J. D., & Brink J. (2010). Confidence and accuracy in assessments of short-term risks presented by forensic psychiatric patients. *Journal of Forensic Psychiatry & Psychology, 21*(1), 1–22.

Dhami, M. K., & Ayton, P. (2001). Bailing and jailing the fast and frugal way. *Journal of Behavioral Decision Making, 14*(2), 141–168. https://doi.org/10.1002/bdm.371

Fast, N. J., Sivanathan, N., Mayer, N. D., & Galinsky, A. D. (2012). Power and overconfident decision making. *Organizational Behavior and Human Decision Processes, 117*, 249–260. https://doi.org/10.1016/j.obhdp.2011.11.009

Faust, D., Hart, K., Guilmette, T. J., & Arkes, H. R. (1988). Neuropsychologists' capacity to detect adolescent malingering. *Professional Psychology: Research and Practice, 19*, 508–515.

Friedman, C. P., Gatti, G. G., Franz, T. M., Murphy, G. C., Wolf, F. W., Heckerling, P. S., Fine, P. L., Miller, T. M., & Elstein, A. S. (2005). Do physicians know when their diagnoses are correct? Implications for decision support and error reduction. *Journal of General Internal Medicine, 20*(4), 334–339. https://doi.org/10.1111/j.1525-1497.2005.30145.x

Goldberg, L. R. (1959). The effectiveness of clinicians' judgments: The diagnosis of organic brain damage from the Bender-Gestalt Test. *Journal of Consulting Psychology, 23*(1), 25–33.

Goldman, L. (2018). Autopsy 2018: Still necessary, even if occasionally not sufficient. *Circulation, 137*(25), 2686–2688. https://doi.org/10.1161/CIRCULATION AMA.118.033236

Haun, D. E., Zeringue, A., Leach, A., & Foley, A. (2000). Assessing the competence of specimen-processing personnel. *Laboratory Medicine, 31*(11), 633–637.

Holzman, G. B., Ravitch, M. M., Matheny, W., Rothert, M. L., Holmes, M., & Hoppe, R. D. (1984). Physicians' judgments about estrogen replacement therapy for menopausal women. *Obstetrics and Gynecology, 63*(3), 303–311.

Huss, M. T., & Zeiss, R. A. (2004). Clinical assessment of violence from inpatient records: A comparison of individual and aggregate decision making across risk strategies. *The International Journal of Forensic Mental Health, 3*, 139–147.

Johnson, C. G., Levenkron, J. C., Suchman, A. L., & Manchester, R. (1988). Does physician uncertainty affect patient satisfaction? *Journal of General Internal Medicine*, *3*, 144–149.

Keren, G. (1987). Facing uncertainty in the game of bridge: A calibration study. *Organizational Behavior and Human Decision Processes*, *39*, 98–114.

Klayman, J., Soll, J. B., Gonzalez-Vallejo, C., & Barlas, S. (1999). Overconfidence: It depends on how, what, and whom you ask. *Organizational Behavior and Human Decision Processes*, *79*, 216–247.

Klein, G. A. (1998). *Sources of power*. MIT Press.

Koehler, D. J. (1991). Explanation, imagination, and confidence in judgment. *Psychological Bulletin*, *110*, 499–519.

Kostopoulou, O., Russo, J. E., Keenan, G., Delaney, B. C., & Douiri, A. (2012). Information distortion in physicians' diagnostic judgments. *Medical Decision Making*, *32*, 831–839. https://doi.org/10.1177/0272989X12447241

Kovacs, R. J., Lagarde, M., & Cairns, J. (2020). Overconfident health workers provide lower quality healthcare. *Journal of Economic Psychology*, *76*, 1–11. https://doi.org/10.1016/j.joep.2019.102213

Kruger, J., & Dunning, D. (1999). Unskilled and unaware of it: How difficulties in recognizing one's own incompetence lead to inflated self-assessments. *Journal of Personality and Social Psychology*, *77*, 1121–1134.

Lord, C. G., Ross, L., & Lepper, M. R. (1979). Biased assimilation and attitude polarization: The effects of prior theories on subsequently considered evidence. *Journal of Personality and Social Psychology*, *37*(11), 2098–2109.

Mele, A. R. (1997). Real self-deception. *Behavioral and Brain Sciences*, *20*, 91–102.

Mendel, R., Traut-Mattausch, E., Jonas, E., Leucht, S., Kane, J. M., Maino, K., Kissling, W., & Hamann, J. (2011). Confirmation bias: Why psychiatrists stick to wrong preliminary diagnoses. *Psychological Medicine*, *41*(12), 2651–2659. https://doi.org/10.1017/S0033291711000808

Meyer, A. N. D., Payne, V. L., Meeks, D. W., et al. (2013). Physician's diagnostic accuracy, confidence, and resource requests: A vignette study. *JAMA Internal Medicine*, *173*(21), 1952–1959. https://doi.org/10.1001/jamainternmed.2013.10081

Miller, D. J., Spengler, E. S., & Spengler, P. M. (2015). A meta-analysis of confidence and judgment accuracy in clinical decision making. *Journal of Counseling Psychology*, *62*(4), 553–567.

Murphy, A. H., & Winkler, R. L. (1984). Probability forecasting in meteorology. *Journal of the American Statistical Association*, *79*, 489–500.

Nadler, J. D., Mittenberg, W., DePiano, F. A., & Schneider, B. A. (1994). Effects of patient age on neuropsychological test interpretation. *Professional Psychology: Research and Practice*, *25*(3), 288–295.

Neil v. Biggers, 409 US 188 (1972). https://caselaw.findlaw.com/court/us-supreme-court/409/188.html

Odeh, M. S., Zeiss, R. A., & Huss, M. T. (2006). Cues they use: Clinicians' endorsement of risk cues in predictions of dangerousness. *Behavioral Sciences and the Law*, *24*, 147-156.

Oskamp, S. (1967). Clinical judgment from MMPI: Simple or complex? *Journal of Clinical Psychology*, *23*(4), 411–415.

Oskamp, S. (1965). Overconfidence in case study judgments. *Journal of Consulting Psychology*, *29*(3), 261–265.

Phillips, L. D. (1987). On the adequacy of judgmental forecasts. In G. Wright & P. Ayton (Eds.), *Judgmental forecasting* (pp. 11–30). Wiley.

Price, P. C., & Stone, E. R. (2004). Intuitive evaluation of likelihood judgment producers: Evidence for a confidence heuristic. *Journal of Behavioral Decision Making, 17*(1), 39–57.

Reason, J., Manstead, A., Stradling, S., Baxter, J., & Campbell, K. (1990). Errors and violations on the roads: A real distinction? *Ergonomics, 33*, 1315–1332.

Rettenberger, M., & Eher, R. (2016). Potential sources of bias and error, the illusion of competence of expert opinion, and some suggestions for the improvement of clinical practice. *Recht & Psychiatrie, 34*(1), 50–57.

Risucci, D. A., Torolani, A. J., & Ward, R. J. (1989). Ratings of surgical residents by self, supervisors, and peers. *Surgical Gynecology and Obstetrics, 169*, 519–526.

Ross, L., Lepper, M. R., Strack, F., & Steinmetz, J. L. (1977). Social explanation and social expectation: Effects of real and hypothetical explanations on subjective likelihood. *Journal of Personality and Social Psychology, 35*(11), 817–829.

Russo, J. E., Medvec, V. H., & Meloy, M. G. (1996). The distortion of information during decisions. *Organizational Behavior and Human Decision Processes, 66*, 102–110.

Schiff, G. D. (2008). Minimizing diagnostic error: The importance of follow-up and feedback. *American Journal of Medicine, 121*(5A), 538–542. https://doi.org/10.1016/j.amjmed.2008.02.004

See, K. E., Morrison, E. W., Rothman, N. B., & Soll, J. B. (2011). The detrimental effects of power on confidence, advice taking, and accuracy. *Organizational Behavior and Human Decision Processes, 116*, 272–285. https://doi.org/10.1016/j.obhdp.2011.07.006

Slovic, P., Fleissner, D., & Bauman, W. S. (1972). Analyzing use of information in investment decision making: Methodological proposal. *Journal of Business, 45*(2), 283–301. https://doi.org/10.1086/295448

Smith, D., & Dumont, F. (1997). Eliminating overconfidence in psychodiagnosis: Strategies for training and practice. *Clinical Psychology: Science and Practice, 4*(4), 335–345.

Tetlock, P. E. (2005). *Expert political judgment: How good is it, how can we know?* Princeton University Press.

Trafimow, D., & Sniezek, J. A. (1994). Perceived expertise and its effect on confidence. *Organizational Behavior and Human Decision Processes, 57*, 290–302.

Van Swol, L. M., Prahl, A., MacGeorge, E., & Brauch, S. (2019). Imposing advice on powerful people. *Communication Reports, 32*(3), 173–187. https://doi.org/10.1080/08934215.2019.1655082

Voytovich, A. E., & Rippey, R. M. (1982). Knowledge, realism, and diagnostic reasoning in a physical diagnosis course. *Journal of Medical Education, 57*(6), 461–467.

Wade, T. C., & Baker, T. B. (1977). Opinions and use of psychological tests: A survey of clinical psychologists. *American Psychologist, 33*, 874–882.

Walfish, S., McAllister, B., O'Donnell, P., & Lamberrt, M. J. (2012). An investigation of self-assessment bias in mental health providers. *Psychological Reports, 110*, 639–644. https://doi.org/10.2466/02.07.17.PRO.110.2.639-644

Wedding, D. (1983). Comparison of statistical and actuarial models for predicting lateralization of brain-damage. *Clinical Neuropsychology, 5*(1), 15–20.

12

The Limits of Insight Alone, the Need for Active Steps, and the Use of Debiasing Strategies

This chapter focuses on cognitive and technological interventions and strategies for reducing bias in one's diagnoses and predictions. We mainly address problems in cold cognition, that is, misjudgments that are not simply reducible to emotional factors. To place this chapter in some context, Chapter 2 focused on implementing careful or meticulous practices in order to avoid basic or preventable errors that have little to do with cognitive biases or strategies for integrating information. Chapter 11 set a framework for the present chapter as well as the next chapter by emphasizing overconfidence and the various problems it can create, in particular its role in building resistance to helpful decision aids and corrective strategies. Chapter 13 builds on the intervention strategies covered in the present chapter, emphasizing practical and specific steps that can be applied to clinical activities for enhancing information gathering, appraising the value of information, and combining or integrating information.

In 1999, the Institute of Medicine published *To Err Is Human* (Kohn et al., 2000). The shocking conclusion of that landmark publication was that medical errors result in up to 98,000 deaths per year in the United States. An estimated 40,000 to 80,000 hospital deaths annually result specifically from misdiagnosis (Leape et al., 2002). More recent publications have substantiated earlier estimates of the large number of deaths caused by diagnostic and judgmental errors (see Chu et al., 2018; Eichbaum et al., 2019; Schnapp et al., 2018). Why is debiasing so important? Chu et al. (2018) found that of the 87 cases reviewed in morbidity and mortality conferences, 48 contained a diagnostic error, and of these, 47 contained a cognitive error that led to the diagnostic error. As a large array of research on such topics as the accuracy of clinical judgment show (e.g., see Chapters 6 and 8), errors and nonoptimal decision making also are common in the mental health field. The goal of this chapter is to debias cognitive errors.

COVERAGE OF DEBIASING

Phillips (2014, p. 75) reminds us that "You cannot detect diagnostic error unless you have a reliable, valid method of making a diagnosis." Of course, physicians in the emergency department (ED) may not have time to do the definitive diagnostic test in order to render an unquestionably accurate diagnosis. In many other medical situations, there often are biomarkers, such as lab tests and biopsies, that can provide a gold-standard diagnosis, even if the gold-standard diagnosis can be ascertained only at autopsy. However, in the case of psychiatric or psychological diagnosis, gold-standard biomarkers or lab tests are usually absent and one is primarily addressing hypothetical constructs versus physical entities. Therefore, ascertaining the accuracy of a diagnosis is much more difficult in this domain. Verifying diagnoses may be secondary in many situations in the mental health field given primary interest in judgmental or predictive accuracy across other domains or outcomes, such as the prediction of improved parental skills following some sort of intervention. However, there are certainly other situations in which diagnostic accuracy is of major interest. There are at least three traditional ways of addressing challenges validating diagnostic accuracy in the mental health field, each of which has its limitations,

The first way is to use the *Diagnostic and Statistical Manual of Mental Disorders* (DSM), and in particular the DSM's recommended diagnostic criteria. Mojtabai (2013) interviewed patients who had been diagnosed with depression during the prior year. He found that only 38% of the patients met the DSM criteria for depression. Many other studies have shown weak correspondence between official definitions of psychological and psychiatric diagnoses in the DSM and the diagnoses assigned by clinicians (see Bruchmuller & Meyer, 2009; Rakofsky & Dunlop, 2015; Ruggero et al., 2010). Because many diagnosticians do not heed the DSM, we conclude that they might not be in favor of a researcher's use of the DSM as the gold standard to decide whether a diagnosis is correct.

The second way of addressing the gold-standard problem in psychiatric and psychological diagnoses is to use expert consensus. One of the authors supervised a master's thesis in which a panel of eight experts was assembled to decide what the gold standard was for each of the cases being presented to the study's diagnosticians. If six of the eight experts agreed on the correct answer, that was supposed to be the gold-standard answer the participants should offer. The master's thesis completely collapsed, because on no case could six of the eight experts agree. We could have selected very easy cases in order to achieve consensus among the experts, but no one was interested in examining diagnostic accuracy only on very easy cases. In addition, setting 75% agreement as a gold standard seems rather lenient in the first place, because the term is often used to describe a lofty bar, such as uniform or nearly uniform agreement or accuracy.[1]

[1] The search for a gold standard is sometimes overemphasized, and often unrealistic, in psychology. There are many instances in the history of science in which valid but fallible indicators are sufficient (although far from ideal) for making progress, or at least getting started. For example, some early devices for measuring heat were tested against touch, which helped move the process forward. Often, as knowledge progresses, valid but fallible indicators are replaced by better methods, a form of bootstrapping common in science. Attempting to identify gold standards prematurely or artificially when the knowledge needed to do so is lacking often causes various undesirable consequences. One such common consequence is the extreme group problem described in Chapter 1, which results in nonrepresentative research groups that inflate

A third way of addressing the gold-standard problem in psychiatric and psychological diagnoses is to monitor long-term follow-up. If a particular diagnosis is characterized by certain long-term sequelae, especially those that are highly predictable and specific to the condition of interest, we could merely wait for the required length of time to ascertain if such sequelae do occur. Their occurrence will tend to confirm the diagnosis, and their nonoccurrence will tend to disconfirm the diagnosis. However, it is often impractical to perform such long-term follow-up, because the length of time one is required to wait can be excessive, and the person under consideration may no longer be available to the researcher. Thus, all three of the strategies for addressing the gold-standard problem in psychiatric and psychological diagnoses are fraught with difficulties.

In this discussion of debiasing, we approach the gold-standard difficulty by citing a large fraction of medical examples where a gold standard is needed to evaluate the validity of diagnoses and therefore the effectiveness of the debiasing technique. However, we also include psychology examples where appropriate. Many of the lessons to be learned from medical research can potentially or easily be transferred to the psychological domain. Also, some of the debiasing research doesn't depend on the validity of any diagnosis. For example, a study might examine which diagnostic strategy generates the most candidate diagnoses.

In addition, as noted, diagnostic categories in the mental health field may be of questionable value or secondary importance as opposed to other judgmental or predictive tasks, such as whether an individual is likely to endanger others. Fundamental judgment errors or shortcomings are almost certain to impact these other types of decisions. Further, Chapter 13 focuses specifically on implementing various procedures in the mental health field that are not aimed so much at reducing biases, but more at increasing use of broadly established normative procedures (e.g., strategies for analyzing the validity of information, and strategies for combining or integrating information). With that said, the discussion of debiasing strategies in this chapter covers a larger fraction of medical studies than are covered in prior chapters.

There is a large group of debiasing articles that we choose not to cover in this chapter, studies in which diagnosticians' awareness of traditional biases is the main dependent variable. From the earliest judgment and decision making research (see Arkes & Blumer, 1985; Fischhoff, 1975) to more recent research (e.g., Aczel et al., 2015; Adame, 2016), we have learned that making people aware of a bias does not inoculate them against succumbing to the bias. Therefore, we don't cover any articles in which mere knowledge of a bias is the primary dependent variable.

accuracy rates and distort qualitative and quantitative diagnostic indicators. A better choice may be accepting some error in group assignment in exchange for more representative groups, and then using means to compensate for error in group assignment, such as mixed validation methods (Dawes & Meehl, 1966; Faust et al., 2021; Jewsbury & Bowden, 2013).

The Dual-Process Framework

The most popular framework in which cognitive bias is examined is the Type 1/Type 2 dual-processing model popularized in Kahneman's (2011) book, *Thinking Fast and Slow*. According to this model, the Type 1 system is intuitive and fast. It uses heuristics, which are cognitive shortcuts that are efficient but occasionally can lead one astray due to heuristics' insufficient and primarily unconscious consideration of all important factors (i.e., automatic processing of information that largely occurs outside of our awareness). Type 2 is a deliberate system that is slow but more thorough and hence uses much more cognitive capacity than does Type 1 processing. Many researchers are quite blunt that Type 1 heuristics are the source of cognitive bias in diagnoses: "Cognitive bias can be defined as the failure of a heuristic strategy" (Altabbaa et al., 2019, p. 91), and "In response to the stressful limitations of the ED, emergency physicians are forced to utilize cognitive short-cutting strategies (i.e., heuristics) for diagnostic decision making. When these strategies fail, they are referred to as cognitive errors" (Chu et al., 2018, p. 144).

For many researchers, the way to minimize diagnostic errors is simply to switch from Type 1 processing to Type 2 processing. This would result in less reliance on such heuristic-driven modes of thought as intuitive pattern recognition and more reliance on analytic thinking: "Debiasing strategies involve the deliberate switching from pattern recognition to analytic thinking" (Daniel et al., 2017, p. 106), and "All [theoretical approaches toward debiasing] share a common feature that involves a deliberate decoupling from Type 1 intuitive processing and moving to Type 2 analytical processing" (Croskerry et al., 2013, p. ii58).

Some debiasing researchers don't think that this traditional Type 1/Type 2 analysis is helpful (Arkes, 2016; De Neys, 2021; Henrikson & Brady, 2013, p. 1). For example, Klein (1998) has shown that ED nurses, firefighters, and other who have to make very fast and highly accurate decisions use "recognition-primed" decision making. They very quickly peruse the situation. This then primes the recognition of the correct diagnosis or assessment due to the similarity of the current situation to prior situations. The appropriate steps are then undertaken. Intuitive Type 1 thinking is not an error-prone culprit in such situations. Instead, slow, deliberate Type 2 thinking might be maladaptive in such high-pressure conditions. We support the view of McLaughlin et al. (2014): Type 1 and Type 2 thinking can both be good, but in different circumstances.

A study by Hoffman et al. (2013, Experiment 1) supports this perspective of differential benefit across differing circumstances. Participants were presented with a multiple-cue judgment task. For example, in judging what dosage of a medication to administer, a doctor might need to consider the weight of the patient, the severity of the symptoms, the age of the patient, and the expected duration of the disease. A participant could approach the task with a rule-based strategy in which these cues are integrated in a linear additive manner. For example, if appraising a possible disgnosis, a patient's case would get a "point" for the presence of each of several symptoms. If the total point value exceeds the threshold for the potential diagnosis, then that diagnosis is deemed appropriate. Alternatively, the participant could use a similarity-based judgment strategy in which the current patient is compared to a prior similar patient. This similarity-based strategy uses far less cognitive capacity than does the rule-based one.

Decision makers adopt one strategy or the other depending on such task characteristics as required cognitive load and the relation between the cues and the diagnosis. While performing the multiple-cue judgment task, some participants also performed a concurrent memory task, thus diverting some of their cognitive capacity from the judgment task to the memory chore. Other participants were not given the concurrent memory task. The cues bore not a linear but a multiplicative relation to the criterion, thus making a similarity-based strategy a much better choice than the complex rule-based one. Because the cognitive load imposed on some participants caused them to utilize the less strenuous similarity-based strategy, these people performed the task more accurately than did the people who used the rule-based strategy, which was less appropriate for solving this particular task. Note that the extra cognitive load imposed on some participants would have prevented so-called Type 2 processing. Hence, the higher performance on this task by persons under cognitive load would be due to their Type 1 processing.

With enough experience, the nurses that Klein (1999) studied were excellent at diagnosing whether a baby had sepsis or whether an adult had a myocardial infarction. Extra deliberation would generally not have been helpful. For an inexperienced intern accompanying the veteran nurse, extra deliberation would have been not only helpful but also necessary. Croskerry et al. (2013) pointed out that a good balance between intuition and deliberation is necessary, depending on the nature of the task and the expertise of the diagnostician. Some environments, such as dermatology, in which the presenting cues are largely visual, foster more recognition-primed intuitive decision making, whereas other tasks, such as integrating several indicators on a checklist, might foster more deliberative decision making. Hammond et al. (1987) made this point long ago: Intuition and deliberation can each be effective, but in different situations.

Figure 12.1 contains two graphs depicting the hypothesized relation between expertise, task difficulty, and type of processing. The graph on the left depicts tasks of below-average or average difficulty; the one on the right depicts tasks of above-average difficulty. Note that for experts, tasks of average or below-average difficulty are done well with intuition. As tasks get more difficult or very difficult, only then

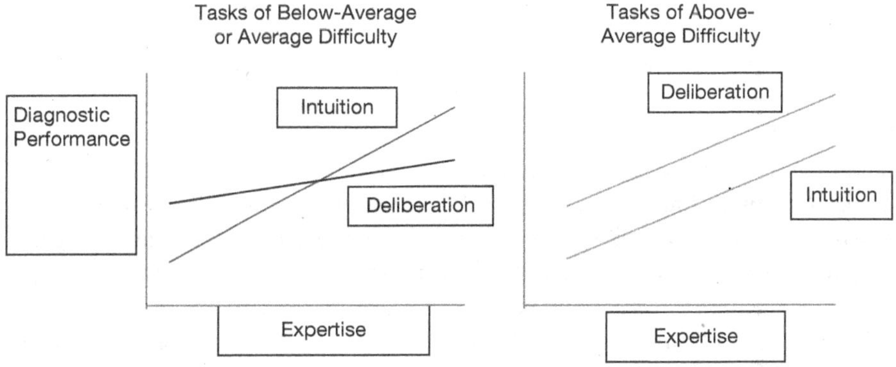

Figure 12.1 Hypothesized relation between expertise, task difficulty, and mode of cognition

might experts be well advised to deliberate. For the less experienced, deliberation is generally superior. Note that deliberation is better than intuition unless one is an expert confronting a diagnostic task whose difficulty level is average or less. A problem occurs if someone who is not an expert overconfidently believes that he or she is one.

Let's first examine the case of a task of average difficulty. If a person assumes that their location is toward the right side of the *x*-axis of the left-hand graph, they will use intuition. When inexpert but overconfident people use intuition rather than deliberation on such tasks, it is likely to result in less accurate diagnostic performance. What if non-experts mistakenly believe that the task is below average in difficulty for the supposedly talented diagnostician they consider themselves to be, but the task is actually quite difficult? Such a person might think they are on the right side of the left-hand graph when they are really on the left side of the right-hand graph, where deliberation is superior.

The problem is thus one of overconfidence, which has long been recognized as a cause of diagnostic error in psychology, counseling, and psychiatry (Berner & Graber, 2008; Rabinowitz & Garelik-Wyler, 1999; Smith & Agate, 2004; Wu & Lowenstein, 2020; see also Chapter 11). If diagnosticians' confidence were well calibrated to their level of knowledge, they would know where they were located on the *x*-axis and could employ the appropriate cognitive strategy depending on task difficulty. Unfortunately, a substantial amount of research suggests that there is only a modest relation between confidence and accuracy. For example, a review of 17 studies (Davis et al., 2006, p. 1094) found that 13 of them "demonstrated little, no, or an inverse relationship" between self-assessment of competence and an objective, external assessment. Podbregar et al. (2001) characterized 126 autopsies as either (a) confirming the clinical diagnosis, (b) demonstrating a new relevant diagnosis that would probably not have influenced the therapy and outcome, or (c) demonstrating a new relevant diagnosis that would probably have changed the therapy and outcome. The investigators found that the level of certainty of the clinical diagnosis was unrelated to the threefold characterization made at autopsy. On the other hand, Friedman et al. (2005), Meyer et al. (2013), and Potchen (2006) found only a "mild" relation between confidence and accuracy of diagnosis. High confidence is associated with fewer requests for additional diagnostic tests (Meyer et al., 2013): "I'm confident in the diagnosis; I don't need another test." Worse yet, overconfidence is associated with a lower quality of healthcare (Kovacs et al., 2020).

A few techniques have successfully reduced overconfidence. The most obvious technique is based on the truism that if one increases one's level of expertise, there is less "room" for overconfidence to be manifested. For example, Smith-Bindman et al. (2003) compared the recall rates for mammogram examinations in the United States and the United Kingdom. A *recall rate* is the rate at which mammographers recommend further evaluation after a mammogram, such as more diagnostic imaging, a biopsy, or an other procedure. A main dependent variable was the rate at which the subsequent biopsy was negative. The recall and subsequent negative biopsy rates were twice as high in the United States as in the United Kingdom, but the cancer detection rates were similar. A probable cause of the discrepancy in accurate detection of cancer is the fact that U.S. physicians are required to read

480 mammograms annually to fulfill required standards, but U.K. physicians are required to read 5,000 mammograms annually. Reading more than 10 times as many mammograms as their U.S. counterparts every year will likely foster a much higher level of expertise among the U.K. physicians, thereby leading to their superior performance. A U.K. physician's reliance on intuition would be more prudent than a U.S. physician's reliance on intuition for the average mammogram according to the analyses depicted in the left-hand graph of Figure 12.1. Also, with their obviously higher level of performance, U.K. physicians would necessarily be less likely to exhibit overconfidence. We hasten to add that greater experience often does not alter accuracy much, or sometimes at all, on many diagnostic and predictive judgments in the mental health field, a major reason being because feedback is often lacking or contains significant error (Faust et al., 1988; Garb, 1998, pp. 14–15). However a strictly visual task, such as reading mammograms, is one in which more experience is likely to be helpful (see Evans et al., 2011).

Another way to diminish overconfidence is to provide intense, unequivocal feedback (Sieck & Arkes, 2005). One possible way to accomplish this aim is through the use of expert systems that provide a large number of test cases. The trainee examining each sample case then renders a diagnosis (see Lincoln et al., 1991). We recommend that each trainee assign a confidence level to the diagnosis for each case so that any discrepancy between confidence and accuracy would be displayed and appreciated (Arkes et al., 1987). Kareken and Williams (1994) had neuropsychologists analyze hypothetical cases and use the case information to estimate level of prior abilities, or the level of functioning at a time before the evaluation. In many situations, to best determine whether a disease or disorder may be present or has impacted cognitive functioning adversely, one needs a pre-event yardstick for purposes of comparison. The researchers found that clinicians' judgments of pre-event functioning deviated from formal methods for evaluating prior functioning, that the strength of association between predictive variables and level of prior abilities was often misappraised, and perhaps most importantly, that level of confidence in estimates was inflated or mistakenly high. The authors subsequently designed workshops in which participants analyzed cases and then were given direct feedback about the accuracy or inaccuracy of their judgments based on pre-evaluation data, in order to encourage greater use of decision aids and better calibration of confidence levels.

Finally, we turn to a very general debiasing strategy, *consider the opposite*, which has been used for a range of purposes, including diminishing overconfidence.

GENERAL COGNITIVE DEBIASING STRATEGIES

Consider the Opposite

The early tests of the consider-the-opposite strategy had nothing to do with diagnosis; they pertained to hindsight bias and overconfidence in one's answers to trivia questions (Koriat et al., 1980; Slovic & Fischhoff, 1977). For example, in Koriat et al.'s study, individuals were asked to consider questions like: Absinthe is

(a) a liquor, or (b) a precious stone. Individuals chose the option they thought was correct and assigned a confidence level to their answer. As usual, over a large series of questions, subjects' confidence significantly exceeded their accuracy. Another group was asked the same questions, but before they indicated their preferred choice and assigned a confidence level to it, they first had to provide a reason why both their preferred answer and the other answer might each be correct and also a reason why each of the possible answers might be incorrect. Koriat et al. (1980) found that in the "reasons" group, overconfidence in preferred choices was only about one third the magnitude of the overconfidence manifested by the group that didn't have to provide any reasons. In other words, considering the opposite answer improved the accuracy–confidence calibration. Subsequently, Hirt and Markman (1995) showed that this debiasing strategy worked well even if the other item to be explained was not a true opposite of the preferred answer—it merely had to be an alternative answer, such as a different explanation of a particular outcome. The consider-the-opposite strategy has been successfully applied to several traditional biases, which is why we characterize it as a general debiasing strategy.

In addition to combatting overconfidence, the consider-the-opposite strategy has been used to mitigate hindsight bias in diagnostic situations. Arkes et al. (1988) asked a subgroup of 194 neuropsychologists to examine a brief case history and then to assign a probability to each of three possible diagnoses. This was the foresight group, because the subjects considered the diagnoses before any outcome information was revealed. The foresight group divided the probabilities about evenly across the three diagnostic options. Three hindsight groups of subjects were each told that one of the three potential diagnoses was correct, but they were asked to assign the probability to each that they would have thought appropriate had they not been told the "true" diagnosis. (Participants and responses were anonymous to avoid social desirability confounding the results.) These three groups manifested hindsight bias, assigning a higher probability to whichever diagnosis they were told was the correct one when compared to the foresight group. There was an additional quartet of subjects who were identical to the prior quartet (one foresight group and three hindsight groups) except that before they indicated the probabilities for each diagnosis, the three hindsight groups had to list one reason why each of the three possible diagnoses was correct. This consider-the-opposite strategy significantly reduced hindsight bias in these groups compared to the "non-reasons" groups.

Mamede et al. (2008, 2010, 2012) used the consider-the-opposite strategy to mitigate availability bias. According to Tversky and Kahneman (1972), people often gauge the probability of an event by the ease with which the instances of the event can be brought to mind, that is, how available the events are in one's memory. Availability bias can pollute diagnostic reasoning, because the likelihood of a diagnosis may be influenced simply by the ease with which similar cases can be recalled. Mamede et al. (2010) presented medical students with eight cases and the students were asked to diagnose the cases with non-analytic reasoning. Some of the cases were somewhat similar to cases the students had seen immediately before and whose diagnoses had been provided. Then the diagnoses were solicited again, but this time using the consider-the-opposite strategy. There were two important results. The second-year medical students succumbed to the availability heuristic more than did the first-year medical students; they diagnosed more cases using the available diagnoses provided for similar cases even though the available diagnosis was incorrect for the cases. The second important result was that both groups rendered more accurate diagnoses in the consider-the-opposite session than they had achieved in the non-analytic session. Mamede et al. (2010) hypothesized that the second-year students would be more likely to fall prey to availability bias than the first-year students because the second-year students had greater experience and would be more likely to use recognition-primed decision making, which considers the similarity of a new case to a prior one. This would foster the use of the availability heuristic, which would sabotage their performance. Both groups benefitted from the consider-the-opposite strategy in the final phase of the study.

In an earlier study, Mamede et al. (2008) found results consistent with their later (2010) research. Internal medicine residents diagnosed either simple or complex cases using an intuitive strategy or a deliberative consider-the-opposite strategy. The consider-the-opposite strategy didn't help significantly with the easy cases, because the intuitive strategy worked well for such cases. As Figure 12.1 shows, on easy cases the residents were able to use their intuition successfully. On the complex cases, the consider-the-opposite strategy led to significantly more accurate diagnoses than did the intuitive strategy, just as the analysis depicted in Figure 12.1 would suggest. Mamede et al. (2010) called the use of consider-the-opposite and other cognitive strategies reflective reasoning, because the application of such strategies leads the diagnostician to reason in a more thoughtful way.

In a third study, Mamede et al. (2012) presented cases with a misleading distracting feature to internal medicine residents and medical students. Each group diagnosed the case with either an intuitive strategy or a multifaceted strategy that contained a consider-the-opposite component. The diagnostic performance of the residents was significantly enhanced by the consider-the-opposite strategy. The medical students' performance was not significantly improved, probably because they lacked sufficient knowledge to distinguish between the incorrect and correct diagnoses.

Jenkins and Youngstrom (2016) performed one of the most ambitious debiasing studies in the mental health domain. Mental health providers mainly in psychiatry and psychology ($N = 137$) were divided into two groups. The experimental group received consider-the-opposite training plus didactic training on cognitive pitfalls in the diagnosis of pediatric bipolar disorder. The didactic training included several elements, such as teaching mnemonics to reduce strain on memory for the appropriate bipolar symptoms, instruction on Bayesian reasoning, and practice in decision making with case information. All participants were then asked to diagnose four cases that were created to detect whether particular decision making errors might take place. The results showed numerous benefits of the training intervention, including a significant increase in overall diagnostic accuracy, sensitivity to possible hypomania or mania, and a doubling in the detection of co-occurring conditions. Because the intervention contained multiple components as well as the consider-the-opposite training, it is not possible to determine the degree to which each of the different components may have contributed to the improvement in diagnostic accuracy.

Maude (2014) pointed out that merely creating a differential diagnosis is itself a way to utilize the consider-the-opposite strategy to enhance diagnostic accuracy. For example, DiNardo et al. (2018) asked 34 postgraduate medical residents to create a differential diagnosis by listing four possible diagnoses for each case. In addition, for each diagnosis, the residents were asked to specify three things: (1) case elements that support that diagnosis, (2) case elements that contradict that diagnosis, and (3) case elements missing if that diagnosis were true. The second component of this assignment is the consider-the-opposite strategy, of course. The overall task of listing four possible diagnoses is the traditional undertaking of creating a differential diagnosis. Those who used this debiasing technique were 8% more accurate in their diagnoses than the residents who did not use that technique. Maude (2014, p. 107) suggested that merely compiling a differential diagnosis "could act as a vital trigger to stimulate thinking at the time of the consultation." If the thinking at the time of the differential includes the consider-the-opposite strategy, it will very likely reduce diagnostic error and improve accuracy–confidence calibration.

Differential diagnoses in medicine and psychology have important common elements (examining positive and negative evidence for a series of possibilities), and direct studies in psychology also show the benefits of consider-the-opposite strategies. Furthermore, studies showing improvement in calibrating confidence, or greater balance in considering positive and negative evidence (e.g., by making negative evidence more salient and thereby diminishing a disproportionate focus on confirming evidence) have clear applicability to important judgment tasks in the mental health field. For example, if one is trying to predict between two or more possible outcomes, such as whether an individual is likely to engage in self-harm or needs to be hospitalized, then reducing overconfidence and the chances of overlooking contrary evidence can produce significant benefits.

Checklists

Checklists have successfully been used in aviation, manufacturing quality control, and other complex domains in order to reduce error (Hales & Pronovost, 2006). In healthcare, checklists have been used primarily in patient care, resource utilization, and guideline adherence, and they have proven to be highly effective in improving patient outcome (see Hart & Owen, 2005). There have also been subsequent attempts to introduce checklists into the diagnostic process (Ely et al., 2011). For example, Ely and Graber (2015) created a set of 4 × 6 cards, each one of which had on its top line a common symptom, such as shoulder pain. Below the top-line symptom was a list of possible diagnoses, some of which were labeled as "Commonly missed" and others labeled as "Don't miss." The latter category included diagnoses that would have very serious consequences if overlooked. The possible diagnoses were ordered according to their base rate. In a small pilot study, the authors compared physicians given checklists to a non-checklist group. Both emergency department (ED) physicians and same-day access clinic (SDAC) physicians participated. Combining the data from both the ED and SDAC physicians, the checklist group committed 11% diagnostic errors in 100 patients and the non-checklist group committed 18% errors, which was not a statistically significant difference because the SDAC physicians showed only a negligible contrast between the checklist and no-checklist groups, with both of these groups making very few errors. However, among the ED physicians, the diagnostic error rate was 19% for the checklist physicians and 45% for the non-checklist ones, which was a statistically significant difference. Another important difference was that the checklist physicians generated almost twice as many diagnoses in their differential diagnosis as did the non-checklist ones. This is a crucial finding, because Schiff et al. (2009) found that the single most frequent cause of diagnostic error was the failure of physicians to consider the correct diagnosis as a possibility. Checklists help conquer this problem. A checklist similar to the one created by Ely et al. (2011) was successfully used to help medical students detect multiple abnormalities on a chest radiograph (Kok et al., 2017).

The use of checklists would seem to be particularly beneficial in psychological diagnoses. The more recent versions of the DSM include lists of symptoms or test results that provide necessary and sufficient conditions for diagnoses. Unfortunately, research on psychological diagnoses reveals that many professionals use "personal criteria" rather than official ones (Brailey et al., 2001; Wade & Baker, 1977). A checklist would seem to be an ideal way to encourage diagnosticians to use the most valid and reliable procedures and not idiosyncratic ones with questionable diagnostic utility. (Whether the most useful and valid diagnostic criteria can be found in the DSM, or how consistently they can be found in that source or other sources, is another matter worthy of consideration.)

Here one might again consider Grove et al.'s (2000) meta-analysis (see Chapter 8), which suggested that all else being equal, structured approaches to collecting information (e.g., structured interviews and formal tests, as opposed to unstructured interviews) significantly enhance the accuracy of decision making in the mental health field. Even simple decision aids, such as checklists, presuming they are well designed and cover important data points, can provide increased structure in obtaining information, and may also include aids to interpretation. As is also covered in Chapter 8, approaches that fall under structured professional judgment, which dictate gathering clinical data systematically by identifying variables that should be appraised, routinely equal or exceed less structured data-collection methods. However, statistical decision methods for integrating or combining information consistently equal or surpass structured professional judgment.

A hypothesized reason that some diagnosticians reject checklists is their feeling that a checklist and other decision aids represent a threat to their autonomy (Hales & Pronovost, 2006). Thus, the use of checklists might seem to impugn the diagnostician's unaided professional judgment. To counteract this attitude, it is important to consider whose welfare is being served. If a checklist helps improve diagnostic accuracy, the patient's welfare is prioritized.

Seek Additional Perspectives

Two literature reviews of the strategies designed to reduce diagnostic errors have concluded that obtaining an additional review of test results has a positive effect (McDonald et al., 2013; Wright et al., 2019). Having multiple people render independent diagnoses takes advantage of the "wisdom of the crowd" or "collective intelligence." Wolf et al. (2015) has shown that as the size of the evaluating group increases to nine people, mammogram diagnostic accuracy increases monotonically. Wolf et al. also showed that any of three rules that combine the diagnoses of the group members, such as a simple majority vote, provide more accurate diagnoses than the most accurate radiologist. Kurvers et al. (2015) obtained the same general advantage of groups over individuals in diagnosing skin cancer.

There are a few simple ways to maximize the wisdom of a crowd. First, the diagnoses must be independent. The person who renders the second opinion should not be made aware of the first opinion. Second, diversity of diagnostic inputs is best. Thomas and Newman-Toker (2016) described a case study in which the input of a physical therapist was crucial in enhancing the diagnostic accuracy of the physicians. The authors suggested that the input of allied health professionals would generally have a salutary influence on diagnostic accuracy.

There is one type of diversity that detracts from diagnostic accuracy. Although Kurvers et al. (2016) confirmed the finding that groups of doctors outperformed any individual doctor in the group, the benefit of a group diminished if the accuracy of the individual group members diverged substantially. In such instances, the weakest members sometimes overruled the diagnoses of the best performers. Thus, highly varying levels of diagnostic accuracy can weaken group performance.

What if there are no other diagnosticians available to comprise a group? Herzog and Hertwig (2009) showed that after a person renders a judgment, that same person can be asked to make the judgment again after taking a new perspective:

> First, assume that your first judgment is off the mark. Second, think about a few reasons why that could be. Which assumptions and considerations could have been wrong? Third, what do these new considerations imply? . . . Fourth, based on this new perspective, make a second, alternative estimate. (p. 234)

Herzog and Hertwig (2009) showed that averaging the two estimates results in half of the improvement that would have occurred had a different person provided the second estimate. This technique, which the authors called dialectical bootstrapping, is actually a combination of consider the opposite and wisdom of the crowd, with both members of the crowd occupying the same brain. To the best of our knowledge, dialectical bootstrapping has not been tested in diagnostic situations.

Hersh's (1971) study (see Chapter 4) exemplified labeling bias. Before intellectual testing with children, psychology graduate students were given information that fostered the hypothesis that each child was either high or low in intellectual ability. This labeling bias resulted in the former group's test results being interpreted as higher than the latter group's test results, even though the bogus labels were randomly assigned to each child. In the domain of forensic science, a type of labeling bias has been found to pollute purportedly scientific testimony. For example, Murrie et al. (2013) paid 108 forensic psychiatrists and psychologists to review the case files of offenders and to score each on two risk assessment scales. Half of the forensic scientists were led to believe that they were working for the prosecution, and the other half that they were working for the defense. The former group gave significantly higher risk scores than the latter group. Findings like this have led to suggestions that "blinding" of forensic scientists should occur with regard to any case information that is not essential to the scientific judgment being requested (see Dror, 2018). Should this recommendation be applied to the diagnostic process, there might be less chance for labeling bias or stereotype bias to occur.

Introspection

There is one general debiasing strategy that is quite unlikely to be effective: introspection. Individuals, professionals included, have very limited access to their own higher-level cognitive processes (Nisbett & Wilson, 1977; see also the section in Chapter 7 on bootstrapping), and thus attempts to identify and then correct biases in one's own thinking will routinely fail. Pronin et al. (2002) coined the term *bias blind spot* to denote one's inability to detect any bias in oneself but to readily perceive it in others. Unfortunately, Neal and Brodsky (2016) found that forensic psychologists thought that introspection was an effective way to identify potential biases in themselves.

TRAINING THAT TARGETS SPECIFIC BIASES

Whereas some general cognitive debiasing techniques, such as the consider-the-opposite strategy, can be used to combat a variety of biases, other interventions target specific biases.

Diagnostic Overshadowing

Diagnostic overshadowing occurs when the presence of one diagnosis interferes with the formulation of an additional diagnosis. One of the many areas in which overshadowing has been demonstrated is in the domain of intellectual disability, a diagnosis that frequently overshadows the diagnosis of comorbidities. Wood and Tracey (2009) divided 220 graduate students who were primarily in clinical and counseling psychology into three groups differing in the intervention they received. The control group received accurate feedback on three training cases with regard to whether they had detected the overshadowed diagnosis. The students in the content-based condition also received accurate feedback on the training cases, but they were also informed of criteria in each training vignette that implicated the overshadowed diagnosis. Students in the principle-based condition received similar feedback to the members of the content-based feedback group but also received information about the phenomenon of overshadowing. On subsequent test vignettes, both intervention groups manifested fewer overshadowing errors than the control group, with the students in the content-based condition generally performing better than those in the principle-based condition. Salutary effects of the training were greater for test stimuli that more closely resembled training stimuli. Because the test vignettes were given shortly after the training vignettes, it is not known what the long-term benefit of either intervention might have been.

Confirmation Bias

Both Morewedge et al. (2015) and Dunbar et al. (2014) developed computer games targeting confirmation bias as well as other biases. The former team of researchers directed their efforts at two additional biases closely related to diagnosis: anchoring and the representativeness heuristic. They defined "anchoring" as "overweighting the first information primed or considered in subsequent judgment" and "representativeness" as "using the similarity of an outcome to a prototypical outcome to judge its probability" (p. 132). The interventions were either a training video or a computer game, each couched in terms of a detective story. The computer games were designed to elicit each of the biases to be subsequently mitigated. Players, mainly college-educated Pittsburgh adults, were given definitions and examples of the biases, and various mitigating strategies were covered in both the game and in the video, including consider the opposite, consideration of base rates, awareness of anchors, instruction in logic, and other strategies. A notable feature of the research was that testing occurred not only shortly after the intervention but also at a follow-up session 8 to 12 weeks after training. The results were that the computer game significantly reduced confirmation bias both at the immediate posttest session and at the delayed posttest session. The game and video were equally effective with regard to debiasing the influence of anchoring at both posttest sessions and at debiasing the use of the representative heuristic at the delayed posttest session. The game was more effective than the video at the immediate posttest session in reducing the use of the representative heuristic. We acknowledge that the Morewedge et al. (2015) and Dunbar et al. (2014) studies did not use medical or psychological diagnoses as their stimulus materials, but it strikes us that the general principles they employed in their computer-based games could readily be applied to such diagnostic tasks.

Analogical Intervention Technique

Aczel et al. (2015) undertook an ambitious program to mitigate a large number of biases. Some of the biases were central to the diagnostic process, such as faulty covariation analysis, whereas others were less so, such as the planning fallacy, which refers to the tendency to be excessively optimistic in estimating the amount of time an endeavor will take. Also, some of the biases pertained to statistical topics, such as ignoring base rates, and others related to nonstatistical issues, such as the outcome bias (see Chapter 5, under the heading, "Hindsight Bias and Outcome Bias"). In addition to the usual control group, there were two intervention groups. One was the awareness group, in which for each bias the participants were provided with a real-life example, an explanation of the bias, and techniques designed to avoid the bias. The third group was the analogical training group, whose training was based on Gentner's (1983) work, which suggested that people could encode the relevant principles if they discovered the principles themselves. An effective way to accomplish this was to ask people to find structural similarities in cases that are superficially similar—leading Aczel et al. to name this debiasing strategy the analogical intervention technique. This approach involved the following components:

1. Participants were asked to find structural similarities between vignettes containing the same bias.
2. Participants received instruction on normative principles.
3. Participants were asked to recall memories of past occasions or anticipation of future occasions when this bias did, or might, occur.
4. Participants were asked to suggest strategies to avoid each bias.
5. Participants were presented with some research-based mitigation strategies.
6. Participants were asked, "How would you use such strategies in real life?"

All participants were tested four weeks after the training. The results were straightforward: the analogical intervention technique was effective, but only for a composite score containing the statistical topics of base-rate neglect, regression to the mean, covariation detection, and insensitivity to sample size. Awareness training was generally ineffective—a typical finding. Another positive effect was that 58% of the individuals provided with the analogical intervention technique reported that the training had made a difference in their real life, whereas only 34% in the awareness group expressed this view. We should also note that the potential effectiveness of debiasing training on statistical concepts had been demonstrated before by such researchers as Fong and Nisbett (1991). However, some of the biases mitigated by Aczel et al. (2015), such as covariation detection, are more closely related to diagnosis and prediction than some of the biases that Fong and Nisbett (1991) tested in their research.

The analogical intervention technique that Aczel et al. (2015) used employs two of the factors Sedlmeier (1999) asserted were important in teaching statistical reasoning: learning by doing and use of flexible training materials. The analogical intervention technique requires trainees to find structural similarities between vignettes, recall memories of past occasions, suggest strategies to avoid each bias, etc. This was not merely a didactic presentation. Instead, participants had to take an active role in their training. Also, by searching for similarities among apparently disparate vignettes, the trainees were exposed to many different manifestations of each bias, thereby enhancing the transfer of the training to more variations of future occurrences.

Use of Natural Frequencies

Research by Gigerenzer and his colleagues (e.g., Gigerenzer & Hoffrage, 1995; Wegwarth & Gigerenzer, 2011) has shown that estimating the probability of a disease is performed much more accurately if the diagnostician uses natural frequencies rather than conditional probabilities expressed as sensitivity and specificity. For example, Hoffrage and Gigerenzer (1998) tested 48 experienced physicians' understanding of a fecal occult blood test (FOBT). In one problem, half of the physicians were given the relevant information in the usual probabilistic way: sensitivity = 50%, false-positive rate = 3%, prevalence = 0.3%. The physicians were asked to estimate the probability of colorectal cancer given a positive test result. The estimates of the probability of colorectal cancer ranged from 1% to 99%, with a modal estimate of 50%. Only 4% of the physicians answered correctly. The other half of the physicians were provided with the equivalent information using natural frequencies: 30 out of every 10,000 people have colorectal cancer; of these 30, 15 will have a positive test result; of the people who do not have cancer, 299 will test positive for cancer. Using these natural frequencies, 67% of the physicians answered correctly; the rest of the physicians were close. The reason for the superiority of natural frequencies is obvious: Using Bayes' Theorem one has to mentally perform three multiplications, one addition, and one division. Using natural frequencies, one has to realize that 15 people who have cancer will have a positive test result, and 299 who don't have cancer will have a positive test result. That means that 15 of the 314 people who test positive have cancer—approximately 5%. One addition and one division are all that is needed. Natural frequencies make estimating disease probabilities far easier and more accurate (if one cannot, or fails to perform, the formal mathematical steps).

DECISION SUPPORT SYSTEMS

One of the most exciting developments in diagnostic debiasing is the advent of expert systems that provide support to the diagnostician. Although the benefits of the early decision support systems (DSSs) were "not convincing" (Hunt et al., 1998), the fraction of successful applications has increased in recent years. Here, we mention only a few from diverse domains and in diverse locales.

Vinny et al. (2019) tested 100 neurology residents in India on 60 clinical vignettes in order to assess their diagnostic accuracy in cognitive neurology. The comparison was between unaided residents and ones using a DSS app. Experts in cognitive neurology generated the differential diagnoses for each vignette and deemed one answer to be the correct response. The unaided residents selected the criterion diagnosis as their most likely diagnosis 35% of the time. The residents who used the app selected the criterion diagnosis 62% of the time.

Martinez-Franco et al. (2018) tested 87 first-year family medicine residents in Mexico City. Half were in the control group and didn't use a DSS. The other half used DXplain. Both groups were presented with 30 cases chosen from internal medicine, pediatrics, gynecology, and emergency medicine. The control group achieved a diagnostic accuracy of 74%. The decision support group achieved a significantly higher accuracy of 82%.

Ramnarayan et al. (2006) tested 76 British diagnosticians (61 physicians, 15 medical students) on 24 simulated cases. The participants reported their differential diagnosis, test orders, and treatment before and after consultation with the diagnostic reminder system. There were two main results. First, use of the diagnostic reminder system achieved a significant decrease in the number of diagnostic errors of omission. Second, the mean diagnostic quality score increased significantly after use of the system.

Various DSSs are now commercially available. They are highly sophisticated, even containing such features as offering a dermatological diagnosis after the diagnostician photographs the skin. A major problem is that DSSs are underutilized. Ridderikhoff and van Herk (1999) asked 20 physicians if "they would accept the advice of the computer if it had been proved that it could do something better than [they] could do." Sixty-five percent of the physicians said No. One of the authors asked a member of the Society of Medical Decision Making why he refuses to use a DSS. He replied, "I didn't go to med school to become a clerk." Vrieze and Grove (2009) reported that only 31% of clinical psychologists used algorithms when making clinical predictions (and even when used may be minimally weighted; see Chapter 8). Thus, a major problem is that many diagnosticians simply won't use a DSS. The following reasons have been offered to explain this reluctance.

First, the reasoning of the DSS is usually opaque. The diagnostician plugs in the various signs and symptoms, and the DSS produces one or more diagnoses. The user cannot access the logic of the DSS diagnostic process, and the user is therefore apprehensive about the output (van Donger & Maanen, 2013).

Second, Dzindolet et al. (2003) suggested that the decision whether to use a DSS depends on the contest between trust in the DSS versus confidence in one's own acumen. Due to typical overconfidence in the latter, the DSS will usually finish in second place in this contest.

Third, diagnosticians may understandably be concerned that use of a DSS may reduce the quality of the diagnostician–patient interaction. For example, Arkes et al. (2007) found that physicians who used a DSS were rated as less competent than physicians who used their own unaided intuition. This result was even obtained when information technology (IT) students did the ratings (Wolf, 2014), whereas one might have hypothesized that IT students wouldn't denigrate a diagnostician who uses a computer. People use confidence as a cue to gauge expertise (Price & Stone, 2004), and consequently diagnosticians who use a DSS might be suspected of being less confident in offering a diagnosis and therefore as lacking sufficient expertise. Sniezek and Van Swol (2001) found that people were more likely to heed the recommendations of more confident advisors, thus providing an explanation for Promberger and Baron's (2006) finding that people are more likely to follow recommendations issued by a confident physician as opposed to recommendations promulgated by a computer. According to Palmeira and Spassova (2015), a physician who seeks patient compliance might therefore want to avoid using a DSS, or alternatively to conceal its use. (We do not feel qualified to judge the ethics of a physician's failing to disclose such a matter, but in the mental health field it would seem questionable.)

Fourth, patients were dissatisfied that the physician looked at the computer rather than at them during the use of the DSS (Porat et al., 2017).

Fifth, even if the DSS was said to be more accurate than the unaided diagnostician, patients thought that the physician could somehow take into account their unique characteristics more than could a DSS, which was thought to be based on people in general rather than on a patient's specific personal situation (Longoni et al., 2019).

Sixth, Dietvorst et al. (2015) found that on an incentivized forecasting task, participants preferred to use human judgment rather than an imperfect algorithm even after they had seen the algorithm outperform the human judge! The authors termed this *algorithm aversion*. Since no algorithm is going to be perfect, this finding means that algorithms will generally be eschewed in favor of less accurate human judgment.

Note that these potential disadvantages of using a DSS are largely psychological—patients' diminished respect for the diagnostician, overconfidence in one's diagnostic ability, use of confidence as a proxy for expertise, aversion to using a superior technique, etc. Therefore, several psychological interventions have been suggested to address these psychological barriers.

First, research has shown that practitioner involvement in the creation of nonmedical decision support systems enhances their adoption (Kaplan et al., 2001). However, this is generally not possible in medical DSSs, because the commercial programs come with the symptoms and logic already preloaded. Fortunately, there is a cheap and surprising way to finesse this problem. Dietvorst et al. (2018) asked participants to use nine cues to estimate 20 high school seniors' scores on a standardized mathematics test. Participants in the "can't change" group could choose between exclusively using their own unaided forecasts or exclusively using a forecast generated by a regression equation. The equation's forecasts were stated to be off by an average of 17.5 percentiles for each student. Participants in the "adjust-by-10" condition could choose between exclusively using their own unaided forecasts or exclusively using a forecast generated by a regression equation, with the proviso that they could adjust the equation's output by up to 10 percentiles. Participants in the "change-10" could choose between exclusively using their own unaided forecasts or exclusively using a forecast generated by a regression equation, with the proviso that they could adjust 10 of the model's 20 forecasts as much as they wished. Participants in the "use freely" could use the model's forecasts as much as they liked when making their 20 forecasts. The results were highly instructive. People in the adjust-by-10 and change-10 conditions used the model's imperfect predictions more than twice as much as did the people in the can't change group. Because people in the can't change group used the model so infrequently, their absolute error significantly exceeded that of the other three groups. Although the model was imperfect, use of the model resulted in superior forecasting performance. Allowing even a very modest amount of modification of the model's prediction fostered use of the model and hence better performance, even though allowing modification of a model generally makes the predictions worse (see Goodwin & Fildes, 1999), much like the literature on countervailing statistical decision procedures shows (see Chapter 8). Enhanced use of a model usually outweighs the detrimental adjustment made by the user (see also Lawrence et al., 2002).

A second strategy to enhance DSS adoption is to emphasize that the DSS is not a substitute for the diagnostician but is instead being used in combination with the diagnostician's own judgment. This strategy can even enhance a patient's regard for the diagnostician compared to the regard the patient would likely have for the diagnostician who works with no DSS assistance (Palmeira & Spassova, 2015). No patient would object to the use of imaging to help diagnose a fracture, because imaging is a useful tool. Similarly, if a DSS is characterized as a tool for the diagnostician rather than as a substitute diagnostician, its acceptance is enhanced.

A third way to increase DSS adoption is to target the DSS to particular points in the diagnostic process. For example, if the DSS detects that the diagnostician is going in the wrong direction, the DSS could then alert the diagnostician to a key test that might provide either disconfirmatory evidence for the current hypothesis or provide potential confirmatory evidence for an alternate hypothesis. This targeting strategy could prevent "alert fatigue," which occurs when diagnosticians get so many alerts and suggestions that they begin to ignore all of them (Berner, 2014).

Nomograms

"The probability nomogram is a graphical method for applying Bayes' Theorem, combining a prior probability (such as the base rate of a condition) with new information from a test," expressed as a likelihood ratio, "to estimate an updated, posterior probability" (Pendergast et al., 2018, p. 345). Figure 12.2 depicts a typical nomogram.

To use it, one places a ruler on the left vertical line corresponding to the pretest probability of the condition. One then pivots the ruler so that it intersects the middle vertical line at the point where the likelihood ratio of the test result or symptom is located. The place where the ruler crosses the right vertical line is

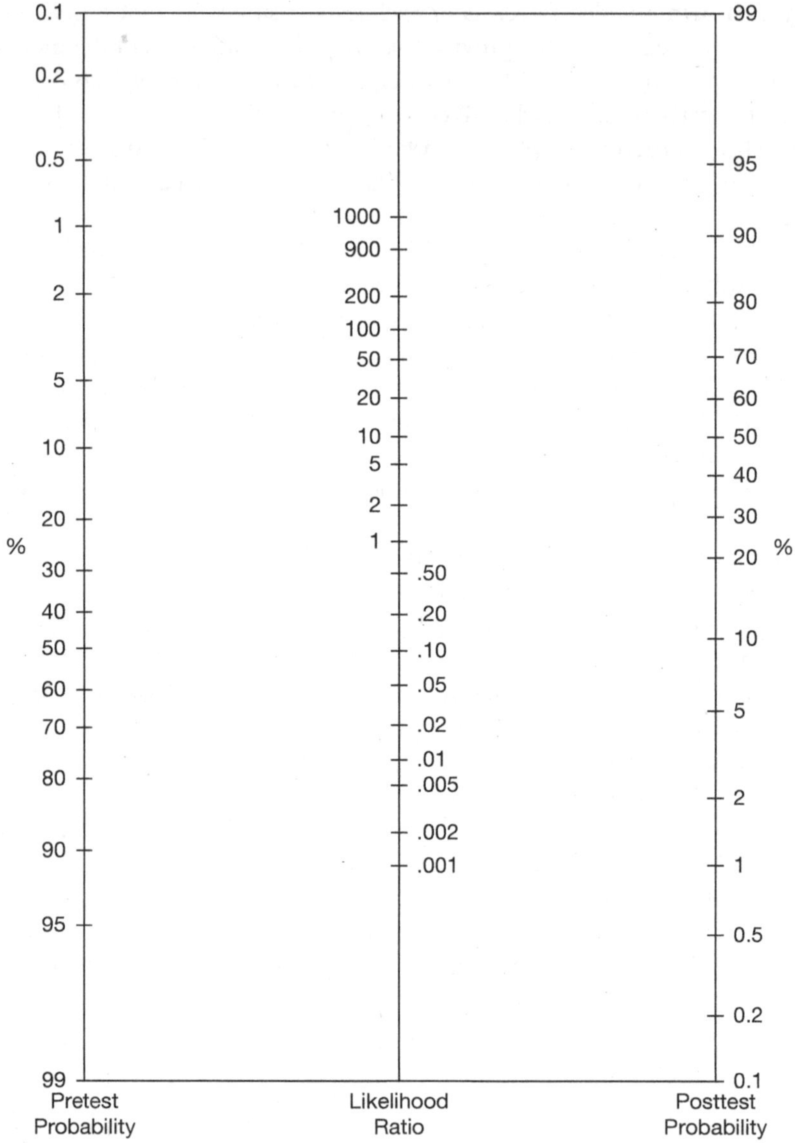

Figure 12.2 Nomogram

the posttest probability given the new test result or symptom. These three vertical lines represent the calculation of Bayes' Theorem without the calculation. Nomograms conquer base-rate neglect, improve accuracy of diagnoses, and heighten inter-rater reliability. No computer is needed; if the convenient Bayes' Theorem app on your smart phone (Kinnear et al., 2019) becomes obsolete due to change in its software, a low-tech nomogram will do just fine. If multiple independent test results are used to make the diagnosis, the posttest probability of test 1 becomes the pretest probability used for test 2.

Nomograms have been used in both medical and clinical psychology contexts. With regard to the latter, Pendergast et al. (2018, p. 346) listed several publications in which likelihood ratios are available: measures of anxiety (Van Meter et al., 2014), attention-deficit/hyperactivity disorder (Algorta et al., 2016), bipolar disorder (Youngstrom et al., 2004), and other conditions (Youngstrom et al., 2015). Van Meter et al. (2018) provided an excellent tutorial on the use of nomograms in the diagnosis of suicide potential in youth.

Nomograms are very helpful even if the precise posttest probability is not required (or available). Chapter 6 (on base rates) discusses a situation in which counselors in a state's community college system were grossly overdiagnosing learning disabilities (LD) among its students, although the base rate of LD at that time in similar circumstances was only around 3%. The counselors estimated that the likelihood ratio for the symptom "tight grip on the pencil" was around 10, probably a serious overestimate, but let's assume for a moment that this estimate was accurate. Use of the nomogram would have very quickly indicated to the counselors that the use of that symptom to diagnose LD would result in a vast number of false-positive errors. Another symptom the counselors used to diagnose LD was "taps feet." The posterior probability calculated from the symptom "tight grip on the pencil" would serve as the prior probability for the calculation of the impact of "taps feet." Of course, it would be a far superior strategy to use a nomogram based upon empirically established likelihood ratios, assuming they are either available or could be established from current data.

A FINAL WORD

Achieving accurate diagnoses and predictions can be highly challenging. The competent decision maker must know how to correctly collect the appropriate data, integrate such data in a statistically appropriate manner, avoid the cognitive pitfalls (discussed in other chapters), and apply debiasing techniques. At the beginning of this chapter, research was cited indicating that diagnostic errors account for a large fraction of hospital deaths every year. As the relation between symptoms and diagnoses, and predictive variables and outcomes, is probabilistic, not all judgment errors can be eliminated, and sometimes the level of success is certainly less than ideal. However, using the techniques described in this chapter and Chapter 13 will help move judgmental accuracy toward the highest possible level.

REFERENCES

Aczel, B., Bago, B, Szollosi, A., Foldes, A., & Lukacs, B. (2015). Is it time for studying real-life debiasing? Evaluation of the effectiveness of an analogical intervention technique. *Frontiers in Psychology*, *6*, 1120.

Adame, B. J. (2016). Training in the mitigation of anchoring bias: A test of the consider-the-opposite strategy. *Learning and Motivation*, *53*, 36–48.

Algorta, G. P., Dodd, A. L., Stringaris, A., & Youngstrom, E. A. (2016). Diagnostic efficiency of the SDQ for parents to identify ADHS in the UK: A ROC analysis. *European Child & Adolescent Psychiatry, 25*(9), 949–957.

Altabbaa, G., Raven, A. D., & Laberge, J. (2019). A simulation-based approach to training in heuristic clinical-decision making. *Diagnosis, 6*(7), 91–99.

Arkes, H. R. (2016). A levels of processing interpretation of dual-system theories of judgment and decision making. *Theory and Psychology, 26*, 459–475.

Arkes, H. R., & Blumer, C. (1985). The psychology of sunk cost. *Organizational Behavior and Human Decision Processes, 35*, 124–140.

Arkes, H. R., Christensen, C., Lai, C., & Blumer, C. (1987). Two methods of reducing overconfidence. *Organizational Behavior and Human Decision Processes, 39*, 133–144.

Arkes, H. R., Faust, D., Guilmette, T. J., & Hart, K. (1988). Eliminating the hindsight bias. *Journal of Applied Psychology, 73*, 305–307.

Arkes, H. R., Shaffer, V. A., & Medow, M. A. (2007). Patients derogate physicians who use a computer-assisted diagnostic aid. *Medical Decision Making, 27*, 189–202.

Berner, E. S. (2014). What can be done to increase the use of diagnostic decision support systems? *Diagnosis, 1*(1), 119–123.

Berner, E. S., & Graber, M. L. (2008). Overconfidence as a cause of diagnostic error in medicine. *The American Journal of Medicine, 121*(5A), S2–S23.

Brailey, K., Vasterling, J. J., & Franks, J. J. (2001). Memory of psychodiagnostics information: Biases and effects of expertise. *American Journal of Psychology, 114*(1), 55–92.

Bruchmuller, K., & Meyer, T. D. (2009). Diagnostically irrelevant information can affect the likelihood of a diagnosis of bipolar disorder. *Journal of Affective Disorders, 116*(1–2), 148–151.

Chu, D., Xiao, J., Shah, P., & Todd, B. (2018). How common are cognitive errors in cases presented at emergency medicine resident morbidity and mortality conferences? *Diagnosis, 5*(3), 143–150.

Croskerry, P., Singhal, G., & Mamede, S. (2013). Cognitive debiasing 1: Origins of bias and theory of debiasing. *BMJ Quality and Safety, 22*(S2), ii58–ii64.

Daniel, M., Carney, M., Khandelwal, S., Merritt, C., Cole, M., Malone, M., . . . Santen, S. A. (2017). Cognitive debiasing strategies: A faculty development workshop for clinical teachers in emergency medicine. *MedEdPORTAL, 13*, 10646.

Davis, D. A., Mazmanian, P. E., Fordis, M., Harrison R. V., Thorpe, K. E., & Perrier, L. (2006). Accuracy of physician self-assessment compared with observed measures of competence. *JAMA, 296*(9), 1094–1102.

Dawes, R. M., & Meehl, P. E. (1966). Mixed group validation. *Psychological Bulletin, 66*, 63–67.

De Neys, W. (2021). On dual- and single-process models of thinking. *Perspectives on Psychological Science, 16*(6), 1412–1427.

Dietvorst, B. J., Simmons, J. P., & Massey, C. (2015). Algorithm aversion: People erroneously avoid algorithms after seeing them err. *Journal of Experimental Psychology: General, 144*(1), 114–126.

Dietvorst, B. J., Simmons, J. P., & Massey, C. (2018). Overcoming algorithm aversion: People will use imperfect algorithms if they can (even slightly) modify them. *Management Science, 64*(3), 1155–1170.

DiNardo, D., Tilstra, S., McNeil, M., Follansbee, W., Zimmer, S., Farris, C., & Barnato, A. E. (2018). Identification of facilitators and barriers to residents' use of a clinical reasoning tool. *Diagnosis, 5*(1), 21–28.

Dror, I. E. (2018). Biases in forensic experts. *Science, 360*(6386), 243.

Dunbar, N. E., Miller, C. H., Adame, B. J., Elizondo, J., Wilson, S. N., Lane, B. L., . . . Zhang, J. (2014). Implicit and explicit training in the mitigation of cognitive bias through the use of serious game. *Computers in Human Behavior, 17*, 307–318.

Dzindolet, M. T., Peterson, S. A., Pomranky, R. A., Pierce, L. G., & Beck, H. P. (2003). The role of trust in automation reliance. *International Journal of Human-Computer Studies, 58*, 697–718.

Eichbaum, Q., Adkins, B., Craig-Owens, L., Ferguson, D., Long, D., Shaver, A., & Stratton, C. (2019). Mortality and morbidity rounds (MMR) in pathology: Relative contribution of cognitive bias vs. systems failure to diagnostic error. *Diagnosis, 6*(3), 249–257.

Ely, J. W., & Graber, M. L. (2015). Checklists to prevent diagnostic errors: A pilot randomized controlled trial. *Diagnosis, 2*(3), 163–169.

Ely, J. W., Graber, M. L., & Croskerry, P. (2011). Checklists to reduce diagnostic errors. *Academic Medicine, 86*(3), 307–313.

Evans, K. K., Cohen, M. A., Tambouret, R., Horowitz, T., Kreindel, E., & Wolfe, J. M. (2011). Does visual expertise improve visual recognition memory? *Attention, Perception, and Psychophysics, 73*, 30–35.

Faust, D., Gaudet, C. E., Ahern, D.C., & Bridges, A. J. (2012). Assessment of malingering and falsification: Continuing to push the boundaries of knowledge in research and clinical practice: Vol. 2. In A. M. Horton & C. R. Reynolds (Eds.), *Detection of malingering during head injury litigation* (3rd ed.). Springer.

Faust, D., Guilmette, T. J., Hart, K., Arkes, H. R., Fishburne, F. J., & Davey, L. (1988). Neuropsychologists' training, experience, and judgment accuracy. *Archives of Clinical Neuropsychology, 3*, 145–163.

Fischhoff, B. (1975). Hindsight is not equal to foresight: Effect of outcome knowledge on judgment under uncertainty. *Journal of Experimental Psychology: Human Perception and Performance, 1*(3), 288–299.

Fong, G. T., & Nisbett, R. E. (1991). Immediate and delayed transfer of training effects in statistical reasoning. *Journal of Experimental Psychology: General, 120*(1), 34–45.

Friedman, C. P., Gatti, G. G., Franz, T. M., Murphy, G. C., Wolf, F. M., Heckerling, P. S., . . . Elstein, A. S. (2005). Do physicians know when their diagnoses are correct? Implications for decision support and error reduction. *Journal of General Internal Medicine, 20*, 334–339.

Garb, H. N. (1998). *Studying the clinician: Judgment research and psychological assessment*. American Psychological Association.

Gentner, D. (1983). Structure-mapping: A theoretical framework for analogy. *Cognitive Science, 7*, 155–170.

Gigerenzer, G., & Hoffrage, U. (1995). How to improve Bayesian reasoning without instruction: Frequency formats. *Psychological Review, 103*, 650–669.

Goodwin, P., & Fildes, R. (1999). Judgmental forecasts of time series affected by special events: Does providing a statistical forecast improve accuracy? *Journal of Behavioral Decision Making, 12*(1), 37–53.

Grove, W. M., Zald, D. H., Lebow, B. S., Snitz, B. E., & Nelson, C. (2000). Clinical vs. mechanical prediction: A meta-analysis. *Psychological Assessment, 12*, 19–30.

Hales, B. M., & Pronovost, P. J. (2006). The checklist: A tool for error management and performance improvement. *Journal of Critical Care, 21*, 231–235.

Hammond, K. R., Hamm, R. M., Grassia, J., & Pearson, T. (1987). Direct comparison of the relative efficiency of intuitive and analytical cognition. *IEEE Transactions on Systems, Man, and Cybernetics, 17*, 753–750.

Hart, E. M., & Owen, H. (2005). Errors and omissions in anesthesia: A pilot study using a pilot's checklist. *Anesthesia and Analgesia, 101*(1), 246–250.

Henriksen, K., & Brady, J. (2013). The pursuit of better diagnostic performance: A human factors perspective. *BMJ Quality and Safety, 22*(S2), ii1–ii5.

Hersh, J. B. (1971). Effects of referral information of testers. *Journal of Consulting and Clinical Psychology, 37*(1), 116–122.

Herzog, S. M., & Hertwig, R. (2009). The wisdom of many in one mind: Improving individual judgments with dialectical bootstrapping. *Psychological Science, 20*(2), 231–237.

Hirt, E. R., & Markman, K. D. (1995). Multiple explanation: A consider-an-alternative strategy for debiasing judgments. *Journal of Personality and Social Psychology, 69*(6), 1069–1086.

Hoffman, J. A., von Helversen, B., & Rieskamp, J. (2013). Deliberation's blindsight: How cognitive load can improve judgments. *Psychological Science, 24*(6), 869–879.

Hoffrage, U., & Gigerenzer, G. (1998). Using natural frequencies to improve diagnostic inferences. *Academic Medicine, 73*, 538–540.

Hunt, D. L., Haynes, R. B., Hanna, S. E., & Smith, K. (1998). Effects of computer-based clinical decision support systems on physician performance and patient outcomes. *JAMA, 280*(15), 1339–1346.

Jenkins, M. M., & Youngstrom, E. A. (2016). A randomized controlled trial of cognitive debiasing improves assessment and treatment selection for pediatric bipolar disorder. *Journal of Consulting and Clinical Psychology, 84*(4), 323–333.

Jewsbury, P. A., & Bowden, S. C. (2013). A description of mixed group validation. *Assessment, 21*(2), 170–180.

Kahneman, D. (2011). *Thinking fast and slow*. Farrar, Strauss & Giroux.

Kaplan, S. E., Reneau, J. H., & Whitecotton, S. (2001). The effects of predictive ability information, locus of control, and decision maker involvement on decision aid reliance. *Journal of Behavioral Decision Making, 14*, 35–50.

Kareken, D. A., & Williams, J. M. (1994). Human judgment and estimation of premorbid intellectual function. *Psychological Assessment, 6*(2), 83–91.

Kinnear, B., Hagedorn, P. A., Kelleher, M., Ohlinger, C., & Toletino, J. (2019). Integrating Bayesian reasoning into medical education using smartphone apps. *Diagnosis, 6*(2), 85–89.

Klein, G. A. (1999). *Sources of power: How people make decisions*. MIT Press.

Kohn, L. T., Corrigan, J., & Donaldson, M. S. (2000). *To err is human: Building a safer health system*. National Academy Press.

Kok, E. M., Abed, A., & Robben, S. G. F.(2017). Does the use of a checklist help medical students in the detection of abnormalities on a chest radiograph? *Journal of Digital Imaging, 30*, 726–731.

Koriat, A., Lichtenstein, S., & Fischhoff, B. (1980). Reasons for confidence. *Journal of Experimental Psychology: Human Learning and Memory, 6*(2), 107–118.

Kovacs, R. J., Lagarde, M., & Cairns, J. (2020). Overconfident health workers provide lower quality healthcare. *Journal of Economic Psychology, 76*, 102213.

Kurvers, R. H. J. M., Herzog, S. M., Hertwig, R., Krause, J., Carney, P. A., Bogart, A., . . . Wolf, M. (2016). Boosting medical diagnostics by pooling independent judgments. *PNAS, 113*(31), 8777–8782.

Kurvers, R. H. J. M., Krause, J., Argenziano, G., Zalaudek, I., & Wolf, M. (2015). Detection accuracy of collective intelligence assessments for skin cancer diagnosis. *JAMA Dermatology, 151*(12), 1346–1353.

Lawrence, M., Goodwin, P., & Fildes, R. (2002). Influence of user participation on DSS use and decision accuracy. *Omega, 30*, 381–392.

Leape, L. L., Berwick, D. M., & Bates, D. W. (2002). Counting deaths due to medical errors: Reply. *JAMA, 289*(19), 2405.

Lincoln, M. J., Turner, C. W., Huag, P. J., Warner, H. R., Williamson, J. W., Bouhaddou, O., . . . Grant, M. (1991). Iliad training enhances medical students' diagnostic skills. *Journal of Medical Systems, 15*(1), 93–110.

Longoni, C., Bonezzi, A., & Morewedge, C. K. (2019). Resistance to medical artificial intelligence. *Journal of Consumer Research, 46*, 629–650.

Mamede, S., Splinter, T. A. W., van Gog, T., Rikers, R. M. J. P., & Schmidt, H. G. (2012). Exploring the role of salient distracting clinical features in the emergence of diagnostic errors and the mechanisms through which reflection counteracts mistakes. *BMJ Quality and Safety, 21*(4), 295–300.

Mamede, S., van Gog, T., van den Berge, K., Rikers, R. M., van Saase, J. L., van Guldener, C., & Schmidt, H. G. (2010). Effect of availability bias and reflective reasoning on diagnostic accuracy among internal medicine residents. *JAMA, 304*(11), 1198–1203.

Mamede, S., Schmidt, H. G., & Penaforte, J. C. (2008). Effects of reflective practice on the accuracy of medical diagnoses. *Medical Education, 42*, 468–475.

Martinez-Franco, A. I., Sanchez-Mendiola, M., Mazon-Ramirez, J. J., Hernandez-Torres, I., Rivero-Lopez, C., Spicer, T., & Martinez-Gonzalez, A. (2018). Diagnostic accuracy in family medicine residents using a clinical decision support system (DXplain): A randomized-controlled trial. *Diagnosis, 5*(2), 71–76.

Maude, J. (2014). Differential diagnosis: The key to reducing diagnosis error, measuring diagnosis and a mechanism to reduce healthcare costs. *Diagnosis, 1*(1), 107–109.

McDonald, K. M., Matesic, B., Contopoulos-Ioannidis, D. G., Lonhart, J., Schmidt, E., Pineda, N., & Ioannidis, J. P. (2013). Patient safety strategies targeted at diagnostic errors: A systematic review. *Annals of Internal Medicine, 158*(5, Part 2), 381–390.

McLaughlin, K., Eva, K. W., & Norman, G. (2014). Reexamining our bias against heuristics. *Advances in Health Science Education, 19*, 457–464.

Meyer, A. N. D., Payne, V. L., Meeks, D. W., Rao, R., & Singh, H. (2013). Physicians' diagnostic accuracy, confidence, and resource requests: A vignette study. *JAMA Internal Medicine, 173*(21), 1952–1959.

Mojtabai, R. (2013). Clinician-identified depression in community settings: Concordance with structured-interview diagnosis. *Psychotherapy and Psychosomatics, 82*(3), 161–169.

Morewedge, C. K., Yoon, H., Scopelliti, I., Symborski, C. W., Korris, J. H., & Kassam, K. S. (2015). Debiasing decisions: Improved decision making with a single training intervention. *Policy Insights from the Behavioral and Brain Sciences, 2*(1), 129–140.

Murrie, D. C., Boccaccini, M. T., Guarnera, L. A., & Ruffino, K. A. (2013). Are forensic experts biased by the side that retained them? *Psychological Science, 24*(10), 1889–1897.

Neal, T. M. S., & Brodsky, S. L. (2016). Forensic psychologists: Perceptions of bias and potential correction strategies in forensic mental health evaluations. *Psychology, Public Policy, and Law, 22*(1), 58–76.

Nisbett, R. E., & Wilson, T. D. (1977). Telling more than we can know: Verbal reports on mental processes. *Psychological Review, 84*, 231–259.

Palmeira, M., & Spassova, G. (2015). Consumer reactions to professionals who use decision aids. *European Journal of Marketing, 49*(3/4), 302–325.

Pendergast, L. L., Youngstrom, E. A., & Ruan-Iu, L. (2018). The nomogram: A decision making tool for practitioners using mulitiered systems of support. *School Psychology Review, 47*(4), 345–359.

Phillips, J., (2014). Detecting diagnostic error in psychiatry. *Diagnosis, 1*(1), 75–78.

Podbregar, M., Voga, G., Krivec, B., Skale, R., Pareznik, R., & Gabrscek, L. (2001). Should we confirm our clinical diagnostic certainty by autopsies? *Intensive Care Medicine, 27*, 1750–1755.

Porat, T., Delancy, B., & Kostopoulou, O. (2017). The impact of a diagnostic decision support system on the consultation: Perceptions of GPs and patients. *BMC Medical Informatics and Decision Making, 17*, 79.

Potchen, E. J. (2006). Measuring observer performance in chest radiology: Some experiences. *Journal of the American College of Radiology, 3*, 423–432.

Price, P. C., & Stone, E. R. (2004). Intuitive evaluation of likelihood judgment producers: Evidence for a confidence heuristic. *Journal of Behavioral Decision Making, 17*(1), 39–57.

Promberger, M., & Baron, J. (2006). Do patients trust computers? *Journal of Behavioral Decision Making, 19*, 455–468.

Pronin, E., Lin, D. Y., & Ross, L. (2002). The bias blind spot: Perceptions of bias in self versus others. *Personality and Social Psychology Bulletin, 28*, 369–381.

Rabinowitz, J., & Garelik-Wyler, R. (1999). Accuracy and confidence in clinical assessment of psychiatric inpatients risk of violence. *International Journal of Law and Psychiatry, 22*(1), 99–106.

Rakofsky, J. J., & Dunlop, B. W. (2015). The over-under on the misdiagnosis of bipolar disorder: A systematic review. *Current Psychiatry Reviews, 11*(4), 222–234.

Ramnarayan, P., Roberts, G. C., Coren, M., Nanduri, V., Tomlinson, A., Taylor, P. M., . . . Britto, J. F. (2006) Assessment of the potential impact of a reminder system on the reduction of diagnostic errors: A quasi-experimental study. *BMC Medical Informatics and Decision Making, 6*, 22.

Ridderikhoff, J., & van Heck, B. (1999). Who is afraid of the system? Doctors' attitude toward diagnostic systems. *International Journal of Medical Informatics, 53*(1), 91–100.

Ruggero, C. J., Zimmerman, M., Chelminski, I., & Young, D. (2010). Borderline personality disorder and the misdiagnosis of bipolar disorder. *Journal of Psychiatric Research, 44*(6), 405–408.

Schiff, G., Hasan, O., Kim, S., Abrams, R., Cosby, K., Lambert, B. L., . . . McNutt, R. A. (2009). Diagnostic error in medicine: Analysis of 583 physician-reported errors. *Archives of Internal Medicine, 169*(20), 1881–1887.

Schnapp, B. H., Sun, J. E., Kim, J. L., Strayer, R. J., & Shah, K. H. (2018). Cognitive error in an academic emergency department. *Diagnosis, 5*(3), 135–142.

Sedlmeier, P. (1999). *Improving statistical reasoning: Theoretical models and practical applications*. Lawrence Erlbaum Associates.

Sieck, W. R., & Arkes, H. R. (2005). The recalcitrance of overconfidence and its contribution to decision aid neglect. *Journal of Behavioral Decision Making*, *18*, 29–53.

Slovic, P., & Fischhoff, B. (1977). On the psychology of experimental surprises. *Journal of Experimental Psychology: Human Perception and Performance*, *3*(4), 544–551.

Smith, J. D., & Agate, J. (2004). Solutions for overconfidence: Evaluation of an instructional module for counselor trainees. *Counselor Education & Supervision*, *44*, 31–43.

Smith-Bindman, R., Chu, P. W., Miglioretti, D. L., Sickles, E. A., Blanks, R., Ballard-Barbash, R., . . . Kerlikowske, K. (2003). Comparison of screening mammography in the United States and the United Kingdom. *JAMA*, *290(16)*, 2129–2138.

Sniezek, J. A., & Van Swol, L. M. (2001). Trust, confidence, and expertise in the judge-advisor system. *Organizational Behavior and Human Decision Processes*, *84*, 288–307.

Thomas, D. B., & Newman-Toker, D. E. (2016). Diagnosis is a team sport: Partnering with allied health professional to reduce diagnostic errors. *Diagnosis*, *3*(2), 49–59.

Tversky, A., & Kahneman, D. (1972). Availability: A heuristic for judging frequency and probability. *Cognitive Psychology*, *4*, 207–232.

Van Dongen, K., & van Maanen, P-P. (2013). A framework for explaining reliance on decision aids. *International Journal of Human-Computer Studies*, *71*, 410–424.

Van Meter, A. R., Algorta, G. P., Youngstrom, E. A., Lechtman, Y., Youngstrom, J. K., Feeny, N. C., & Findling, R. L. (2018). Assessing for suicidal behavior in youth using the Achenbach system of empirically based assessment. *European Child and Adolescent Psychiatry*, *27*, 19–169.

Van Meter, A. R., Youngstrom, E., Youngstrom, J. K., Ollendick, T., Demeter, C., & Findling, R. L. (2014). Clinical decision making about child and adolescent anxiety disorders using the Achenbach system of empirically based assessment. *Journal of Clinical Child & Adolescent Psychology*, *43*(4), 552–565.

Vinny, P. W., Gupta, A., Modi, M., Srivastava, M. V. P., Lal, V., Sylaja, P. N., . . . Vishnu, V. Y. (2019). Head to head comparison between neurology residents and a mobile medical application for diagnostic accuracy in cognitive neurology. *QM: An International Journal of Medicine*, *112*(8), 591–598.

Vrieze, S. L., & Grove, W. M. (2009). Survey on the use of clinical and mechanical prediction methods in clinical psychology. *Professional Psychology: Research and Practice*, *40*(5), 525–531.

Wade, T. C., & Baker, T. B. (1977). Opinions and use of psychological tests: Survey of clinical psychologists. *American Psychologist*, *32*(10), 874–882.

Wegwarth, O., & Gigerenzer, G. (2011). Statistical illiteracy in doctors. In G. Gigerenzer & J. A. Muir Gray (Eds.), *Better doctors, better patients, better decisions: Envisioning health care 2020* (pp. 137–152). MIT Press.

Wolf, J. R. (2014). Do IT students prefer doctors who use IT? *Computers in Human Behavior*, *35*, 287–294.

Wolf, M., Krause, J., Carney, P. A., Bogart, A., & Kurvers, R. H. J. M. (2015). Collective intelligence meets medical decision making: The collective outperforms the best radiologist. *PLOS One*, *10*(8), e0134269.

Wood, D. S., & Tracey, T. F. G. (2009). A brief feedback intervention for diagnostic overshadowing. *Training and Education in Professional Psychology*, *3*(4), 218–225.

Wright, B., Faulkner, N., Bragge, P., & Graber, M. L. (2019). What interventions could reduce diagnostic error in emergency departments? A review of evidence, practice and consumer perspectives. *Diagnosis*, *6*(4), 325–334.

Wu, J., & Lowenstein, E. (2020). Balancing confidence and humility in the diagnostic process. *Diagnosis*, *7*(1), 11–15.

Youngstrom, E. A., Choukas-Bradley, S., Calhoun, C. D., & Jensen-Doss, A. (2015). Clinical guide to the evidence-based assessment approach to diagnosis and treatment. *Cognitive and Behavioral Practice*, *22*(1), 20–35.

Youngstrom, E. A., Findling, R. L., Calabrese, J. R., Gracious, B. L., Demeter, C., Bedoya, D. D., & Price, M. (2004). Comparing the diagnostic accuracy of six potential screening instruments for bipolar disorder in youths aged 5 to 17 years. *Journal of the American Academy of Child & Adolescent Psychiatry*, *43*(7), 847–858.

13

Approaches for Improving Information Gathering, Appraising the Utility of Information, and Combining and Interpreting Information

Prochaska and DiClemente developed an influential model of behavioral change that describes different steps in the process (Prochaska & DiClemente, 1977; Prochaska & Velicer, 1997). A particularly important step is the transition from precontemplation to contemplation, in which an individual moves from thinking minimally about altering certain behaviors to a point at which they start considering such possibilities more actively. Prochaska and colleagues found that emphasizing the potential pros of altering behaviors seemed to do more to move individuals forward than emphasizing the cons of continuing ongoing behaviors. Keeping this in mind, we know that some decision researchers show a propensity for criticizing, if not berating, certain problematic decision practices. That passion is sometimes driven by laudable concern about the potential costs of increased error. However, in the spirit of Prochaska's and his colleagues' work, we wish to emphasize the benefits of improving or changing certain decision practices. Such benefits include, but are not limited to, increased diagnostic and predictive accuracy, improved client care, and the reassurance of knowing that one is aligning one's practices with methods supported by sound research in domains in which that knowledge can provide considerable assistance.

Chapter 12 focuses mainly on debiasing methods. Debiasing methods are one side of a two-sided approach to enhancing judgmental accuracy. The second component, which is the focus of this chapter, is normative decision practices, or methods that are known to enhance accuracy but are often underutilized or misapplied. Underuse of such methods may relate minimally to biases and instead simply reflect a lack of familiarity. For example, it took the genius of Bayes to recognize the benefits of formally incorporating prior odds into prediction and to develop ways of doing so. One would not say decision makers unaware of these methods are biased because the methods are not being used, an attribution sometimes made by decision researchers that seems misplaced.

Although we touch on some additional debiasing procedures and beneficial clinical practice habits, we now turn primarily to normative methods and related strategies. The materials that follow are divided into three sections: foundational materials that apply broadly to decision making, information gathering, and the integration or interpretation of information. The three areas are often interrelated, and thus discussion of any one of the areas often has implications for, or overlaps with, other areas. For example, when combining information, one wishes to focus on a composition of items that maximize accuracy, but if one does not gather that information in the first place, then integration efforts are compromised.

FOUNDATIONAL MATERIALS FOR GATHERING AND INTERPRETING INFORMATION

Methodical Adherence to the Best Validated Methods Increases Judgmental Accuracy

As previously emphasized, the greatest general contributor to diagnostic and predictive accuracy in the mental health field is methodical adherence to the best validated methods, such as the use of properly-developed statistical decision methods. If one examines studies addressing clinical decisions or the comparison of clinical and statistical decision methods, one finds that the clinical and statistical methods sometimes tie, but when there is a difference, the statistical method exceeds the clinical method nearly all of the time. The differences may be relatively small or they may be substantial. For example, accuracy levels that fail to exceed chance levels occur about two to three times more often with clinical judgment versus statistical decision methods, and statistical decision methods achieve high levels of accuracy considerably more often than clinical judgment. Similarly, if one compares effect sizes obtained in studies examining clinical judgment versus studies examining the effectiveness of well-developed tests and assessment methods, one often finds that the latter demonstrate a substantial, or even a twofold or greater, advantage.

Outcomes favoring statistical decision methods and well-validated tests and assessment methods over impressionistic judgment may be jarring, but the positive side to all of this is that decision researchers, many of whom are mental health professionals themselves, have developed procedures that can enhance our diagnostic and predictive accuracy and thereby provide better care. This voluminous research provides us both with critical guidance that is disregarded at one's peril and clear directions for increasing our success.

Formal Tests of Efficacy, Not Subjective Confidence, Are the Better Guide to Accuracy

Decisions to use or reject methods and strategies rest substantially on an accurate determination of their efficacy. For example, if the best evidence suggests that a certain structured interview method is clearly better than another structured interview method for a particular decision task at hand, and that decisions are less accurate when the results of the two methods are combined than when using the first method alone, the course of action should be clear. Thus, it is important to be as accurate as possible when evaluating the efficacy of methods.

Most individuals, clinicians in the mental health field included, are pervasively more confident in their accuracy than is warranted (see Chapter 11). The naturalistic features of everyday clinical practice often create the misimpression that our rate of accuracy exceeds our actual level of performance, due to such factors as nonrepresentative feedback from clients and self-fulfilling prophecies. Hence, calibrating one's confidence accurately through impressionistic methods is subject to multiple sources of misinformation that foster inflated beliefs. Overconfidence creates a host of problems. For example, overconfident practitioners often reach conclusions too soon, or before critical information has been obtained, and tend to make overly extreme or risky decisions. In addition, overconfident decision makers often fail to take corrective actions, are less likely to detect their errors, and tend to reject potentially helpful decision aids or research innovations. Suppose a decision maker believes they achieve, say, a 90% level of accuracy, when their true accuracy is 70%. Consequently, a statistical prediction method that generates an 80% accuracy rate and could thereby decrease their error rate from 30% to 20%, would likely be rejected due to the misperception that it's a downgrade relative to their current performance.

Rather than relying on subjective impressions about our level of performance, we can look to research on the effectiveness of the methods we use (assuming the methods are applied as designed and studied). Self-impressions about decision accuracy are vulnerable to various cognitive failings, such as confirmatory bias and hindsight bias (see Chapters 4 and 5). For example, confirmatory bias can lead us to focus disproportionately on outcomes that seem to support our judgments, and hindsight bias can lead us to mistakenly recall our predictions as more consistent with outcomes than is actually the case.

In addition, placing main reliance on subjective impressions reduces our opportunity to use various research methods that attenuate biases, such as single- or double-blind appraisal. We also usually lack control or comparison groups, and thus, for example, do not know what outcomes would have occurred had we decided otherwise. We may think that a positive outcome with a client reflects a sound or optimal decision about the treatment approach we selected, and that could be true, but perhaps a similar or better outcome would have been obtained with another selection. Overall, for these and other reasons, the quality of evidence one uses to appraise one's judgmental accuracy often does not approach the quality of evidence about the success of methods yielded by a series of well-designed studies and perhaps a meta-analysis of the results.

Hence, in determining a method's accuracy and the success one is likely to achieve if using it properly, one can look to research conducted in settings similar to one's practice and with similar clients. In some cases, there will be a considerable body of literature that has demonstrated results in general accord with one another. These outcomes should provide evidence that is at least as good, and often considerably stronger, than subjective impressions. If practitioners argue that the research does not apply to them because they do something different or modify standard procedures, then research on such topics as countervailing suggests that if these changes do impact accuracy, the result is far more likely to be negative than positive. One who assumes otherwise would seem to bear the burden of proof.

In the moment when clinical decisions have to be made, one will rarely have definitive evidence establishing whether one's self-impressions about accuracy, or a body or research on accuracy, is the better source. However, considering the extensive literature showing pervasive overconfidence, and the quality of evidence and the conditions under which information about accuracy levels is obtained, it seems clear that one should usually bet on the research evidence, especially when the studies are methodologically sound and have generally yielded consistent results. In applied psychology, as is true in many other professions, often the best we can do is to go with the usually superior choice. Identifying exceptions is frequently hazardous, degrades the percentage of correct decisions, and requires a method to identify exceptions effectively that probably does not yet exist (and if available and feasible would probably have been used in the first place).

Strategies to reduce overconfidence are discussed in Chapter 12, such as actively considering contrary evidence. One can also keep track of one's hits and misses. When tracking one's accuracy, it is advantageous to record predictions or judgments when they are made. If one fails to keep such a record, then once outcomes are known, hindsight bias and the resultant reconstruction of initial predictions can make it seem like one's accuracy was greater than was truly the case. That misperception, in turn, is likely to attenuate or negate the potential value of feedback for adjusting one's level and calibration of confidence. If possible, one can also try to focus on outcomes that can be appraised without too much ambiguity, such as whether a client's score on a PTSD screening measure or a depression inventory decreases by more than a standard deviation after five treatment sessions.

The same data upon which the original predictions were based and subsequent outcomes were observed might be sufficient to create a statistical decision method that can be used with new cases. For new cases, one could see how the accuracy of the statistical predictive method compares to one's own or other's clinical judgments. For example, if clients in a setting are reviewed by a group of practitioners at the time of intake, attendees might complete a short rating scale containing variables believed to have potential predictive value (e.g., quality of initial rapport, level of insight, motivation for treatment, number of prior treatment attempts, level of social support, etc.). The data coding and analysis needed to create statistical prediction methods, given modern computing power, would likely require a relatively small investment of time and might well improve accuracy.

Limits of Insight

We will not reiterate the need to take active steps to improve decision making, as opposed to depending on insight alone, but simply wish to mention one other factor limiting the utility of self-reflection on decision processes. As modeling studies show, individuals' introspections about their cue use or subjective cue utilization may bear limited relation to objective measures of their cue use. For example, cues that individuals believe they rely on heavily may have negligible impact on their decisions, and cues they believe have little or no impact may have a sizeable influence (for an example see Werner et al., 1983). Therefore beliefs about one's current cue use and the changes that are needed, as well as self-instructions to alter one's cue use, might seem to have been implemented effectively, but that is no assurance these aims have actually been achieved. For example, an individual might humbly acknowledge that they have held incorrect beliefs about certain minority group members and set out to alter their practices. Despite good will and the belief that this worthwhile goal has been accomplished, judgments might still be similarly biased. In such circumstances, other steps are needed, such as potentially blinding a person to sociodemographic factors that degrade their judgments.

Experience Is Not Necessarily the Best Teacher

Experience and practice can be invaluable tools for skill development and self-improvement, such as learning the fine-motor movements needed to write in cursive or to play a musical instrument. However, for improving performance on other types of tasks, experience may have restricted value, quickly reach a point of diminishing returns, be minimally helpful, frankly misleading, or highly costly. Furthermore, there may be better, or far better and more efficacious, ways to learn or to improve performance than relying heavily on direct personal experience. (How many times might an employee at the deli counter practice guessing the weight of various items before realizing that a proper scale is more accurate and can be mastered far more rapidly? Does a person really need to jump off the roof of a house at least three times to learn it's a bad idea?) We often encourage others to avoid learning the hard way. However, we may miss opportunities to apply this advice to ourselves when it might serve us well. The mental health field is a culture onto itself, and certain things, whether truly warranted or not, are repeated so often that we may take them as givens and not question them sufficiently.

There are circumstances in which one cannot blend two different sources of information. For example, a dichotomous choice may be necessary, one cannot delay too long, and two different sources of information may be in direct conflict with one another. Thus, we must elevate one source of information over the other. It is here that practitioners often face the dilemma of siding with their experience versus research findings.

Many studies have examined the impact of experience on judgmental accuracy in the mental health field. We believe it is fair to say that across these studies, the relative benefits of experience are often considerably less robust than many practitioners assume. It is not unusual to find rather modest effect sizes, and sometimes no overall change in accuracy at all, and a fairly early point of diminishing returns (Spengler et al., 2009). Often, experience leads to a larger increase in confidence than in accuracy and creates a growing gap between the two (i.e., level of confidence increasingly greater than accuracy), along with all of the problems that come with overconfidence.

We are not dismissing the major benefits of experience across various tasks and endeavors, and its value for generating potentially remarkable ideas and hypotheses that may later be verified through formal studies. However, typical effect sizes for the benefits of experience in enhancing clinical judgment and prediction are relatively modest or small when compared to the gains achieved by the proper use of base rates, statistical decision procedures, and well-validated assessment methods. An additional major advantage of the latter types of information and methods is that unlike the hundreds or thousands of hours of experience one may believe are needed to achieve true judgmental proficiency in the mental health field, proper use of such decision aids as base rates and statistical decision methods can require far less time to master. To the extent time is saved and proficient methods are available to a wider array of mental health professionals, we can extend the reach of professional services. (We would note that the relation between training and decision accuracy often diverges from the literature on experience and accuracy. In general, poor training can lead to no gains or even diminished accuracy despite the number of hours involved, whereas proficient training, such as tutorials in the application of Bayes' Theorem, can increase a range of skills rapidly.)

In addition to studies examining the impact of experience on judgmental accuracy and the comparison to other methods for enhancing decision accuracy, key methodological contrasts between learning via clinical experience versus well-conducted research are worth considering. First, research data can serve as a way of condensing important aspects of experience and large amounts of empirical/experiential information. (By *empirical*, we are referring here to its original formal meaning, as denoting information gained by observation, and not as synonymous with research evidence.) For example, a researcher who gathers 5,000 MMPI-2 profiles may have compiled a database that exceeds a clinician's personal exposure to such information during an entire career. Thus, perceptions of what does and does not count as experiential (or empirical) information is not always as clear-cut as it might seem; the researcher's amalgamation of MMPI-2 profiles comprises a trove of experience. Certainly, research data will never capture the richness and salience of direct experience. Nonetheless, direct experience often does not come solely with potential advantages, but also with potential disadvantages or misleading elements that can be partly offset by proper research methods. For example, the salience of information or aspects of a client's presentation may affect judgment considerably but show limited association with diagnostic or predictive value for the issue at hand. In addition, depending primarily on experience to sharpen one's skills, as opposed to applying existent research knowledge, can lead to otherwise avoidable errors that exact a high toll.

Furthermore, and arguably most importantly, clinical practice is primarily driven by client needs (as it should be), and not by maximizing opportunities to learn from experience. Consequently, a practitioner: (1) rarely gets to fill the four cells of a covariation table with sufficiently large, representative samples; (2) selects a course of action and therefore does not know what would have happened had a different course of action been selected (i.e., the clinician lacks a control or comparison group); (3) does not select treatments across clients through random assignment; and, (4) being the one providing the treatment, cannot be blinded to the treatment being offered when appraising outcome. Thus, when trying to learn through clinical experience, these four powerful tools for acquiring knowledge are attenuated, at best, and often impractical or simply unavailable. Other differences or disadvantages could be discussed, but the central issue seems clear: when trying to learn certain types of things (e.g., presence and strength of association between variables; comparative treatment effectiveness; base rates of occurrence across different groups of individuals), scientific methodology can offer major advantages. How can one, for example, determine the presence and strength of association as effectively, or effectively at all, when the conditions of clinical practice prevent one from filling the four cells of a covariation table, in comparison to conducting a study that meets this essential need?

Thus, for acquiring knowledge about various matters essential to maximizing diagnostic and predictive accuracy, experience by itself may not be a very effective guide or can even be frankly misleading (see the discussion of illusory correlation in Chapter 3), whereas well-conducted research is likely to offer a better alternative. This is not to suggest that every study is well conducted, or that a study or two alone is likely to provide much certainty in a field that can be as challenging as psychology. However, when a body of methodologically sound research achieves reasonable consistency in outcomes (e.g., that therapy helps a substantial percentage of individuals), it is worth taking note. As also follows, when a compilation of well-conducted and generally consistent research indicates one conclusion and experiential impressions suggest a conflicting conclusion, such as whether a client has bipolar disorder, we should be humble and realize that the research is more likely to be correct than our impressionistic judgment. Of course, there are exceptions, but as discussed in reference to Einhorn's (1986) landmark article, and despite the angst it might create, we often have to accept some degree of error to make less error. Identifying exceptions with sufficient accuracy to do better overall would often require a method better than experiential learning and competently conducted scientific research, which has yet to be identified or created. Thus, if we have to make a decision in real time to maximize benefit to the client, then despite internal reservations, we should generally go with well-conducted research that has generated convergent outcomes (or have a compelling reason to bet against it, as discussed in this chapter and in Chapter 8 in the sections "Sawyer's Review" and "I know an exception when I see one").

When evaluating support for self-appraisals of one's judgmental accuracy or level of confidence, or when evaluating the comparative accuracy of conclusions based on experience versus scientific studies, two broad questions are essential: (1) What is the evidence? (2) How sound is the evidence, or what are the knowledge credentials? For clinical judgments and decisions, one is often most interested in evidence bearing on predictive accuracy in important domains or in the area of immediate interest. Knowledge credentials often relate to the type of evidence under consideration. For example, the evidence may be based primarily on subjective impressions of efficacy under limited or poor conditions for learning, which, as noted, often occurs in practice settings. Alternatively, did conditions allow one to gather information from all four cells of a covariation table and to obtain sufficiently large and representative samples, and were methods used to attenuate bias, such as single- and double-blinding? Further, did studies yield relatively consistent results across independent investigators and facilitate rigorous meta-analyses that generated robust findings?

The mental health field, especially in psychology, has often pushed for a model dictating active engagement in both research and practice. We will not enter into what sometimes seem more like ideological than evidence-based debates about science-practice models. However, whether one does or does not support models advocating that care providers engage regularly in both research and clinical practice (a science-practice model), we do support the model of the scientific-practitioner, in which those providing services have good familiarity with research that can inform practice and are capable consumers of research. It is not that we oppose clinicians engaging in both research and practice, which is not at all the case, but only that we question whether the benefits of engaging in both have been overstated.

In domains in which scientific knowledge enhances practice, there is good basis to argue that practitioners should be informed consumers of scientific research, because such knowledge can make an important difference. Examples include multicultural research on determinants of treatment effectiveness, knowing how to distinguish between a proficient meta-analysis and a shaky one, or facility with critical dimensions for appraising assessment measures or other forms of information-gathering. It seems to us that decision research is one of the most important areas in which knowledge can be put to pragmatic use in clinical practice and when applied properly is almost certain to enhance diagnostic and predictive accuracy.

Psychometrics Really Matter: Selecting the Best Available Methods

Psychometric qualities are a little like gravity—if you release a rock, it will fall, and if psychometric qualities are poor, methods will almost surely follow a downward path. Psychometric qualities are not solely applicable to tests; they are also essential to other types of information intended for applied use. For example, if an interview impression or datum is extremely variable or cannot be appraised accurately, then it is unlikely to have predictive utility. A number of years ago, the use of anatomically detailed dolls for assessing potential child sexual abuse came under challenge due to insufficient scientific support. (We wish to state as loudly and clearly as we can that we in no way question the importance of identifying abuse. Rather, it is the effectiveness of methods that is at issue, and especially the use of methods that might be considerably less accurate than better alternatives.) In response to concerns raised about the use of anatomically detailed dolls, some defended the practice by arguing their use could be conceptualized as a variation in interview methods, and consequently that knowledge of psychometric qualities did not matter. This is a highly questionable rationale. If a method does not generate valid or accurate results, it should not be used, whether it is a test, a questionnaire, a structured or unstructured interview method, or some other form of information gathering.

The quality of assessment and prediction methods varies enormously, and thus making sound selections is vitally important. Surveys of professional test usage sometimes suggest limited association between frequency of use and level of validity (see Archer & Newsom, 2000; Piotrowski, 1985; Wright et al., 2017). In a number of these surveys the word *validity* does not even appear, and other considerations frequently seem to drive test selection. How accuracy becomes relegated to secondary status is hard to grasp, but it may stem from such factors as insufficient awareness of technical qualities, choices being passed down across generations, or a belief we have commonly encountered that clinical judgment can overcome or compensate for relatively weak technical qualities, especially if one gathers extensive information.

Throwing noise and error into a pile of information, such as results from a technically poor test, is far more likely to degrade, rather than enhance, decision making. Further, how could subjective judgment elevate one beyond the technical limits of highly flawed methods? For example, if a test generates a score that is primarily error, what subjective means would allow one to extract something useful from it? Eliminating that test result from consideration and depending instead on more useful variables could lead one to surpass the test's accuracy, but that strategy is different from somehow miraculously exceeding the informational value of a highly flawed measure and using it in the hopes of elevating one's judgment. If we could routinely exceed the predictive value of a variable or data point using clinical judgment, then clinical judgment should surpass statistical decision methods regularly. Such a result would be expected because statistical decision methods are bounded by the technical limits of the information on which they are based. However, numerous comparative studies have shown just the opposite outcome, with statistical decision methods almost always equaling or exceeding clinical judgment (see Chapter 8).

Practitioners may sometimes ascribe more stature to test companies than is justified. There are numerous tests with respectable or strong psychometric qualities, but tests also abound that are plagued by such problems as clearly deficient normative samples, major floor or ceiling effects, or grossly deficient reliability. For example, one compilation or battery of neuropsychological measures in wide use for about two decades provides no reliability data for a number of the tests or subtests, and where reliability data are reported, one often finds disturbing outcomes, such as reliabilities on measures for different age groups as low as .20, .19, .13, and .06. How can one justify the use of a measure that approaches or exceeds 90% error? And how could clinical judgment correct for results that are little different than pulling random numbers out of a hat? It is highly likely that base rates alone will often outperform such deficient measures, at times by a wide margin.

It can be helpful to apply a few basic psychometric "go or no-go" guidelines, especially if better potential choices are available. Under the great majority of circumstances (although not all, for technical reasons we do not go into here), if test–retest reliability is deficient, one can just say No to that test or its problematic subcomponents. If reliabilities are not reported for certain test components and are not available elsewhere, those components should not be used unless circumstances are truly exceptional. One reason for such a default option is that including weak predictors in diagnostic or predictive formulations is often a more serious mistake than excluding good predictors, especially in areas in which various other valid measures are available (for further details, see the subsequent heading, "Three Steps for Screening Information"). Hence, one should be conservative about including questionable variables.

Similarly, at least for certain variables, if measures of validity generate feeble outcomes (in cases in which the test is not already doomed by deficient reliability), and especially if there are better options, those variables should be disregarded. Also, if there is little or no formal validity data for anything resembling the application being considered, it renders the potential value of the measure highly questionable or ambiguous. Under such conditions, it is once again better to exclude it, especially when other methods are available and research has supported their positive qualities. One can also see that decision policies advocating a readiness to exclude variables when they are demonstrably weak or lack supportive evidence clash with the common, but often questionable or counterproductive, dictate to integrate all of the available information.

There is a tendency to think of validity as a global quality, as in a statement like, "The MMPI-2 is a valid test." Global statements of this type are essentially non sequiturs, because a test may be an excellent choice for some questions and groups and useless for other applications. Hence, validity is a specific, not a global, quality. If one switches application to a different question or group, one might obtain a very different accuracy rate. Additionally, although use of a test will rarely mirror the conditions of validation studies exactly, the broader the level of generalization or extrapolation required, the more likely validity figures drawn from the original application will become more and more questionable. There is a truism that goes as follows: "Conclusions cannot be better than the data upon which they depend." Although there can be exceptions, in general the quality of conclusions is limited by the quality of the information one uses. The prediction of human behavior is hard enough without adding avoidable error by choosing weak or deficient methods, especially when better options are available.

Exercise Care

The refrain we have emphasized repeatedly in this book, "methodical adherence to the best validated methods," starts by emphasizing the need for meticulousness. Even the best psychological assessment methods can be completely spoiled by error or non-adherence to prescribed procedures. One of the authors was involved in research on scoring objective tests. We found that one hospital created a computer scoring program for a popular measure that mistakenly changed the designations for answers on the Beck Depression Inventory-2 from what should have been a range of 0 to 4 to a range of 1 to 5, thus elevating the score on every item by one point. Consequently, even if an individual answered an item in the most benign way possible and should have been assigned a score of 0, they were assigned a score of 1. Given the 21 items on the measure, this increased all total scores by 21 points and resulted in the lowest possible score (21) falling within the level of moderate depression. Even individuals who had answered in a manner that should have produced a total score that fell within normal limits often produced (mistaken) total scores classified as indicating severe depression. In such cases one wonders just what took place when clinicians accessed the test results, yet patients had reported that they were minimally depressed or not really depressed at all. Remarkably, this scoring fiasco had gone on for some time before we discovered it during the course of our research, and the call to the site was disturbing for all involved, especially for the dedicated clinician on the receiving end.

Chapter 2 provides multiple examples of basic or clerical errors drawn from actual cases. In a number of those cases, erroneous practices had become routinized, and therefore occurred time and again. In one case, a clinician had repeatedly used the wrong normative table for an alternative version of a test that he had mistaken for the original version, and that generated standard scores that were considerably lower than they should have been. In another case, as amazing as it seems, a clinician who administered a certain memory test regularly and was working from a copy, failed to realize he was missing the back side of this two-page measure. The referrals he received generally addressed concerns about cognitive capacities, and the neuropsychologist came to think that the low scores that one test taker after another obtained on this particular memory measure demonstrated its remarkable sensitivity to impairment. One might think that the mistakes occurring in both these examples would have been detected quickly. However, as Chapman and Chapman's (1969) classic research on illusory correlation found, remarkably strong and consistent evidence may be needed to recognize or unlearn mistaken beliefs about associations between variables (in this case a low test score and memory impairment). As research on confirmatory bias indicates, it is often far easier to form initial hypotheses than to correct such impressions once formed.

Further, as is common in clinical practice, the lack of feedback or clear feedback, as well as cognitive biases, such as overweighting supportive evidence and underweighting negative evidence, can impede the recognition of error.

Simple steps can often greatly reduce clerical, and sometimes extremely damaging, errors. Redundancy often provides excellent protection. For example, having two individuals enter data independently may cut keyboarding errors down to nearly 0% if a procedure is put in place for identifying inconsistent entries and then making the needed corrections. If two individuals each make keyboarding errors, say, 2% of the time, and if the errors are not caused by systematic factors or different item characteristics but are more or less random, then the chances of the same item being entered incorrectly by both individuals is $1/50 \times 1/50 = 1/2{,}500$. Double-checking scoring on psychological measures can also eliminate many errors.

Having a detail-oriented clinician occasionally check one's evaluations and scoring procedures, and offering the same service in return, can also assist in spotting flawed procedures that generate repeated errors across cases. In one case, a clinician used copies of the Stroop test instead of the original materials. A frequently used component of the test involves rapid color naming of items. The copying process had resulted in some fading of the colors, and thus especially for individuals with reduced color discrimination (which is not what this test is intended to measure), scores were often depressed significantly. The clinician, who had been given the copies, had never seen the originals and thus was unaware of the problem. Another clinician familiar with the way the test should have looked noticed the problem immediately, but unfortunately not until after the first clinician had used it many times.

In many professions in which quality control is essential, equipment needs to be checked or recalibrated regularly, so why not clinical protocols as well? Yes, taking these extra steps is a time drain, and sadly one often will not be reimbursed for the effort. However, consider how often many individuals, due to awareness of their fallibility, double-check a motel room before leaving in order to avoid forgetting some item worth $10 or $20. The far greater potential costs of avoidable diagnostic or predictive error thus might be worth contemplating.

All Else Being Equal, Increase Structure, Be Systematic

All else being equal, structured or systematic forms of data gathering generate greater overall accuracy than more variable methods, such as unstructured interviews (see Grove et al.'s 2000 meta-analysis and Dana et al.'s 2013 series of studies documenting the shortcomings of unstructured interviews). All else being equal, given their benefits in enhancing accuracy, structured or systematic approaches to data gathering should generally be preferred to less structured methods, or at least included as a component of data gathering.

Our focus here is on increasing structure in order to enhance judgmental accuracy, but we recognize that various clinical activities sometimes call for less structured approaches. For example, therapy sessions may place a premium on natural interactions, especially when building a therapeutic relationship, and little good may come from treatment without accomplishing that aim. Alternatively, a new client may present at intake in such emotional turmoil that reducing distress may be a much greater immediate need than implementing structured approaches to gathering information. None of this makes accuracy irrelevant, but there are situations in which the benefits of structured approaches can be offset or postponed by clients' current needs. Nevertheless, in many situations, clients are fine with structured approaches, especially if one explains their benefits and clinicians do not act robotically. Structured approaches can be implemented in a friendly and supportive manner, and if they enhance accuracy in critical areas without compromising other central goals, one is placing the client's needs at the forefront.

Various procedures can be used to provide or increase structure, such as checklists (see Chapter 12), lists of essential topics or variables to evaluate (see, for example, the discussion of structured professional judgment in Chapter 8), structured interview methods, and tests and questionnaires. Structured interview techniques, tests, and questionnaires often provide additional benefits that go beyond systematic data gathering. For one, sophisticated approaches may have been used during their development to achieve representative sampling of content domains. For example, when creating a vocabulary test, rigorous methods can help reduce the item pool to a manageable level that still provides a good approximation of overall word knowledge. Such a test is likely to be considerably more trustworthy than, for example, depending on an evaluator's subjective impressions of a person's word use during an interview.

In addition, tests, questionnaires, and structured interview techniques often provide advantages for combining or interpreting the information they generate. Potential examples include normative or reference samples for purposes of comparison, quantification that facilitates various forms of sophisticated data analysis that would otherwise be excluded, and formal decision or interpretive procedures, such as statistical decision methods. Such advantages help explain why as far back as 1966, Sawyer found that statistical decision procedures based on tests alone equaled or exceeded procedures based on unstructured interviews. Of interest, unstructured interviews also made unique contributions or improved overall accuracy when added to test results, but only when statistical decision methods were used.

The value of structured methods can be compromised or reversed if practitioners do not adhere to specified procedures. Chapter 2 provides examples in which clinicians violated or altered standard procedures, sometimes in minor ways and sometimes substantially. For example, during test administration, clinicians may provide help that is not allowed, or not provide help that is supposed to be offered. Test administrators may also make minor or major changes in specified test instructions. Such alterations in procedures may result from substandard training, carelessness, or insufficient concern about potential consequences. Lee et al.'s (2003) detailed review of research on alterations in prescribed test procedures showed how difficult it can be to anticipate their impact. Seemingly significant alterations sometimes change outcomes negligibly, yet at other times, seemingly minor changes impact results substantially. Changing a few words of instruction (e.g., "Work as quickly as you can without making mistakes" vs. "Work as quickly as you can") can create striking differences in test results. Considering that an individual's results on structured methods are often compared to the results of normative or reference groups, if one alters the conditions of testing, the comparison can be distorted, rendered useless, or even worse, become highly misleading.

We are not suggesting that standardized procedures should never be altered. If items from a structured interview trigger a severe emotional reaction, one should almost surely attend to the client's distress, rather than insisting the interview must move forward. Various other circumstances, such as substantial fatigue, evident noncooperation, or confusion, can also provide good reason to halt a procedure, or perhaps to try some intervention to regain sufficient engagement. Alternatively, limits in comprehension due to testing an individual in a secondary language, or a previously unrecognized disability, such as a reading or motor impairment, may also necessitate changes or require one to switch to an alternative method. Thus, various circumstances might call for a break in standardized procedures, documentation of what occurred, and accompanying cautions when interpreting results, or perhaps disregarding results entirely and seeking alternative methods. However, there is a major difference between altering procedures for a compelling rationale as opposed to doing so for no good reason, such as an overly casual attitude toward standardized procedures or insufficient familiarity with prescribed methods. Decision making in the mental health field is often hard enough without adding noise or error to the process that could have been easily avoided.

Interpretation

Determining What Information to Include and Exclude

The common adage to include and integrate as much information as possible when drawing conclusions often does more harm than good. Information can conflict directly and thus cannot really be aligned, such as when one test score falls well below the cutoff for abnormality and a second score on a similar test falls far above that cutoff. Further, some information might be plainly erroneous and other information weaker or far weaker than stronger predictors. Also, spending considerable time and effort collecting highly redundant information typically does little or no good and is wasteful.

Compared to integrating all the information or as much data as possible, a much better guide is: *Within the bounds of feasibility, gather and use the piece or combination of information that maximizes accuracy for the decision task of interest*. In many cases, even a relatively small amount of information, such as three or four of the strongest, least redundant variables, will approach or reach a ceiling in predictive accuracy. This does not mean obtaining the needed information will necessarily be easy or require minimal time. For example, painstaking searches may be necessary, or obtaining the data needed to compute cumulative indices may take hours. In other cases, one needs to make multiple decisions, and the outcomes of interest may show minimal associations with one another. Thus, the best predictive variables for each outcome may be largely non-redundant, and gathering even a limited number of variables or indicators for each judgment task can require extended information gathering.

In contrast, collecting more or far more information than is needed adds time and, ironically, carries considerable risk of reducing accuracy. For example, the weakest variables stand the greatest chance of conflicting with the strongest variables. To the extent the weakest variables, which may not be recognized as such, influence decisions, it will usually be in the wrong direction. One might also consider the abundant literature suggesting that unstructured interviews can elicit helpful information, but decision makers often have difficulty separating what is and is not useful. Studies on subjective data integration also suggest that variables we know may have limited utility and that we intend to downplay or disregard may nevertheless have a substantial impact on our judgments (see Chapter 7).

Hence, effective decision making often includes more acts of exclusion than inclusion of information. In the many situations in which a relatively small number of variables approach or reach the upper limits of predictive accuracy, the far greater number of surplus predictors will likely add little or nothing to accuracy, or, far worse, may well diminish accuracy when combined with better predictors. Properly developed decision procedures are designed to identify and use the best combination of predictors and to eliminate variables with no positive influence, or especially a negative influence. In contrast, subjective decision methods are often considerably less efficacious in achieving these aims.

Three Steps for Screening Information

To the extent one chooses to combine information using subjective or clinical judgment, notwithstanding what the literature might show, or when there is no other viable option, we suggest one consider three sequential questions when deciding what information to gather and to use for decision tasks. These three determinations are, in order:

1. Is it valid?
2. Does it beat the base rates?
3. Does it enhance incremental validity?

We will examine the three inquiries one by one.

Is it valid? A negative answer to the first of the three steps is logically dispositive. If a variable is not valid, it should not be used. In practice, the negative evidence pertaining to validity may not be as certain as we would like, but that is often our lot in the mental health field, and if the evidence is predominantly negative or almost certainly negative, the course of action should be clear.

One may also obtain levels of validity that are so low that for the great majority of circumstances, they have little or no practical value. Certainly, if other variables are available that show at least modest levels of validity, there is little reason to use variables with minimal levels of validity.

Again, validity is not strictly cumulative, and often far from it. Adding one robust predictor to another robust predictor will realize little improvement if they are highly redundant. Or if one identifies 101 variables that each account for 1% of the variance and combine them, one will not account for 101% of the variance, because these variables will not all be entirely independent of one another, and may well have considerable overlap. Here again, believing that everything is important often degrades decision making, partly because one is then likely to collect poor information that may still exercise a considerable influence on judgment, especially if it is salient (e.g., a seemingly dramatic human figure drawing). Discarding valid but feeble variables, especially if there are other variables of superior validity, is almost always a good choice.

Of the various methods that can be used to evaluate validity, covariation analysis is among the most useful. The efficacy of a variable can be grossly overestimated if one focuses mainly on Cell A of a covariation table (the present-present condition). For example, one could uncover many instances in which individuals with psychological disorders acted violently. However, many individuals experience psychological disorders. Consequently, if even a very small percentage of individuals with psychological disorders act violently, one can still accumulate large numbers. Nonetheless, a high percentage of individuals with such disorders do not act violently, and in addition, one must compare the proportion of occurrence among those with such disorders to the proportion of occurrence among those without such disorders to determine whether the data suggest an association.

We emphasize covariation here because it is easy to be fooled into thinking two variables are associated when they really are not related to one another, as has often occurred in the history of psychology, medicine, and other fields, especially when individuals focus excessively or exclusively on the present-present cell. The present-present cell may include dramatic instances that capture our attention (e.g., shark attacks). Alternatively, two cells of a covariation table may be considered (e.g., how often sharks attack people as opposed to leaving them alone), but if one wants to determine if sharks are more aggressive than, say, barracudas, then one has to compare proportions of attacks across the two species. Similarly, if one wishes to determine whether adolescents have a greater frequency of psychological disorder (PD) than adults, one has to compare proportions of positive versus negative cases across the two groups, as in:

adolescents with PD/adolescents without PD
vs.
adults with PD/adults without PD

If these ratios are the same or nearly so (e.g., ~1:10 vs. ~1:10), then it suggests that the belief adolescents have greater rates of psychological disorder than adults is mistaken. Alternatively, a practitioner might assume that a certain result on a psychological test is indicative of major depressive disorder because it occurs 75% of the time when the disorder is present. However, if the test result is just as common among those without major depressive disorder, then at least as far as the analysis goes, the assumed relationship does not hold and the test result should not be used for this differentiation. Of course, there are other formal methods for analyzing possible associations between variables, and if well-conducted studies generate negative results, a variable should be excluded unless subsequent, more positive, evidence emerges.

Does it beat the base rates? A variable that is known to be invalid should not be used, in which case the course of action is clear. Similarly, variables that technically cannot be called invalid because they do show a minimal association with one or another outcome, but that have little or no true utility and are outpaced by stronger predictors, can almost always be excluded as well. In contrast, a negative answer to the present question—Does it beat the base rates?—may not settle the decision to use or to discard a variable.

If maximizing overall accuracy is the primary goal and one is facing a dichotomous choice, then if the base rates achieve greater predictive accuracy than the variable (or combination of variables) under consideration, one should use the base rates. There are too many situations in psychology in which needless tests and evaluative methods are used when one should have known from the start or early on that the base rates provide equal or greater predictive power. The result is wasted time and expense, and even worse, when the base rates achieve greater accuracy but are not used, increased error. Again, a valid test, and even one that achieves an impressive level of accuracy, may still fall short of the accuracy achieved playing the base rates, in particular when base rates are extremely high or low.

Nevertheless, there are times that assessment methods do not beat the base rates but might still warrant use. Achieving the greatest level of overall accuracy is not always the primary goal, especially when the potential consequences of false-negative and false-positive errors are unequal. For example, false-negative errors may result in much greater harm than false-positive errors. Failing to detect or predict certain conditions or outcomes can have catastrophic results (e.g., missing a major psychological disorder with a high morbidity and mortality rate, or the intent to cause self-harm or harm to others). Thus, in such situations, one might accept more error, or considerably more error, to reduce the frequency of the more damaging type of error.

Even here, however, when the resultant increase in error rate begins to far outstrip the accuracy achieved by playing the base rates, as can occur especially with exceedingly low or high frequency events, decision policies may require a second look. For example, committing major resources to preventative initiatives may result in far less good than redirecting resources in another direction (e.g., increasing access to life-saving antibiotics). It is certainly not our intent to treat the value of human welfare as a math exercise, or to suggest that decision researchers' personal values should usurp or supersede others' views. Rather, decision research can help develop methods that enhance diagnostic and predictive accuracy and clarify the consequences of our decision policies, and thereby assist in actualizing benevolent intent. With this in mind, if one goes to great lengths to avoid false-positive errors but consequently increases overall error extensively, one might be faced with a situation in which for every life saved, one loses the opportunity to save dozens of lives or more.

In addition, although the base rates may provide greater accuracy than a single variable achieves, combinations of variables may beat the base rates. However, such a shift will not necessarily occur just because one is adding variables. Once more, adding new information to other information, even if that new information is valid, may not increase accuracy at all, and may degrade accuracy when valid but weaker predictors are combined with stronger predictors. Given what seems to be a decided tendency to overestimate the value of adding new variables or accumulating large bodies of information, it is best to check the impact of such additions formally or by accessing research that might be available on the topic, rather than just assuming a favorable outcome.

Although other variables, tests, or methods may not beat the base rates across the totality of cases, subsets of results may do so. For example, suppose the use of the base rates in a certain treatment setting produces a 75% level of accuracy in identifying individuals with serious substance use problems. (For purposes of this example, we do not address the potential asymmetry in costs between different types of errors.) A researcher has developed a test that achieves a 70% overall accuracy rate, which does not beat the base rates. Nonetheless, if one selects, say, the 20% of individuals with the highest scores on this test, accuracy for this subgroup may be greater than it is for the overall group. (Such alterations are often part of the rationale for creating receiver operator curves, which analyze shifts in accuracy across the range of outcomes or scores a method produces.) Thus, although the test is not as good as the base rate when all cases are taken together, in a subset of individuals with extreme results, the test might beat playing the base rate and be given priority when the two conflict.

Finally, in other situations, one is not trying to determine whether the base rates versus other diagnostic signs or predictors should take precedence when the two conflict. Rather, one is interested in combining base rates and other predictors to formulate more accurate probability estimates than is possible with either type of information alone. Diagnostic or predictive tasks may involve differential diagnosis, potential outcome of alternative treatment choices, the expected recovery period or outcome from some type of condition, or prediction of various behaviors. Here, if both types of information (base rates and predictive variables) have value and are not simply redundant, then combining them should improve the accuracy of likelihood estimates, especially if determined formally using Bayes' Theorem. When different events have equal or nearly equal base rates, then base rates will have little or minimal value and chance guessing will do about as well, as is also the case when predictive variables have minimal validity. If one of the informational sources has nominal predictive utility, then it should not be used; combining it with other information will not help things, and consequently the stronger source should be used instead.

Does it enhance incremental validity? When one adds information to other available information, one can examine its impact on accuracy. The new information may increase accuracy, it may not change it, or it may decrease accuracy. To the extent new information increases accuracy, it can be said to generate *incremental validity*. Whenever possible, one wants to start with the strongest possible predictor, and then use formal methods to determine the impact of adding new predictors to that variable. Rather than having to attempt what can be a complex analysis of incremental validity on one's own or in one's head, it is preferable to select combinations of variables for which incremental validity has been studied carefully (and that are feasible to access or appraise in one's setting of interest). Where the best combinations differ across individuals or settings, one wishes to know what variables, such as demographic factors or individual differences, influence incremental validity and how selections can be tailored to the client's specific situation.

Evaluating incremental validity seems to be a far better guide to collecting and utilizing information than the familiar recommendation to gather and integrate as much information as possible, the latter of which also often emphasizes clinical (impressionistic) judgment and complex pattern analysis. Again, validity is not cumulative, and as more and more information is added, especially if one starts with high-quality information, new information is increasingly unlikely to produce a positive yield and may well direct attention away from the strongest predictors. In addition, the attempt to integrate large and diverse informational sources, which preferably takes into account their precise level of validity and redundancy and other characteristics, exceeds what even very bright minds can accomplish without formal decision aids. Fortunately, other very bright minds have developed highly effective formal procedures that can carry out these analyses for us at lightning speed, such as properly developed statistical decision methods, so why not benefit from their advantages as opposed to using weaker methods?

For predictive or diagnostic tasks, it is hard to justify seeking information that does not enhance accuracy, especially when one can identify and collect the most useful information early in the data-gathering process. At times, additional information will inadvertently reduce accuracy, especially if insufficient attention is given to its likely value or potential limitations. Should the client bear the burden or cost for these wasteful efforts, especially when practices are more likely to increase, rather than diminish, error? (We understand there are other situations in which acquiring additional information could provide other types of benefits, such as a therapist coming to know a client more fully in order to increase an empathic connection.) Again, just a few pieces of information, such as base rates and perhaps two or three other variables selected for their level of validity and independent contribution to accuracy, may approach or reach a ceiling in predictive success.

As with base rates, the result of analyzing incremental validity is not dispositive, and choices may rest on other priorities. For example, reducing the more harmful type of error might be a greater priority than overall accuracy. In such circumstances, one seeks a combination of variables that best serves that purpose without reducing overall accuracy an unsatisfactory amount. None of this, however, negates either the value of incremental validity as a key guide for evaluating what information should be sought and included in decision making, or its clear advantages over the far more common advice to integrate all the information, an approach that also often prioritizes clinical judgment over formal methods. For example, test manual after test manual emphasizes the need to gather broad information sources, but they rarely mention the need to consider incremental validity.

One who wishes to prioritize incremental validity may also encounter practical obstacles. The ideal combination of variables might not be feasible to collect in one's setting given limitations in time, resources, or access. For example, a neuropsychologist might want to obtain educational records to help determine whether current testing reflects a decline in cognitive abilities after a soldier's exposure to explosive blast waves, but the clinician may need to act well before those records can be obtained. Unfortunately, despite the obvious importance of incremental validity, the biggest obstacle may be insufficient research in areas of interest.

There are, of course, thousands of studies examining whether adding variables increases accuracy, such as using multiple predictors to identify brain dysfunction or PTSD. Many of these studies are of limited scope and do not draw from a wide enough range of predictors. For example, all the predictors may be tests, as opposed to the use of more diverse variables. To maximize incremental validity, one seeks variables that make the greatest independent contribution to accuracy—variables that are both strong predictors and as nonredundant with other worthwhile predictors as possible. For example, suppose one first examines the association of different variables, one at a time, with an outcome, such as level of response to some type of treatment. One then ranks the variables in order of predictive accuracy from highest to lowest. One might think that combining the first and second strongest variables would achieve greater predictive accuracy than, say, the first and fourth strongest variables, but that depends on the level of redundancy between variables. If the strongest and second strongest variables are highly correlated with one another (are highly redundant), but the first and fourth strongest variables are considerably less redundant, then the latter combination may generate greater overall accuracy when combined than the first and second strongest variables. Hence, when seeking combinations of predictors that maximize incremental validity, examining diverse classes of variables that may not show excessive overlap can enhance success. These diverse classes may include tests, clinical features, diagnostic indicators, historical occurrences, sociodemographic characteristics, and family history. Broad analyses of incremental validity are far less extensive than one might imagine and can be frustratingly difficult to find.

Alternatively, new potential predictors may be validated against outcome variables that generate favorable results when the new predictors and outcome variables are highly correlated with one another. For example, a new measure for assessing depression may be validated against one or two well-validated measures of depression. The validity of the new predictor may be measured by its level of association with the well-validated measures, with the validity coefficient increasing to the extent the new predictor overlaps or correlates with the well-validated measures, and not to the extent it yields incremental validity. The result will be to identify new potential measures or predictors as being effective when they correlate highly with previously validated tests or outcome criteria, eventuating in compilations of highly correlated measures. In such situations, when multiple tests with high levels of redundancy generate consistent outcomes, the impact on bolstering the clinician's confidence is likely to be considerably greater than any actual increase in incremental validity.

If one reads various assessment texts and manuals, one often finds recommendations to build redundancy into assessment practices, for example, by including two or more measures that assess similar areas with the intent of catching anomalous results. Redundancy can have its benefits, such as when a patient is asked multiple times by various hospital personnel whether they have had anything to eat or drink in the hours preceding upcoming surgery, or when two individuals input data independently and consistency checks are performed. However, when a clinician selects a combination of tests to conduct an assessment, redundancy may be ill-advised, especially if one starts with a test that is clearly better than other alternatives, and then adds additional tests that are less accurate but purportedly measure the same variables or constructs. To the extent one obtains inconsistent results across the measures, the weaker tests will be wrong more often, or far more often, than the stronger test, and thus to the extent the weaker measures influence decision making, that influence is more likely to degrade than enhance accuracy. (In isolated circumstances one might be able to make an argument for a weaker measure shifting the ratio of false-positive and false-negative errors in a favorable direction, but an inferior test often will not achieve these ends, and such properties cannot be assumed but should be established through formal study.)

Short of comprehensive research on incremental validity, one can at least look for studies that examine less extensive combinations of variables, or simply investigations that provide formal decision procedures. Formal decision methods, when properly developed, usually take validity and redundancy into account. One will often find, especially if statistical decision procedures are properly cross-validated (or, one might say, properly validated in the first place), that considerably fewer variables are required than one might assume to exceed the accuracy of clinical judgment.

If one cannot find any studies on incremental validity for all, or even some, of the predictors under consideration for the decision task at hand, one can at least look at articles or test manuals that provide correlation matrices. One may find that various tests, scales, or predictive variables one could use contain highly redundant elements. For example, one analysis reported correlations in the .80s and .90s between four MMPI-2 scales designed to assess potential overreporting or exaggeration of symptoms (see Greene, 2012, p. 62), and which all seem to have robust validity when used for such purposes. However, given these correlations, one should not think of the scales as providing four separate indications of overreporting that, especially when taken together, provide nearly definitive evidence. Rather, the scales are essentially four different options for measuring the same thing. Given the test–retest reliabilities of such scales, their correlations with each other approach maximum levels, and thus there is very little more here than reappraisal of the same phenomenon with a little measurement error thrown into the mix.

As a rule of thumb, in such cases, and even those in which correlations do not reach the levels in the above example, one is usually better off selecting the strongest of the redundant measures (especially if that measure has high psychometric test–retest reliability) and excluding the other redundant scales. If the best measure and the next best measure align, there is nothing to resolve, and given high redundancy, the second measure will likely produce minimal, or no, incremental validity. Alternatively, if the strongest and next best measure conflict, or especially the best measure and a considerably weaker measure conflict, then the stronger measure is likely to be right and the weaker measure to be wrong. The ability to identify exceptions—when the weaker measure is right and the stronger measure is wrong—with sufficient consistency to exceed the level of accuracy achieved by always deferring to the stronger measure, would usually require a better method than the stronger method; if such a better method were available and feasible to use, it should have been selected in the first place. After selecting the strongest option among the redundant measures, one then looks for other strong predictors that show limited correlations with that initial measure and other potential predictors. Of course, much of the guesswork and approximations could be attenuated or eliminated if the best combinations were identified through the needed research.

Incremental validity also helps in making what can be excruciating decisions to not seek certain information or to disregard other information that has been obtained. If one gets past the oft-repeated but questionable dictate to integrate all the information, it can become clear that one often has to be more active in excluding predictive variables than in including them. The thought that not seeking or excluding information could result in error is understandably troubling. However, unfortunately, whatever decision policies one selects are likely to fall well short of perfection, and it is a painful fact of clinical life that we are going to make errors (and a major reason we often have to defer to the conservative or less risky choice). The question is whether our decision policy results in less error or in a more favorable balance in the types of errors we reduce, when compared to the alternative we are considering. The choice is not between a perfect decision policy and a worse one, but between a better or worse one. The better choice often comes down to selecting the predictors that maximize incremental validity, or that shift the ratio of false-positive and false-negative errors in the desirable direction without going too far. Thus, it might be better to frame our situation as improving decision making through carefully selecting predictive variables and weeding out variables that move us further from our goal.

Here one encounters a variation of the "broken leg" example, where if one becomes too rigid and unbending, bad things can happen. For example, if the best combination of predictors suggests that a client is very unlikely to act on suicidal ideation, but just before leaving the office the client adds a comment that suggests severe risk, one must obviously reassess the situation or disregard the initial appraisal. Revising predictions or erring on the side of caution is often advisable given the uncertainty of our predictive methods and the imbalance that may be present between the costs of false-positive and false-negative errors. However, knowing that countervailing may be called for at times is not a rationale for adopting a decision policy, such as trying to integrate all the information, that is almost certain to be less effective than placing incremental validity at the forefront.

Further Considerations: Errors of Inclusion Can Be More Costly than Errors of Exclusion

In many situations in the mental health field, there are multiple measures with similar predictive utility (e.g., depression scales, measures of anxiety, measures of effort on cognitive tests, measures of verbal memory). Such measures often have relatively high correlations with one another, and when they generate conflicting outcomes, it can be very difficult to determine on a case-by-case basis which result (if any) is accurate. When one has multiple correlated or redundant measures, excluding one of them is not going to change results much, if at all, and if their levels of validity vary significantly, then all else being equal, it is generally better to defer to the strongest measure(s) as opposed to the weaker measures. Thus, in such situations, errors of exclusion will often have minimal impact.

In contrast, including a weak measure has greater potential to do harm, especially when subjective judgment is used to combine information. Additionally, we often lack sufficient awareness of the impact that variables might have on our thinking, and thus information we believe we depend on heavily may have minimal influence, and information we believe we largely disregard might have considerable impact. We may tell ourselves that some test, predictor, or method has limited value, and thus that we will be very cautious about using the results it generates, but that does not ensure that this intention will be realized.

One of the authors (D.F.) was trained in the use of the House-Tree-Person "test," in which a client is asked to draw a separate picture of each of these three items. The author's professor went through an array of possible interpretive cues; for example, if the client drew a knot in the tree, it suggested the occurrence of trauma, and if one measured the location of the knot from the bottom to the top of the tree trunk, one could estimate the time of the trauma. Thus, if the individual was 20 years old and the knot appeared at a height half way up the trunk, the time of the trauma was supposedly at about age 10. The professor then offered a caution about the use of the method but indicated it could serve as an effective ice breaker with the client, and especially with a child. Even then, the author thought the method was likely bunk (almost no scientific studies were cited during the lecture), but not that it was a bad idea to use the method early in an evaluation to help ease a child's anxiety.

When this same author taught a graduate course in assessment, a couple of the students mentioned their training in these types of projective drawings. Much of what they described sounded all too familiar. For example, they noted they were told that such assessment methods could be used as potential ice breakers, and that the results needed to be interpreted with caution. How sad it seemed that such poor methods were passed on from generation to generation when so many better methods had been created. In any case, by that point, having acquired more knowledge, especially about decision science, the author raised the point that these pictures could be dramatic. Further, regardless of what we told ourselves about limiting our reliance on them, that did not mean we would actually do so, especially given their salience. Additionally, if one had the children draw pictures right at the beginning of the evaluation, it could easily lead to faulty initial hypotheses that might then be strengthened through confirmatory bias. Thus, highly problematic information—something considerably more likely to produce obfuscation than illumination—could have the greatest relative impact on judgment. The author suggested to the students that they find a more benign way to break the ice (maybe by learning a magic trick or two), but if they still wanted to have clients do drawings, not to charge for any time involved, and to pick up the pictures without ever looking at them.

The weaker a variable, the more likely it is to diverge from accurate variables. Thus, to the extent weak or invalid variables influence judgment (quite possibly without our recognizing the presence or extent of the influence), the more likely our judgmental accuracy will be eroded rather than enhanced. As such, especially when multiple effective predictors are available that have considerable redundancy, errors of exclusion will often have minimal impact, whereas errors of inclusion can overturn what would otherwise be accurate judgments or predictions. If variables are weak, if their validity is poor, or if their status is uncertain, then it is generally better to exclude them than to include them, especially when good predictors with an established scientific track record are available. Again, the advice to collect extensive information and integrate it often runs contrary to fundamental decision making principles.

Separate Statistical Fact and Artifact

Regression toward the Mean

It is easy to confuse statistical fact with artifact. Kahneman (2011) provided a noteworthy example involving the training of pilots. Pilot instructors were curious to see whether verbal praise or criticism affected performance differently. After smooth landings, they praised the pilots, and after bumpy or less satisfactory landings, they criticized them. The instructors observed that praise resulted in a decline in performance more often than criticism, with criticism more often followed by improvement. However, a satisfactory landing is determined partly by skill and partly by atmospheric conditions, such as wind speed and direction. All else being equal, an especially good landing is likely to be followed by a less exemplary landing, and a less exemplary landing by a better landing. Thus, the quality of landings was partly determined by random conditions, and a change from one landing to the next by variation in those conditions, as opposed to verbal praise or criticism. Similarly, a baseball manager who praises players after an especially impressive win and criticizes them after an unusually sloppy loss may underestimate the role of chance in outcomes and come to believe that criticism works better than praise.

Shifts from more extreme outcomes to less extreme outcomes that stem in part from chance are referred to as regression toward the mean. Extreme outcomes are often followed by less extreme outcomes. The greater the extent to which an outcome falls outside the mean and is a product of chance, the greater the extent to which a subsequent outcome will tend to move in the direction of the mean. For example, suppose that a person earns a very high (or very low) initial score on an ability test with poor test–retest reliability. If the test is re-administered at a later date (practice effects aside) and the individual's capacities have not changed, the second score will likely be considerably closer to the mean than the initial score. (For those who may be less familiar with the concept, *practice effect* refers to improvement in performance that may result from merely having taken a test earlier, or the benefits of prior experience with the measure.) An initial score that exceeded 19 of 20 individuals may be followed by a second score that barely falls above the mean; conversely, a first score that fell below 19 of 20 individuals might be followed by a second score that barely falls below the mean.

One of the authors has reviewed many initial and repeat neuropsychological evaluations. Perhaps surprisingly, quite a few of the evaluations included multiple measures with weak or clearly deficient test–retest reliability. As a result, especially on tests with deficient test-retest reliability, retesting often led to substantial changes, with the highest scores trending downward and the lowest scores trending upward, largely due to regression effects. Nevertheless, in many instances, regression effects were not discussed, and the changes were apparently viewed as signaling true alterations in underlying capacities. For example, when low scores on tests with deficient reliability improved considerably, but not beyond the level expected by regression toward the mean, they might be interpreted as showing recovery of neurocognitive functions. In a number of cases, the neuropsychologists accepted the improvements as genuine. In contrast, they might have expressed skepticism about high scores that decreased considerably. For example, they might note that the declines were unexpected given the condition at issue and thus raised doubt about the individual's cooperation with testing, perhaps without realizing that such changes aligned closely with expected regression effects.

Similarly, suppose an investigator develops an intervention program for children with serious reading problems. A screening test is administered, and children who score more than 2 standard deviations (SD) below the mean (or at about the 2nd percentile) are selected for intervention. Suppose the particular screening test has a test–retest reliability of .50 and a mean practice effect of ½ standard deviation. Suppose further we are trying to predict performance on retesting, even if there had been no change in reading ability, Given the level of test–retest reliability, the best prediction of the score on retesting is the SD × test–retest reliability, or in this case -2.0 × .50 = -1.00 SD (or at the 16th percentile). If one next adds on the ½ SD for practice effects, the expected score now falls at -.5 SD below the mean (or at the 31st percentile). (We realize calculating scores on retesting that take practice effects into account may be more nuanced than we are portraying, but we are just trying to illustrate the combined impact of test-retest reliability, practice effects, and regression toward the mean.)

Now suppose the intervention had absolutely no impact. One would still see a mean change in scores from -2.0 SD to -.5 SD, or from the 2nd percentile to the 31st percentile! In fact, even if the intervention was harmful and decreased proficiency by, say, ½ SD, one would still see an illusory benefit, with the children increasing from the 2nd percentile to the 16th percentile (-2.0 SD × .50 = -1 SD; with the +.5 for the practice effect offset by the -.5 harm caused by the intervention, leaving an outcome of -1.0 SD). In a converse example, with children scoring 2 SD above the mean, it might seem like a program with absolutely no impact had caused harm by reducing mean level of performance.

An important predictive principle follows from regression toward the mean: In general, predictions should be no more extreme than the variables upon which they are based. Rather, all else being equal, predictions should be regressed toward the mean. For example, suppose an occupational aptitude test has been administered, and for a particular job of interest the individual obtains a score that falls 1 SD above the mean (or at the 84th percentile). Background research shows a correlation of about .40 with performance on that job, a level of validity that would often be described as moderately robust. One follows the same basic procedure used when predicting scores on a re-administration of a test, but here one is instead trying to predict level of performance for that particular occupation. Hence, one is not using the test to predict itself, but to predict something else, and with this latter type of application one uses the validity coefficient, not the test–retest reliability coefficient.

Given the score of +1.0 SD and the validity coefficient of .40, the best prediction is: SD × validity coefficient = +1.0 SD × .40 = +.40 SD (or performance at about the 66th percentile). Note that the original test score, which fell at +1.0 SD, or the 84th percentile, diminishes to +.40 SD, or the 66th percentile, so the regressed estimate is less extreme than the variable upon which it is based. We might add that when performing these calculations, individuals sometimes overlook the direction of the SD. Thus, if the score fell 1 SD below the mean, or at -1 SD, the result would be: -1 SD × .40 = -.40 SD (or at the 34th percentile).

Again, the degree of regression depends on the level of the original score and the validity coefficient, or the robustness of the predictor(s). One sees violations of this predictive principle in many common circumstances: for example, a very promising graduate school applicant is predicted to equal or exceed the best student in the last 10 years, despite prediction of graduate school performance often lacking precision; a young golfer is predicted to be the next Annika Sörenstam or to exceed her; a person on a poker hot streak decides to bet the house (even though the recent good hands have no direct bearing on the quality of the next hand). Likewise, when a client has a particularly good session, the next session might not be quite as good, and a not-so-good session may well be followed by a better session. We are not suggesting that predictions should never exceed the level of the variable(s) upon which they are based. Other factors may be relevant, such as improvement after systematic practice or training, or a big payoff if an exceptional outcome does occur and a capacity to absorb losses without too much difficulty if the prediction fails. Nonetheless, without a compelling reason, as opposed to blind hope, predictions should be regressed, and especially with weaker predictors, regressed predictions are almost sure to achieve greater overall accuracy across a series of occurrences than insufficiently regressed or more extreme predictions.

One should also be alert to situations in which predictive variables could be degraded due to a variety of factors, such as application to questions or groups for which they may be less suited, or the attempt to extend predictions over somewhat longer time periods than were examined in background studies. For example, some combination of variables might be effective for predicting aggressive behavior over a 48-hour period, but even extending the length of prediction to an additional day or two may reduce accuracy. When there are solid reasons to believe that predictive success might be reduced by altered circumstances, and in particular the presence of factors that commonly do reduce accuracy, such as extended time intervals, predictions should be regressed more than would otherwise be the case. One hopes that such adjustments can be based on studies that provide formal guidance, or that potentially questionable variables given changed circumstances can be replaced by better options.

Beware of Small Samples

A common statement at a case conference starts with something like, "I once had a client who . . ." An *N* of 1 may be better than an *N* of 0, but often by very little. As Tversky and Kahneman (1971) demonstrated in their memorable article, "Belief in the Law of Small Numbers," individuals, including sophisticated methodologists and mathematicians, often treat small samples as if they are, or nearly are, as representative of their respective populations as considerably larger samples. Insufficient recognition of the need for adequate sample size often leads researchers to underpower studies or creates alarm among sports fans if their favorite team loses their first two games of a 162-game baseball season. Underappreciating the limits of small samples can also lead mental health professionals to overweight normative or reference samples that are much too small to produce representative information, or to grant that *N* of 1 at the case conference more credence than is merited. It is often worth asking whether samples of individuals or behaviors are large enough to draw firm conclusions, and when planning studies, to conduct formal analysis of power to reduce the probability of false-negative results or Type 2 errors.

Increase the Use of Base Rates

Surveys and research spanning across decades (see Furman, 2005; Kahneman & Tversky, 1972; Kennedy et al., 1997; Meyers, 2015) suggest that base rates are often underutilized or disregarded by laypersons and mental health professionals alike.

This tendency to underuse base rates seems to be heightened when case-specific information is provided, even when that information is less informative than base rates and sometimes of little or no value for diagnostic or predictive purposes. Of course, in many applied clinical situations, whether a case conference or an intake or therapy session, practitioners are inundated with case-specific information. That material is likely to contain information of varying utility, and when it is applied for diagnostic or predictive purposes, one hopes primary attention will be given to the most valuable data points. However, to the extent case-specific information redirects attention away from base rates, it may compromise or negate use of this helpful, and at times most helpful, information.

We discuss the use of base rates at length in Chapter 6 and will not reiterate that material here. What we would suggest for present purposes is that one's decision making procedures or checklist include material on base rates. One can always ask if there is base rate information available for the decision(s) at hand, thinking in sufficiently broad terms to identify possible sources, much in line with Appendix 1. Many studies and publications will not use the term *base rates*, but they provide exactly that type of information. For example, epidemiological research and a wide range of outcome studies routinely generate base-rate information, such as how often individuals recover from mild head injuries, the percentage of individuals who experience subsequent episodes of major depressive disorder if they have already had two or more prior episodes, the frequency that a child will experience some form of affective disorder if both biological parents have an affective disorder, the rates at which various life events cause PTSD, the differential frequency with which certain symptoms (e.g., visual hallucinations) are associated with schizophrenia versus an acute organic brain disorder, how often normal individuals obtain at least one deviant score on a certain psychological test, and on and on. Scientific research and data gathering in the mental health field, as well as various agencies, have generated large stores of information about base rates, which, sadly, despite their tremendous potential for improving diagnostic and predictive accuracy, are far too often underused, or not used at all.

One's procedural checklist could contain entries on base rates like:

1. *Before proceeding with a psychological evaluation or predictive tasks, consider whether base rates are available for the judgments at issue.*
2. *What are the strongest reasons to use base-rate information in the present case*? (We generally prefer the positive form of this question as opposed to a negative or more neutral form, given the compelling evidence that base rates are frequently underused or underweighted. For a practitioner who uses base rates routinely, items that appear here and across the other two entries may already be applied regularly.)
3. *When there is a choice between base rates developed for different groups or subgroups, then in most circumstances use the most narrowly applicable base rates.* (As described in Chapter 6, narrowness in this context is defined as features that change the base rates and are applicable to the individual. For example, a variable might change the base rates for

pre-adolescents versus adolescents, but if one is working with an older client, those changes in base rates will not be relevant. In addition, the reason for use of the qualifier "in most circumstances" is that one set of base rates may have been gathered using much stronger methods, such as far more comprehensive and representative sampling, than another set of base rates. Hence, at times, although one set of base rates may seem to achieve a somewhat better fit with the current client than an alternative set does, clear differences in methodological quality might sway the ultimate selection. Unfortunately, at present, there is limited formal guidance for selecting among alternative sets of base rates, making seemingly close calls more difficult than they otherwise might be.)

4a. *If base rates are available and the most applicable source has been selected, is one faced with a dichotomous decision? If so, what is the accuracy that can be achieved by simply playing the base rates?*

4b. *Given the accuracy achieved by playing the base rates, are there any other sources of information, alone or in combination, that can beat the base rates? If not, is there a compelling rationale for doing something other than deferring to the base rates and omitting any other assessment method?* (Although underuse of base rates seems to be a far more common problem than excessive use, and practitioners are often better served by asking whether they are underutilizing base rates, the answer to this question might be affirmative. For example, administering tests might not achieve greater accuracy than the base rates, but could shift the ratio of false-negative versus false-positive errors in a favorable direction in situations in which one error type is far worse than the other type. Other potentially compelling reasons for countervailing base rates are discussed in Chapter 6.)

5a. *Are any of the judgments or predictions that need to be made not purely dichotomous, and is there interest in determining the likelihood of outcomes? If so, and if there are applicable base rates and other valid predictors, combine the two sources of information to determine likelihoods.*

5b. *Use formal methods, rather than subjective judgment, to combine the base rates and other valid predictors, such as Bayes' Theorem or a nomogram.*

Increase Use of Statistical (Actuarial) Judgment Methods

Many of the same points presented in the immediately preceding section on underuse of base rates apply similarly to underuse of statistical judgment methods. Here again, surveys show underutilization or complete disregard of statistical decision methods, despite the overwhelming body of literature showing that they almost always equal or exceed clinical judgment, sometimes by a large margin, and thus are superior overall. Assertions that statistical decision methods are often unavailable usually fail to distinguish between the lack of studies comparing clinical and statistical judgment methods in a particular domain as opposed to studies that generate statistical decision procedures that can be applied directly in clinical work in that domain or used with minor modification (see Chapter 8).

When it is truly the case that no statistical methods are available for a pending decision, and base rates are also lacking or using them alone is not the best available option, one cannot fault a practitioner for relying primarily on clinical judgment. Additionally, although about one third of the studies examining the accuracy of clinical judgment demonstrate high error rates or even chance levels of performance, the majority of studies demonstrate at least modest levels of validity. Thus, although high levels of confidence are rarely warranted and overconfidence should be avoided, clinical judgment may certainly contribute to decision accuracy. (The option of combining clinical and statistical methods is covered in Chapter 8, and we would simply note here that such approaches are often less feasible than may be assumed, especially when the two methods generate conflicting outcomes.)

In other situations, clinicians face decision tasks for which studies comparing clinical and statistical decision making are lacking, but separate studies are available that have generated statistically based outcomes, formulae, or algorithms that can be applied directly in clinical work or used with minor modifications. As is discussed in Chapter 8, such studies run into the thousands. Consequently, in many situations, the clinician has or can gain access to applicable statistical or actuarial decision procedures. This then leaves the choice of using clinical judgment or such statistically based decision procedures.

When selecting between clinical judgment and statistically based decision methods in the absence of comparative studies between the two methods for the task at hand, one still has access to an exceptionally helpful source to guide the decision. One can use the track record of outcomes across the hundreds of studies comparing the two methods to determine the prior odds or base rates for the relative success of one or the other method. If, in at least 95% of the comparative studies, statistical methods have equaled or exceeded clinical methods, then there should be at least a 95% chance that the same outcome would occur were a new comparative study performed. Countervailing this high or extreme base rate successfully would require a very accurate means to identify exceptions, such as a demonstrated relation to the highly unusual counterexamples (i.e., clinical method exceeding the statistical method) in the mental health field. These exceptions have been so unusual that uncovering possible systematic factors is largely reduced to speculation, and their occurrence may be explained mainly by statistical artifact, because their frequency does not necessarily exceed the rate expected due to Type 1 error or chance.

Therefore, in situations in which one lacks an applicable comparative study in the decision domain of interest, but one has access to a well-developed statistical decision method, there is a very good chance that using the statistical method will lead to equal or better overall success than using clinical or impressionistic judgment. Certainly the comparative record of success would make statistical judgment a much stronger choice. Suppose you had to place a million dollar bet on whether horse A or horse B would win a race on the occasions they did not end up in a dead heat. Suppose further that in past races, when one of the horses won, horse A beat horse B less than 5% of the time, and horse B beat horse A at least 10 times more often than horse A beat horse B. (This estimation takes into account the frequency of ties versus the relatively superiority of one or the other method across the comparative studies.) Those odds overwhelmingly favor one decision policy over another, and they approximate the likelihoods in new situation in which either clinical or statistical decision methods could be used. If one also takes ties into account (in which case it doesn't really matter which method is selected), the prior odds of doing as well or better by selecting the statistical decision method is at least 95%.

Thus, in the many cases in which statistical decision procedures are available, then even absent comparative studies on the specific decision task(s) at hand, the better choice seems clear. One can then take the step that follows logically of eliminating the unwarranted requirement (or rationale) that a comparative study needs to be available before selecting a statistical decision procedure over the clinical judgment method. If one instead considers the availability of comparative studies a preferred, but not necessary, condition for using statistical judgment methods, the world of available statistical decision methods multiplies from the hundreds to the thousands. Many, many research studies yield useful statistical algorithms or procedures pertinent to applied clinical decisions, whether they involve predictors of suicide attempts, the benefits of alternative treatments, the chances of spontaneous recovery from one or another type of disorder, or the occurrence of child sexual abuse, to name a few of numerous abundant possible examples.

Recognizing the overall superiority of statistical decision making and the wide availability of choices, we can apply some of the checklist suggestions for making greater use of base rates with only minor modifications and add a couple of others specific to statistical decision procedures. One's procedural checklist could contain items like:

1. *For decision tasks under consideration, determine whether statistical decision procedures are available. Do not limit yourself to comparative studies, but expand the scope of the search to studies that generate statistical analyses or formalisms that can be applied directly, or with minor modification, to the decision tasks of interest.* (If one addresses certain decision tasks regularly, one might well have collections of pertinent literature readily available.)
2. *What are the strongest reasons to use statistical decision methods in the present case*? (As with base rates, we generally prefer the positive form of this question, given the compelling evidence that statistical decision methods are frequently underused or underweighted.)
3. *If one has used a statistical decision method and is leaning toward countervailing the outcome, try to first generate the best reason (or reasons) the statistical outcome is correct and more likely to be accurate*

than the alternative conclusion one is contemplating. (Considerable research indicates that many clinicians countervail statistical decision methods freely and often, but that these decision practices rarely improve things overall and commonly increase error, sometimes substantially. When one contemplates going against the statistical decision method, overconfidence may lead to a counterproductive choice. Unwarranted confidence levels may stem from being overly focused on reasons the statistical method may be wrong, a potential form of confirmatory bias. Generating plausible reasons that the statistically based result may be correct and one's contemplated countervail may be incorrect makes contrary evidence more salient and can reduce excessive confidence and the chances of diminishing overall accuracy—see Chapter 12 for further details. Again, we are not suggesting that one should never countervail statistically based decision rules, but rather that one should feel wariness in doing so. Countervailing regularly is a problematical and counterproductive approach. Some arguably compelling reasons to contemplate countervailing are described in Chapter 8, under the heading "Sawyer's Review" and in the subsection on broken leg examples.)

Delay/Deliberate When Possible

Literature on premature closure suggests that more accurate decision makers often wait longer before reaching conclusions, whereas other clinicians may form initial impressions within minutes or even seconds of initial contact with a client that remain unaltered thereafter. Clinicians commonly overestimate the amount information that truly influences their decision making, and often even a modest number of the most valid and least redundant variables approach a ceiling in accuracy when combined properly. Nevertheless, the odds are poor that such information will be obtained within a few minutes or, say, 30 seconds of client contact. Further, although the demarcation between rapid and more deliberate information processing may be less distinct than is sometimes described, when circumstances do not create urgent demands for rapid decision making, taking the opportunity to deliberate and think things through often benefits decision accuracy. Additional time might allow one to check one's work for accuracy, to identify important informational sources from a checklist that had been overlooked, to conduct a full, well-validated structured interview, and to execute hypothesis testing that increases the chances of disconfirming erroneous impressions.

Consider the following analogy. A witness takes the stand. His or her lawyer walks the witness through the initial (direct) examination, which may be brief. Often, such testimony seems compelling. Thus, the jurors are in a position somewhat like the clinician who forms an early impression or conclusion. Next, the opposing lawyer conducts a cross-examination, which may change impressions dramatically. The opposing lawyer catches the witness in an inaccuracy or two pertaining to critical facts, such as uncovering a major flaw in an alibi. Suddenly things seem very different. The first lawyer wanted to create an immutable impression almost immediately and solicited confirmatory evidence to support it. The opposing lawyer has the goal of gathering and presenting potential disconfirming evidence.

One of the authors has consulted in numerous forensic cases, and lawyers often fear that jurors' impressions will become too hardened before they get their chance to cross-examine an opposing expert or put on their own witnesses. If they can somehow prevent premature, fixed impressions, then given sufficient opportunity to get jurors to "consider the opposite," they may well be able to change impressions. As for mental health professionals, deliberation and delay in forming final conclusions can have significant benefits when circumstances do not force earlier decisions.

If one reminds oneself that things that appear clear early on may not be as clear as they seem, and if one continues to seek the most valuable information, makes proportional efforts to uncover and consider potential contrary evidence, and uses decision methods that are not subject to initial biases or swayed by the order in which information is received, one is more likely to ultimately reach accurate conclusions. For example, if one is entering information into a statistical decision method, the order in which that information was originally obtained will not change the outcome (except under unusual circumstances, which we do not explore here). Furthermore, the statistical method is not sentient and thus not subject to forming hypotheses that will bias analysis of later information. (The same cannot always be said for machine learning or artificial intelligence–see Chapter 10.)

Make Active Attempts to Disconfirm Hypotheses; Try Not To Just Prove, But Also To Disprove

Nuanced philosophical debates about the role of confirmation and disconfirmation in the development of scientific fields aside, from a practical standpoint, because many hypotheses or conclusions in fields as difficult as mental health are prone to error, we require some mechanism to help identify when conclusions need to be revised or are wrong. The benefits of recognizing error, and preferably doing so efficiently, comprise an area in which balancing efforts to disprove versus prove hypotheses and initial judgments can prove very helpful.

As already discussed, actively considering possible negative evidence for one's initial conclusions can have salutary effects, such as bringing confidence and accuracy into greater alignment and reducing the potential deleterious impact of such cognitive pitfalls as hindsight bias. In addition, confirmatory strategies can appear to generate abundant supportive evidence for hypotheses that are overly extreme, need modification, or are simply wrong. One reason confirmatory strategies can create illusory support for a questionable or false hypothesis rests on the variability of human behavior, and another reason originates in the way individuals often go about testing hypotheses, which can create conditions in which a false belief seems to receive piece after piece of supportive evidence.

First, given variability in human behavior over time and circumstances, one can uncover supportive evidence for many hypotheses about individuals, even if they are off base or more wrong than right. For example, individuals with introverted tendencies (unless very extreme) may engage in extroverted behavior at times, and vice versa. Suppose a client is nervous during the initial stages of an intake interview, and under such circumstances is more talkative and loud than usual. The practitioner may form an initial impression of extroverted tendencies, and may ask questions that probe to see whether this initial impression is supported, such as, "Do you find that you are outgoing at times?" or, "Are there times when you enjoy being the center of attention?" Given that such behaviors may well be present at times even with an individual who is more introverted than outgoing, the initial impression of extroversion may be strengthened (Snyder & Swann, 1978). Alternatively, for an individual who is more outgoing than internalizing, that same initial anxiety may manifest as somewhat atypical reticence, leading the clinician down a different path of questioning that again would tend to "confirm" a mistaken initial belief. Individuals commonly focus on seeking confirmatory evidence. They may well do so with the sincere intent of obtaining the correct answer rather than proving they are right, but without fully appreciating potential shortcomings of such strategies.

Understandably, readers might view this example of confirming initial hypotheses about extroversion or introversion to be somewhat contrived or extreme. One might consider instead the evaluation of such characteristics as level of anxiety, lapses in judgment, instances of impulsive behavior, or memory slips in a person concerned with declining cognitive functions. Undoubtedly, normal individuals get anxious at times, do not always think problems through sufficiently, and may act without sufficient deliberation, such as starting with one potato chip and proceeding to polish off half the bag despite a vow to avoid that first bite given the ultimate outcome in nearly all prior occasions. Memory slips are also common, such as forgetting what one was originally watching after channel surfing, or one's parking spot in a large lot.

Probing for the presence of such types of common human fallibilities or traits is likely to generate multiple supportive instances, even if someone falls well within normal limits in these areas. For example, behaviors proposed as potential indicators of concussion (e.g., concentration difficulties, fatigue, or restlessness), upon further study, turned out to be considerably more common in the general population than was often assumed (see Faust, 2012, pp. 392–393). One can also see how such misimpressions might be reversed almost immediately if the evaluator made equal efforts to obtain disconfirmatory evidence, such as by asking, "Are these impulsive behaviors common for you, or do you show self-restraint about as often or more often?" or, "You mentioned memory slips? Are there times your memory seems especially strong?" or, "You mentioned that your job often requires you to update your knowledge. Do you find that your ability to keep your work knowledge up to date has remained stable?" One might argue instead that questions inquiring into these or other areas should usually be posed in a nonleading manner. However, with some clients, open-ended questions elicit minimal responses that are not very helpful.

Second, main or sole reliance on confirmatory strategies can be highly inefficient and generate less conclusive outcomes than disconfirmatory strategies (Wason, 1968). We can start with an abstract illustration and then move on to a clinical example. Suppose one is testing a hypothesis about the number series 1-2-3-4, with the researcher providing accurate feedback about inquiries in every instance. A natural hypothesis about the series is that the numbers ascend by 1. In theory, one could continue testing this hypothesis ad nauseam by starting with 5, asking if it's consistent with the underlying concept, receiving a positive response, and then proceeding likewise to 6, 7, 8, 9, and well into the night, receiving affirmative feedback every time.

However, suppose after receiving a few affirmative responses, one instead tries to disprove the hypothesis that the numbers ascend by one. One goes back to the original string (1-2-3-4), and asks if the 4 was followed by a 3, would this fit the underlying concept? If one was then informed that it does, then one should realize immediately, assuming the feedback is accurate, that the original hypothesis is wrong. One would still be left to uncover the correct concept, but at least the erroneous hypothesis would have been eliminated and one could examine other possibilities (such as numbers that fall 1 number above or below the prior number). (The next section sets forth some strategies that might be used to disconfirm hypotheses or rule out different diagnostic possibilities.)

As a clinical example, suppose a practitioner is attempting to rule in or rule out a mild traumatic brain injury (MTBI). One could spend considerable time gathering information on presenting symptoms associated with MTBI. However, given the overlap between MTBI symptoms and the symptoms of various other conditions, such as PTSD and problem substance use, considerable ambiguity may remain. Attempts to disconfirm MTBI may prove far more efficient and accurate. Multiple conditions must be present for a MTBI to occur, one of which is an event that generates sufficient forces to damage the brain. Thus, if inquiry shows that no such event occurred, it should be possible to eliminate MTBI as a plausible diagnostic possibility. For example, a car accident may have been so minor that there is almost no chance it could have caused a brain injury.

Holistic (Scenario) Thinking Is Not the Whole Story

We often think in scenarios or stories. There is the success story of the underdog, the rise and fall of the shining star, or the resentful social recluse who meets the right partner and is transformed through loving kindness. The tendency to think holistically or in scenarios is one factor underlying the conjunction fallacy, or the mistaken belief that the likelihood of two (or more) events occurring together exceeds the likelihood of any of the component events occurring alone (e.g., that A + B is more likely than either A or B alone). Take the following hypothetical example:

> Jack is a 12-year-old child with a troubled past, poor impulse control, and a history of two prior foster placements that each had to be terminated in less than two months. He has just started a third placement. Which of the following do you think is the most likely outcome?

A. Jack will quickly develop serious conflicts with his foster parents.
B. The placement will have to be terminated.
C. Jack will quickly develop serious conflicts with his foster parents, and the placement will have to be terminated.

The temptation is to pick option C, because it seems to be the most likely scenario. However, C, which is the composite of A and B, cannot be more likely that either A or B alone: some children develop serious conflicts with their foster parents but their placements are not terminated, and some children's placements are terminated even though they have not developed serious conflicts with their foster parents. Thus, A + B cannot be more likely than A or B alone. Nevertheless, given tendencies to think about events holistically or in scenarios, the conjunction fallacy is committed regularly (Arkes, Aberegg, & Arpin, 2022; Tversky & Kahneman, 1971).

The culture of mental health often strongly encourages holistic thinking or thinking in scenarios (consider the usual format for a case conference, or the very common advice to integrate all the information). We do not question whether looking at the bigger picture can have benefits. However, at other times or as a supplemental strategy, thinking analytically or in terms of component elements can have considerable value and improve judgmental accuracy. A number of examples and guidelines follow.

Break Down Links in a Chain or Sequence of Events to Achieve More Accurate Estimates of Occurrences

A client is meeting with his therapist. After a prolonged struggle, the client has finally decided to ask an acquaintance on a date. The therapist has concerns about the decision. The client is hypersensitive to rejection, tends to develop self-destructive thoughts when rebuffs occur, and made a serious suicide attempt two years earlier. Further, the client has just started to make progress on these issues, and considerable therapeutic work remains to be done to develop more sufficient adaptive capacities and coping skills.

Assume for purposes of this example that the client will not change his mind, and further that if three negative events all occur, the client will likely act self-destructively. (We realize these hypothetical examples, which are mainly used for illustrative purposes, often contain elements of artificiality and oversimplification.[1]) The three negative events are: (1) the acquaintance declines the client's invitation, (2) the acquaintance's response is harsh, and (3) the client has ready access to lethal means for committing self-harm. Further, assume that the probabilities for each of these occurrences are as follows: 1 = 50%, 2 = 15%, and 3 = 95%. Finally, for purposes of this example, each of the component events is treated as independent of the others (e.g., that the response to the invitation will not change the likelihood of access to lethal means).

Treating each of these elements or links in the chain as independent of one another, we can calculate the probability of this highly adverse event by multiplying the three probabilities together, as in: $.50 \times .15 \times .95 = \sim 7\%$, which is considerably higher than we would like, given the horrific nature of this potential outcome. Now, again for illustrative purposes, suppose the therapist must choose to prioritize one of the three elements, and that the absolute level of impact would be about the same across the three possible selections. We will set that level at 10%. The natural tendency is to select the most likely occurrence—ready access to lethal means—which falls at .95. If we reduce the .95 to .85, the result is: $.50 \times .15 \times .85 = \sim 6\%$, achieving a very modest reduction from about 7% to about 6%. We have accomplished something, but not much. Instead, assume we focus on the least likely event, thereby reducing the .15 to .05, resulting in an overall risk of $.50 \times .05 \times .95 = \sim 2\%$, cutting the overall risk to one third of the original figure (after eliminating rounding). The underlying principle that follows is that all else being equal, in order to achieve the greatest reduction in the chance that a chain of events will all occur, focus on reducing the likelihood of the least (not most) probable element.

Conversely, if one is trying to increase the probability of a desired outcome (e.g., the opportunity to attend an excellent graduate program), then all else being equal, focus on increasing the probability of the least likely component. Therefore, if overcoming financial barriers is the most likely obstacle, doubling down on finding funding opportunities could well be the highest priority. These hypothetical examples are purer than one finds in the great majority of clinical settings and when one has to make applied clinical decisions. For example, it might not be clear how independent the different links of the chain really are, the extent to which attempts to alter the odds are likely to succeed, and the extent to which the magnitude of impact differs across the factors. One may need to make adjustments for such ambiguities by taking steps like appraising impact as one goes along and revising estimates as needed, or by recognizing that the probabilities are approximations subject to at least modest error, leading one to default more readily to less risky courses of action, such as suggesting a higher level of intervention. Even given the kind of painful uncertainties one often encounters in applied

[1] We readily acknowledge that the real world often cannot be divided into such neat boxes, and again emphasize that such examples are used to illustrate important guiding principles. At times, such principles will have straightforward applications, but at other times circumstances and limits in knowledge create ambiguities that can become vexing. As we proceed with the current example, we will go on to discuss potential ambiguities in real-world applications.

settings, the fundamental principles still apply, and it is better to use them to guide decision making than to implement misdirected strategies that are almost certain to magnify overall error.

When Available, Focus on Criteria of Inclusion and Exclusion, Not Associated Indicators

Strictly speaking, *criteria of inclusion* are diagnostic signs or indicators that, if present, rule in a disorder, and *criteria of exclusion* are signs or indicators that, if absent, rule out a disorder. In contrast, *associated signs or indicators* are variables related to a condition, but they are not definitive in ruling in or ruling out a condition. Associated signs or indicators are often present in multiple disorders and may show considerable overlap across individuals with and without a disorder.

An example of an inclusionary criterion is blatant thought disorder in the absence of clouded consciousness or delirium, which is almost a certain indictor of some type of schizophrenia spectrum or other psychotic disorder. Given the relative rarity in the mental health field of finding definitive indicators, the terms *inclusion* and *exclusion* are often meant to convey something like very strong or nearly definitive evidence, as opposed to infallible criteria. As an example of a presumed exclusionary criterion, a child being evaluated for autism spectrum disorder may show no impairments in social interactions. An example of an associated symptom might be elevated distress, which does not rule in or rule out a wide range of disorders. In addition, although many associated symptoms are more common among those with, versus those without, psychological problems, they still may be seen with fairly high frequency among individuals without significant maladjustment. One might say that associated symptoms are neither necessary or sufficient to rule in or rule out a particular psychological disorder, and sometimes to even rule in or rule out the presence of any psychological disorder at all (given the overlap that is often seen across those with and without disorder).

Given their limited utility, chasing down associated signs and symptoms may not help much in clarifying diagnostic possibilities or outcomes, or even in distinguishing normal individuals from individuals with psychological conditions. Of course, symptoms themselves may become the focus for treatment, although here we are primarily focusing on their potential value for diagnostic and predictive purposes. We also understand that various diagnostic categories in the mental health field do not really offer much practical guidance, but surely there are exceptions, such as bipolar disorder and various eating disorders, given their potential treatment responsiveness and the high rate of morbidity and mortality among those who go untreated.

To avoid wasted time and to increase accuracy when performing differential diagnosis, one can start by asking whether there may be potential criteria of inclusion or exclusion. If such criteria can be identified, then if feasible (e.g., the needed information is available or potentially available), they can serve as early starting points. As noted, for example, if a child's social relations are normal, that finding goes a long way toward ruling out autism spectrum disorder; if an individual followed over time shows cognitive weaknesses, but these problems have been present for years and have not gotten any worse, one can likely rule out a progressive neurocognitive disorder; or if someone shows no formal thought disorder, that essentially rules out various forms of schizophrenia spectrum disorders. We should note that the structure of the *Diagnostic and Statistical Manual of Mental Disorders* (currently the fifth edition, DSM-5) can sometimes facilitate, and sometimes hinder, such attempts. For example, for a range of disorders in DSM-5, the client needs to present with only one or a few symptoms among a longer list of possible symptoms within a diagnostic criterion, and the manual provides clear latitude for going outside or beyond those criteria in formulating diagnoses. Thus, two individuals classified as having the same disorder may have little in common with each other, and determining what might rule in or rule out a disorder can become a confusing exercise.

Finally, distinguishing between those with and those without psychological disorder may not get the clinician very far, and signs, symptoms, and characteristics that might help with that very broad differentiation may have little or no utility when further narrowing is attempted. For example, the DSM-5 includes a generic requirement for distress or impairment in social, occupational, or other areas of functioning for identifying a supposed psychological disorder. Even if the presence of such distress or impairment provides some help in distinguishing between those with or those without psychological disorders, accomplishing this general categorization will often assist little in differentiating one condition from another, because distress/impairment is supposed to be a defining feature across psychological disorders. (Evaluation of severity levels, however, may provide some help.)

As a second example, both PTSD and concussion can have multiple symptoms in common (e.g., significant disruption in attention and concentration, marked irritability, and persistent negative emotional states). Any or all of these features may help separate individuals who might have one or both of these conditions from those without mental health or related disorders. However, once the first determination is made (that one or both of the conditions are likely present), the same symptoms that facilitated that initial determination may not help in differentiating between the two potential diagnoses given the degree of symptom overlap. As one proceeds to narrow down possibilities, signs and symptoms that got one past the prior step may lose their differentiating value for the next step. Hence, at each step along the way, one is looking for variables that are both valid and have differentiating value. As the possibilities narrow, variables with differentiating value can undergo change in their efficacy. Previously useful variables often become ineffective or less effective, and in the latter case, when possible, should be replaced by stronger variables.

Closing Thoughts

We humbly and sincerely hope that materials in this chapter, and throughout the book, will provide information and guidance that help realize the book's goal of enhancing decision making and thereby improving client outcomes. We view this work as our vote for the role of rationality and applied science in enhancing human welfare.

Reconsidering or altering long-established thinking patterns and widely held "givens" in the mental health field about judgment and decision making is not a light lift. Likewise, recognizing instances of problem practices and applying stronger methods often require dedication and practice. For example, recognizing that one has drawn a conclusion about the association between two variables that did not account for all four cells of a covariation table, or identifying and applying base rates, can take practice and repetition. Toward that end, the six appendices to this text provide practical information and practice materials that are designed to facilitate application of the decision literature. We hope those materials will prove to be useful.

REFERENCES

Archer, R. P., & Newsom, C. R. (2000). Psychological test usage with adolescent clients: Survey update. *Assessment, 7*(3), 227–235.

Arkes, H. R., Aberegg, S., & Arpin, K. A. (2022). Physicians' probability estimates of a sequence of events. *JAMA Network Open*. doi.org/10.1001/jamanetworkopen.2022.18804

Chapman, L. J., & Chapman, J. P. (1969). Illusory correlation as an obstacle to the use of valid psychodiagnostic signs. *Journal of Abnormal Psychology, 74*, 271–280.

Dana, J., Dawes, D., & Peterson, P. (2013). Belief in the unstructured interview: The persistence of an illusion. *Judgment and Decision Making, 8*(5), 512–520.

Einhorn, H. J. (1986). Accepting error to make less error. *Journal of Personality Assessment, 50*(3), 387–395.

Faust, D. (2012). *Coping with psychiatric and psychological testimony* (6th ed.). Oxford University Press.

Furman, A. L.-E. (2005). *Clinicians' knowledge and use of decision making research* [Unpublished master's thesis]. University of Rhode Island, Kingston, RI.

Greene, R. L. (2012). *The MMPI-2/MMPI-2-RF: An interpretive manual* (3rd ed.). Allyn & Bacon.

Grove, W. M., Zald, D. H., Lebow, B. S., Snitz, B. E., & Nelson, C. (2000). Clinical versus mechanical prediction: A meta-analysis. *Psychological Assessment, 12*(1), 19–30.

Kahneman, D. (2011). *Thinking, fast and slow*. Farrar, Straus and Giroux.

Kahneman, D., & Tversky, A. (1972). On the psychology of prediction. *Psychological Review, 80*, 237–251.

Kennedy, M. L., Willis, W. G., & Faust, D. (1997). The base-rate fallacy in school psychology. *Journal of Psychoeducational Assessment, 15*(4), 292–307.

Lee, D., Reynolds, C. R., & Willson, V. L. (2003). Standardized test administration: Why bother? *Journal of Forensic Neuropsychology, 3*, 55–81.

Meyers, J. F. (2015). *Development and psychometric evaluation of a clinical beliefs questionnaire for licensed psychologists* [Doctoral dissertation]. https://doi.org/10.23860/diss-meyer-joseph-2015

Piotrowski, C. (1985). Clinical assessment: Attitudes of the Society for Personality Assessment membership. *The Southern Psychologist, 2*, 80–83.

Prochaska, J. O., & Velicer, W. F. (1997). The transtheoretical model of health behavior change. *American Journal of Health Promotion, 12*, 38–48.

Snyder, M., & Swann, W. B. (1978). Hypothesis-testing processes in social interaction. *Journal of Personality and Social Psychology, 36*(11), 1202–1212.

Spengler, P. M., White, M. J., Ægisdottir, S., Maugherman, A. S., Cook, R. S., Nichols, C., Lampropoulos, G. K., Walker, B. S., Cohen, G. R., & Rush, J. D. (2009). The meta-analysis of clinical judgment project: Effects of experience on judgment accuracy. *The Counseling Psychologist, 37*(3), 350–399.

Tversky, A., & Kahneman, D. (1983). Extensional versus intuitive reasoning: The conjunction fallacy in probability judgment. *Psychological Review, 90*(4), 293–315.

Tversky, A., & Kahneman, D. (1971). Belief in the law of small numbers. *Psychological Bulletin, 75*(2), 105–110.

Wason, P. C. (1968). Reasoning about a rule. *Quarterly Journal of Experimental Psychology, 20*, 273–281.

Werner, P. D., Rose, T. R., & Yesavage, J. A. (1983). Reliability, accuracy, and decision making strategy in clinical predictions of imminent dangerousness. *Journal of Consulting and Clinical Psychology, 51*(6), 815–825.

Wright, C. V., Beattie, S. G., Galper, D. I., Church, A. S., Bufka, L. F., Brabender, V. M., & Smith, B. L. (2017). Assessment practices of professional psychologists: Results of a national survey. *Professional Psychology: Research and Practice, 48*(2), 73–78.

Introduction to the Appendices

The six appendices are intended to illustrate and augment materials presented throughout the book, and to provide practice applying guides, strategies, and normative procedures arising from decision literature. Appendix 1 presents some exemplar sources for base rate information. Although there are limited articles or texts primarily devoted to base rates, base rate information is available in a wide variety of sources and publications, such as epidemiological studies and outcome studies (e.g., frequency of good recovery from a mild traumatic brain injury, frequency of substantial gains from some type of therapeutic intervention). Thus, as illustrated in Appendix 1, a literature search will often yield useful base rate information for numerous clinical decision making tasks.

Appendix 2 provides a nomogram, which can assist in analyzing the impact of base rates and combining base rates with other information without having to perform mathematical calculations (see also Chapter 6). Appendix 3 reviews and details formal procedures for combining base rates with other information, such as test results and other forms of diagnostic and predictive information. Illustrations are also provided for various applications of base rates, such as differential diagnosis or assistance with dichotomous choices.

Appendix 4 provides a sample of recent publications on machine learning and artificial intelligence pertaining to clinical practice. Appendix 5 presents an array of practice cases and illustrative clinical scenarios, along with opportunities to apply information presented in this book and receive feedback on these efforts.

Appendix 6 offers both a detailed and condensed summary of guides and steps for increasing the accuracy of clinical judgment and decision making that appear throughout this book. Either of these summaries might serve as a checklist for clinical practices.

APPENDIX 1

A Sampling of Base-Rate Sources

OVERVIEW OF APPENDIX 1

The following is intended as a sampling of sources that provide base rate information for various diagnoses and conditions. As described earlier in the book (see Chapter 6), sources of base rate information may not always be obvious. Often, reporting of base rate information is a secondary contribution of a text or peer-reviewed publication. This applies to many, but not all, of the texts and articles that follow. For the sources listed below, we have attempted to describe the nature of the base rate information included in each source.

TEXTS

American Psychiatric Association. (2013). *Diagnostic and statistical manual of mental disorders* (5th ed.). https://doi.org/10.1176/appi.books.9780890425596

The American Psychiatric Association's *Diagnostic and Statistical Manual of Mental Disorders* (DSM), currently in the 5th edition, provides prevalence estimates or base rates for a wide range of diagnostic categories, making it a rich source for identifying base rate information. However, given the difficulties and status of psychiatric classification in general, limitations in DSM prevalence data deserve consideration.

The quality of DSM prevalence data varies in relation to a number of variables, such as the breadth and quality of research, and especially in relation to the status of the categories and the efficacy of the diagnostic criteria for identifying the conditions. For some diagnostic categories, scientific foundations are well-established, and diagnostic criteria and methods for identification are available that often lead to unambiguous results and good levels of agreement across diagnosticians. However, other categories have shaky or questionable foundations, with criteria that may create considerable ambiguities, place heavy burden on subjective judgment, and easily lead to differing appraisals. Thus, reported prevalence rates will have differing margins of error. In addition, many diagnoses do not rest on an invariant set of symptoms that are required to identify a disorder, but rather various options or ways to satisfy what are often relatively general criteria (e.g., two or more of five possible characteristics). Consequently, two individuals who fall within the same category may have multiple differences in their presentations or in their overall combination of symptoms.

McCaffery, R. J., Palav, A. A., O'Bryant, S. E., & Labarge, A. S. (Eds.) (2003). *Practitioner's guide to symptom base rates in clinical neuropsychology*. Kluwer Academic/Plenum Publishers.

"This recent text... provides tables and procedures for estimating the positive and negative predictive values of our tests given varying base rates of the condition of interest. They include numerous symptoms associated with traumatic brain injury, neurological disease, and psychological disorders... This is a valuable resource for clinical, forensic, and research use." (Lees-Haley, P.R. (2007). A review of: "McCaffrey, R. J., Palav, A. A., O'Bryant, S., & Labarge, A. S. (2003). Practitioner's Guide to Symptom Base Rates in Clinical Neuropsychology", *Applied Neuropsychology, 14*(3), 230–231.)

JOURNAL ARTICLES

General Psychiatric and Neurodegenerative Disorders

Kitchen Andren, K. A., Gabel, N. M., Stelmokas, J., Rich, A. M., & Bieliauskas, L. A. (2017). Population base rates and disease course of common psychiatric and neurodegenerative disorders. *Neuropsychology Review, 27*(3), 284–301.

This article is intended to provide an easily accessible and comprehensive reference source for age of onset, as well as prevalence and incidence data, for common neurodegenerative and psychiatric disorders in adults. Epidemiological data were compiled from multiple sources and presented in several tables and a figure, which can be helpful to students and clinicians across healthcare disciplines.

Auerbach, R. P., Mortier, P., Bruffaerts, R., Alonso, J., Benjet, C., Cuijpers, P., Demyttenaere, K., Ebert, D. D., Green, J. G., Hasking, P., Murray, E., Nock, M. K., Pinder-Amaker, S., Sampson, N. A., Stein, D. J., Vilagut, G., Zaslavsky, A. M., Kessler, R. C.; WHO WMH-ICS Collaborators. (2018). The WHO World Mental Health Surveys International College Student Project: Prevalence and distribution of mental disorders. *Journal of Abnormal Psychology, 127*(7), 623–638.

This study reports initial results from the first stage of the WHO World Mental Health International College Student project, in which a series of surveys were carried out in 19 colleges across eight countries (Australia, Belgium, Germany, Mexico, Northern Ireland, South Africa, Spain, and the United States). The main aim was to estimate prevalence rates and basic sociodemographic correlates of common mental disorders among first-year college students. Web-based self-report questionnaires administered to incoming first-year students (45.5% pooled response rate) screened for six common lifetime and 12-month DSM-IV mental disorders, such as major depression and generalized anxiety disorder. There were 13,984 respondents, all full-time students: 35% of whom screened positive for at least one of the common lifetime disorders assessed and 31% of whom screened positive for at least one 12-month disorder. Syndromes typically had onsets in early-middle adolescence and persisted to the time of the survey.

Although relatively modest, the strongest correlates of screening positive were older age, female sex, unmarried or deceased parents, no religious affiliation, non-heterosexual identification and behavior, low secondary school ranking, and extrinsic motivation for college enrollment. As a reminder, variables that narrow base rates can augment the power of base rates as predictors (see Chapter 6). More specifically, suppose base rates for one or another condition or outcome differs among certain subgroups, such as those of varying ages, and the difference is relevant to the current client or examinee. For example, one might find differences between individuals in their 30's versus their 40's, but if the current client is a 10-year-old child, then those differences are not relevant. In the present study, the relatively low levels of association with background variables suggest that they will have little impact on the base rates and thus may not change things much. In other cases and studies, one should be alert to modifying variables, such as demographic characteristics, that are associated with changes in prevalence rates or outcomes, especially when these associations are robust.

Wichstrøm, L., Berg-Nielsen, T. S., Angold, A., Egger, H. L., Solheim, E., & Sveen, T. H. (2011). Prevalence of psychiatric disorders in preschoolers. *Journal of Child Psychology and Psychiatry*, *53*(6), 695–705.

Many disorders seen in childhood and adolescence start in the preschool years, although available prevalence (base) rates for psychiatric disorders in young children are often limited. For this study, all children born in 2003 or 2004 in the city of Trondheim, Norway, who attended the regular community health check-up for 4-year-olds (97.2% of eligible children), and whose parents consented to take part in the study (*N* = 2,475, 82.0%), were screened for behavioral and emotional problems. A subgroup of 1,250 children took part in a more comprehensive study, including a structured diagnostic interview, which 995 parents (79.6%) completed. The estimated population rate for any psychiatric disorder (excluding encopresis–6.4%) was 7.1%. The most common disorders were attention-deficit/ hyperactivity disorder (ADHD, 1.9%), oppositional defiant disorder (1.8%), conduct disorder (0.7%), anxiety disorders (1.5%), and depressive disorders (2.0%). Co-occurring disorders were common. More emotional and behavioral disorders were seen in children whose parents did not live together and in those of low socioeconomic status. (Again, these are factors that would or might modify base rates.) Overall, the prevalence of disorders among preschoolers was lower than in previous studies from the United States. In either case, when base rates are low, one often needs powerful diagnostic tools to increase accuracy over levels achieved by playing the base rates alone. For example, for a disorder with a prevalence rate of 1%, one would be correct 99% of the time assuming that the particular condition was not present, and thus one would need diagnostic methods that are more than 99% accurate to increase overall hit-rates. Of course, we are not suggesting that a mental health professional should always guess that no particular disorder is present, but rather that the comparative accuracy of playing the base rates versus using diagnostic methods should be keep in mind and can significantly impact decision procedures and policy.

Performance Validity and Symptom Validity

The following articles report on the frequency of performance or symptom validity. Broadly, performance validity typically refers to whether, or the extent to which, an examinee is sufficiently engaged on a test measuring cognitive functioning to generate representative indications of ability; symptom validity typically refers to an examinee's reporting style on self-report measures of symptoms, such as potential tendencies to over-state or exaggerate difficulties. There are individual tests designed solely for assessing performance validity or symptom validity (i.e., stand-alone tests). Although significant progress has been made with respect to procedures for assessing performance and symptom validity, considerable methodological gaps remain, a comprehensive discussion of which is beyond the scope of this book. The articles below report base rates of performance or symptom validity in various contexts and populations; however, as described below, the reader should take note of cautions and caveats when considering the reported base rates.

Aparcero, M., Picard, E. H., Nijdam-Jones, A., & Rosenfeld, B. (2022). Comparing the ability of MMPI-2 and MMPI-2-RF validity subscales to detect feigning: A meta-analysis. *Assessment*, *30*(3), 744–760.

The Minnesota Multiphasic Personality Inventory-2 (MMPI-2) and Minnesota Multiphasic Personality Inventory-2 Restructured Form (MMPI-2-RF) are commonly used measures to assess for psychological symptoms. These measures include several scales that have proven useful in differentiating among examinees who are overreporting, underreporting, or forthrightly or sincerely reporting symptoms. This study provides effect sizes and central tendency statistics for various MMPI-2 and MMPI-2-RF scales divided by groups (e.g., "honest responders," individuals instructed to overreport, or individuals identified as over-reporters based on their reporting on a different symptom report measure) and symptom types (i.e., medical versus psychological).

McCaffery, R. J., & Lynch, J. K. (2020). Base rates of performance validity test failure among children and young adult litigants with histories of elevated blood lead levels. *Journal of Pediatric Neuropsychology*, *6*, 198–202.

Assessing performance validity among children and young adults is a challenging task. It is further complicated by the presence of diagnoses or conditions that may interfere with cognitive functioning. The following article provides an example of narrowing a base rate, in this case narrowing it to children and young adults with a history of elevated blood lead exposure and who are currently involved in litigation. As with the majority of performance validity research, this study is subject to several caveats and limitations. The study lacks a control group, hence the reader is unable to draw conclusions regarding the discriminative utility of the performance validity criterion applied in the research study. Additionally, inferences involving whether failure on measures of performance validity was due to poor purposeful effort, involvement in litigation, or an alternative factor are tenuous due to study design limitations.

Schroeder, R. W., Clark, H. A., & Martin, P. K. (2021). Base rates of invalidity when patients undergoing routine clinical evaluations have Social Security Disability as an external incentive. *The Clinical Neuropsychologist*. https://doi.org/10.1080/13854046.2021.1895322

This study provides another example of narrowing base rates of performance validity failure on neuropsychological assessment, in this case among individuals either receiving or seeking Social Security Disability as compared to individuals without known incentives. This study provides base rate information for four groups that were clinically referred for neuropsychological evaluation: (1) individuals already receiving Social Security Disability, (2) individuals actively seeking Social Security Disability, (3) individuals considering seeking Social Security Disability and, (4) individuals without known external incentives. As can be seen, narrowing the base rate by Social Security Disability status yields sizeable differences in the frequency of invalid performance on multiple performance validity measures.

Mild Traumatic Brain Injury and Concussion

Asken, B. M., Snyder, A. R., Smith, M. S., Zaremski, J. L., & Bauer, R. M. (2017). Concussion-like symptom reporting in non-concussed adolescent athletes. *The Clinical Neuropsychologist, 31*(1), 138–153.

Symptoms commonly associated with concussion (e.g., headache, sleep difficulties, cognitive difficulties) are prevalent among individuals who have not sustained concussions. Consequently, the extent to which such symptoms offer discriminative utility in differentiating between individuals who have and have not sustained concussions may be limited. This study assessed 349 adolescent student athletes prior to sport participation (i.e., no concussion). Results yielded base rate information for individual "concussion-like symptoms" such as headache (12.9%), feeling slowed down (14.0%), and trouble falling asleep (16.0%) among adolescents without concussion. Such base rate information may guide symptom appraisal when combined with base rate information among adolescents with concussion at varying post-injury time intervals.

Rao, V., Bertrand, M., Rosenberg, P., Makley, M., Schretlen, D. J., Brandt, J., & Mielke, M. M. (2010). Predictors of new-onset depression after mild traumatic brain injury. *The Journal of Neuropsychiatry and Clinical Neurosciences, 22*, 100–104.

Psychiatric symptoms following mild traumatic brain injury are common; however, persistent psychiatric symptoms are far less common. This study provides base rate information regarding the prevalence of depression following mild traumatic brain injury in the first-year post injury. The study reported that 18% of individuals developed depression in the first-year following mild traumatic brain injury, which can be interpreted as approximately one in five individuals developing new onset depression. Notably, this base rate is based on a relatively small sample (*N*=43) and included considerable variability in age, education, race, income, and mechanism of injury.

Schretlen, D. J., & Shapiro, A. M. (2003). A quantitative review of the effects of injury on cognitive functioning. *International Review of Psychiatry, 15*(4), 341–349.

Assessing for diminished cognitive functioning following traumatic brain injury requires awareness of base rate information narrowed by both brain injury severity and amount of time elapsed since the injury. This study narrows base rate information by both of these factors through the provision of effect sizes computed from 39 studies totaling 1,716 individuals with traumatic brain injuries and 1,164 control subjects. As determined by the study (in the figures), among individuals with mild traumatic brain injuries, there are minimal differences in cognitive functioning after approximately one month post injury. Relative to base rates, at 30 or more days following injury, this information indicates that we should expect equivalent proportions of individuals with mild traumatic brain injuries and healthy individuals to show intact cognitive functioning on formal testing. In contrast, individuals with moderate to severe traumatic brain injuries perform worse on cognitive testing compared to control subjects to varying extents and at varying post injury intervals.

Inter-Subtest Variability or Scatter

Gontkovsky, S. T., Kreiner, D. S., Ryan, J. J., Golden, C. J., & Teichner, G. (2022). Relative subtest scatter on the WAIS-IV in a clinical sample referred for outpatient neuropsychological evaluation. *The Clinical Neuropsychologist, 36*(8), 2205–2220. https://doi.org/10.1080/13854046.2021.1975827

Inter-subtest variability, or scatter, refers to the difference between the highest and lowest scores on a battery of tests. Understanding the extent to which scatter is common among healthy individuals is requisite to determining whether certain levels may indicate the presence of cognitive impairment on a given cognitive test battery. This study reported base rates of scatter on the Wechsler Adult Intelligence Scale-Fourth Edition (WAIS-IV). Results of this study indicate that roughly equivalent levels of scatter are produced by both healthy and clinical populations.

APPENDIX 2

Nomogram

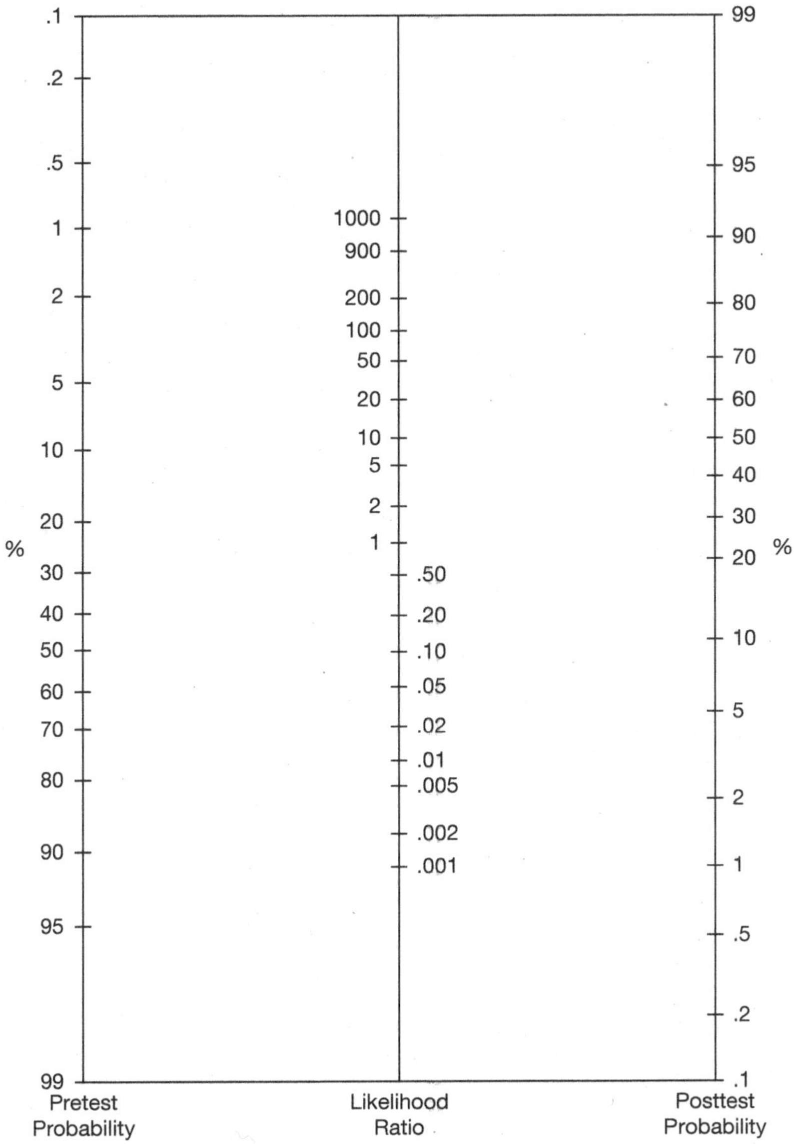

Figure A2.1 Nomogram

APPENDIX 3

Examples of Combining Base Rates with Other Diagnostic Signs, Indicators, and Test Results

The following materials are intended to guide the use of base rates and combining them with other signs or indicators. Please note that likelihood ratios are used throughout. To combine likelihood ratios and base rates (or probabilities), base rates are converted to ratio form. Consider the following example, a probability of 90% equates to a ratio of 90/10, such that the condition of interest is present in 90 cases and not present in 10. We provide general principles, which we believe may prove helpful by themselves, and also more technical information that permits more exacting determinations.

Guides for Combining Base Rates with Other Signs/Indicators

If the base rate and diagnostic sign/indicator are both valid and each contributes to the accuracy of prediction, then:

Compare the base rate and the diagnostic indicator:

A. If they are in the same direction (adjust the more extreme variable):

- a. If both are positive: The probability of the outcome is higher than the more likely of the two indicators. Therefore, take the higher probability and adjust it upward.
- b. If both are negative (again, adjust the more extreme indicator): The probability of the outcome is lower than the less likely of the two indicators. Therefore, take the lower probability and reduce it.

B. If they are in opposing directions:

- a. The probability of the outcome is lower than the probability of the affirming (positive) indicator and higher than the probability of the negative indicator.

b. The magnitude of the adjustment is related to the gap between the two indicators. The greater the gap, the larger the adjustment that is necessary. Sometimes the change will be very substantial (e.g., a 9 in 10 chance may be reduced to a 1 in 10 chance).

It is best to calculate likelihoods using Bayes' Theorem (see Waller et al., 2006, *A Paul Meehl Reader*, Chapter 9).

The formula is:

Prior probability × likelihood ratio/positive + negative cases

–or–

Base rate × likelihood ratio/positive + negative cases

For example, assume a base rate of 90% and a likelihood ratio of 5/1, thus:

Step 1: Base rate × likelihood ratio = 90/10 × 5/1 = 450/10
Step 2: Numerator remains as is, but for the denominator, one adds the numerator to the initial denominator to obtain the total for both positive and negative cases, as in 10 + 450 = 460
Step 3: Calculate the odds of a positive case by dividing the numerator by the denominator, as in: 450/460 = 97.8%

Two other examples:

1. Base rate = 90%, likelihood ratio = 1/9, thus
   Step 1: 90/10 × 1/9 = 90/90
   Step 2: 90 + 90 = 180
   Step 3: 90/180 = 50%
2. Base rate = 10%, odds ratio = 1/9
   Step 1: 10/90 × 1/9 = 10/810
   Step 2: 10 + 810 = 820
   Step 3: 10/820 = .012%

Although formal calculations are most accurate, a very rough rule of thumb for making these adjustments is to:

1. Convert base rate and the likelihood ratio to percentiles;
2. Convert percentiles to *z* scores (assuming a normal curve; for a handy online *z*-score calculator, see https://measuringu.com/calculators/pcalcz/);
3. Combine the two (do not forget to retain the direction of the *z* score, that is, if the score is above the 50th percentile, the *z* score is in the positive direction, and if it is below the 50th percentile, the *z* score is in the negative direction), and then convert back to percentiles.

For example, suppose the following results are obtained:

Base rate = 10%
Likelihood ratio = 90%
10% = z = −1.28;
90% = z = +1.28;
Then, simply sum the z scores:
−1.28 plus + 1.28 = 0
z = 0.0 = 50%

We have 50/50 odds. Certainly an increase in probability over the base rate, but still resulting in considerable uncertainty.

In another example:

Base rate = 10% = z = −1.28
Test = 95% = z = +1.64
Again, simply sum the z scores:
−1.28 plus + 1.64 = +.36
z = +.36 = 64%

In this case, given the strength of test result (95% probability), the probability increases from a base rate of 10% to 64%, suggesting that it is more probable than not that the condition of interest is present.

ILLUSTRATIONS

Please note that some of the following illustrations are more advanced examples of combining base rates and diagnostic or treatment indicators. Some such examples may be difficult to follow for those who lack familiarity with certain statistical methods. As such, for students early in their training, the examples may best serve as a guide for instructors to demonstrate the pragmatics underlying how base rates and diagnostic or treatment indicators are combined.

Furthermore, as a guide to properly interpreting the examples below, consider the following. Each column (i.e., "Base Rate," "Ratio for Diagnostic Indicator / Diagnostic Sign / Test" and "Conclusion") is distinct. We are illustrating how the information from the first two columns (i.e., "Base Rate" and "Ratio for Diagnostic Indicator / Diagnostic Sign / Test") is combined to address the clinical question. The rows that follow the ratios (i.e., "% conversion," "z-score conversion" and "z to %") represent alternative ways of representing the above ratios and arriving at more precise probabilities that inform the conclusion. Additionally, for the "A" examples (i.e.,

"A.1" and "A.2"), the base rate and the indicator both point in the same direction, or one is neutral. In contrast, for the "B" examples (i.e., "B.1," "B.2") the base rate and indicators point in opposing directions.

Diagnosis

Clinical question: What is the likelihood that brain damage is present? Or, Is brain damage present?

	Base Rate		Ratio for Diagnostic Indicator		Conclusion
Example A.1	8:1		4:1		> 8:1 (YES, Present)
% conversion	*89%*		*80%*		
z score conversion	*1.23*	+	*0.84*	=	*2.07*
z to %				=	*98.1%*
Example A.2.	1:8		1:4		< 1:8 (NO, Not present)
Example B.1	8:1		1:4		< 8:1, or about 62% (YES, Present)
Example B.2	1:8		4:1		>1:8, or about 38% (NO, Not present)
Example B.3	8:1		1:8		Equal Odds (Cannot determine)

Clinical Question: What is the likelihood that multiple personality disorder (MPD) is present? Or, Is MPD present?

	Base Rate		Ratio for Diagnostic Indicator		Conclusion
Example A.1	1:1,000 = no		1:10 = no		< 1:1000 (NO, MPD not present)
Example B.1	1:1,000 = no		10:1 = yes		<< 10:1, or about 1% (NO, MPD not present)
Example B.2	1:1000 = no		100:1 = yes		<< 100:1, or about 22% (NO, MPD not present)
% conversion	*0.1%*		*99.0%*		
z score conversion	*−3.09*	+	*+2.32*	=	*−0.77*
z to %				=	*22.1%*

Use of Base Rates in Differential Diagnosis

Clinical Question: Is PTSD or generalized anxiety disorder (GAD) present?

	Base Rate	Ratio For Diagnostic Sign	Conclusion
Example A.1	2:1 = PTSD	2:1 = PTSD	> 2:1 (PTSD more likely)
Example A.2	2:1 = PTSD	1:1 = either PTSD or GAD	2:1 (PTSD more likely)
Example B.1	2:1 = PTSD	2:1 = GAD	Equal Odds (Cannot Determine)
Example B.2	2:1 = PTSD	4:1 = GAD	< 4:1 (GAD more likely)

Use of Base Rates for Evaluating Likely Success of an Intervention or Selecting Among Alternative Interventions

1. Likely Success of Intervention A

	Base Rate	Test Result	BR + Test
Example A	70%	90%	> 90% (Intervention has more than a 90% chance of success)
Example B	5%	90%	<<90% (Intervention has far less than a 90% chance of success)

2. Likely Success of Alternative Interventions (A vs. B)

Example A	Base Rate	Test Result	BR + Test
Treatment A	70%	70%	> 70%
Treatment B	50%	70%	≤ 70%

Therefore, all else being equal, select Treatment A over B.

Example B	Base Rate	Test Result	BR + Test
Treatment A	90%	70%	> 90%
Treatment B	60%	90%	> 90% (But by a smaller magnitude than Treatment A above)

Therefore, all else being equal, select Treatment A over B.

APPENDIX 4

A Sampling of Recent Publications in Five Areas of Machine Learning and Artificial Intelligence Related to Applied Clinical Practice

ATTENTION-DEFICIT/HYPERACTIVITY DISORDER

2022

- Tang, Y., Sun, J., Wang, C., Zhong, Y., Jiang, A., Liu, G., & Liu, X. (2022). ADHD classification using auto-encoding neural network and binary hypothesis testing. *Artificial Intelligence in Medicine, 123*, 102209.

2021

- Cervantes-Henríquez, M. L., Acosta-López, J. E., Martinez, A. F., Arcos-Burgos, M., Puentes-Rozo, P. J., & Vélez, J. I. (2021). Machine learning prediction of ADHD severity: Association and linkage to *ADGRL3*, *DRD4*, and *SNAP25*. *Journal of Attention Disorders, 26*(4), 587–605. https://doi.org/10.1177/10870547211015426
- Faraone, S. V., Gomeni, R., Hull, J. T., Busse, G. D., Melyan, Z., O'Neal, W., Rubin, J., & Nasser, A. (2021). Early response to SPN-812 (viloxazine extended-release) can predict efficacy outcome in pediatric subjects with ADHD: A machine learning post-hoc analysis of four randomized clinical trials. *Psychiatry Research, 296*, 113664. https://doi.org/10.1016/j.psychres.2020.113664
- Jafari, P., Mehrabani-Zeinabad, K., Javadi, S., Ghanizadeh, A., & Bagheri, Z. (2021). A machine learning approach to assess differential item functioning of the KINDL Quality of Life Questionnaire across children with and without ADHD. *Child Psychiatry & Human Development, 53*(5), 1–12.
- Kim, S., Lee, H., & Lee, K. (2021). Can the MMPI predict adult ADHD? An approach using machine learning methods. *Diagnostics, 11*(6), 976.
- Öztekin, I., Finlayson, M. A., Graziano, P. A., & Dick, A. S. (2021). Is there any incremental benefit to conducting neuroimaging and neurocognitive

assessments in the diagnosis of ADHD in young children? A machine learning investigation. *Developmental Cognitive Neuroscience, 49*, 100966.
- Zhang-James, Y., Hoogman, M., van Rooij, D., Buitelaar, J., Franke, B., & Faraone, S. V. (2021). Machine learning classifiers for ADHD and comorbid disorders. *Biological Psychiatry, 89*(9), S23–S24.

2020

- Dubreuil-Vall, L., Ruffini, G., & Camprodon, J. A. (2020). Deep learning convolutional neural networks discriminate adult ADHD from healthy individuals on the basis of event-related spectral EEG. *Frontiers in Neuroscience, 14*, 251.

AUTISM SPECTRUM DISORDERS

2021

- Ghosh, T., Al Banna, M. H., Rahman, M. S., Kaiser, M. S., Mahmud, M., Hosen, A. S., & Cho, G. H. (2021). Artificial intelligence and Internet of things in screening and management of autism spectrum disorder. *Sustainable Cities and Society, 74*, 103189.
- Zhao, Z., Tang, H., Zhang, X., Qu, X., Hu, X., & Lu, J. (2021). Classification of children with autism and typical development using eye-tracking data from face-to-face conversations: Machine learning model development and performance evaluation. *Journal of Medical Internet Research, 23*(8), e29328.
- Zhao, Z., Zhu, Z., Zhang, X., Tang, H., Xing, J., Hu, X., Lu, J., & Qu, X. (2022). Identifying Autism with Head Movement Features by Implementing Machine Learning Algorithms. *Journal of Autism and Developmental Disorders, 52*(7), 3038–3049. https://doi.org/10.1007/s10803-021-05179-2

2020

- Küpper, C., Stroth, S., Wolff, N., Hauck, F., Kliewer, N., Schad-Hansjosten, T., Kamp-Becker, I., Poustka, L., Roessner, V., Schultebraucks, K., & Roepke, S. (2020). Identifying predictive features of autism spectrum disorders in a clinical sample of adolescents and adults using machine learning. *Scientific Reports, 10*(1), 4805. https://doi.org/10.1038/s41598-020-61607-w
- Leblanc, E., Washington, P., Varma, M., Dunlap, K., Penev, Y., Kline, A., & Wall, D. P. (2020). Feature replacement methods enable reliable home

video analysis for machine learning detection of autism. *Scientific Reports, 10*(1), 21245. https://doi.org/10.1038/s41598-020-76874-w

- Rahman, M., Usman, O. L., Muniyandi, R. C., Sahran, S., Mohamed, S., & Razak, R. A. (2020). A review of machine learning methods of feature selection and classification for autism spectrum disorder. *Brain Sciences, 10*(12), 949.
- Thabtah, F., & Peebles, D. (2020). A new machine learning model based on induction of rules for autism detection. *Health Informatics Journal, 26*(1), 264–286.

2019

- Bertoncelli, C. M., Altamura, P., Vieira, E. R., Bertoncelli, D., & Solla, F. (2019). Using artificial intelligence to identify factors associated with autism spectrum disorder in adolescents with cerebral palsy. *Neuropediatrics, 50*(03), 178–187.
- Hyde, K. K., Novack, M. N., LaHaye, N., Parlett-Pelleriti, C., Anden, R., Dixon, D. R., & Linstead, E. (2019). Applications of supervised machine learning in autism spectrum disorder research: A review. *Review Journal of Autism and Developmental Disorders, 6*(2), 128–146.
- Thabtah, F., Abdelhamid, N., & Peebles, D. (2019). A machine learning autism classification based on logistic regression analysis. *Health Information Science and Systems, 7*(1), 1–11.

BORDERLINE PERSONALITY DISORDER

2021

- Avarzamani, L., Hosein Mozafarian, M., Shahmiri Barzoki, H., Mohsen Rahnejat, A., & Ebrahimi, M. (2021). Comparison of emotional intelligence in young male patients with borderline personality disorder or traits and healthy controls. *Professional Psychology: Research and Practice, 52*(4), 352–359.
- Jiménez, S., Angeles-Valdez, D., Rodríguez-Delgado, A., Fresán, A., Miranda, E., Alcalá-Lozano, R., Duque-Alarcón, X., Arango de Montis, I., & Garza-Villarreal, E. A. (2022). Machine learning detects predictors of symptom severity and impulsivity after dialectical behavior therapy skills training group in borderline personality disorder. *Journal of Psychiatric Research, 151*, 42–49. https://doi.org/10.1016/j.jpsychires.2022.03.063
- Keefe, J. R., Kim, T. T., DeRubeis, R. J., Streiner, D. L., Links, P. S., & McMain, S. F. (2021). Treatment selection in borderline personality disorder between dialectical behavior therapy and psychodynamic psychiatric management. *Psychological Medicine, 51*(11), 1829–1837.

- Palmer, B. A., Pahwa, M., Geske, J. R., Kung, S., Nassan, M., Schak, K. M., Alarcon, R. D., Frye, M. A., & Singh, B. (2021). Self-report screening instruments differentiate bipolar disorder and borderline personality disorder. *Brain and Behavior, 11*(7), e02201. https://doi.org/10.1002/brb3.2201

2019

- Salem, H., Ruiz, A., Hernandez, S., Wahid, K., Cao, F., Karnes, B., Beasley, S., Sanches, M., Ashtari, E., & Pigott, T. (2019). Borderline Personality Features in Inpatients with Bipolar Disorder: Impact on Course and Machine Learning Model Use to Predict Rapid Readmission. *Journal of Psychiatric Practice, 25*(4), 279–289. https://doi.org/10.1097/PRA.0000000000000392

MOOD DISORDERS

2021

- Cavallo, F., Semeraro, F., Mancioppi, G., Betti, S., & Fiorini, L. (2021). Mood classification through physiological parameters. *Journal of Ambient Intelligence and Humanized Computing, 12*(4), 4471–4484.
- Kim, S., Lee, H. K., & Lee, K. (2021). Screening of mood symptoms using MMPI-2-RF scales: An application of machine learning techniques. *Journal of Personalized Medicine, 11*(8), 812.
- Maes, M., Moraes, J. B., Bonifacio, K. L., Barbosa, D. S., Vargas, H. O., Michelin, A. P., & Nunes, S. O. V. (2021). Towards a new model and classification of mood disorders based on risk resilience, neuro-affective toxicity, staging, and phenome features using the nomothetic network psychiatry approach. *Metabolic Brain Disease, 36*(3), 509–521.
- Richter, T., Fishbain, B., Fruchter, E., Richter-Levin, G., & Okon-Singer, H. (2021). Machine learning-based diagnosis support system for differentiating between clinical anxiety and depression disorders. *Journal of Psychiatric Research, 141*, 199–205.

2020

- Cho, C. H., Lee, T., Lee, J. B., Seo, J. Y., Jee, H. J., Son, S., An, H., Kim, L., & Lee, H. J. (2020). Effectiveness of a Smartphone App With a Wearable Activity Tracker in Preventing the Recurrence of Mood Disorders: Prospective Case-Control Study. *JMIR Mental Health, 7*(8), e21283. https://doi.org/10.2196/21283
- Mellem, M. S., Liu, Y., Gonzalez, H., Kollada, M., Martin, W. J., & Ahammad, P. (2020). Machine learning models identify multimodal

- measurements highly predictive of transdiagnostic symptom severity for mood, anhedonia, and anxiety. *Biological Psychiatry: Cognitive Neuroscience and Neuroimaging, 5*(1), 56–67.
- Webb, C. A., Cohen, Z. D., Beard, C., Forgeard, M., Peckham, A. D., & Björgvinsson, T. (2020). Personalized prognostic prediction of treatment outcome for depressed patients in a naturalistic psychiatric hospital setting: A comparison of machine learning approaches. *Journal of Consulting and Clinical Psychology, 88*(1), 25.

2019

- Cho, C. H., Lee, T., Kim, M. G., In, H. P., Kim, L., & Lee, H. J. (2019). Mood prediction of patients with mood disorders by machine learning using passive digital phenotypes based on the circadian rhythm: Prospective observational cohort study. *Journal of Medical Internet Research, 21*(4), e11029.

SUBSTANCE USE DISORDERS

2021

- Lu, H., Xie, C., Lian, P., Yu, C., & Xie, Y. (2021). Psychosocial factors predict the level of aggression of people with drug addiction: A machine learning approach. *Psychology, Health & Medicine, 27*(5), 1168–1175.

2020

- Barenholtz, E., Fitzgerald, N. D., & Hahn, W. E. (2020). Machine-learning approaches to substance-abuse research: Emerging trends and their implications. *Current Opinion in Psychiatry, 33*(4), 334–342.
- Symons, M., Feeney, G. F., Gallagher, M. R., Young, R. M., & Connor, J. P. (2020). Predicting alcohol dependence treatment outcomes: A prospective comparative study of clinical psychologists versus "trained" machine learning models. *Addiction, 115*(11), 2164–2175.

2019

- Afzali, M. H., Sunderland, M., Stewart, S., Masse, B., Seguin, J., Newton, N., Teesson, M., & Conrod, P. (2019). Machine-learning prediction of adolescent alcohol use: a cross-study, cross-cultural validation. *Addiction, 114*(4), 662–671. https://doi.org/10.1111/add.14504

- Symons, M., Feeney, G. F., Gallagher, M. R., Young, R. M., & Connor, J. P. (2019). Machine learning vs addiction therapists: A pilot study predicting alcohol dependence treatment outcome from patient data in behavior therapy with adjunctive medication. *Journal of Substance Abuse Treatment*, *99*, 156–162.
- Wetherill, R. R., Rao, H., Hager, N., Wang, J., Franklin, T. R., & Fan, Y. (2019). Classifying and characterizing nicotine use disorder with high accuracy using machine learning and resting-state fMRI. *Addiction Biology*, *24*(4), 811–821.

APPENDIX 5

Practice Cases and Clinical Scenarios

COVARIATION ESTIMATION IN THE WILD

Gerri A. Smith, Ph.D., has been hired as a staff psychologist in a geriatric primary care clinic. His primary expertise is in brief treatments for mood disorders; however, in his new position, he has been tasked with conducting brief cognitive screenings for mild cognitive impairment (MCI) as a component of patients' annual evaluations. Results of the screenings will determine whether patients are referred for more thorough (and costly!) neurological/neuropsychological evaluations. According to clinic policy, all individuals with suspected MCI should be referred for further evaluation.

First, Dr. Smith acquires MCI base rate estimates in his setting. With limited access to formal academic search engines (i.e., PubMed), he conducts a brief literature search on Google Scholar. His search yields an article that provides MCI base rates in a U.S. urban setting (Manly et al., 2005). The sample's demographics appear to align well with the patients seen in the clinic. The study reported the following data based on a sample of 1,313 community-dwelling individuals age 65 and older:

Age Group	**Base Rate of MCI (%)**
65–75	24.0
>75	32.6

Dr. Smith identified age as the most salient variable by which to predict the presence or absence of MCI. Therefore, he now prepares the foundation for his covariation estimates.

For individuals between the ages of 65 and 75, he produces the following (using 100 as the population estimate):

		Disease Status	
		Present	Absent
Test Result	Positive		
	Negative		
		24 (% of individuals w/ MCI)	76 (% of individuals w/o MCI)

And for individuals over age 75, he produces the following (using 100 as the population estimate):

		Disease Status	
		Present	Absent
Test Result	Positive		
	Negative		
		33 (% of individuals w/ MCI)	67 (% of individuals w/o MCI)

Given the base rate estimates, Dr. Smith gains the following insight: upon encountering patients between the ages of 65 and 75, if he does not refer any for additional cognitive testing, his decision not to refer will be accurate 76% of the time. However, he will fail to refer approximately 1 in 4 (24%) who are appropriate for further neurological/neuropsychological evaluation. Such additional workup may identify a reversible cause of cognitive impairment, gain access to a clinical trial for a patient, or facilitate treatment that may slow progression to a dementia. The 24% figure increases to 1 in 3 (33%) if Dr. Smith follows the same referral practice for individuals over age 75. The scenarios illustrate the cost of a false-negative error.

Conversely, if Dr. Smith were to refer all patients for additional evaluation, he would erroneously refer between 75% and 66% of patients in their respective age brackets. Such false-positive errors are also costly. For example, the neurology or neuropsychology service that receives the referral will likely become inundated with cases, thereby creating extensive wait times. As a result, those who might benefit most from an evaluation could be forced to wait weeks or months. Additionally, patients and their families may be forced to assume costs for unnecessary procedures.

Given the consequences associated with false-positive and false-negative errors, Dr. Smith would prefer not to rely on base rates alone. His clinic has access to a common cognitive screening measure, the Montreal Cognitive Assessment (MoCA), and he hopes to determine whether its use might improve referral accuracy above and beyond the base rates.

After conducting another brief literature review, he identified a systematic review and meta-analysis that provided sensitivity and specificity rates for differentiating between those with and without MCI (Tsoi et al., 2015). According to a meta-analysis of nine studies, when using a cutoff of 26/30, the MoCA yielded a sensitivity of 0.89 and specificity of 0.75. Consequently, the MoCA will detect 89% of the cases with MCI accurately; and 75% of those without MCI accurately. Dr. Smith proceeds to update his covariation estimates with these data.

For individuals between the ages of 65 and 75, he produces the following (using 100 as the population estimate):

		Disease Status	
		Present	**Absent**
Test Result	**Positive**	21	19
	Negative	3	57
		24	76

Positive Predictive Value (PPV) = 21/(21 + 19) = 21/40 = **52.5%**
Negative Predictive Value (NPV) = 57/(57 + 3) = 57/60 = **95.0%**

And for individuals over age 75, he produces the following (using 100 as the population estimate):

		Disease Status	
		Present	**Absent**
Test Result	**Positive**	29	17
	Negative	4	50
		33	67

Positive Predictive Value = 29/(29 + 17) = 29/46 = **63.0%**
Negative Predictive Value = 50/(50 + 4) = 50/54 = **92.6%**

Dr. Smith can now accurately appraise how use of the MoCA will impact his referral accuracy above and beyond reliance on the base rates alone. Again, if he relies on estimated population base rates of MCI alone for individuals between ages 65 and 75 and does not refer any cases, he will be correct 76% of the time and fail to appropriately refer about 1 in 4 patients.

Continuing our focus on individuals ages 65 to 75, if Dr. Smith does not refer patients who score above the MoCA cutoff, he will be correct 95% of the time; or stated differently, he will fail to refer only 1 in 20 patients with MCI (false-negative error). Alternatively, if he refers patients who score below the MoCA cutoff, he will be correct approximately 52.5% of the time; or stated differently, 1 in 2 patients referred will not have MCI (false-positive error). As can be seen in the tables above, in the older age bracket (>75) with a higher base rate of MCI, the PPV improves considerably and the NPV declines slightly.

So, will administration of the MoCA improve his referral accuracy? In short, the answer is yes. Referring on the basis of MoCA test results will marginally improve his overall accuracy relative to using only the base rates and thereby electing not to refer any individuals for further assessment (ages 65 to 75: Base rate of MCI = 24%, base rate of no MCI = 76%; using MoCA = 78% accuracy, which is the sum of the proportion of positive test results when MCI is present plus the proportion of negative test results when MCI is absent). MoCA administration provides value through its reduction of false-negative errors (i.e., failing to detect a condition when present), which in this scenario likely outweighs the cost of a false-positive error. Specifically, in the patients ages 65 to 75, when Dr. Smith uses the MoCA to determine referral appropriateness, his false-negative rate declines from 24% (if he used only the base rate and deemed every person to have no MCI) to 5% (the false-negative rate if he used the MoCA). This seemingly small difference results in approximately 1 in 5 patients receiving further workup who otherwise would not have received a referral. Moreover, whereas no individuals would have been referred if the base rate were used by itself, we would now expect approximately 87.5% of patients with MCI to score below the MoCA cutoff (21/24 = 87.5% sensitivity), resulting in a sizeable proportion of individuals with MCI receiving workup who would not have otherwise. (The sensitivity differs very slightly from 89% in the literature (Tsoi et al, 2015), because this example had to use whole numbers rather than fractions of people in the four cells of the covariation matrix.)

In sum, this brief clinical vignette illustrates the relative ease with which clinicians can improve their decision making accuracy and acquire data to properly fill all four cells of a covariation table. As can be inferred from the PPVs and NPVs, Dr. Smith is comfortable accepting a higher rate of false-positive errors in relation to false-negative errors. This largely aligns with his appraisal of relative costs associated with these errors (i.e., failing to identify and treat a reversible dementia [false negative] vs. increased financial costs to patients and providers [false positive]). Although acquiring precise data for unique settings may not always be possible, we hope we have conveyed how informed estimates may yield appreciable improvements in accuracy and understanding of test results.

REFERENCES

Manly, J. J., Bell-McGinty, S., Tang, M., Schupf, N., Stern, Y. & Mayeux, R. (2005). Implementing diagnostic criteria and estimating frequency of mild cognitive impairment in an urban community. *Archives of Neurology, 62*, 1739–1746.

Tsoi, K. K., Chan, J. Y. C., Hirai, H. W., Wong, S. Y. S., & Kwok, T. C. Y. (2015). Cognitive tests to detect dementia: A systematic review and meta-analysis. *JAMA Internal Medicine, 175*(9), 1450–1458.

THE POWER OF A PRIOR INCORRECT HYPOTHESIS

A father and son were camping in central Michigan. The son suddenly fell unconscious. The alarmed father placed his son in the car and drove quickly to the nearest local doctor. The doctor did a quick evaluation, wrote the diagnosis on a sheet of paper, put the paper in the shirt pocket of the boy, and told the father to drive his son quickly to a hospital in Ann Arbor. The father sped down Route 23 to Ann Arbor and took his son into the ER. The physicians in the ER read the diagnosis on the piece of paper and provided the care appropriate for that diagnosis. The boy's condition worsened. The staff called my friend Bob, who was the chief resident at the time. They explained that the boy's condition was becoming dire. Bob asked what the symptoms were. Upon hearing the list of symptoms, Bob said that this was an obvious case of X. Because the staff at the Ann Arbor hospital had based the boy's treatment upon the incorrect diagnosis Y written on the sheet of paper, they hadn't considered any other diagnosis that the symptoms clearly implied. Bob was insulated from this problem, because he hadn't seen the incorrect diagnosis on that fateful piece of paper. The staff began appropriate treatment of X, and the boy recovered.

DR. D. DANGEROUS

Referral has been made to a psychologist by the family physician, who has observed that patient Jones has voiced various physical complaints over the years. The complaints have become far more frequent during the past few months and do not have any detectable physical cause, and the family doctor has become concerned that Jones may have a serious psychological disturbance. The psychologist conducts an assessment and files the following report. Your task is to critique the report. Note: As will probably be obvious, this is a fictional case designed to provide practice in identifying flaws in judgment or decision making. It certainly is not intended as commentary on the field of psychology or practitioners.

The Report

Dear Dr. Physician:

Thank you for referring this most interesting patient. Given the importance of the referral question, I performed an interview and conducted a very lengthy battery of psychological tests. Unfortunately, just as I suspected from the beginning, the results provide unquestionable evidence of serious psychological disturbance.

I started by asking Jones what he thought was the purpose of the evaluation. He indicated he was not entirely sure, which, along with other evidence, suggests a tendency to deny or repress anxieties or fears. In fact, as I will further describe below, he again displayed such tendencies when I shared my findings with him, refusing to accept some of my conclusions. Unfortunately, this type of resistance, and Jones's lack of personal insight into his problems, are negative prognostic indicators.

Jones's family history is significant. In describing his relationship with his two sisters, he noted that there were more than occasional disagreements, and that at times family relations were tense. He also described sibling rivalry, which sometimes intensified to the point that the siblings felt anger or resentment toward one another. He noted that his father had a number of nervous mannerisms, and that at one point, during a slump in his business, complained that he was under considerable strain. His mother worked at a variety of jobs, apparently unable to make stable career commitments. Although the parents have remained married, they have had ups and downs in their relationship, and at least once considered divorce. As such, the home environment was not always a warm and nurturing one, and Jones sometimes feared that his parents would separate.

On intellectual testing, Jones's overall score fell within the high average range. Scores across the subtests, which have a mean of 10 and a standard deviation of 3, were relatively consistent. However, Jones's score on a measure of vocabulary was a full standard deviation higher than his score on a measure of visual-motor speed. Such discrepancies are very unusual, suggest far greater strength in acquired word knowledge than eye–hand coordination, and raise serious questions about Jones's vocational plans (i.e., furniture making). In fact, this vocational choice may well represent a form of overcompensation for personal weaknesses or deficits in the visual-motor area. Of interest, despite ongoing psychological problems, Jones did not have difficulty on items emphasizing attention and concentration. The reasons that the test failed to detect this area of dysfunction are unclear in this case.

On personality testing, I began with human drawing tasks, mainly with the intent of "breaking the ice." Although Jones produced some interesting responses, I did not place much weight on them in my analysis of materials. An initial objective measure suggested mild depression but did not produce results that, in my opinion, accurately portrayed this individual. Of the two subsequent depression screening inventories, the second detected the more serious level of depression that is present and obvious on interview. My experience with these various depressive inventories shows that in cases of inconsistent results, it is usually this last one that produces the most valid outcome. Other personality testing results were largely within normal limits.

The overall conclusion is an intensification in a long-standing anxiety disorder with significant depressive features. As noted, at the completion of my evaluation, I shared my results with Jones. Although he agreed with some of my interpretations, he disagreed with others. For example, when I discussed his inability to form close interpersonal relations, he insisted he had some close friendships. Most likely, these supposedly close friendships involve situations in which Jones places his needs in the background and caters to others, likely those types of individuals who have an excessive desire to be cared for. Jones also revealed a number of life events that, on the surface, might seem surprising or unexpected in light of the evaluation results, but, on closer analysis, are expectable given what was learned about Jones.

Given my busy practice, I do not have time to see Jones and would suggest referral to a new therapist in town. I have referred three or four patients her way and have heard good reports from two of these patients and nothing negative from the other two.

Again, my thanks for the referral.
Sincerely,
Dr. D. Dangerous

Critiques

1. *"Given the importance of the referral question, I performed an interview and conducted a very lengthy battery of psychological tests."*
   — More is not necessarily more. A combination of information may not be more accurate than a result from a single test or a few tests.
2. *"Unfortunately, just as I suspected from the beginning, the results provide unquestionable evidence of serious psychological disturbance."*
   — Possible examples of hindsight bias and overconfidence.
3. *"I started by asking Jones what he thought was the purpose of the evaluation. He indicated he was not entirely sure, which, along with other evidence, suggests a tendency to deny or repress anxieties or fears."*
   — What is the base rate for being unsure of the purpose of an evaluation? It is likely quite high. Dr. Dangerous may be ignoring base rate information, thereby engaging in overpathologizing (i.e., over-identifying disorder), and/or premature closure, and/or illusory correlation.
4. *"He again displayed such tendencies when I shared my findings with him, refusing to accept some of my conclusions."*
   — As in Item 3 (above), Dr. Dangerous is likely overpathologizing a relatively high base rate behavior. This statement may also reflect premature closure and/or an illusory correlation.
5. *"He noted that there were more than occasional disagreements, and that at times family relations were tense. He also described sibling rivalry, which sometimes intensified to the point that the siblings felt anger or resentment toward one another. He noted that his father had a number of nervous mannerisms, and that at one point, during a slump in his business, complained that he was under considerable strain. His mother worked at a variety of jobs, apparently unable to make stable career commitments. Although the parents have remained married, they have had ups and downs in their relationship, and at least once considered divorce. As such, the home environment was not always a warm and nurturing one, and Jones sometimes feared that his parents would separate."*
   — Again, what is the base rate for familial conflict? It is likely high. Additionally, Dr. Dangerous' characterization of the patient's mother's work history may reflect a personal bias.
6. *"Jones's score on a measure of vocabulary was a full standard deviation higher than his score on a measure of visual-motor speed. Such*

discrepancies are very unusual, suggest far greater strength in acquired word knowledge than eye–hand coordination, and raise serious questions about Jones's vocational plans (i.e., furniture making)."

— This score discrepancy is likely the result of normal variation. A discrepancy of this magnitude is highly probable based on chance alone. Additionally, it is unclear whether evidence supports a score comparison in this instance (i.e., what is the correlation between measures?).

7. *"Of interest, despite ongoing psychological problems, Jones did not have difficulty on items emphasizing attention and concentration. The reasons that the test failed to detect this area of dysfunction are unclear in this case."*
   — This may represent confirmatory bias, or applying more rigorous evidentiary standards when outcomes conflict with one's beliefs.
8. *"On personality testing, I began with human drawing tasks, mainly with the intent of 'breaking the ice.' Although Jones produced some interesting responses, I did not place much weight on them in my analysis of materials."*
   — Often, as diagnosticians, we do not know what influences our judgments, so our intent (e.g., to use a task only as an ice breaker) does not ensure we will not be influenced. Also, adding less valid data or poor data to better data may well have a negative influence on accuracy.
9. *"An initial objective measure suggested mild depression but did not produce results that, in my opinion, accurately portrayed this individual."*
   — Countervailing here is questionable and may reflect a form of confirmation bias.
10. *"Of the two subsequent depression screening inventories, the second detected the more serious level of depression that is present and obvious on interview."*
    — This is a possible example of the effects of confirmation bias on data interpretation and data collection strategies. Also, does adding measures produce incremental validity in this instance?
11. *"My experience with these various depressive inventories shows that in cases of inconsistent results, it is usually this last one that produces the most valid outcome."*
    — There may be serious limits to the use of experience in this context, especially if used to overturn better established interpretive procedures.
12. *"The overall conclusion is an intensification in a long-standing anxiety disorder with significant depressive features."*
    —What is the basis for concluding this condition is long standing?
13. *"Although he agreed with some of my interpretations, he disagreed with others."*
    — What is the base rate for a patient disagreeing with a clinician's impression? Is the examiner showing confirmation bias (e.g., if

examinee agrees with me, the examinee has insight, but if disagrees, lacks insight)?

14. *"Jones also revealed a number of life events that, on the surface, might seem surprising or unexpected in light of the evaluation results, but, on closer analysis, are expectable given what was learned about Jones."*
    — This is another possible example of hindsight bias.
15. *"Given my busy practice, I do not have time to see Jones and would suggest referral to a new therapist in town. I have referred three or four patients her way and have heard good reports from two of these patients and nothing negative from the other two."*
    — Dr. Dangerous is using a small sample to draw conclusions. Also, the sample is inadequate for proper covariation analysis, so Dr. Dangerous is not able to determine such associations. (What about patients that Dr. Dangerous has not heard from? What about individuals with the same problems treated by a different clinician?).

SELF-ASSESSMENT

For the following items, identify the key judgment flaw or the main problematic judgment practice:

1. Jones scored at the 95th percentile on a measure of reading ability with a moderate to high validity coefficient for predicting overall reading capacity. Therefore, I expect him to perform at least within the top 5% of the group in reading.
   a. Being overly influenced by availability bias
   b. Failure to regress estimates or predictions
   c. Hindsight bias
   d. Conjunction fallacy
2. When I told Jones in a firm manner that he was not ready for therapy, he stormed out of my office, therefore further verifying the conclusion.
   a. Reversal bias
   b. Failure to consider statistical artifact
   c. Channeling effects
   d. Representative heuristic
3. I find that children who experience feelings of anger toward their parents often have an attention disorder, and thus I think this type of anger is an important indicator of such disorders.
   a. Failure to consider population base rates
   b. Overdependence on hypothetical case analysis
   c. Failure to recognize standard error of measurement of the difference
   d. Variation co-actuarial fallacy

4. Upon receiving follow-up information about my patients, I often find that the outcome was predictable.
   a. Use of a disjunctive strategy
   b. Improper bootstrapping
   c. Hindsight bias
   d. Failure to consider Cell C of a covariation table
5. I know you think Mary will have academic difficulties, but I think it is more likely she will have academic difficulties and drop out of school.
   a. Hindsight bias
   b. Failure to consider base rates
   c. Conjunction fallacy
   d. Failure to separate statistical fact from artifact
6. The child I am treating seems to intentionally undermine therapeutic progress. Almost every time we have an excellent therapy session, the session that follows is not nearly as good.
   a. Failure to distinguish the antecedent from the consequence
   b. Conjunction fallacy
   c. Failure to consider the nonrepresentativeness construct
   d. Failure to consider regression toward the mean
7. So what if the combination of the Clinical Sign A and Clinical Sign B produces the highest validity coefficient? You've got to obtain much more information to maximize accuracy.
   a. Overreliance on experience
   b. Failure to consider incremental validity
   c. Ignoring the impact of extreme groups on the appraisal of accuracy
   d. Ignoring content validity
8. What's so bad about Psychologist James, anyway? The two or three clients I've referred to him seem to have progressed well in their treatment.
   a. Mistakenly embracing the "law of small numbers"
   b. Having inadequate data to perform covariation analysis
   c. Using a sample that may be skewed or nonrepresentative
   d. All of the above
9. I know the test is biased because one group obtained higher scores than the other.
   a. Failure to consider face validity
   b. Failure to perform variation/covariation analysis
   c. Confusing regression effects with true variance
   d. Failure to consider what the actual state of things might be
10. I do use computerized test interpretation, although I am very cautious about accepting interpretations that conflict with my clinical impressions.
    a. Confirmatory bias
    b. Conjunction fallacy
    c. Failure to consider internal consistency data
    d. Failure to consider regression to the mean

11. I know our interview procedures are effective, because almost 85% of the individuals we admit go on to succeed.
    a. Failure to consider the base rate for success across all applicants
    b. Inadequate data for proper covariation analysis
    c. Possible self-fulfilling prophecy
    d. All of the above
    e. None of the above
12. In diagnosing learning disability, I integrate information across dozens and dozens of variables when reaching a decision.
    a. Hindsight bias
    b. Probable lack of insight into cue utilization
    c. Failure to consider Cell A when performing covariation analysis
    d. Failure to consider obsolescence
13. I use the Draw-a-Person test only as an ice-breaker, am very aware of its major scientific shortcomings, and do not allow it to influence my impressions.
    a. Pseudo-verification of an untestable hypothetical construct
    b. Failure to consider standard error of measurement
    c. Ignoring differences in individual variation
    d. Knowing we should not be influenced is no guarantee it will not occur

Answer Key: 1, b; 2, c; 3, a; 4, c; 5, c; 6, d; 7, b; 8, d; 9, d; 10, a; 11, d; 12, b; 13, d

APPENDIX 6

Checklists and Guides

OVERVIEW OF APPENDIX 6

In healthcare and other fields, checklists have often proven highly effective in reducing error and improving outcomes (see Chapter 12). Checklists can provide increased structure in obtaining information, and they may also include aids to guide interpretation. For example, as covered in Chapter 8, approaches for gathering clinical data that specify variables of interest routinely equal or exceed less structured data-collection methods. In addition, various guides for decision making appear across diverse sections of the book, and we thought it might be helpful to draw across chapters and present the materials in a central location. Given these considerations, we developed something akin to a checklist for clinical decision making.

Some of the materials in the book can easily be framed as relatively narrow checklist items (e.g., Did I use base rates when such information was available?). Other materials are broader and best captured as principles that do not fit neatly into a checklist format (e.g., gather information that maximizes incremental validity). To enhance user friendliness and convenience, the compilation of items that follows includes both materials that read like typical checklist queries and affirmative statements that present critical principles for gathering and interpreting information, hence the switches back and forth at times between both types of entries. We still refer to these materials as checklists for the sake of convenience, while recognizing their heterogeneous nature. The common element is that all items can serve as cross-checks for clinical work that strives to maximize effective decision making. All items or guides are bolded and italicized for ease of identification.

CHECKLISTS: MORE DETAILED AND CONDENSED VERSIONS

We provide the checklist in two versions. In the first version, for a number of the listings, we provide supplementary explanations or foundational bases. Further details about the items, their research bases, and specifics of their application can be found in the main text. In the second version, the items are presented in the same order but generally with minimal or no explanation, so that the user can proceed through the listings quickly and efficiently, as one might wish to do in the course of an assessment or before finalizing a report. The checklists are divided into three sections: (I) broad or overarching issues, (II) procedures for gathering information, and (III) procedures for interpreting or integrating information. The topics in the sections overlap to a degree, and thus placement into various sections, and especially into sections II and III, was somewhat arbitrary and required some cross-referencing. Finally, multicultural considerations often fit into multiple potential sections. Comments about multicultural considerations are included in various passages in the first two sections, but we felt it would be most helpful to keep checklist items and guides exclusively devoted to multicultural considerations together and to present them in section III, given the emphasis on interpreting and integrating information.

APPENDIX 6.1

Comprehensive Checklist and Guides

PART I: BROAD OR OVERARCHING POINTS

I.1 Exercise care to maximize decision accuracy.

- ***Have you exercised methodical adherence to the best validated methods, such as careful adherence to standard procedures and selection of the best available decision methods*?**
- ***If feasible, have a detail-oriented and trusted colleague, who is blind to your conclusions, occasionally check your evaluations and scoring procedures to avoid having systematic error creep into your work (perhaps in exchange for providing similar services to that colleague).***

The adage we have referenced multiple times before—"*methodical* adherence to the best validated methods"—starts by emphasizing the need for meticulousness. Even the best psychological assessment methods can be completely spoiled by error.

Simple steps can often greatly reduce clerical, and sometimes extremely damaging, errors. Redundancy often provides excellent protection. For example, having two individuals enter data independently may cut keyboarding errors down to nearly 0% if a procedure is put in place for identifying inconsistent entries and then making the needed corrections.

I.2 Insight or introspection alone provides little help; active steps are needed to enhance diagnostic and predictive accuracy.

- ***Recognizing the possibility of biases and problem judgment practices, by itself, often does little to improve judgmental accuracy. Have you taken active steps to improve performance*?**

  Among various factors restricting the value of introspection alone, individuals, professionals included, often have limited access to their own higher-level cognitive processes. Consequently, attempts to identify and then correct biases in one's own thinking will often be unsuccessful.

I.3 Take active steps to avoid or attenuate inflated confidence.

- ***Overconfidence has long been recognized as a major cause of diagnostic and predictive error and is associated with various problematic judgment practices, such as forming nearly immutable conclusions far too early in the diagnostic or interpretive process or before critical information has been gathered. Have you taken steps to diminish unwarranted confidence?***

One technique for reducing overconfidence is the general debiasing strategy of considering the opposite, as described in detail in Chapter 13. Variations of this approach include actively considering alternative possibilities, generating the best evidence or argument one can think of for a contrary conclusion, or seeking out independent second opinions or divergent points of view. The propensity to overvalue supportive evidence is a major factor bolstering confidence to inappropriately high levels; hence, implementing strategies that bring potential contrary evidence to mind or make it more salient can reduce confidence to more appropriate levels.

Another potential way to diminish overconfidence is to record predictions in advance and subsequently to check one's accuracy rates. To the extent initial predictions are specific rather than overly general, and the outcome information is readily appraised, the more likely such feedback will be helpful. Checking outcomes against previously recorded predictions will likely provide more accurate information than retrospective impressions of one's success. The tendency to recall predictions as more consistent with outcomes than is actually the case once outcomes are known can easily distort subjective appraisal of our proficiency (see the section in Chapter 5 on hindsight bias). In addition, it can be helpful to assign a confidence level to each prediction so that the match or discrepancy between confidence and accuracy can also be appraised.

I.4 Is the evidence I'm planning to gather to make a prediction or reach a decision most likely to maximize decision accuracy? Am I taking an even-handed approach to appraising the quality of evidence, especially when clinical experience and research evidence point in conflicting directions?

Considerable evidence suggests that practitioners too readily defer to their experience over even well-conducted and strongly supported scientific evidence or formal decision procedures and consequently increase error (see Faust & Furman, 2023). Thus, one might ask such questions as:

- ***Have I distinguished between the context of discovery (or hypothesis formation) and the context of verification (or the strength of methods for testing hypotheses)?***

- ***Has the salience or immediacy of information led me to overweight its strength when compared to blander, but potentially stronger, information, such as very high or very low base rates?***
- ***Have I carefully appraised the strength of the scientific findings, and before countervailing those findings, have I considered the strongest argument for going with the scientific evidence over my personal experience or impressions?***

Although underweighting scientific evidence may well be the more common tendency or process diminishing accuracy, there are times one might argue that alternative sources of information should be considered more actively and that the question should be stated in the converse form.

PART II: DATA GATHERING

II.1 Increase structure when gathering information.

Research shows that structured or more systematic methods of data gathering, such as well-developed tests and structured interview methods, as opposed to unstructured interviews, tend to increase diagnostic and predictive accuracy. Structured or systematic approaches to data gathering, given their benefits in enhancing accuracy, should generally be preferred to less structured methods, or at least should be included as a component of data gathering.

Even simple decision aids, such as checklists (presuming they are well designed and cover important topics and procedures), can serve to increase structure. Similarly, approaches that fall under *structured professional judgment*, which dictate gathering clinical data systematically by identifying variables that should be appraised, routinely equal or exceed less structured data-collection methods (see Chapter 8). However, it should be recognized that statistical decision methods for integrating or combining information consistently equal or surpass structured professional judgment.

The value of structured methods can be compromised or reversed if practitioners do not adhere to specified procedures. Practitioners may also make minor or major changes in prescribed or standard test instructions. Lee et al.'s (2003) detailed review of research on alterations to prescribed test procedures showed how difficult it can be to predict the impact of the changes and how sizeable these influences can be even if the changes seem minor. Certainly, when alterations in standard procedures are taken lightly or result from insufficient care in practices, they are simply adding potentially costly error.

Understandably, certain circumstances might justify altering standardized procedures, although one might wish to actively consider reasons to avoid such changes before proceeding. When changes are made, it is important to document what occurred and to adjust confidence downward, making more conservative judgments, or proceeding with the assumption that the accuracy of results is likely to be diminished when compared to results obtained in studies based on standard procedures. Presumably, a diligent practitioner would likely reserve altering standard procedures for situations in which even greater reductions in accuracy would seemingly result if changes were not made. However, such a forecast may be speculative and lack good quality evidence to guide decisions.

II.2 Have I identified (collected information on) the best predictors or combination of predictors, while bypassing information that cannot help, and may only compromise, decision accuracy?

- ***Maximizing incremental validity should often be the primary guide for gathering information.***
- ***One should avoid tests and assessment methods that are so psychometrically flawed or limited that they are highly unlikely to enhance accuracy and may well decrease accuracy, especially when better sources of information are available.***

Reasons to gather information or interact with clients may of course serve other purposes than predicting outcomes, such as building the therapeutic relationship. However, when the primary aim of information gathering is to maximize diagnostic or predictive accuracy, then to the extent possible, one should seek out information that best serves those aims. It is a waste of a client's time and money, as well as professional resources, to gather information that is far more likely to degrade rather than enhance accuracy, and that has little potential to reduce the type of errors one most wants to avoid, such as missing a major disorder.

One might wish to apply a few psychometric "go or no-go" guidelines, especially if better potential choices are available. In the great majority of circumstances (although not in all circumstances, for technical reasons we will not go into here), if measurements of test–retest reliability yield clearly deficient outcomes, one can eliminate that test or its problematic subcomponents. If reliabilities are not reported or available for certain test components, those components should not be used unless circumstances are truly exceptional. Similarly, at least for certain test components or predictive variables, if validity studies generate feeble outcomes, and especially if there are better options, those variables should be disregarded. Also, if there are few or no formal validity data for anything resembling the application or use under consideration, the potential value of predictors is rendered highly questionable or ambiguous. Under such conditions, it is once again better to exclude those predictors, especially when other predictors are available, and research has supported their positive qualities for the decision task(s) at hand.

II.3 Have I taken needed steps to decrease reliance on memory?

Memory is a reconstructive process and can easily become degraded or distorted over time as additional information is gathered or impressions have been formed. Thus, make sufficient and careful contemporaneous notes/records as close in time to a clinical encounter as possible. Alternatively, if appropriate, and subject to the client's approval, use formal recording methods to decrease strain on memory and the likelihood of later errors in recall.

PART III: DATA INTEGRATION AND INTERPRETATION OF INFORMATION

III.1 Increase the use of decision aids.

III.1.1 Have I made maximal use of base rates?

Professionals often underuse or disregard base rates. The tendency to underuse base rates increases when case-specific information is provided, as is typically the circumstance in applied clinical work, and even when such information has negligible value for diagnostic or predictive purposes and base rates have greater predictive utility. One can always ask if base rate information is available for the decision(s) of interest, thinking in sufficiently broad terms to identify various possible sources (see Appendix 1). Many studies and publications will not use the term *base rates* but will provide exactly that type of information. For example, epidemiological research and a wide range of outcome studies routinely generate base rate information.

One's procedural checklist might contain entries on base rates like:

- ***Before proceeding with a psychological evaluation or predictive task, consider whether base rates are available for the judgments at issue.***
- ***What is/are the strongest reason(s) to use base rate information in the present case?***
- ***When base rates are available for different groups or subgroups, have I selected the most narrowly applicable base rates when they are a better choice than using more general base rates?***

Narrowness is defined here as features that change the base rates and that are applicable to the individual. For example, a variable might change the base rates for pre-adolescents versus adolescents, but if one is working with an older client, those changes are irrelevant.

- ***If base rates are available and the most applicable source is selected, am I faced with a dichotomous decision? If so, what level of accuracy can be achieved by simply playing the base rates?***

- ***Given the accuracy achieved by playing the base rates, are there any other sources of information, alone or in combination, that can beat the base rates? If not, isn't deferring to the base rates likely to be the best decision policy? Or, before using other assessment methods, what is the most compelling reason I can think of to just defer to the base rates?***

The usual tendency seems to be to underuse or neglect base rates, especially as more and more information is gathered about a client. Consequently, actively considering reasons to defer to the base rates seems to be in order, rather than focusing primarily or exclusively on reasons to countervail the base rates, or just proceeding to do so with limited hesitation or deliberation. (This approach, which is intended to make counterevidence more salient, is a variation of the strategies discussed in greater detail in Section III.2.2 below). With that said, even when base rates achieve the greatest level of accuracy, there can be sound reasons to gather and use other information along with, or in place of, base rates. For example, in some situations, false-negative or false-positive errors are far worse than the converse error. Administering tests might not achieve greater accuracy than the base rates but could nonetheless shift the ratio of false-negative to false-positive errors in the desirable direction. (One does need to balance the shift in type of error against changes in accuracy level, because overall error rate may increase to an extent that the tradeoff is not justified.) Other potentially compelling reasons for countervailing base rates are discussed in Chapter 6.

- ***Are any of the judgments or predictions under consideration not purely dichotomous, and is there value in determining the likelihood of outcomes? If so, and if there are applicable base rates and other valid predictors, have I combined the two sources of information to determine likelihoods?***
- ***Have I used formal methods, rather than subjective judgment, to combine the base rates and the other valid predictors, such as Bayes' Theorem or a nomogram?***

III.1.2 Increase the use of statistical (actuarial) judgment methods and other decision aids.

Assertions that statistical decision methods are often unavailable frequently do not distinguish between the availability of: (a) studies that compare clinical and statistical judgment methods in a particular domain, as opposed to (b) studies that have generated statistically based outcomes, formulae, or algorithms that can be applied directly in clinical work or used with minor modification. Consider the situation in which only the latter type of studies (as described under "b") are available for a specific judgment or domain. Here, one can look at the track record of outcomes across the hundreds of studies that compare the two methods across other domains. Given the number of comparative studies, the diversity of decision tasks examined, and the uniformity of outcomes, one can project the odds or base rates for the relative success of the two alternative methods in a new area of application. If, in at least 95% of the comparative studies, statistical methods have equaled or exceeded clinical methods, there is a high likelihood that the same outcome will occur in a new area of application.

Therefore, in situations in which one lacks an applicable comparative study in the decision domain of interest but has access to a well-developed statistical decision method, there is a very good chance that using the statistical method will lead to equal or better overall success than using clinical or impressionistic judgment. Certainly, the comparative track record of success would make statistical judgment a much stronger bet, and to predict otherwise would seem to require a powerful reason to believe the current circumstance is somehow different, a common assumption but one that comparative studies show is very often misplaced. Here again, overconfidence may be counterproductive.

- ***For decision tasks under consideration, are statistical decision procedures available? Have I looked beyond comparative studies to research that generates statistical analyses or formalisms that can be applied directly, or with minor modification, to the decision tasks of interest?***
- ***What are the strongest reasons to use statistical decision methods in the present case?***

As with base rates, we generally prefer the positive form of this question, given the compelling evidence that statistical decision methods are frequently underused or underweighted. (Similar approaches, which are intended to make counterevidence more salient, are discussed in greater detail in Section III.2.2 below.) One could argue that if the situation were reversed, the question could be stated in the obverse form, such as when a clinician uniformly adhered to a statistical decision method that was highly questionable in certain applications (e.g., when predictive variables that loaded heavily on English mastery were used for a person who barely speaks the language).

- ***If I'm considering countervailing the outcome of a statistical decision method, what is the best reason (or reasons) I can think of that the statistical outcome may be correct and the alternative conclusion I'm considering wrong?***

Considerable research indicates that many clinicians countervail freely and often, but that these decision practices rarely improve overall accuracy and commonly increase error, sometimes substantially. When one contemplates going against the statistical decision method, overconfidence may lead to a counterproductive choice.

III.2 Cognitive strategies/debiasing

III.2.1 Deliberate and delay when possible

- ***When circumstances do not create urgent demands for rapid decision making, taking the opportunity to deliberate and think things through often benefits decision accuracy.***

More accurate decision makers often wait longer before reaching conclusions, whereas other clinicians may form initial impressions within minutes or even seconds of initial contact with a client, impressions that remain unchanged thereafter. The odds are poor that the information needed to make the most accurate judgments possible will be obtained within a few minutes or seconds of client contact.

III.2.2 Consider the opposite, make active attempts to disconfirm hypotheses, and direct similar attention to positive and negative evidence and to client's strengths and weaknesses

Various studies described in Chapter 12 suggest that the strategy we refer to as *consider the opposite* can reduce overconfidence, hindsight bias, and confirmatory bias. Merely creating a differential diagnosis offers a potential means for utilizing the consider-the-opposite strategy because it can stimulate thinking about alternative possibilities and contrary evidence that otherwise may be overlooked given the common tendency to focus disproportionately on confirming evidence.

Furthermore, studies showing improvement in calibrating confidence and greater balance in considering positive and negative evidence (e.g., by making negative evidence more salient and thereby diminishing primary focus on confirming evidence) have clear applicability to important judgment tasks in the mental health field. For example, if one is trying to select between two or more possible outcomes, such as whether or not an individual needs to be hospitalized, then reducing overconfidence and the chances of overlooking contrary evidence can produce significant benefits.

Implementing disconfirmatory strategies can be very helpful in recognizing error, and doing so efficiently, as opposed to relying primarily or exclusively on confirmatory strategies. Overreliance on confirmatory strategies can be highly inefficient and may yield less conclusive outcomes than disconfirmatory strategies. Confirmatory strategies can appear to generate abundant supportive evidence for faulty hypotheses given such factors as the variability in human behavior. For example, even generally deliberate individuals will probably make hasty decisions at times, and generally upbeat individuals will experience periods of sadness, so seeking supportive evidence for a hypothesis about problems with impulsivity or low mood could well "succeed" whether warranted or not.

It is also important to direct balanced attention to clients' strengths and weaknesses. You might wish to review your notes and reports and see if an appropriate balance has been achieved between clients' positive attributes and problem areas. For example, if you've administered a questionnaire or rating scale, you might check if the draft of your report disproportionately references responses indicating problems and underrepresents responses indicating normal functioning or positive qualities, or simply tally the respective percentages of positive and negative statements in the draft and compare it to the original rating scale responses themselves. We understand that disproportionality may be warranted for various reasons. For example, certain problems require urgent attention and emphasis. However, there is often considerable continuity between those who do and do not seek or need professional help, with both groups showing a combination of strengths and weaknesses and positive and not so positive characteristics. Further, effective intervention often builds on a client's strengths and positive attributes. Nevertheless, many reports we have reviewed resemble a newscast emphasizing human fallibilities and misfortune, with perhaps a token wave to something brighter.

The risks of overlooking strengths or misidentifying positive capacities as problems may be increased when working with clients from diverse backgrounds. Behaviors and coping strategies that might be ineffective or dysfunctional in one set of circumstances, such as fluid family boundaries, may represent effective adaptive behaviors under different situations.

III.2.3 Holistic thinking (thinking in scenarios) is not the whole story.

In certain circumstances, thinking holistically or in stories or scenarios is not the most effective approach to diagnosis or prediction. At times, such strategies should be supplemented or replaced by more analytic approaches that break down problems or decision tasks to component parts.

The tendency to think holistically or in scenarios is one factor underlying the conjunction fallacy, or the mistaken belief that the likelihood of two (or more) events occurring together exceeds the likelihood of any of the component events occurring alone (e.g., A + B is more likely than either A or B alone). The culture of mental health often strongly encourages holistic thinking or thinking in scenarios, as is seen in common formats for case conferences or the very frequent advice to integrate all the information. At times, looking at the big picture has benefits, but at other times, thinking analytically or in terms of component elements can have considerable value and improve judgmental accuracy. Some examples and guidelines follow.

- ***When estimating the likelihood of occurrences, rather than thinking holistically, it is often more effective to break down the links in a chain or sequence of events.***
- ***When predicting the likelihood of outcomes, if: (a) more than one component is involved, (b) all components must be present or occur, and (c) the components are relatively independent of one another, multiplying all the probabilities jointly (e.g., A × B × C) will often provide a more accurate determination of likelihood than formulating impressions holistically or thinking in scenarios.***
- ***All else being equal, to decrease the probability of an adverse outcome, focus on decreasing the probability of the least probable link in the chain, and not on the most likely (and possibly most salient) one.***

All else being equal, lowering the probability of the least likely component in a chain of events has the greatest impact on reducing the chances the adverse event will occur. For example, if there are two links in the chain with respective probabilities of 90% and 10%, decreasing the probability of the first event by 5%, or from 90% to 85%, will have minimal impact. With the original figures, the probability = .90 × .10 = 9%. If the more probable link is lowered by 5%, the result is .85 × .10 = 8.5%. In contrast, lowering the second link by 5%, or from 10% to 5%, will have considerable impact: the result becomes .90 × .05 = 4.5%, which cuts the risk in half. Conversely, as enumerated below, when one seeks to achieve a positive outcome, all else being equal, one still focuses on the least likely event but instead attempts to increase it to the extent possible.

- ***All else being equal, to increase the probability of a desired outcome, focus on increasing the probability of the least probable link in the chain, and not on the most salient or most likely (and possibly most salient) one.***
- ***If a series of conditions all must be present or occur for an outcome or condition to be present, analytic appraisal of one or more components may quickly show that the condition or outcome is highly improbable.***

Suppose, for example, one is considering whether an accident caused a clinically significant concussion. Careful review of the original incident, as opposed to more holistic consideration of reported symptoms and symptom onset, may show clearly that any potential forces generated during the event were far from sufficient to cause such an injury, thereby ruling out its occurrence (or more specifically, the event in question as a possible cause).

III.2.4 When appropriate and available, start by focusing on criteria of inclusion or exclusion, not on associated indicators.

To avoid wasted time and to increase accuracy when performing differential diagnosis, one can start by asking whether there may be potential criteria of inclusion or exclusion. If such criteria can be identified, then if feasible (e.g., the needed information is available or potentially available), they can serve as early starting points.

Strictly speaking, *criteria of inclusion* are diagnostic signs or indicators that, if present, rule in a disorder, and *criteria of exclusion* are signs or indicators that, if absent, rule out a disorder. In contrast, *associated signs or indicators* are variables that are related to a condition but are not definitive in ruling in or ruling out that condition. Associated signs or indicators are often present across multiple disorders and may show considerable overlap across individuals with and without the disorders.

Given the relative rarity in the mental health field of finding definitive indicators, the terms *inclusion* and *exclusion* are often meant to convey something like very strong or nearly definitive evidence, as opposed to infallible criteria. One might say that associated symptoms are neither necessary or sufficient to rule in or rule out a particular psychological disorder, and sometimes even whether any type of psychological disorder is present (given the overlap often seen in those with and without disorder).

Chasing down associated signs and symptoms, given their limited utility, may not help much in clarifying diagnostic possibilities or outcomes, or even in distinguishing normal individuals from individuals with psychological conditions. One might argue that diagnostic categories in the mental health field often fail to offer much practical guidance in any case. Nonetheless, there seem to be clear counter-examples, e.g., bipolar disorder and various eating disorders, given potential treatment responsiveness and the high rate of morbidity and mortality among those who go untreated.

III.2.5 Seek additional perspectives, second opinions, and input from diverse thinkers

It can be very difficult to recognize our own problematic judgment habits, cognitive biases, and errors, and to avoid overconfidence. Various factors operate in naturalistic practice settings that often inflate confidence beyond the level that is warranted and create systematic misimpressions or "illusory correlations." Such factors include, for example, (a) insufficient feedback, (b) nonrepresentative feedback, (c) channeling effects, (d) not knowing what would have happened had one acted otherwise, (e) tendencies to misremember initial judgments as more consistent with outcomes than is actually the case, and (f) reduced opportunities to implement formal, scientific procedures designed to attenuate judgmental biases. Hence, seeking alternative or second opinions, especially from someone who is blind to our judgments, can prove helpful and lead us to carefully re-examine our conclusions. Given the operation of hindsight bias, if the individual rendering a second opinion is informed of our opinion, then even without their realizing it, that information may sway their judgment toward confirming our initial conclusion. Consequently, the more independent the second opinion, and the freer it is from potential contaminating influences, the better.

Research covered in Chapter 12 also describes the potential value of obtaining opinions from a group, at least in certain circumstances, and especially input from divergent or diverse individuals. Individuals who think differently than us may be more likely to know, or think of, things that we ourselves might not know or consider.

III.3 Managing information; data integration and interpretive strategies

III.3.1 When determining what information to include and exclude when reaching a decision, to the extent possible and all else being equal, use the piece or combination of information that maximizes accuracy (incremental validity).

The common adage to include and integrate as much information as possible when drawing conclusions often does more harm than good. For example, if one adds weaker information to stronger information, it can dilute or reverse the impact of the stronger information, and thereby not only fail to increase accuracy but potentially increase error. In many cases, even relatively small amounts of information, such as three or four of the strongest, least redundant variables, will approach or reach a ceiling in predictive accuracy.

- ***Three Steps for Screening Information***

We suggest that one consider three sequential questions when deciding what information to gather and use for decision tasks. These three determinations are, in order:

1. Is it valid (for the specific question being asked and the individual being evaluated)?
2. Does it beat the base rates?
3. Does it enhance incremental validity?

Step 1: Is it valid? A negative answer to the first question is logically dispositive. If a variable is not valid, it should not be used. In practice, negative evidence about a variable's utility might not be as certain as we would like, but that is often our lot in the mental health field, and if the evidence is predominantly negative or nearly definitive, the course of action should be clear. Similarly, validity may be so low that variables have negligible practical utility and should be discarded, especially if there are better alternatives.

Validity is a specific, not a global, quality, and hence its appraisal should be directed at the particulars of the task and the individual under consideration. In a later section of this appendix, we examine the application of tests and predictive methods developed for certain groups to other groups, or across diverse populations. Although our scientific knowledge base is increasing, we still often lack sufficient information on generalization to groups other than those in test development samples, or to what may be rather narrow groups with whom most of the validation research has been conducted.

Additionally, validity can shift depending on the stage in the decision process. For example, we may initially be screening individuals to evaluate their need for some type of mental health services. However, once this broad determination is made, one may move on to narrower determinations, such as the choice of intervention approach. At this point, variables that helped in gauging whether individuals had a general need for mental health services may not assist in making these finer determinations. Hence, at each step along the way or as one narrows things down, one is looking for variables that are both valid and have differentiating value. As the possibilities proceed to greater levels of specificity or narrower distinctions, the differentiating value of variables may decline considerably or completely.

For example, a variable like significantly diminished concentration may assist in differentiating soldiers exposed to blast injuries who have resultant PTSD or concussion (or both) from soldiers without these conditions. However, diminished concentration is commonly present with both PTSD and concussion. Suppose one is now trying to differentiate between the presence of PTSD, the presence of concussion, or the co-occurrence of the two conditions, differentiations that presumably would affect treatment planning. Diminished concentration, which helped with the initial separation of those with and without PTSD or concussion, would likely not assist in the differentiation of the two conditions because the symptom is present in both conditions. In these and related circumstances when one moves from the more general to the more specific, previously useful variables can become less effective or ineffective and, when possible, should be replaced by variables that can assist in making the narrower determinations in question.

Step 2: Does it beat the base rates? A negative answer to this question may not settle the decision to use or discard a variable. If maximizing overall accuracy is the primary goal and one is facing a dichotomous choice, then if the base rates achieve greater predictive accuracy than the variable (or combination of variables) under consideration, one should use the base rates. However, even assessment methods that do not surpass the base rates might still warrant use, especially when the potential consequences of false-negative and false-positive errors are unequal. One may accept more overall error in order to reduce the frequency of the more damaging type of error. Even here, however, when the resultant increase in error rate begins to far outstrip the accuracy achieved by playing the base rates, as may occur with exceedingly low- or high-frequency events, decision policies may require a second look.

Furthermore, although the base rates may provide greater accuracy than a single variable, combinations of variables may beat the base rates. In addition, although other variables, tests, or methods may not beat the base rates across the totality of cases, subsets of results may do so, such as cases in which individuals obtain particularly high or particularly low scores on tests measuring depression. The frequency with which these sorts of exceptions occur may be overestimated and difficult to evaluate subjectively, and formal methods (e.g., appropriate multivariate methods) should be used whenever possible.

In other situations, one is not selecting between the base rates versus other diagnostic signs or predictors when the two conflict and a dichotomous choice is needed. Rather, the aim may be to combine base rates and other predictors to formulate more accurate probability estimates than one could achieve with either type of information alone. (Procedures for combining base rates with other information, and other circumstances in which one might override the base rates, are covered in Chapter 6.)

Step 3: Does it enhance incremental validity? To the extent new information increases accuracy, it can be said to generate incremental validity. Rather than attempting what can often be a complex analysis of incremental validity on one's own, one prefers to select combinations of variables for which incremental validity has been studied carefully and which are feasible to obtain in one's setting of interest. When the best combinations change across different individuals or settings, one wishes to know what variables, such as demographic factors or individual differences, influence incremental validity and how the selection of variables can be tailored to the clinician's specific circumstances.

To maximize incremental validity, one seeks variables that make the greatest independent contribution to accuracy—that is, that are both strong predictors and as nonredundant as possible. Hence, examining diverse classes of variables that may not show excessive overlap, such as tests, clinical features or diagnostic indicators, historical occurrences, and sociodemographic characteristics, can enhance success. Studies providing such broad analyses of incremental validity are far less common than one might imagine (as opposed to studies examining a narrower range of variables) and can be frustratingly difficult to find.

- ***Errors of inclusion are often more costly than errors of exclusion. In most circumstances, if in doubt, it is better to eliminate weak or unestablished variables than to include them when reaching conclusions.***

When one has multiple correlated or redundant measures, excluding one of them is not going to change results much, if at all, especially if levels of redundancy are relatively high. If one cannot find needed studies on incremental validity to guide the selection of variables or to pare down the number of variables used, the following rule of thumb may help. Redundancy is not all or none, and the level of redundancy will likely vary, even among measures that tend to have strong correlations. All else being equal, one targets variables for inclusion that (a) have relatively lower levels of redundancy with other variables and (b) the highest levels of validity with the outcomes of interest. In such situations, and applying these criteria, it is better to defer to the highest quality measures as opposed to the weaker measures, and again, errors of exclusion will often have minimal impact.

In contrast, including a weak measure has greater potential to do harm, especially when subjective judgment is used to combine information. If variables are weak, if their validity is poor, or if their status is uncertain, then it is generally better to exclude than include them, especially when good predictors with an established scientific track record are available.

As with base rates, determining what maximizes incremental validity is not necessarily dispositive, and choices may rest on other priorities, such as reducing the more harmful type of error. In such circumstances, one seeks a combination of variables that best serves that purpose without reducing overall accuracy an unacceptable amount (see Chapter 13 for further details on appraising incremental validity and handling situations in which insufficient information is available).

III.3.2 Separate statistical fact and artifact

- ***Are findings likely genuine, or best explained by regression toward the mean?***

Shifts from more extreme outcomes to less extreme outcomes that stem partly from chance are referred to as *regression toward the mean*. Extreme outcomes are often followed by less extreme outcomes. The greater the extent to which an outcome falls outside the mean and is a product of chance, the greater the extent to which a subsequent outcome will tend to move in the direction of the mean. For example, suppose one administers a battery of tests and then repeats the same tests at a later date to track a client's progress. If a number of the tests have mediocre or weak test–retest reliability, then the highest scores are likely to decline substantially and the lowest scores to increase substantially. Practice effects aside, if a test with a .50 test–retest reliability generates a score 3.0 standard deviations (SD) above the mean, then even if the client's status has not changed at all, the best prediction of the score on retesting is the SD multiplied by the test–retest reliability, or $3.0 \times .50 = 1.5$ SD. Consequently, on retesting, one obtains a score that has declined on average by 1.5 SD. Likewise, an original score that fell 3.0 SD below the mean, again assuming no true change and absent practice effect, will increase by a mean of 1.5 SD. Some tests or subtests that practitioners may use may have reliabilities in the .30's or even lower, and thus the level of regression is even greater.

An important predictive principle follows from regression toward the mean:

- ***Predictions should be no more extreme than the variables upon which they are based. Rather, all else being equal, predictions should be regressed toward the mean to the degree chance or randomness enters into outcomes.***

One should also be alert to situations in which predictive variables could be degraded due to various factors, such as application to questions or groups for which they may be less suited, or by extending predictions over longer time periods than were examined in background studies. For example, suppose most studies involve relatively short time intervals, such as a few weeks, but predictions are made extending over months or years, such as the educational level a child will ultimately achieve. As one extends the time frame, the level of predictive accuracy usually declines, and sometimes to the point that validity approaches zero. One hopes that such adjustments for level of regression toward the mean as time frames expand can be based on studies providing formal guidance. Further, if possible, variables that are likely to degrade considerably given changed circumstances can be replaced with better options, or at least updated assessments can be performed as needed.

- ***Beware of small samples: Is sample size sufficient to draw firm conclusions? Are you being sufficiently cautious given limits in sample size?***

Individuals often treat small samples as if they are more representative of population parameters than is genuinely the case. For example, a statement like, "I once had a client who . . ." may be better than assertions based on a sample size of 0, but often not much better. Similarly, failure of a well-established decision method on one or two occasions may lead us to abandon it prematurely. Alternatively, some tests in common use in neuropsychology have alarmingly small normative or reference samples (e.g., 15 or 10 individuals, or fewer). The problem of small sample size for cognitive and psychological tests and structured interview methods often plagues assessment of diverse groups. Furthermore, and importantly, methods that may not generate formal psychometric data or that have not been formally appraised for psychometric standing do not escape the hazards created by inadequate sample size, as may be the case with unstructured interviews.

III.4 Multicultural considerations

This text focuses on decision making; therefore, the discussion below on multicultural considerations mainly addresses assessment, prediction, and other judgment tasks. Clearly, there are many critical issues in multicultural psychology we do not cover and that extend beyond this text and our expertise.

III.4.1 Do I have the education, training, and background to perform a cross-cultural evaluation with a potential client?

Despite welcome strides in recent years, a number of past surveys examining the quality of multicultural assessments have shown, and sometimes still show, unflattering overall results and a disturbing frequency of problem practices. Although cross-cultural evaluations call on certain general skills and knowledge, much of what is needed in addition is not generic, but is specific to such factors as a client's race, ethnicity, nationality, economic status, and language. For example, a psychologist who evaluates a farmer from rural Guatemala with little formal education one day and a CEO from Barcelona who attended graduate school in London the next day may be encountering two individuals with overlapping primary languages, but many areas of marked contrast. A mental health practitioner who believes, say, that a graduate class in multicultural psychology, a couple of continuing education classes, and perhaps a month of living in Tokyo has prepared them for multicultural work across a broad and widely varied swath of humanity is badly mistaken. Thus, there is no shame in being as realistic as possible about one's limits performing cross-cultural evaluations with certain clients, or consulting with those with specialized knowledge to determine whether one should refer the client to another practitioner. This is an additional area in which overconfidence can be especially harmful, and previous suggestions for attenuating inflated self-beliefs may be useful.

One can also perform a self-appraisal of readiness to perform cross-cultural work and the validity of assessment methods and techniques one is considering for use by consulting the guides and standards provided by a group like the International Test Commission (ITC). The ITC has incorporated the findings and recommendations of various eminent psychologists and cross-cultural experts. Although the ITC guides and standards may be discounted as being aspirational or ideological, the ITC does not seem to view them that way, but rather as essential steps in adapting tests across cultures.

One can perform a straightforward count of the number of issues the ITC covers and how familiar one is with the respective content, and one can also use the guides and descriptions as helpful ways of gauging the scientific status of the methods one is considering using with the client in question. Various ITC documents and guides are readily available on the Internet, and one may especially wish to review "ITC Guidelines for Translating and Adapting Tests" (2nd ed., version 2.4, 2017; https://www.intestcom.org/files/guideline_test_adaptation_2ed.pdf).

III.4.2 If proceeding with the evaluation seems to be the best option despite apparent limitations and shortcomings, such as gaps in my knowledge, should I seek consultation from individuals with the needed expertise I lack to enhance the quality of my work?

Rapidly expanding resources are available to mental health professionals performing cross-cultural assessments. In addition to an increasing number of high-quality texts, research studies, and professional guidelines, one may well be able to connect with experts in the field, who might be easily identified by their publication track records or continuing education activities. One of the authors has often found it helpful to contact university departments (e.g., psychology, sociology, anthropology) and search for someone with expertise directly bearing on a client's or examinee's race, ethnicity, and cultural background.

III.4.3 Have the assessment procedures/tests and interpretive procedures I've used, or plan to use, been validated for groups of individuals like my client? Similarly, do base rates and statistical decision procedures generalize effectively to my client?

Although the knowledge base is improving, there is often a dearth of research evidence addressing the application of assessment methods, base rate information, statistical decision methods, and other interpretive procedures and bodies of knowledge to diverse populations. Often, one might feel at a particular loss with a client who differs in critical respects from the groups for whom at least a substantial literature and knowledge base are available. Furthermore, questionable or mistaken beliefs about cross-cultural evaluations are not uncommon (see Chapter 9). For example, it is often assumed that language tests are considerably more susceptible to cultural influences than nonverbal tests, despite research showing that biasing influences can be just as great, or greater, with nonverbal items. Additionally, although cross-cultural differences may lead to decreased scores on some tests or subcomponents of tests compared to results obtained by original normative groups or so-called members of the mainstream culture, these differences may lead to increased scores on other tests or subtests. The result may be, for example, a wide divergence in two test scores using mainstream norms that actually represent equal abilities for the individual in question relative to the performance of individuals from similar backgrounds and life experiences.

Although it probably goes without saying, just because a measure for assessing cognitive abilities, psychological status, or cooperation with assessment procedures (e.g., a response set scale) is effective with certain groups does not mean it will be effective with other groups or when applied cross-culturally. Once again, validity is a specific, not a global, quality. Therefore, even tests or assessment methods that are highly effective in addressing specific questions with specific groups may achieve far from comparable results with diverse groups, unless they are adapted properly for cross-cultural application. Likewise, the base rates generated for some groups may not generalize to, or even approximate, the base rates for other groups, and interpretive procedures and statistical decision methods may show altered effectiveness when applied cross-culturally. Additional research, reviews, and meta-analyses examining cross-cultural influences on base rates and the effectiveness of decision methods are much needed.

- ***Have I adequately assessed such factors as acculturation and/or linguistic/reading skills in ESL clients (i.e., clients for whom English is a second language), such as their oral English competency?***
- ***Am I capable, if needed, of conducting the assessment in the client's preferred language?***

The use of an interpreter, although often better than making no modifications when an assessment should be administered in a client's primary language, has various complications that can appreciably degrade validity (see the aforementioned "ITC Guidelines for Translating and Adapting Tests"). For example, a psychologist may lack sufficient familiarity with the client's language to determine whether the interpreter conveyed the meaning of test items and the client's responses properly. When evaluating responses on intellectual testing, for example, fine distinctions may be needed to assign credit correctly, to decide whether answers should be queried, and to determine whether to continue or to terminate subtests. In addition, exemplars for responses meriting full, partial, or no credit may have unclear application because even minor changes in answers (e.g., "large" versus "gigantic") can alter scoring, and the psychologist may not know whether the interpreter reproduced these subtleties exactly. Other language factors can also create problems. For example, idioms or content may be difficult to translate, may be more or less familiar across cultural groups, or may be understood differently. A statement like, "I do things when the spirit moves me," can mean very different things among individuals with contrasting cultural backgrounds.

- ***Given limitations in scientific and professional knowledge that are often present or exacerbated in cross-cultural work, have I adjusted for the greater level of uncertainty involved in formulating diagnostic or predictive judgments?***
- ***Have I openly acknowledged in reports or communications with others, where and as appropriate, the increased level of uncertainty in diagnostic and predictive judgments given limits in the scientific and professional knowledge base in cross-cultural work?***

Again, being more confident than is warranted is associated with increased error and overly risky decisions. Thus, as uncertainty mounts, one usually needs to be more conservative in decision making. For example, if uncertainty about the risk for self-harm increases, one may have to move more quickly to implement protective measures.

III.5 Glitter does not necessarily equal gold: Beware of overblown claims about artificial intelligence (AI) or machine learning (ML).

Chapter 10 reviews some of the impressive accomplishments and promises of AI and ML. However, some supposed AI and ML programs are something less dressed up in misleading packaging, or they may be flawed procedures that, among other things, are contaminated by biased information processing that can greatly disadvantage certain groups. Moreover, even if an interpretive program is automated, or appears sophisticated, it may not be well supported or helpful in enhancing accuracy. Thus, careful appraisal of programs, and perhaps consulting with an expert in the area, can help practitioners reach informed judgments about the credibility of AI or ML claims.

REFERENCES

Faust, D., & Furman, A. (2022).When clinical judgment and science conflict, how does one decide? The epistemological status of learning from experience vs. science. In C. L. Cobb, S. J. Lynn, & W. O'Donohue (Eds.), *Toward a science of clinical psychology* (pp. 71–104). Springer.

Lee, D., Reynolds, C. R., & Willson, V. L. (2003). Standardized test administration: Why bother? *Journal of Forensic Neuropsychology*, *3*(3), 55–81.

APPENDIX 6.2

Condensed Checklist Items and Guides

This condensed checklist is divided into three sections: (I) broad or overarching issues, (II) procedures for gathering information, and (III) procedures for interpreting or integrating information. The order of items is the same as in the "Comprehensive Checklist and Guides" (CCG). The difference between the two checklists is that the Condensed Checklist provides the items with minimal elaboration, whereas the CCG provides considerably greater explanation for many items. Anyone using this checklist who would like further explanation can always find the corresponding entry in the CCG or refer to the original text. As is true for the CCG, topics in the three sections overlap to a degree, and thus placement into various sections, and especially in Sections II and III, was somewhat arbitrary and required some cross-referencing.

PART I: BROAD OR OVERRIDING POINTS

I.1. Exercise care to maximize decision accuracy

- ***Have you exercised methodical adherence to the best validated methods, such as careful adherence to standard procedures and selection of the best available decision methods?***
- ***If feasible, have a detail-oriented and trusted colleague, who is blind to your conclusions, occasionally check your evaluations and scoring procedures to avoid having systematic error creep into your work (perhaps in exchange for providing similar services to that colleague).***

I.2 Insight or introspection alone provides little help; active steps are needed to enhance diagnostic and predictive accuracy.

- ***Recognizing the possibility of biases and problem judgment practices, by itself, often does little to improve judgmental accuracy. Have you taken active steps to improve performance?***

I.3 Take active steps to avoid or attenuate inflated confidence.

- ***Overconfidence has long been recognized as a major cause of diagnostic and predictive error and is associated with various problematic judgment practices, suchand forming nearly immutable conclusions far too early in the diagnostic or interpretive process or before critical information has been gathered. Have you taken steps to diminish unwarranted confidence?***

I.4 Is the evidence I'm planning to gather to make a prediction or to reach a decision most likely to maximize decision accuracy? Am I taking an even-handed approach to appraising the quality of evidence, especially when clinical experience and research evidence point in conflicting directions?

One might ask such questions as:

- ***Have I distinguished between the context of discovery (or hypothesis formation) and the context of verification (or the strength of methods for testing hypotheses)?***
- ***Has the salience or immediacy of information led me to overweight its strength when compared to blander, but potentially stronger, information, such as very high or very low base rates?***
- ***Have I carefully appraised the strength of the scientific findings, and before countervailing those findings, have I considered the strongest argument for going with the scientific evidence over my personal experiences or impressions?***

Although underweighting scientific evidence may well be the more common tendency or process diminishing accuracy, there are times one might argue that alternative sources of information should be considered more actively and that the question should be stated in the converse form.

PART II: DATA GATHERING

II.1 Increase structure when gathering information.

Research shows that structured or more systematic methods of data gathering, such as proper use of psychological tests or structured interviews, tend to enhance the accuracy of diagnostic and predictive judgments.

II.2 Have I identified (collected information on) the best predictors or combination of predictors, while bypassing information that cannot help, and may only compromise, decision accuracy?

- ***Maximizing incremental validity should often be the primary guide for gathering information.***
- ***One should avoid tests and assessment methods that are so psychometrically flawed or limited that they are highly unlikely to enhance accuracy and may well decrease accuracy, especially when better sources of information are available***?

II.3 Have I taken needed steps to decrease reliance on memory?

Memory is a reconstructive process and can easily become degraded or distorted over time as additional information is gathered or impressions have been formed. Thus, make sufficient and careful notes/records as close in time to a clinical encounter as possible. Alternatively, if appropriate, and subject to the client's approval, use formal recording methods to decrease strain on memory and the likelihood of later errors in recall.

PART III: DATA INTEGRATION AND INTERPRETATION OF INFORMATION

III.1 Increase the use of decision aids.

III.1.1 Have I made maximal use of base rates?

One's procedural checklist might contain entries on base rates like:

- ***Before proceeding with a psychological evaluation or predictive task, consider whether base rates are available for the judgments at issue.***
- ***What is/are the strongest reason(s) to use base rate information in the present case?***

- ***When base rates are available for different groups or subgroups, have I selected the most narrowly applicable base rates when they are a better choice than using more general base rates?***

Narrowness is defined as features that change the base rates and are applicable to the individual. For example, a variable might change the base rates for preadolescents versus adolescents, but if one is working with an older client, those changes will be irrelevant.

- ***If base rates are available and the most applicable source is selected, am I faced with a dichotomous decision? If so, what level of accuracy can be achieved by simply playing the base rates?***
- ***Given the accuracy achieved by playing the base rates, are there any other sources of information, alone or in combination, that can beat the base rates? If not, isn't deferring to the base rates likely to be the best decision policy? Or, before using other assessment methods, what is the most compelling reason I can think of to just defer to the base rates?***

Not simply deferring to the base rates may be a sound choice at times, even when they generate the highest level of accuracy among alternative methods. For example, a test or structured interview method might not achieve greater accuracy than the base rates, but their use could shift the ratio of false-negative versus false-positive errors in a favorable direction when one type of error is far worse than the other type. Other potentially compelling reasons for countervailing base rates are discussed in Chapter 6.

However, the usual tendency is to underuse or neglect base rates, especially as increasing amounts of information are gathered about a client. Consequently, actively considering reasons to defer to the base rates seems to be in order in most situations, rather than just countervailing or disregarding them with little hesitation or deliberation.

- ***Are any of the judgments or predictions under consideration not purely dichotomous, and is there value in determining the likelihood of outcomes? If so, and if there are applicable base rates and other valid predictors, have I combined the two sources of information to determine likelihoods?***
- ***Have I used formal methods, rather than subjective judgment, to combine the base rates and the other valid predictors, such as Bayes' Theorem or a nomogram?***

III.1.2 Increase the use of statistical (actuarial) judgment methods and other decision aids.

- ***For decision tasks under consideration, are statistical decision procedures available? Have I looked beyond comparative studies to research that generates statistical analyses or formalisms that can be applied directly, or with minor modification, to the decision tasks of interest?***
- ***What are the strongest reasons to use statistical decision methods in the present case?***

As with base rates, we generally prefer the positive form of this question, given the compelling evidence that statistical decision methods consistently yield equal or greater accuracy than clinical judgment, and thus are the stronger method overall. Even so, well-validated statistical decision methods are frequently underweighted, countervailed, or entirely neglected.

- ***If I'm considering countervailing the outcome of a statistical decision method, what is the best reason (or reasons) I can think of that the statistical outcome may be correct and the alternative conclusion I'm considering wrong?***

III.2 Cognitive Strategies/Debiasing

III.2.1 Deliberate and delay when possible

- ***When circumstances do not create urgent demands for rapid decision making, taking the opportunity to deliberate and think things through often benefits decision accuracy.***

III.2.2 Consider the opposite, make active attempts to disconfirm hypotheses, and direct similar attention to positive and negative evidence and to clients' strengths and weaknesses

Various studies (see Chapter 12) suggest these strategies can reduce overconfidence, hindsight bias, and confirmatory bias.

It is also important to direct balanced attention to strengths and weaknesses. You might wish to review your notes and reports and see if you have struck a reasonable and accurate balance between a client's positive and negative characteristics and areas of functioning.

III.2.3 Holistic thinking (thinking in scenarios) is not the whole story.

In certain circumstances, thinking holistically or in stories or scenarios is not the most effective approach to diagnosis or prediction. At times, such strategies should be supplemented or replaced by more analytic approaches that break down problems or decision tasks into component parts. Some examples and guidelines follow.

- ***When estimating the likelihood of occurrences, rather than thinking holistically, it is often more effective to break down the links in a chain or sequence of events.***
- ***When predicting the likelihood of outcomes, if: (a) more than one component is involved, (b) all components must be present or occur, and (c) the components are relatively independent of one another, multiplying all the probabilities jointly (e.g., A × B × C) will often provide a more accurate determination of likelihood than formulating impressions holistically or thinking in scenarios.***
- ***All else being equal, to decrease the probability of an adverse outcome, focus on decreasing the probability of the least probable link in the chain, and not on the most salient or most likely (and possibly most salient) one.***
- ***All else being equal, to increase the probability of a desired outcome, focus on increasing the probability of the least probable link in the chain, and not on the most likely (and possibly most salient) one.***
- ***If a series of conditions all must be present or occur for an outcome or condition to be present, analytic appraisal of one or more components may quickly show that the condition or outcome is highly improbable.***

III.2.4 When appropriate and available, start by focusing on criteria of inclusion or exclusion, not on associated indicators.

To avoid wasted time and increase accuracy when performing differential diagnosis, one can start by asking whether there may be potential criteria of inclusion or exclusion. If such criteria can be identified, then if feasible (e.g., the needed information is available or potentially available), they can serve as early starting points and sometimes quick paths to endpoints.

III.2.5 Seek additional perspectives, second opinions, and input from diverse thinkers.

It can be very difficult to recognize our own problematic judgment habits, cognitive biases, and errors, or to avoid overconfidence. Hence, seeking alternative or second opinions, especially from someone who is blind to our judgments and may think in ways that differ from us, can prove very helpful and lead us to carefully re-examine our conclusions.

III.3 Managing information; data integration and interpretive strategies

III.3.1 When determining what information to include and exclude when reaching a decision, to the extent possible and all else being

equal, use the piece or combination of information that maximizes accuracy (incremental validity).

The common adage to include and integrate as much information as possible when drawing conclusions often does more harm than good. For example, if one adds weaker information to stronger information, it can dilute or reverse the impact of the stronger information, and thereby not only fail to increase accuracy, but potentially increase error. Often, even relatively small amounts of information, such as three or four of the strongest, least redundant variables, will approach or reach a ceiling in predictive accuracy.

- ***Three steps for screening information***

We suggest one consider three sequential questions when deciding what information to gather and to use for decision tasks. Greater details about these three steps, including their rationale and application, can be found in the comprehensive checklist and in Chapter 13.

The three questions, in order, are:

1. Is it valid (for the specific question being asked and the individual being evaluated)?
2. Does it beat the base rates?
3. Does it enhance incremental validity?

Step 1: Is it valid? A negative answer to the first of the three questions is logically dispositive. If a variable is not valid, or if the evidence is predominantly negative, it should not be used. Similarly, the validity of variables may be so low that they have negligible practical value and should be discarded, especially if there are better alternatives.

Step 2: Does it beat the base rates? A negative answer to this question may not settle the decision to use or discard a variable. If maximizing overall accuracy is the primary goal and one is facing a dichotomous choice, then if the base rates achieve greater predictive accuracy than the variable (or combination of variables) under consideration, one should use the base rates. However, even assessment methods that do not surpass the base rates might still warrant use, especially when the potential consequences of false-negative and false-positive errors are unequal. In other situations, one wishes to combine base rates and other predictors to formulate more accurate probability estimates than one could achieve with either type of information alone. (Chapter 6 details procedures for combining base rates with other information, and other circumstances in which one might override the base rates.)

Step 3: Does it enhance incremental validity? To the extent new information increases the level of accuracy achieved with methods or variables already in use, it can be said to generate *incremental validity*. As with base rates, the result of analyzing incremental validity is not dispositive, and choices may rest on other priorities, such as reducing the more harmful type of error. In such circumstances, one seeks a combination of variables that best serves that purpose without reducing overall accuracy an unsatisfactory amount. To maximize incremental validity, one seeks variables that make the greatest independent contribution to accuracy—that are both strong predictors and as nonredundant as possible.

Errors of inclusion are often more costly than errors of exclusion. In most circumstances, if in doubt, it is better to eliminate weak or unestablished variables than to include them when reaching conclusions.

When one has multiple correlated or redundant measures, excluding one of them is not going to change results much, if at all, and if their levels of validity vary significantly, all else being equal, it is generally better to defer to the highest quality measure(s) as opposed to the weaker measures. Thus, in such situations, errors of exclusion will often have minimal impact. In contrast, including a weak measure has greater potential to do harm, especially when subjective judgment is used to combine information. If variables are weak, if their validity is poor, or if their status is uncertain, then it is generally better to exclude than include them, especially when good predictors with an established scientific track record are available.

III.3.2 Separate statistical fact and artifact

- ***Are findings likely genuine, or best explained by regression toward the mean?***

Shifts from more extreme outcomes to less extreme outcomes that stem in part from chance are referred to as *regression toward the mean*. Extreme outcomes are often followed by less extreme outcomes. The greater the extent to which an outcome falls outside the mean and is a product of chance, the greater the extent to which a subsequent outcome will tend to move in the direction of the mean.

An important predictive principle follows from regression toward the mean:

- ***Predictions should be no more extreme than the variables upon which they are based. Rather, all else being equal, predictions should be regressed toward the mean to the degree chance or randomness enters into outcomes.***

One should also be alert to situations in which predictive variables could be degraded due to various factors, such as application to questions or groups for which they may be less suited, or the attempt to extend predictions over somewhat longer time periods than were examined in background studies.

- ***Beware of small samples. Is the sample size sufficient to draw firm conclusions? Are you being sufficiently cautious given limits in sample size?***

Individuals often treat small samples as if they are more representative of population parameters than is often the case, potentially creating judgment errors or leading decision makers to overlook or underweight potentially more useful information.

III.4 *Multicultural considerations*

This text focuses on decision making; therefore, the items on multicultural considerations mainly address assessment, prediction, and other judgment tasks. Clearly, there are many critical issues in multicultural psychology we do not cover and that extend beyond this text and our expertise. For further details and explanation of the items that follow, please see the Comprehensive Checklist and Guides.

III.4.1 Do I have the education, training, and background to perform a cross-cultural evaluation with a potential client?

Despite welcome strides in recent years, a number of past surveys examining the quality of multicultural assessments have shown, and sometimes still show, unflattering overall results and a disturbing frequency of problem practices. Additionally, cross-cultural evaluations often require more than general skills and knowledge in multicultural psychology, but also specialized knowledge and competencies specific to such factors as a client's race, ethnicity, nationality, economic status, and language. Various sources and guides can assist in appraising one's readiness to perform specific cross-cultural tasks or work with particular clients, as well as methods one is considering using (see, for example, the International Test Commission's *"ITC Guidelines for Translating and Adapting Tests,"*2nd ed., version 2.4, 2017) https://www.intestcom.org/files/guideline_test_adaptation_2ed.pdf).

III.4.2 If proceeding with the evaluation seems to be the best option despite apparent limitations and shortcomings, such as gaps in my knowledge, should I seek consultation from individuals with the needed expertise I lack to enhance the quality of my work?

Rapidly expanding resources are available to mental health professionals performing cross-cultural assessments. In addition to an increasing number of high-quality texts, research studies, and professional guidelines, one may well be able to connect with experts in the field, who might be easily identified by their publication track records or continuing education activities.

III.4.3 Have the assessment procedures/tests and interpretive procedures I've used, or plan to use, been validated for groups of individuals like my client? Similarly, do base rates and

STATISTICAL DECISION PROCEDURES GENERALIZE EFFECTIVELY TO MY CLIENT?

Although the knowledge base is improving, there is often a dearth of research evidence addressing the application of assessment methods, base rate information, statistical decision methods, and other interpretive procedures and bodies of knowledge to diverse populations.

- ***Have I adequately assessed such factors as acculturation and/or linguistic/reading skills in ESL clients (i.e., clients for whom English is a second language), such as their oral English competency?***
- ***Am I capable, if needed, of conducting the assessment in the client's preferred language?***

The use of interpretive services, although often better than making no modifications when an assessment should be administered in a client's primary language, carry various complications that can appreciably degrade validity (again, see the "ITC Guidelines for Translating and Adapting Tests"). For example, a psychologist may lack sufficient familiarity with the client's language to determine whether the interpreter conveyed the meaning of test items and the client's responses properly.

- ***Given limitations in scientific and professional knowledge that are often present or exacerbated in cross-cultural work, have I adjusted for the greater level of uncertainly involved in formulating diagnostic or predictive judgments?***
- ***Have I openly acknowledged in reports or communications with others, where and as appropriate, the increased level of uncertainty in diagnostic and predictive judgments given limits in the scientific and professional knowledge base in cross-cultural work?***

Being more confident than is warranted is associated with increased error and overly risky decisions. Thus, as uncertainty mounts, one usually needs to be more conservative in decision making.

III.5 Glitter does not necessarily equal gold: Beware of overblown claims about artificial intelligence (AI) or machine learning (ML).

Chapter 10 reviews some of the impressive accomplishments and promises of AI and ML. However, some seemingly impressive AI and ML programs are something less dressed up in misleading packaging, or may be flawed procedures that, among other things, are contaminated by biased information processing that can greatly disadvantage certain groups. Thus, careful appraisal of programs, and perhaps consulting with an expert in the area, can help practitioners.

INDEX

For the benefit of digital users, indexed terms that span two pages (e.g., 52–53) may, on occasion, appear on only one of those pages.

Note: Tables and figures are indicated by *t* and *f* following the page number